Mark D Karau is a lecturer of history a
Colleges. His published articles inc
The Journal of the Great War Society anc

The Naval Flank *of the* Western Front
The German MarineKorps Flandern 1914–1918

MARK D KARAU

Seaforth

PUBLISHING

For Jacqui, Alex and Katherine

In Memoriam

Bernhard Karau (1908-1980)
Willard Doering (1917-1996)

This edition first published in Great Britain in 2014 by
Seaforth Publishing,
Pen & Sword Books Ltd,
47 Church Street,
Barnsley S70 2AS

www.seaforthpublishing.com

British Library Cataloguing in Publication Data
A catalogue record for this book is available from the British Library

ISBN 978 1 84832 231 8

Fist published 2003 under the title *Wielding the Dagger:
The Marinekorps Flandern and the German War Effort, 1914–1918*

Typeset in Ehrhardt and Avenir by M.A.T.S Leigh-on-Sea-Essex
Printed and bound in Great Britain by CPI Group (UK) Ltd, Croydon, CR0 4YY

CONTENTS

LIST OF CHARTS

Plate section located between pages 52 and 53

Preface

I FIRST BEGAN MY INVOLVEMENT with this project six years ago as a dissertation. Now that it is finally complete the list of debts I have incurred is so extensive that I am almost bound to forget someone! Any list of those who aided me in this project has to begin with the man who guided me through the initial stages of the work, my dissertation advisor Professor Paul Halpern. Without the benefit of his assistance and expertise I seriously doubt that this project would ever have seen the light of day. I also owe a tremendous debt to Professor Dennis Showalter who graciously volunteered to read the work even though we had only just met. His encouragement and advice have made this a vastly better work than it would have been otherwise. Thanks as well are due to the members of my doctoral committee: Professors Jan K. Tanenbaum; Nathan Stoltzfus; Winston Lo; and Patrick O'Sullivan, all of whom provided suggestions on ways to improve the manuscript. I must also thank the staff of the Bundes Archiv in Freiburg for their assistance running down materials pertaining to the MarineKorps and the war in Flanders. The staff of the inter-library department at Strozier Library also deserve commendation for handling my reams of inter-library loan requests.

Thanks are also due to several colleagues I have taught with over the last six years, all of whom encouraged me to finish the project and some of whom read and commented on parts of the manuscript. They are: Professor David Mock of Tallahassee Community College; Professor Michael O'Brien of the University of Wisconsin Fox Valley College; Ms. Susan Strauss of Santa Fe Community College and especially Professor Barbara Oberlander of Santa Fe Community College. My sincere thanks to all of you.

I would also like to thank Professor Jim Sloan and Ms. Sheila Ann Wiest who provided the maps for the work.

I must also thank my editor at Greenwood, Dr. Heather Staines for her work on my behalf and especially for her patience during the revising process.

Thanks are also due to my family, especially my parents, Donald and Karen

Karau, who, I suspect often wondered what I was doing and why it was taking so long, but nevertheless accepted what I was doing and supported it. Finally, I would be especially remiss not to mention the debt I owe to my wife, Jacquelynn Karau, without whose unfailing support and encouragement this project would have been stillborn. Not only did she accept the greater burdens of child rearing and house maintenance that were required while I devoted countless hours to this work, she also assisted in the editing and word processing. This work is as much hers as it is mine.

Last but not least I'd like to thank a series of individuals who had little to do with the project directly but without whose help or inspiration this would never have been written: Mr. George Ackermann, who first interested me in German history and the German language; Professors Michael Phayer, Julius Ruff, Ronald Zupko, and Father J.P. Donnelly for inspiring a young undergraduate; and finally, Professor Donald Horward, whose passion for his profession is contagious.

My sincere thanks to you all. Needless to say what errors and shortcomings remain are mine and mine alone.

Introduction

Belgium, the 'dagger held at the throat of England'; this small collection of provinces which first attained independence in 1830 had long been a critical factor in British foreign policy. The British were traditionally concerned that Belgium, especially the Flanders coast, would fall under the permanent control of the strongest continental power. This is not the place to detail the struggles engaged in by the various powers during the 17th, 18th, and early 19th centuries; suffice it to say that from the conclusion of the Dutch Wars of the 17th century through the long struggles against France in the 18th and early 19th centuries one of Great Britain's primary military and foreign policy aims was to ensure that Belgium, and especially the ports along the Channel coast, was either neutral or controlled by a weak nation such as the Netherlands. Following the victorious conclusion of the Napoleonic Wars, the area now known as Belgium was granted to the Kingdom of the Netherlands in order to create a large buffer state on the northern frontier of France. This arrangement lasted barely fifteen years.

In 1830 a revolution occurred against the rule of the Dutch and, over the course of an eight-year struggle, Belgium attained independence from the Netherlands. English concerns over the future security of the new state were allayed by the signing of a treaty between the major powers which guaranteed Belgium's perpetual neutrality. This treaty was aimed primarily at France, at that point still England's most threatening rival. The strategic situation in Europe changed slowly and, despite France's defeat at the hands of Prussia in 1871, France remained Britain's most dangerous foe until 1904. It was a combination of the growing military and economic might of the new German nation and the naval building policy of Admiral Alfred von Tirpitz which resulted in Germany taking the place of France as Great Britain's top rival.[1]

The situation was complicated further by the existing tensions between France and Germany. The enmity that had existed between those two countries since 1871 put Belgium in a singularly uncomfortable position. Any German attack on France, or vice versa, could easily spill over into Belgium and might bring Great Britain to war against the aggressor. Due to the gradual solidification of the Entente Cordiale between 1904 and 1914 it should have been clear to the German leadership that an attack upon Belgium would bring Germany to war against Great Britain; yet the Germans deluded themselves into believing that this was not so. This begs the question: just how did Belgium fit into German military plans?

There is no need here to go into a discussion of the famous (or infamous) Schlieffen Plan arranged by Alfred von Schlieffen of the German General Staff.[2] Of more relevance to our purposes are the relatively unknown plans of the German navy regarding Belgium. After all, in any war between Germany and England the opposing fleets would be of critical importance.[3]

In the 1890s the Germans began to recognise the important role that the Belgian harbours could play in a war between Germany and Great Britain. The importance of these harbours stemmed from their location. Any enterprise undertaken by the German navy against England would have a much shorter distance to travel if it began in Flanders than if it started from the Helgoland Bight. This would correspondingly reduce the risks of such an operation and improve its potential for surprise. With this in mind the head of section AIII of the Naval Staff, which was responsible for formulating war plans dealing with Western Europe and the Mediterranean, KorvettenKapitän Ludwig von Schröder, the future commander of the MarineKorps Flandern, prepared a plan for a surprise seizure of Antwerp by the German navy as the first step in a war against England.[4] The plan involved the smuggling into Antwerp, on a cargo ship, of 11,000 German soldiers whose mission was to take and hold Antwerp and the banks of the Scheldt until the German army could arrive to relieve them. This force would then be freed for an attack upon England.

This rather fanciful plan existed in a vacuum. There was no input from the German army because the two German services did not co-operate and did not share their war plans with each other. As a result there was no comprehensive plan of operations. German naval planning occurred without input from the army and vice versa.[5] This lack of communication meant that when war came in 1914 the German navy was unable to appreciably assist the army. Furthermore, despite plans such as those of von Schröder the navy was even unprepared to take over control of the Flanders harbours.

The potential value of the Flanders coast does not appear to have been widely recognised within the Kaiserliche Marine.[6] One of the few individuals within the navy who did recognise the strategic potential of the area was Admiral Alfred Tirpitz, the head of the German Naval Office and architect of the German battle fleet. In October 1915, as part of the internal debate over war aims, he penned a denkschrift entitled 'Die Bedeutung Belgiens und seiner Häfen für unsere Seegeltung'. In the denkschrift Tirpitz laid out his views on Belgium and its potential economic and military value for Germany.[7]

Belgium's primary economic importance derived from the port of Antwerp and the control of the river traffic moving through it to the sea. Holding Antwerp would give Germany a number of advantages, for example, they would be able to impose tariffs on non-German commercial traffic moving through the harbour and free their own goods from such taxes. Most importantly however, Antwerp would provide a direct link to the sea for the German industries in the Ruhr and the Rhineland. Tirpitz believed that only the possession of Antwerp would allow the German government to repair the economic damage done by the war and avert an internal economic catastrophe that might topple the current social structure.

Of more immediate import and greater interest for the topic at hand were Tirpitz's military concerns. In this instance Antwerp was less important than what Tirpitz referred to as 'the Triangle'. This consisted of the three ports of Ostend, Zeebrugge, and Bruges.* These three ports, the former two directly on the coast and the latter linked to them by twelve miles of inland canals, would provide Germany with several advantages in a war with England. The most obvious was that these ports were significantly closer to the heart of the British Empire than were the German bases in the Bight. For example, the Flanders bases brought German forces within seventy nautical miles of the mouth of the Thames. Additionally, these bases could provide shelter for any German forces based in the area because they could retreat to Bruges to avoid enemy attacks from sea and still sortie whenever they desired. A third advantage was that the Flanders bases allowed the Germans to employ sizable numbers of small submarines, the UB and UC-classes, in the English Channel.[8] These small vessels did not have the range to reach the Channel if they were forced to operate from the main German harbours. Taken as a whole, Tirpitz believed that these factors would force the British to maintain a tight watch on the eastern Channel. Tirpitz claimed this would be a major victory for the German fleet. In addition, Tirpitz argued that control of the Flanders coastline would allow the Germans to introduce close co-operation between the fleet and the new German air force. According to Tirpitz the German naval threat would force the British to maintain more forces in vulnerable forward positions than they would otherwise. These forces could then, in turn, be attacked by German aircraft.

* Spelt Brugges in contemporary German documents.

Finally, Tirpitz laid out his intention to eventually expand the harbours of Ostend, Zeebrugge, and Bruges in order to make them usable by large surface warships.[9] Since basing in Flanders would drastically shorten the distance to safe harbours the German battle fleet would be able to seek out the Royal Navy in the western half of the North Sea. Finally, Tirpitz hoped that by forcing the British to maintain a sizeable force in the eastern Channel the Germans could engage the British fleet piecemeal and slowly whittle down its numerical advantage. In other words, proper use of the Belgian harbours would allow a more effective implementation of the strategy of *Kleinkrieg*.[10]

These ideas first occurred to Tirpitz several months earlier, in August 1914. In that month he sponsored the creation of the MarineDivision Flandern. This study is an examination of the MarineDivision and its later incarnation, the MarineKorps Flandern. In it I will examine the creation of the unit, its purpose, career, and final demise in the general collapse of 1918. In the process a number of issues will be examined: the impact of the MarineKorps upon German naval strategy; the disputes over resources between the various sectors of the fleet; additional disputes between the German army and navy over resources, and the impact of the Flanders flotillas and the MarineKorps on the outcome of the war.

The Flanders harbours, as Tirpitz argued and as the British clearly recognised early in the war, provided the German navy with bases that, if properly utilised, would have allowed it to strike dangerous blows at the vital British traffic in the English Channel and southern North Sea. The MarineKorps Flandern was the instrument by which this naval war was to be carried out. For various reasons the MarineKorps was unable to fulfill the great expectations Tirpitz had for it. This history of the MarineKorps, then, is an attempt to explain not only how the Germans conducted operations in one of the most critical theatres of the war; it also attempts to explain why they allowed the opportunities presented by their occupation of the Flanders coast to waste away.

1

Creation of the MarineKorps

PRECISELY WHEN ADMIRAL ALFRED von Tirpitz decided to create a naval unit to garrison the Flanders coast is unknown. The first mention of such a unit is in a telegram from Grosses Hauptquartier in Coblenz to Berlin on 23 August 1914. The document recommended the creation of a marine division to defend the French and Belgian coastlines.[1] This date was confirmed by Edgar Erich Schulze, Tirpitz's son-in-law and an Admiral Staff Officer on the MarineKorps Flandern, in his article 'Das MarineKorps in Flandern 1914–1918'. He claims that on that day Tirpitz telephoned General Headquarters and requested the creation of a naval division which would garrison the coastlines.[2] What exactly led Tirpitz to this recommendation and what did he hope to accomplish? Any study of the MarineKorps needs to begin with an examination of these elemental issues

There were three factors which were central to Tirpitz's thinking. The first of these resulted from the adoption of the strategy of *Kleinkrieg*. In order for this strategy to be employed effectively Germany required bases from which the light forces of the Kaiserliche Marine could sortie. The Heligoland Bight was simply too far from the English coastline to be useful unless the English attacked the Bight itself (as they did on 28 August 1914). The Belgian coastline was perfectly situated. A German force based in Belgium would be in a position to attack the vulnerable commercial and military shipping in the English Channel.[3] The plan was for the newly created MarineDivision to build and defend the naval bases that these forces would use.

In his memoirs, Tirpitz pointed to a second factor that influenced his thinking in August 1914. Due to the successes in the west Tirpitz had begun to consider the possibility of Germany splitting Belgium and creating an independent Flemish state. This state was to be little more than a German puppet and, according to Tirpitz, Germany was to have the right to permanently occupy the harbour and city of Zeebrugge.[4] He wanted the navy to take the leading role there and the MarineDivision would allow the navy to get its foot in the door, so to speak.

1

The most important factor however appears to have had little to do with the future of Flanders or even with the future course of the war against England. The decisive factor leading to the creation of the MarineDivision was an internal conflict between the German army and the navy. The conflict stemmed from their varying priorities for the war and from their differing war aims. However it also, and perhaps most importantly, resulted from their conflicting demands on Germany's already severely strained reserves of manpower and material.[5] The core of the issue for Tirpitz was the fact that in Germany's hour of need the army was winning tremendous victories while the navy sat idle. According to both Tirpitz and Schulze the MarineDivision was created both to provide the navy with a greater role in the war and to provide a point of co-operation between the army and the navy.[6] While the unit succeeded in attaining the first of these aims, it was a dismal failure at the second. In fact, much of the history of the MarineKorps Flandern revolved around the push and pull of its conflicting duties to both of the German forces. That history began in late August 1914.

As was mentioned, the spark that began the creation of the MarineDivision came on 23 August 1914. There had been discussions between the General Staff and the Reichs Marine Amt[7] (hereafter RMA) over the path that the German advance through Belgium was to take. The army intended to strictly follow the Schlieffen Plan and continue to maintain the greatest possible pressure on the French. Tirpitz and the RMA, believing the French were beaten, were beginning to look to the next stage of the struggle; the naval war with England. Tirpitz and the navy considered it essential to capture the Belgian and northern French harbours as quickly as possible in order to prevent the destruction of the harbour facilities and the shipping therein. To this end the RMA attempted to force the General Staff to alter their path of advance to encompass at least the Belgian harbours, most importantly, the city of Ostend. The army adamantly refused, stating that they could not afford to weaken the right wing by detaching units for secondary concerns. Acquiring extra shipping material for the navy was not worth disrupting the carefully scripted campaign plan.[8] This was a continuation of the deplorable state of pre-war relations between the two services, the most notable consequence of which was the lack of any coherent combined war plan. It was because of this that Tirpitz began to push for the creation of a naval division which could take over the coastal sector of the front and ensure that the interests of the navy were attended to.

From the beginning however there were questions as to what role such a hybrid could or would play. Vice-Admiral Eduard von Capelle for example, was determined that the unit, if it were created, would be used only as an occupation force and for naval purposes. He was wary lest the unit be taken over by the army for use in the frontlines. This would leave the Kaiserliche Marine once again without influence in Belgium.[9] His concerns were well founded. Tirpitz's attempt to create a naval division set off a series of debates between the highest leaders of the General Staff and the RMA.

The debates between the army and the navy revolved around two issues: control of the new unit and the role it would play in the war. These debates went on for four days, from the 24th to the 28th of August. The navy's primary concern was that the unit remain under naval control and not become simply a military garrison, similar to the various Landwehr units which were intended for the occupation of Belgium. The army, on the other hand, intended to make use of the unit to ease the strain on its manpower in the west. They hoped to use the division to garrison northern Belgium until sufficient Landwehr forces were available to take over. Only at that point would the division be able to concentrate on naval affairs. On one point however the two sides were in agreement; the division was *not* intended for frontline combat.

In an attempt to avoid placing the unit under the command of the army, the navy tried to place the division under the direct command of the Kaiser. The army countered this move by arguing that the troops were needed to assist in garrisoning Belgium and therefore they would have to be under the army's command. Over the course of a series of meetings from the 24th to the 27th of August a compromise was eventually reached: the MarineDivision was to be created and modelled upon an army division. It would be placed under the *temporary* command of the German army and would be used to garrison conquered Belgium. That status would last until the MarineDivision arrived on the Belgian coast. At that point it would be removed from the control of the army. Its commander, who would be chosen from the fleet, would be given the right of *Kommandogewalt*; the right to report directly to the Kaiser. This arrangement was finalised in a conference with the War Minister, General Erich von Falkenhayn, on 29 August. On that same day the order was issued creating the MarineDivision Flandern.[10] For the time being the debate between the army and navy was closed; this was destined though to be only a temporary truce.

The official order announced the creation of a naval division roughly approximate in strength to a full army division. It was to consist of marines, naval artillery and units of the naval reserve, the Seewehr (the naval equivalent of the Landwehr). The division was placed temporarily under the control of the German army and was to be used as an occupation force in Belgium but it was also to prepare the northern French and Belgian harbours for use in the *Kleinkrieg* against England. The final composition of the division was to be determined by the division's commander in co-operation with the chiefs of the Baltic and North Sea naval stations. The latter, though, proved unwilling to see their roles in the war diminish, and were not very co-operative.[11]

The division was to consist of a naval battalion from Kiel of roughly 3,000 men, two Landwehr artillery batteries from Kiel (300 men), 1,400 men of the naval artillery detachment at Kiel and 150 men for the dockyards in Flanders as well as a 1,000 man detachment from the naval defence (Seewehr) force in Kiel. Even larger numbers were requested from Wilhelmshaven: a 4,500 man naval battalion; 3,000 men from the naval artillery; 300 men for the dockyards and 2,000 men from the Seewehr. In addition, the division was assigned a cavalry squadron and a 300 man medical unit. For the dockyard personnel there was a particular stress on individuals who had experience with the submarines and torpedo boats of the Imperial fleet. This represented a serious drain on the resources of the two station commanders.[12]

The station commanders attempted to prevent the loss of these men by claiming that their ability to defend the German coastline would be gravely compromised. This argument was countered by several memoranda from the RMA, reiterating that the state of the war was such that a British landing on the German coast was not likely in the near future and that therefore the commanders were to comply and release the requisite forces. The two stations then tried to subvert the order by sending sub-par men to the new command. This was swiftly countered by Tirpitz who sent a personal memorandum informing the station chiefs that the personnel sent to the MarineDivision had to be fully capable of fulfilling their new assignments. In the end the station chiefs had little choice but to acquiesce in the demands of the RMA, though a compromise was once again struck. Roughly 10,000 new recruits were sent to the naval stations in late 1914 to allow the station chiefs to recoup their losses.[13] This did nonetheless place quite a drain on the Imperial navy, particularly its officer corps. For example the creation of the MarineDivision reportedly led to the decommissioning of the entire Sixth Battle Squadron (largely obsolete pre-dreadnoughts) and the reduction of the Fifth Battle Squadron.[14]

Once this issue was decided preparations for the dispatch of the unit proceeded rapidly and smoothly. The first section of the division, consisting of naval infantry, was to leave Kiel and Wilhelmshaven on 31 August with the artillery and the remainder of the infantry to follow on 3 September.[15] Training in their new duties would take place in Brussels once the entire division had arrived. Things moved smoothly and the requisite forces left the naval stations as planned.[16] Once the station commandants were brought in line and the troops were made available the MarineDivision Flandern quickly came into being.

Initially the division was composed of two regiments of naval infantry. The first regiment consisted of the I, V and VIII battalions and twelve heavy guns drawn from the Landwehr. The second regiment was made up of the II, IV, VI and VII battalions with an additional 3,500 men drawn from the naval artillery. These two regiments were combined into a 14,000 man Marine Brigade.[17] In addition to these forces there was a naval artillery regiment and a regiment of men drawn from the Seewehr. The division was rounded out with one and one-half cavalry squadrons, one section of Landwehr artillery, two companies of engineers (pioniere), five batteries of landing guns and five machine gun companies. There was supposed to be a contingent of aircraft as well but these did not arrive until 1915. As it stood in September 1914 the actual strength of the MarineDivision was 16,544 men and 421 officers with forty-four machine guns and twelve larger calibre guns.[18] Most of the guns were small- to medium-calibre though the division was equipped with three 28cm Krupp cannons. Also included was material for the construction of a radio station on the Belgian coastline which would be used to direct German submarines to targets in the Channel and southern North Sea. The force was rounded out with fifty pilots, the kernel of the future air arm.[19]

In late August and early September this hybrid hodge-podge of reservists and a few, mostly inexperienced, regulars was sent off to Brussels for what they expected would be easy occupation duty and a period of training to last for a month or two while the army concluded its campaign in France. That, however, was not to be their fate. Instead they became a frontline unit in both the war on the Western Front and the war at sea.

The division was given several missions. First of all, to mollify and assist the army, it was to be used as a garrison force in Belgium and northern France, but only until the successful conclusion of the war against France, thereafter it was to provide for the defence of the Flanders coastline against a potential landing by the British. More importantly to Tirpitz, it was to establish a forward base on the Flanders coast which could be used to launch attacks on shipping in the English Channel and along the southern coastline of Britain. Finally, Tirpitz and the commander of the MarineDivision, Admiral Ludwig von Schröder, hoped that these attacks might force the British to bring their battle fleet to the southern North Sea, where it could be engaged by the High Seas Fleet in favorable conditions.[20]

The lack of training which the unit received made Tirpitz's choice of the overall commander for the unit a critical one. He very quickly selected a retired admiral living in Berlin named Ludwig von Schröder. He would become known to friend and enemy alike as the 'Lion of Flanders.'

LUDWIG VON SCHRÖDER

Von Schröder came into the Imperial German Navy in the days of its infancy. He entered service as a cadet in the newly created navy in 1871 and served continually from that point until the end of the German empire in 1918 with only a brief retirement from 1913 to 1914. Von Schröder spent his initial time on board the training vessel *Niobe*. Over the course of his first year in the fleet he went on training cruises to the West Indies and to Venezuela. The following year, 1872, he was transferred as a SeeKadet to the cruiser *Friedrich Karl* while it was stationed in Barbados. It was while on board the *Friedrich Karl* that he met a young Leutnant zur See who would have a tremendous effect on his career. That officer was Alfred Tirpitz.[21]

Von Schröder served aboard the *Friedrich Karl* with Tirpitz until 1874 and apparently made an impact on the future founder of the German battle fleet since Tirpitz, once he became influential in the German navy, brought von Schröder into his inner circle.

In 1874 von Schröder transferred from the *Friedrich Karl* to the artillery school ship *Renown* where he served with two other men who would make their name in Wilhelmine Germany, Henning von Holtzendorff and Georg Alexander von Müller. Following that brief stay he entered an officer training course in 1875 and in 1876 began his affiliation with the naval infantry. In that year he was assigned to the *Deutschland* as part of the Second MatrosenDivision. That August he received his first-officers commission as signal officer of the *Kronprinz* which was stationed in the Mediterranean during the early stages of the Balkan crisis.[22]

From there he moved rapidly up in postings. He spent two months in 1877 as watch officer in the *Preussen* before being posted as an instructor on board the *Niobe* where one of his students was the brother of the future Kaiser, Prince Heinrich.[23] Following a tour of Asia as watch officer in the *Freya* he returned to Germany and was briefly posted to a naval artillery division before becoming an instructor to the First MatrosenDivision in 1881-82. In 1885 he joined Tirpitz once again when von Schröder was appointed as first officer in the torpedo flotilla leader *Blitz*, a ship commanded by Tirpitz.[24] From the *Blitz* von Schröder moved on to the *Blücher*, the school ship of the torpedo service. He spent the next five and a-half years as an instructor in the torpedo service before moving to Kiel in 1892 as an instructor for the Torpedo and Mine school. At the same time he was placed on the Naval Cadet Examination Commission.[25]

In 1895 von Schröder moved from the torpedo service to the Naval Staff where he succeeded August von Heeringen as head of section A3 and was made responsible for planning mine and torpedo attacks against Britain.[26] While he was here, von Schröder completed a study of how the Germans could best make use of the Belgian and Dutch coastlines in the event of a war against Great Britain. This study singled out the ports of Ostend and Zeebrugge as possible sites for advanced naval stations.[27] In 1912 von Schröder left the Naval Staff for what appeared to be his final assignment; he was appointed head of the Baltic naval station. In 1913 he retired and took up residence in Berlin where he remained until he was pulled back into service in August 1914 as commander of the MarineDivision Flandern.[28]

Clearly there were a number of factors in von Schröder's background which made him a desirable commander for the new unit. First of all was his knowledge of the Belgian coastline and the advantages it could give Germany in a war against Britain. He was the logical choice since the navy was clearly intending to put into practice what he had spent several years studying. His lengthy experience in the torpedo and mine service also weighed in his favor. Due to the nature of the ports in Flanders which, with the exception of Antwerp, were rather small, the use of larger warships would be at best problematical and probably impossible. This made it desirable to have someone in command of the division who was experienced in the use of small craft and their primary weapons, the torpedo and the mine. It was expected that the campaign carried on from Flanders would be fought out between the light forces of Germany and Britain.

A third factor in von Schröder's favor was his experience as a station chief. Tirpitz wanted a commander who was experienced in running a naval station since the navy was proposing to create a new naval station on the Flanders coast.

The affiliation von Schröder had early in his career with the naval infantry and the naval artillery was another reason for his selection. Due to the unusual nature of the MarineDivision as a hybrid naval/military unit his prior experience with those two branches of the service would also be useful.

Furthermore, it seems logical that, given the ragtag nature of the Marine-Division and the haphazard way in which it was put together, von Schröder's background as an instructor was also important. Most of the troops he was to command had never worked together before and few were properly trained. His background in training and educating the officers of the Kaiserliche Marine must have recommended him to Tirpitz.

Doubtless a final factor in his favor was his long-term association with Tirpitz. Tirpitz required a strong willed commander for this rather awkward post; someone whom he could rely on to preserve the interests of the navy in any conflict with the German army. It was only natural that he would turn to someone he had known and trusted for many years. In addition, Tirpitz recognised that he and von Schröder shared similar views regarding the use of the navy during the war. Von Schröder was an aggressive admiral who favoured an active naval policy; Tirpitz agreed. For all of these reasons von Schröder was called out of retirement and made commander of the MarineDivision Flandern on 24 August 1914.

It was now the responsibility of von Schröder and his staff to pull the division together and to prepare them for their role in the war against Britain. They anticipated that they would have several weeks to train while the army mopped up the French. They soon discovered that this was not to be the case. The defeat at the Marne drastically altered the plans that had been established for the use of the MarineDivision.

The history of the division and, later, the MarineKorps Flandern, can be broken into three phases, each based upon which of the division's assignments was most pressing at the time. The first of these phases ran from the inception of the MarineDivision until the creation of the MarineKorps in November 1914 and was characterised by the unit's use for purely military purposes. The second and longest phase consisted of the period from November 1914 to March 1918. During this phase the dominant concern of the MarineKorps was the conduct of the naval war in the Channel. The final phase began with the great offensive of 1918 and continued until the end of the war and was marked once again by the dominance of the military duties of the Korps.

THE FIRST PHASE: DOMINATION BY THE ARMY

The early stage of the MarineDivision's existence turned out to be dominated by the needs of the German army. The original intention was for the division to serve only as a garrison behind the army as it advanced through Belgium and into France. Later, once the war against France had concluded, it would be possible for the division to revert to its primary mission of preparing the Belgian and northern French coastlines for use in the *Kleinkrieg* against England. This was the understanding that was reached on 29 August 1914 when the order creating the unit was issued. Obviously no one expected the sudden reversal of fortunes on the western front that took place at the Marne in early September. That reversal drastically altered the role of the MarineDivision. When the war stalemated the conflict between the army and the navy over the use of the division was renewed.

The initial units of the MarineDivision left Kiel and Wilhelmshaven on 31 August as planned. They consisted of only two marine battalions and one machine gun company. The remainder of the unit followed on 3 September.[29] Von Schröder and his staff arrived in Brussels on 5 September as the Anglo-

French counterattack at the Marne began. As a direct result the MarineDivision was moved out of Brussels and placed under the command of the VII Army. The division was then moved to a position just outside of Antwerp to help maintain the watch upon the Belgian army fortified in the city. This was supposed to be a quiet sector where the division could begin training and still perform a useful function. It turned out not to be very quiet after all.

The division saw its first combat when the Belgians attempted to break out of the city on 9 September. The attempt was repulsed by the Germans with the MarineDivision acquitting itself well.[30] That same day saw the beginning of the retreat of the German armies from the Marne and the failure of the Schlieffen Plan. In the chaos following the mental collapse of Helmuth von Moltke, the head of the General Staff, and the German retreat the Marine-Division went from being a garrison unit to being pressed into frontline duty. They were soon to take part in heavy fighting.

On 9th September the division was placed under the command of the III Reserve Korps and assigned to take part in the capture of Antwerp.[31] A few rushed attempts were made to provide the division with some rudimentary training though, in essence, the unit was forced into battle well before it was ready.

The taking of Antwerp was left to General Hans von Besseler. According to von Besseler's plan the MarineDivision was to cover the western sector of the advance into the city. Besseler knew this would be a difficult task but justified it by saying that it (naval participation) would forever seal 'the brotherhood and co-operation between the army and navy.'[32] The assault began on 27 September.

Most of the division's fighting was done by the Marine brigade which advanced against some of the outer forts. By the end of the 28th the division had penetrated through the outer defences and into the suburbs of Antwerp, albeit with heavy losses.[33] At that point they ran into serious opposition from Fort Waelhelm, one of the Belgian strongpoints. The advance was held up there for three days while the German marines took heavy losses from Belgian artillery fire which the MarineDivision quite simply was not equipped to handle and could not effectively reply to. The losses led to a decision by von Schröder to commit the division's reserve, the Seewehr forces, to the battle on 1 October. These troops had even less combat training than the marines; they were only naval reservists and, consequently, their arrival had little impact on the battle and the bulk of the fighting continued to be done by the marines. Eventually the marines were able to subdue Fort Waelhelm, albeit only with the assistance of artillery from the III Korps. On 2 October the division resumed its advance into the city.[34]

The Belgians, for their part, were aware that Antwerp probably would be unable to hold out against the German artillery that had been so effective in demolishing Liège and Namur, and in early September they called for the British and French to help their army fight its way out of the city and to the Allied lines in the west. The British and French preferred to have the resistance in Antwerp continue since they were engaged in what became known as the 'race to the coast' and continued Belgian resistance could only benefit them. However, on 2 October the Belgians announced that, since they had not received the assistance they had requested, they were now pulling their army out of the city and leaving behind only a token garrison force.[35]

To assist the retreat of the Belgian army the British and French planned an attack in the direction of Bruges. They needed time however to make necessary arrangements. In order to buy that time the First Lord of the Admiralty, Winston Churchill, went to Antwerp along with the Royal Marine Brigade to try and rally Belgian resistance. Churchill arrived on 3 October and convinced the Belgians to try and hold for another ten days. He promised that if the Belgians did not receive favorable assurances from Britain and France regarding the latter's planned attack toward Bruges within three days they were free to withdraw and British troops would be sent to Ghent to cover the retreat. In the meantime they would continue to be supported by the Royal Marines. To make good on that promise the remainder of the British Naval Division was sent on 6 October. The Royal Marines took positions along the Nethe river, directly across from the German MarineDivision.[36] This arrangement had the desired effect and the resistance of the Belgians was temporarily bolstered.

The German marines meanwhile encountered significant trouble attempting to cross the Nethe river in the face of their better-trained British counterparts. They finally succeeded but it took an additional five days of bombardment by the heavy guns of the III Korps. The river was crossed on 7 October by four battalions of marines, but only after being abandoned by the British. The men of the Seewehr Brigade followed and occupied the positions captured by the marines. The advance continued against the inner line of fortifications until 10 October when the last of the Belgian forts surrendered to the Germans.[37] That same day von Schröder moved his headquarters into the city and was made defacto governor of Antwerp.[38]

While the resistance within Antwerp continued the British VII division landed at Zeebrugge on 7 October and a cavalry division landed at Ostend. This force was to relieve Antwerp with the aid of the French but the French force never materialised, and when the retreat from Antwerp began the British forces at Zeebrugge and Ostend were left trying to hold a perimeter through which the

Belgian army could retreat. In this they were successful. Though Antwerp fell to the Germans the Belgian army escaped to the west where it remained for the duration of the war.[39]

Within Antwerp itself most of the materials which might have been useful in the upcoming naval war had been destroyed by the Allies to prevent their falling into German hands. However the Germans were able to find two radio broadcasting stations in useable condition, and these were rapidly converted to naval use. Later in the war these were used to communicate with ships moving toward the Flanders area and with the RMA.[40] For the most part however the materiel rewards of the battle were slim.

The MarineDivision had acquitted itself well during its first serious test and as a result von Schröder was visited over the following days by Admiral Alexander von Müller, the head of the Kaiser's naval cabinet, and by Tirpitz. During his visit the State Secretary reminded von Schröder that he wanted the navy to take on a larger role in the war once von Schröder and his troops were able to occupy and fortify the Belgian coastline. Tirpitz foresaw future opposition from the army to his plans and hinted to von Schröder that he had begun to consider expanding the MarineDivision into a MarineKorps.[41]

The day following the visit of the State Secretary, 14 October, the bulk of the MarineDivision was moved out of Antwerp and began an advance toward the harbours of Bruges, Ostend and Zeebrugge, called by von Schröder, 'the Triangle.' For the purposes of the advance they were placed under the command of the new IV Army which the new head of the General Staff, Erich von Falkenhayn, had created to cover the extreme right wing of the German advance during the 'race to the sea.' The division was to be associated with the IV Army for the remainder of the war.[42]

The same day the MarineDivision began its renewed advance, the IV Reserve Division captured Ostend and Bruges against only light resistance and, much to the surprise of the Germans, the two ports were largely intact. Though the allies had caused extensive damage to Antwerp they retreated through the 'triangle' (Ostend, Zeebrugge, and Bruges) without taking the time to destroy the port facilities. The harbours were left intact, despite the protests of the Royal Navy, at the request of the British army which expected to turn the German flank and drive the Germans out of Belgium. When that happened they would need to be able to use both Ostend and Zeebrugge as supply points for their own advance.[43] This meant though that when the war stalemated the ports remained in German hands and the MarineKorps was able, in 1915, to develop them into important naval bases. By the 20th and 21st of October all three harbours were captured and the division began to construct coastal defences.

The capture of the three harbours and the new conditions of the war in the west led to a change in the activities of the MarineDivision. By the end of October and start of November it was increasingly evident to both sides that the race to the sea would not succeed in turning either's flank. Attempts were still made to break through, most notably the First Battle of Ypres where the Germans committed a newly created and largely untrained reserve army to battle in an effort to break through the enemy line[44], but the war now began to settle into trench warfare. The MarineDivision was involved in skirmishes along the front line into early November and, in fact, remained a frontline unit for the rest of the war. Their main operations though, now began to change.

The new primary objective was to begin the fortification of the coast and to prepare it for use in the *KleinKrieg* against England. On 23 October the entire Flanders coastline was placed under von Schröder's command.[45] He had several immediate problems to deal with. He had to repair the losses his unit had taken during the battles around Antwerp and during the advance. He also had to prepare defences for a coastline which was under ceaseless bombardment by the Royal Navy during late October and November 1914 and he also had to prepare for the eventual construction of a new German naval station in Flanders. At the same time he was forced to deal with a situation on the land front which was, to say the least, less than ideal. His division was frequently forced into combat and this in turn left him at least partially subject to control by the German army. Some of these issues were taken out of his hands: the conflict with the army was largely resolved by the expansion of the Marine-Division to the MarineKorps; the question of choosing a site for the new German naval station was taken up by an RMA committee led by the future commander of the Flanders submarine flotillas, KorvettenKapitän Karl Bartenbach; and the difficulties caused by the perpetual bombardment by British warships were eased to a certain extent by the dispatch of submarines to the area. However, von Schröder and his staff still had plenty of work to do.

Von Schröder had begun to prepare for the creation of his naval station as soon as Antwerp fell. He ordered the men of the division to gather all the salvageable material they could find in Antwerp. Those vessels which were still seaworthy were dispatched to Bruges via the Belgian canal system. Von Schröder was already planning on using Bruges as his primary naval base, even should the advance of the army bring Germany into possession of Dunkirk and Calais.[46] In addition, he had taken steps to convert the captured Belgian broadcasting stations into a Flanders radio station.[47] This was a small beginning on what was a very large task and his efforts were hampered by problems he experienced trying to get reinforcements from the Baltic and North Sea naval stations.

Von Schröder had argued since early September that his forces were insufficient to carry out his orders. On 12 September he requested two additional battalions of marines and four batteries of 10.5 or 15cm guns.[48] His requests were vigorously opposed by the heads of the naval stations and sparked a renewed debate over precisely what the size of the MarineDivision should be. It was during this debate that the first discussions concerning the expansion of the division into a corps took place.

The argument of the naval station commanders was that they had already been too severely weakened by the creation of the MarineDivision and could not afford any further depletions. The division should instead look to the army for additional personnel and equipment.[49] This led in turn to bitter recriminations from the staff of the MarineDivision that the troops in the stations at home should not be allowed to 'play war' while real fighting went on in Flanders.[50] These recriminations continued until 20 October when the decision was finally made to reinforce the division. The garrisons of the forts in Kiel and Wilhelmshaven were reduced to skeleton crews and older ships were left with only maintenance crews in order to come up with the needed forces.[51] These new forces were used to create a second MarineDivision. This decision clearly showed a growing commitment to the Flanders theatre.

EXPANSION TO THE MARINEKORPS

As October turned to November and the final German attempt to turn the Allied left flank at Ypres failed, it became evident that the nature of the war itself was changing. What followed was what the Germans termed *Stellungskrieg*, or 'positional warfare.' As the two sides began the construction of the elaborate trench systems which would become the lasting image of the First World War the role of the MarineDivision also began to change. Though they were to remain in the front lines for the duration of the war the division's focus now shifted to the naval war. This was made possible by two factors: the stalemate on the Western Front and the expansion of the division into a MarineKorps. This was accomplished by creating a second MarineDivision.

The decision to expand the division into a corps was taken with relatively little discussion. The idea of expansion was first brought up during the reinforcement debates in October. The discussions at that time envisioned a second division of two naval brigades, a half squadron of cavalry, an engineer company and a Landwehr field battery section.[52] This proposal was followed up on 3 November when Tirpitz suggested that the MarineDivision be expanded into a corps and that von Schröder be given direct access to the Kaiser, otherwise known as *Immediatstellung*.[53]

As it was in the creation of the MarineDivision, the position of the German army was critical in these discussions. Their attitude was largely shaped in October when the Kaiser decided that it was time for the MarineDivision to take up its primary mission; prosecuting the *KleinKrieg* against England.[54] For this to take place it would be necessary for the units of the division which were engaged in other tasks to be returned as soon as possible. Since units of the division were currently in use along parts of the western front this decision meant that the German army would lose valuable resources at a critical point in the war. Even though the units of the division were untrained they still filled a valuable role by holding down quiet sectors of the front, thereby freeing up more highly trained units for offensives or for transfers to the east. Not wishing to lose these resources the army was willing to compromise and therefore supported the creation of a second naval division with the proviso that the new division would fill the place in the front lines that the first division was vacating.[55]

With the support of the army assured the discussions now centered on the shape which the new division was to take. These were also brief. On 5 November a proposal was created, and eventually adopted, setting the strength of the new division at just over 20,000 men; 4,000 of these were to be marines with an additional 2,000 from the naval artillery and the bulk of the force, 13,000 men, coming from the Seewehr. They were to be equipped with forty machine guns and fourteen 6cm quick-firing artillery pieces. The division was to be shipped out gradually over the course of November and December, only reaching its full strength at the end of the year.[56] The bulk of these forces, over 12,000 men, were drawn from the North Sea naval station with the remainder coming from the Baltic station. The unit was organised as follows: one Marine regiment; two Seewehr brigades of two regiments each; one regiment of naval artillery; two engineer companies and various sanitation and supply services.[57]

On the following day, an *Allerhöchste Befehl* was issued to Falkenhayn and the German Chancellor, Theobold von Bethmann-Hollweg, informing them of the Kaiser's decision to create a second MarineDivision which would join with the first to form the MarineKorps Flandern. Admiral von Schröder, the commander of the 1st MarineDivision, was to relinquish that position and take command of the MarineKorps. He was to be placed directly under the command of the Kaiser and was to have the same rights and privileges as the North Sea and Baltic station commanders.[58] An area extending from the Dutch border in the east to the French border in the west and from the coast south to a line from the Yser river to the village of Moerhuizen was designated as the Flanders naval station.[59] The headquarters of the MarineKorps was to remain in Bruges and the 1st MarineDivision, which was placed under the command of Vice-Admiral Hermann Jacobsen, was now moved to the coast to take up its defence and begin preparing the area for use in the naval war. The 2nd MarineDivision, under the command of Vice-Admiral Friedrich Schultz, was to take the place of the 1st MarineDivision in the frontline. It was however to remain under the command of the MarineKorps, not the army. It formally took over its sector on 4 December[60] and the MarineKorps Flandern was born.

The decision to expand the MarineDivision appears to have been taken primarily for reasons of efficiency. The division was originally created to assist in the prosecution of the naval war against Britain but due to the setbacks of the German army in the west it was forced into participation in the land campaign. Though the unit generally acquitted itself well, it was hampered by disputes over the role it was to play and over whether it was to be controlled by the army or the navy. By creating a second MarineDivision it was possible to alleviate most of these problems. With one division assigned to purely naval duties and a second taking over the military requirements on the land front it appeared to the German leadership that the naval/military conflict which first arose in August would be laid to rest. Furthermore, both the purposes for which the unit had been created and the duties which it had since taken on could best be served by this arrangement. This did indeed succeed in easing the problems between the army and the navy, but they did not disappear. The creation of the MarineKorps Flandern, with its commander possessing *ImmediatStellung*, created an essentially independent force on the Western Front which was not always willing to bow to the needs of the German army. Some inkling that the disputes between the two services would continue appeared early in 1915.

These initial disputes were minor but were, none the less, signs that there were still areas of conflict between the army and navy; primarily over jurisdiction in Flanders. The disputes revolved around three areas: the always touchy issue of reinforcements and supplies; the jurisdiction of the Marine-Korps as opposed to the Governor-General of occupied Belgium; and the insistence of the army that, in the event of a major allied attack, they would have the full support of the MarineKorps.

In nearly every one of these instances the MarineKorps acceded to the wishes of the army. For example, on the issue of reinforcements, the army prevailed upon the MarineKorps in February 1915 to relinquish, from the coastal sector, two 38cm guns for use against Verdun and Dunkirk.[61] The MarineKorps also agreed to build its coastal batteries, especially those around Ostend, so that they could be pivoted and used against the land front.[62] Of more import, the MarineKorps, in early 1915, released some of its officers for assignment to the army due to the general shortage of officers.[63] The MarineKorps also agreed in

March 1915 that in the event of a major allied offensive in the west they would co-operate fully with the army.[64]

The one area in which the MarineKorps prevailed over the army concerned the issue of jurisdiction in Belgium. The MarineKorps felt that it was necessary for them to have control over the civilian population in their station area so that they could, among other things, requisition labour to assist in building the naval bases and coastal fortifications. A decision was reached on this matter on 20 February 1915 in a meeting between the Chief of Staff of the MarineKorps and representatives of the General-Government of occupied Belgium. At that meeting the MarineKorps was given control over the civil administration of its station area.[65]

These minor disputes were signs that a neat division of duties between the army and the MarineKorps was not possible. There would continue to be areas of tension for the remainder of the war, however, by the end of 1914 the MarineKorps was free to begin concentrating on its main task; the naval war against Great Britain.

2

Building the Naval Bases and Fortifying the Coast

THE MARINEKORPS FLANDERN WAS initially created to give Germany a geographic advantage in a naval war with Great Britain by occupying the harbours along the Belgian and French coasts. Tirpitz intended to have it to construct naval bases along the coast that would aid the German navy in the prosecution of the war; in particular the *Kleinkrieg*, by which the Germans intended to whittle away at Britain's superiority in battleships with an aggressive campaign of mine-laying and subsidiary operations by submarines. The Germans were particularly interested in the harbours along the northern French coast, especially Calais, but due to the setbacks in the west they were never able to reach them. As a result the MarineKorps concentrated its efforts on the Flanders harbours.

These harbours had a number of advantages over the main German fleet bases in the Heligoland Bight. The first and most obvious was simply their geographic position. The bases in the Heligoland Bight were roughly 450 nautical miles from the main British harbours on the west coast of England. The Flanders harbours, on the other hand, were only 250 nautical miles from those ports.[1] The advantage is obvious. The closer German ships and submarines were to their area of operations the less time they would have to spend in transit; therefore more time could be spent on station.

The shorter distance to the British bases also allowed the Germans to make use of smaller types of submarines and torpedo-boats which were specially constructed for use in Flanders and which, due to their limited radius of action, would not have been able to operate from the Bight. Their short construction time made it possible to rapidly expand the German submarine forces.

Another advantage these ports possessed were the excellent connections they had with one another via the canals in Belgium. This was particularly true in the case of what Tirpitz and von Schröder both called the 'Triangle': Ostend, Zeebrugge, and Bruges. It was possible for German forces to shelter in Bruges out of the range of British warships and still sortie through the canals connecting Bruges with Ostend and Zeebrugge. This created a very difficult situation for the British. However, The advantages of these three harbours were by no means obvious in late 1914.

Once the MarineDivision was expanded into the MarineKorps in November 1914 the Germans could concentrate on developing the Flanders area for use in the naval war. However, the situation in Flanders in November and December of 1914 was chaotic at best. No plans existed for using these harbours and there were no naval bases to hand. The MarineKorps was forced to start from scratch. Their first mission was to find a suitable port which could be developed into a naval base.

In October 1914 the Naval Staff examined the three harbours of Ostend, Zeebrugge, and Bruges and laid out its requirements for a useable naval base. They were: 1) easily navigable entrances and exits; 2) facilities for the repair and maintenance of the boats; 3) the possibility for reconnaissance by land and sea based planes and 4) protection against an enemy naval bombardment.[2] With these criteria in mind the Naval Staff, throughout late October and November of 1914, studied the possible bases in Flanders in an attempt to discover which, if any, would qualify. A commission was appointed under KorvettenKapitän Karl Bartenbach, a long time officer in the submarine arm, to undertake this study.[3] The commission's work was supplemented by a study prepared in October that was based on pre-war reports by German naval officers. The two studies concerned themselves primarily with Antwerp, Ostend, Bruges, and Zeebrugge though the latter study also covered the French harbours. It is worth examining their results in some detail.

SEARCHING FOR NAVAL BASES

The French Channel Ports[4]

The Naval Staff study of October 1914 considered, in addition to the Belgian harbours, the French harbours of Dunkirk, Calais, Boulogne, Le Havre, and Cherbourg in an effort to determine which would be the most suitable for use against Britain. Of course, given the result of the 'race for the coast' and the German defeat therein, the results of the study were never implemented. Nonetheles, they shed light upon what the Naval Staff was looking for in a base and provide a basis of comparison for the Belgian harbours.

The first harbour considered was Dunkirk. The study found that, due to the narrow channels and shallow waters around the port, it would not be very useful as a submarine base. However, these same navigational problems as well

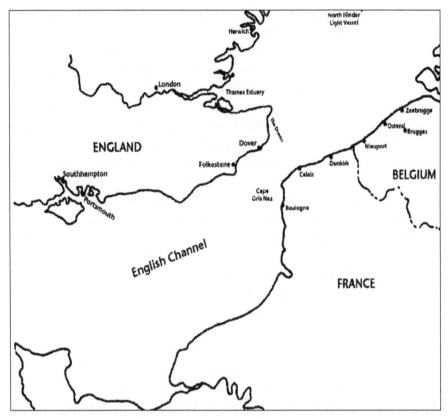

The English Channel and the surrounding coasts.

as the position of the harbour made it easily defensible against an assault by sea. Furthermore, it was very well equipped with workshops, dockyards and repair facilities. It was therefore considered to be an excellent advanced base for torpedo-boats.

Calais was the closest port to Great Britain and hence of great importance to the British. The Germans were somewhat less impressed with it. Calais had far fewer navigational problems than Dunkirk did, for example, the depth of the water was sufficient to allow submarines to dive immediately after leaving port, and the port itself, like that in Dunkirk, was well equipped with dry-docks, but it was considered very vulnerable to attack. It would therefore require the construction of a massive series of coastal artillery barrages for defence before it could be used by naval vessels. Overall, though it was useable by submarines, the Naval Staff considered it inferior to Dunkirk.

Boulogne, like Calais, posed little difficulty as far as navigation was concerned and had sufficient depth to allow submarines to dive soon after leaving port.

However, also like Calais, it was in an exposed position and would require the installation of numerous batteries of heavy guns for defence. In fact, Boulogne was even more vulnerable than Calais to naval bombardment because the railway lines connecting the harbour with its hinterland ran along the coast and could be cut by a naval bombardment. This would leave the port partially isolated. Boulogne also had only limited resources for the repair of warships and was therefore labeled as 'barely passable' for a torpedo-boat and submarine base.

Le Havre, the fourth French port studied, seemed to be very promising. Though it had serious navigational problems that the Naval Staff thought might even force the Germans to place French pilots on their warships it was exceptionally well equipped with dry-docks, repair facilities, magazines and supply depots. It also had extensive defensive works which, supplemented by coastal artillery, would provide excellent protection for any forces based there. Finally, as with Ostend and Zeebrugge there was a canal connecting the harbour with the inland areas. In the event of a naval bombardment German light forces could shelter in this canal out of the reach of enemy guns.

Cherbourg was even more promising. The channels leading into the harbour were deep enough to be useable not only by submarines and torpedo-boats but also by small cruisers. As with Le Havre it was very well equipped with dockyards and dry-docks and was protected by old French fortifications. Furthermore Cherbourg was only seventy nautical miles from Portsmouth and 150 nautical miles from either end of the English Channel. Overall it was considered a first class and highly desirable base which could prove to be of decisive importance if the Germans decided to launch a commercial war with their submarines. Of course, there was the problem of getting forces to Cherbourg through the Dover Strait, but this was not discussed in the report.

However, the German offensive was halted at Ypres and these ports remained in Allied hands throughout the war. The Germans were left with only the Belgian harbours. These were much less desirable.

The Belgian Harbours

The one major port within Belgium was of course Antwerp. There were, however, two significant problems preventing the Germans from using Antwerp as a naval base. First of all, the Allies sank block ships in the harbour channels and destroyed most of the facilities within the port before leaving the city.[5] Even after the damage was repaired there was still the problem of the neutrality of the Netherlands. The main channel in the Scheldt river, which ran from Antwerp to the North Sea and which was navigable by large warships, the Oostgat, ran through Dutch territorial waters and directly past Walcheren Island.[6] This ruled out the use of Antwerp as a base unless the Germans were willing to violate Dutch neutrality which, at this stage of the war, they were not ready to do. Even though Antwerp could not be used as a naval base the Germans could still make use of the considerable ship building facilities in the city.

There were two major shipbuilding factories and six dry-docks within the harbour. True, these had been severely damaged by the retreating Allies but once they were repaired Antwerp could be used as a centre for the construction of small submarines and torpedo-boats.[7] One of these factories for example had four slipways, each of which was more than 100 meters long, more than sufficient for the building of torpedo-boats and submarines. This factory, the Chantiers Navales Anvernois, was the site at which the Germans later assembled the majority of the UB and UC-class submarines that eventually made up the Flanders Submarine Flotilla. By the end of February 1915 the Germans had repaired the damage to the harbour facilities and were building four submarines every three weeks in Antwerp.[8] The Germans still needed a base in Belgium though. With Antwerp unavailable they turned their eyes to the 'Triangle': Ostend, Bruges, and Zeebrugge.

The Germans captured these ports relatively intact on 15 October and promptly began looking into their possible use as military bases. The Naval Staff studied these harbours using the same criteria they used in regard to the French harbours and concluded that both Ostend and Zeebrugge presented navigational problems due to the shallowness of the water, which was only five-to-six metres deep, and the tendency of the entrances of both ports to become clogged with sand due to the strong currents along the coast. In addition, neither port was fortified and both were therefore very vulnerable to enemy attack, though the canals connecting them with the inland harbour of Bruges would allow any ships stationed in the coastal harbours to retreat from a naval bombardment. Neither harbour had much in the way of repair and main-tenance facilities either. Zeebrugge had no repair shops or dry-docks that could be used for military purposes and Ostend was only slightly better equipped, with two dry-docks and some workshops which could be converted to naval use. The conclusion of the Naval Staff was that both harbours would need significant work and were only suitable as stopgaps until the army could acquire the better equipped French harbours.[9]

The study undertaken by the Bartenbach Commission confirmed these gloomy conclusions. Bruges was hardly considered by the Commission at all due to a general lack of necessary facilities. It was only considered useful as a supply station and a safe harbour for ships stationed along the coast.[10] Most of the study concentrated on the two coastal ports of Ostend and Zeebrugge.

Zeebrugge was, as the Naval Staff study suggested, very poorly equipped. The only available facilities were storage sheds, a very small repair shop twenty minutes-walk from the harbour and a modern electrical plant; there were no dry-docks.[11] The Commission also confirmed that the harbour was essentially defenceless and noted it would be necessary to construct a massive array of coastal artillery batteries to ensure the security of the harbour. Zeebrugge did have two advantages however. One was the large mole which surrounded the harbour and could provide some shelter against bombardment.[12] The other was the fact that the canal connecting Zeebrugge with Bruges, unlike the canal from Bruges to Ostend, was large enough to be used by light cruisers as well as torpedo-boats and submarines.[13] In general however, it was not considered a desirable base.

Ostend was only slightly better. Like Zeebrugge, it had no defences and would require a significant investment in coastal artillery to make it safe enough to use as a naval base. It did however, have more repair facilities and a few dry-docks. It also had the advantage of being located only sixty nautical miles from the mouth of the Thames. The Bartenbach Commission concluded that of the three harbours Ostend was the best suited for development and that it should become the new German submarine base in Flanders. The Commission also decided that, despite its problems, Zeebrugge should be prepared as a secondary base. Before any forces could be stationed in either harbour though, the MarineKorps would need to construct defensive works and make improvements to the harbours themselves.[14]

Once the choice of a base was made it fell to the MarineKorps to begin the work of improving the harbours. In order to accomplish this a special section of the Korps was created, the *Abteilung Hafenbau*. This section, headed by Kapitän zur See Friedrich Pohl, was responsible for constructing and maintaining the harbours, canals, and airfields in the station area.[15] It was continually understaffed and at its height consisted of only 5,000 men.[16]

The Abteilung Hafenbau undertook several projects. Priority was given to developing repair and supply stations in both Ostend and Zeebrugge. Once these were completed then emphasis was placed on developing Bruges as a repair and auxiliary supply station.[17] The canals linking Bruges with Antwerp were also widened so that the small submarines that were to be built in Antwerp could be transferred through the canals to Ostend and Zeebrugge.[18]

The Abteilung also created a string of radio stations along the coast that were to be used to communicate with German submarines. The idea of creating a system of radio stations to broadcast intelligence concerning British shipping movements to German submarines had been discussed in October and was now implemented, although it did not work as effectively as had been hoped.[19]

Most of the supplies for these projects were taken, once again, from the naval stations in Germany, particularly the Baltic station, but the actual labour was done by requisitioned Belgian workers.[20] Roughly 5,000 Belgians were drafted from various areas and sent to the coast to build the repair facilities, radio stations, and dry-docks in Ostend and Zeebrugge. They were also put to use dredging the harbours to prevent them from silting up.[21] The most critical work, that of building the coastal fortifications, was also done by forced Belgian labour.[22]

By the end of February and the start of March 1915 the conditions in the harbours at Ostend and Zeebrugge had improved sufficiently that they could begin receiving naval forces from Germany. There were however still concerns over whether the ports were adequately defended.

FORTIFYING THE COAST

From the beginning of November 1914 until the middle of the following year, the MarineKorps was busy preparing a series of heavy artillery emplacements which, it was hoped, Would protect the new naval bases from British attack. The creation of this elaborate defensive system was given extra emphasis following the British landing at the Dardanelles, when legitimate concern arose on the German side that a similar landing would be attempted in Flanders.

The German concerns over the defence of the Flanders coast were a result of British operations along the coast during late October and early November 1914. During those months the British undertook several naval bombardments of German positions along the coast in a successful attempt to slow down the German advance to the west.[23] The attacks began on 17 October and continued until 9 November when they were temporarily halted. They were renewed in late November when the forces of the Dover Patrol bombarded Zeebrugge from the 21st to the 26th of November. The bombardments then continued on a haphazard basis throughout the first winter of the war while the British debated their next course of action. There was some sentiment in the British government for a Flanders offensive in 1915 but it was only one of several plans being discussed. The latter included schemes to seize part of the German Baltic coastline and land Russian forces just north of Berlin as well as plans to seize an island such as Heligoland or Borkum which would allow the implementation of a close blockade of Wilhelmshaven. The British eventually chose to pursue the assault on the Dardanelles Straits instead.[24]

The Germans anticipated that an attack in Flanders might be on the British agenda for 1915. In early December von Schröder was warned by the head of the High Seas Fleet, Friedrich von Ingenohl, that the British had concentrated a group of old steamers in southern British harbours. Von Ingenohl believed that the British intended to use these vessels as block ships. Though personally convinced the ships were meant for the German bases in the Bight, he wanted von Schröder aware of the concentration just in case they were intended instead for Zeebrugge.[25] As a result von Schröder ordered his staff to prepare a study evaluating the chances for success of a British blocking operation aimed at Zeebrugge. They concluded that an attempt to block the harbour would probably succeed because there were insufficient defences along the coast. In order to defend against an attack it would be necessary to sew all approach routes with mines and also maintain a submarine patrol off the coast. Von Schröder accordingly requested that additional submarines be assigned to the Flanders theatre.[26]

Nor was Flanders the only area of concern for the Germans. They were also very concerned about the possibility of an allied landing in the mouth of the Scheldt. They feared that a landing there would drive the Dutch from the coast and turn the German flank. A report from the military attaché in the Netherlands in April 1915 called attention to the large number of troops now available to the British for a landing in the Scheldt estuary. He considered it likely that a landing would be followed by a rapid offer of peace to the Dutch, which if not accepted, would cost them their colonial empire. In his opinion the Germans could not count on significant Dutch resistance and would have to anticipate having their flank turned.[27] This gave the navy still more reason to be concerned over the defences along the coast and as a result the MarineKorps began studying possible countermeasures to such a British move.[28] These concerns led to the acceleration of defensive measures which had begun in late 1914.

The planning of the German defences for Belgium had begun in October 1914. The same day that the RMA sent out the Bartenbach Commission to examine the ports they also telegraphed to von Schröder to find out which, if any, of the guns that had been captured from the Belgians could be used for the defence of the coast.[29] The MarineKorps responded three days later, reporting that the MarineKorps had captured several light, rapid-firing 5cm Belgian guns which, unfortunately, would only be suitable for guarding the mouths of the harbours against close range torpedo-boat attacks. Since he had no suitable guns on hand von Schröder requested that sixteen 15cm guns, sixteen 10.5cm guns, and sixteen 8.8cm guns be assigned to the MarineKorps so that he could begin setting up the defences of the harbours.[30] The 8.8cm were to be used primarily as air defence guns while the 10.5 and 15cm were intended for use against enemy ships.

Heavier calibre guns were also requested from the fortresses in home waters. In late October von Schröder requested several 28 and 35cm guns from the

North Sea station, justifying his request by arguing that the British would never attempt a landing in the Bight because of the strength of the High Seas Fleet. Therefore Flanders was much more vulnerable and the heavier calibre guns could be put to much better use there.[31] What von Schröder envisioned was an array of guns ranging from the captured Belgian 5cm up to and including heavy 35cm guns similar to those intended for the *Mackensen*-class battle cruisers.[32] By the end of November he expected to have in place fourteen 15cm guns, twenty-four 12.5cm guns, twenty-nine 10.5cm, and sixteen 8.8cm. These were to be placed mostly around the two harbours. By the end of the year he anticipated widening the defensive field by constructing additional batteries containing fourteen 15cm and fifty-four 8.8cm guns. These batteries were to be supplemented by four 24cm and twelve 28cm guns. Eventually he hoped to add another sixteen 15cm, eight 21cm, four 24cm, and twenty 28cm. This would give the MarineKorps a total of 218 artillery pieces along a roughly 50km stretch of the Flanders coastline.[33]

To supplement the artillery defences of the coast von Schröder also requested a half-flotilla of submarines and a half-flotilla of torpedo-boats. Five of each were considered to be the minimum necessary to defend the coast while the artillery defences were being constructed. Once the artillery defences were completed the torpedo-boats could still be used to maintain a watch on the channel and the submarines could be used to attack British shipping.[34] Unlike the artillery however, these forces were not granted to the MarineKorps. With the exception of a few submarines occasionally sent into the Channel, the MarineKorps was forced to rely on its artillery for defence.

Over the course of the next few months construction of the fortifications moved along rapidly. By the end of February 1915 the MarineKorps could report that excellent progress was being made and that they expected the fortifications to be complete by the end of March.[35] They met that date. By 31 March the fortifications were complete. They consisted of an array of batteries extending from the Dutch border in the east to just west of Ostend. However, they were not quite as extensive as von Schröder had hoped for. The following tables present a complete listing of the coastal defences as they existed in March 1915 (they were augmented as the war progressed).[36]

These were only the main batteries. They were supplemented by a wide array of 8.8cm guns used for air defence. Furthermore, the westernmost 15cm guns were constructed on a pivoting base so that they could also be used against the enemy positions around Nieuport. In addition, there were a number of mobile batteries consisting of captured French and Belgian guns varying in calibre from 5.7cm to 15cm.[37] The fortifications were under the

Table 1: German Batteries on the Flanders Coast March 1915

Ostend Sector

Battery Name	Number and Calibre	Range
Aachen	4 x 15cm	13.7km
Antwerp	6 x 10.5cm	10.8km
Beseler	4 x 15cm	13.7km
Cecilie	4 x 15cm	13.2km
Hindenburg	4 x 28cm	12.3km
Irene	3 x 15cm	12.6km

Zeebrugge Sector

Battery Name	Number and Calibre	Range
Hertha	4 x 21cm	16.2km
Kaiserin	4 x 15cm	13.7km
Mittel Batterie	7 x 10.5cm	10.8km
Groden Batterie	4 x 28cm	10.5km
Friedrichsort	4 x 28cm	10.0km
Freya	4 x 21cm	16.2km
Augusta	3 x 15cm	12.6km

NOTE: Listings are from west to east. Information from: Von Schröder to von Tirpitz and Kaiser Wilhelm II, 31st March 1915, RM3:5639.

command of Rear-Admiral Max Witschel, Artillery Inspector of the MarineKorps.[38]

The gun emplacements were supplemented by three minefields that were laid off the Flanders coast. One of these was just northwest of Nieuport in order to make it more difficult for the British fleet to support allied land operations in Flanders. The second was laid north of Blankenberg along the probable route of advance of any British fleet moving on Zeebrugge, and the last was laid north of the Scheldt to hamper any British attempt to land in the Netherlands.[39]

These defences were augmented throughout the war with additional batteries which gradually made the Flanders coast one of the most heavily defended sections of coastline in the world. For example, the *Kaiser Wilhelm II* battery was completed in the spring of 1916 and consisted of four 30.5 cm guns. The *Deutschland* battery followed in the spring of 1917 with three 38cm guns. Finally, in the last year of the war, a large number of mobile 17cm and 28cm railway guns were added as well.[40] For the most part the batteries did what they were intended to do; with the exception of the Zeebrugge and Ostend raids of 1918, they deterred the Royal Navy from making any close range attacks on the Flanders coast.[41]

In preparing their defences the MarineKorps also had to take into account the newest element in warfare; the aeroplane. The British began to launch air raids against the Flanders harbours in early 1915 once it became apparent that the Germans were basing submarines in them. The first attack occurred on 22nd January but did little damage.[42] The raids soon became a regular occurrence and most had little or no effect. However, on the night of February 12th, a British air raid on Zeebrugge succeeded in doing significant damage to *U-14*.[43] The submarine was taken out of service for several months. This raid had two very important results: first it was a decisive factor in the decision of Admiral von Pohl not to assign a flotilla of fast destroyers to the Flanders front;[44] and secondly it resulted in a major effort to increase the air defences of the bases.

One of the measures undertaken, as we have seen, was the erection of 8.8cm anti-aircraft guns. As additional precautions the MarineKorps directed that submarines in port were to have their guns manned at all times and at night were to move to different berths. In addition, the machine gun defences of the harbours were to be manned at all times.[45] The RMA also suggested that false submarine hulls be built and placed about the harbours to draw the fire of British planes while shelters were built for the actual submarines. (These were primitive pre-cursors to the more elaborate shelters built in 1917 and 1918.)[46] These initial efforts were improved upon as the war progressed.

The MarineKorps slowly created an entire air defence system for the ports. First, the MarineKorps' station area was organized into four sectors, each of which was responsible for its own air defence. One sector was based in Bruges, another covered the coastal batteries, and two others were based in Ostend and Zeebrugge respectively.[47] They also constructed a number of watch stations along the Belgian coastline from Mariakerke to Knocke. The stations were all connected with each other and with a central directory by telephone. Any appearance of enemy aircraft was to be phoned to the MarineKorps' head-quarters in Bruges and then relayed to the ports. As a backup measure signal rockets were also to be set off when enemy aircraft were sighted.[48] Furthermore, all essential facilities were equipped with spotlights and machine guns. The spotlights were arranged in groups of three or four and were to serve a dual purpose; to illuminate the enemy planes and blind the enemy pilots.[49] In addition, all German planes were forbidden to fly over the ports and any planes flying over the coastal batteries were required to make recognition signals and to schedule their flights in advance.[50] By the end of 1917 these measures covered the entire coastline. These measures were moderately effective, though it was necessary to assign fighters to the Flanders area in 1916 and 1917 as support for the anti-aircraft guns.

By the middle of 1915 the harbours of Ostend and Zeebrugge had been converted into useable and extremely well defended naval strongpoints. The air defences appeared to be sufficient to keep allied air attacks at bay and the coastal gun emplacements provided the harbours with an unequalled measure of security. It now remained to be seen just what the Germans could do with these bases. The MarineKorps' next mission was to acquire naval and air forces from the German fleet. This proved to be difficult.

Creation Of The Flanders Naval Air Station

One of the MarineDivision's original missions had been to create a naval air station on the Flanders coast. To begin that project a small detachment of pilots and mechanical personnel had been sent out with the MarineDivision.[51] These plans were first formed in late August 1914 and envisioned a naval air station commanded by Admiral von Schröder in conjunction with a member of the Naval Air Service. The station's initial missions were simply to train pilots and maintain the few aircraft the division possessed. These duties were to be expanded as the war progressed.[52]

Despite the clear intentions to create a new naval air station it took prodding by the MarineDivision to get this done. In a report sent to the RMA on October 20th von Schröder urged that immediate steps be taken to create the air station since he needed aircraft for patrols along the coastline. He also pointed out that there was an excellent site near Zeebrugge for an airfield.[53] Tirpitz responded to this request by assigning a full airship company to the MarineKorps and by accelerating plans to create a full air station in Flanders.[54] As a result of pressure from Tirpitz, the Flanders Naval Air Station was officially created on 5 December 1914;[55] initially it consisted of two seaplanes and the airship company and was commanded by Kapitän zur See Hans Herr.[56] Herr also had at his disposal a fixed balloon section for air defence and a carrier pigeon section to relay messages from the planes to the ground and vice versa.[57]

In May of 1915 the MarineKorps formed the 'Volunteer Naval Air Corps' as a supplement to the air station. This consisted of Germans who had volunteered for service in Belgium. They were assigned as pilots, mechanics or observers based upon their experience. A brief mention of what was required for a volunteer to be made a pilot serves as a reminder of just how new airpower truly was. In order to be commissioned as a Petty Officer 3rd Class a volunteer only needed three hours of flying experience. Higher grade officers needed only similar flight time but had to have 'sufficient social standing' as well.[58] This auxiliary force, not surprisingly, had only a marginal impact on the war.

Initially, the Flanders air station was forced to get by with older models of aircraft but by the later stages of the war they were equipped with two fine types of planes: the Brandenburg W12 single seater bi-plane with a 200 horsepower engine capable of speeds approaching 160km/hour and armed with one or two machine guns; and the superior W29 monoplane two-seater armed with three machine guns and capable of staying aloft for over three hours. The latter's maximum speed peaked at 178 km/hour; it allegedly gave Germany 'virtual air superiority over the Channel.'[59]

The Flanders planes were generally used for four purposes. First of all they served as auxiliaries to the air defences of the bases. In that role they were used primarily as interceptors against British bombing raids. This began almost immediately after the founding of the air station and continued throughout the remainder of the war.[60] The planes also served as spotters for the coastal artillery which were, for the most part, indirect firing weapons. The planes of the Flanders air station became their eyes. They watched the fall of shot from the German guns and reported back to the gunners so that the latter could make the necessary adjustments and close in on their targets.[61] In a memorandum from January 1915, von Schröder urged that spotters be used as often as possible to assist the gunners.[62]

In a similar vein, the Flanders craft were also used to provide reconnaissance for the submarines and torpedo-boats based in Flanders. In fact, in a memorandum from late 1914, this was listed as the primary use for aircraft based in Flanders.[63] It was even believed that it would be possible to use aerial spotters to guide German submariners to their targets. This idea never quite lived up to its promise due to communications problems between the submarines and planes, however. The German reconnaissance efforts eventually expanded to include aerial searches for minefields and they eventually covered the entire area from the Dover-Calais straits out to the seas north-east of the Netherlands.[64]

Lastly, planes based out of Flanders were used to attack English shipping both at sea and in port. The Germans hoped that repeated air attacks on the British patrols off the Belgian coast would drive them out of the area completely. Unfortunately for the Germans aircraft in the First World War were not nearly as deadly to shipping as they were in the Second World War and this scheme did not succeed.[65] The offensive activity of the planes was initially directed against Dunkirk, Le Havre, the Thames and Harwich.[66] Bombing campaigns against these harbours began in November of 1914 and continued throughout the war. They had only minimal success.[67]

London was another potential target for German air attacks. In a rather chilling memorandum written in October 1914 by a young naval officer who had some familiarity with London, the notion of firebombing the city was discussed. The London firefighter's shortage of vehicles and manpower was examined in great detail. The memorandum concluded by urging the navy to attack the city with large numbers of small incendiary devices because it was believed that the fires would spread rapidly and that the understaffed fire service would be unable to cope with them. London would then burn to the ground.[68] The High Seas Fleet responded favorably to this memorandum and urged that the necessary bombs be developed.[69] Fortunately the plan was never implemented due to reservations on the part of the Kaiser.[70] This memorandum led to several serious studies examining the idea of attacking London from the air. These studies resulted in the Zeppelin and Gotha raids of 1916-1918. The rationale for overlooking the Hague conventions and international law was that these agreements did not apply to war in the air, only to war on land and at sea.[71] The MarineKorps, however, was not involved in these latter raids. Their offensive actions were directed almost exclusively against the major harbours in northern France and southern Britain.

The presence of aircraft not under the control of the army in the Flanders area led almost immediately to disputes between the German army and the MarineKorps over the assignment of pilots and first-rate aircraft. The shortage of pilots was a particular problem by early 1915 and this proved to be an area where, not surprisingly, the demands of the MarineKorps were secondary to those of the army. Many pilots were taken from the MarineKorps and reassigned to Germany where they were used to train new pilots for the army. Others were claimed for other sectors of the front or were given to other corps, while still others, though this more often was the lot of mechanics, were taken and used as infantry due to the exceptionally heavy casualties. By the beginning of March 1915 von Schröder was receiving complaints from his air commanders that, since the start of the year, over 100 men, both pilots and mechanics, had been taken by other commands to serve as infantry.[72] There was however little that von Schröder could do to ease the problem. In fact, the policy of the army regarding the supply of aircraft in early 1915 only made the situation worse.

It had been decided in September of 1914, prior to the Battle of the Marne, that the army was to have priority in the supply of aircraft until the land campaign in the west was concluded at which point the needs of the navy would be addressed.[73] Due to the fact that the war stalemated and the western land campaign was never completed, this original agreement between the Naval Staff and the General Staff came under fire from the navy.

Starting in late March 1915 the navy began to question the arrangement. Two measures in particular led to a demand that the situation be reassessed. On 23 March, because of the shortage of planes, the Naval Staff acceded to a request that all captured planes, both land based and sea planes, were to be turned over to the army.[74] This was not appreciated by Admiral von Schröder and the situation was aggravated a few weeks later when the army insisted that it take over full control of all production orders for aircraft. It would assign to the navy what it could spare. The decision resulted from a dispute between the army and navy over an order the navy had placed in February for ten Albatross fighters that were to be sent to the Flanders air station. The War Ministry had intervened and taken over those planes for the army. Tirpitz was incensed and replied that these planes were *absolutely* essential for defending the Flanders bases against air attack.[75] (Emphasis original.) He also argued that the naval station in Flanders was so important that its needs should be placed before those of the army and demanded a reappraisal of the September agreement concerning the allocation of forces.[76] To Tirpitz the army did not appear to take the needs of the navy seriously, considering airplanes as something of an 'ornament' for the fleet.[77] Von Schröder, for his part, was vehemently opposed to having to place orders for aircraft with the War Ministry since he believed this left the interests of the navy too much in the hands of the army.[78] The dispute was eventually resolved in favour of the army. As a result the Flanders station received only one of the new Albatross fighters.[79] The issue however did not vanish and disputes over aircraft remained a thorn in the relations between the two services for the remainder of the war.

Though the establishment of an air station in Flanders was important it was not the reason for which the MarineKorps had been created and certainly was not the reason for the building of the Flanders naval bases. The air station was merely to serve as an adjunct to the primary mission of the MarineKorps, which remained the vigorous prosecution of the war at sea. However, if this mission was to be fulfilled then von Schröder would need to have submarines, torpedo-boats and destroyers under his command. Since these would have to come from the High Seas Fleet and the naval stations in Germany von Schröder soon had another fight on his hands. In early 1915 the leadership of the German navy had to decide which of its many theatres, the North Sea, the Baltic Sea or Flanders would have strategic priority.

3

The Creation
of the Flanders Flotillas

THE ORIGINS OF THE FLANDERS flotillas lie in the disputes between the various German naval commands. As we have seen the value of the Flanders coastline was recognised early in the war by Admiral Tirpitz and he took steps, by creating the MarineDivision, to take advantage of this favourable geographic position. However, due to the compromises that attended the creation of the MarineDivision and its peculiar position as a hybrid naval-military unit, no provision was made for the assignment of light naval forces to the division. Once the coast was occupied it was up to Admiral von Schröder to persuade the higher commands to assign him the light forces he needed in order to make full use of the Flanders positions. This proved to be a very difficult task.

DEBATES OVER FORCE ALLOCATION

During October 1914, while the Bartenbach Commission was engaged in studying the Belgian harbours, a memorandum discussing the type of operations that could be carried out from the 'Triangle' was written by Rear-Admiral Paul Behncke. In the memorandum Behncke examined the possibilities for action by submarines, torpedo-boats and minelayers.

He made a very strong argument for the employment of submarines in Flanders, stating that the geographic position of the new bases would allow the submarines to spend more time on station. The bases would also extend the radius of action of the German submarines. Additionally, the harbours on the Belgian coast would allow the Germans to make use of smaller coastal submarines in the narrow waters of the English Channel. He hoped that an aggressive submarine campaign in the eastern portion of the Channel would force the British to divert their transports to France from ports such as Le Havre and Calais to more westerly ports, for example, Brest.[1]

However, Behncke argued against the use of torpedo-boats in Flanders because

British destroyers were faster and better armed than the small German craft. He was also very concerned about the dangers presented by British minefields. He argued that because of the danger from the British destroyers it would be necessary to assign light cruisers to protect the torpedo-boats. This would in turn expose the light cruisers to serious danger from mines and the likely results of such an operation were simply not worth the risk. A similar evaluation applied to the use of minelayers. The expected benefit from any transfer of minelayers to Flanders was simply not worth the dangers they would face in transit.[2] These same arguments were used by both Admiral von Ingenohl and Admiral von Pohl during the upcoming debates over the allocation of forces to Flanders.

In the meantime the course of events was forcing the German naval leadership to seriously consider assigning submarines to Flanders. During the crucial land battles along the coast during October 1914 the Royal Navy intervened with cruisers, destroyers, and occasionally battleships against the German positions. This fire support was critically important in halting the German drive on Nieuport.[3] In an effort to end these bombardments the German navy began to dispatch submarines to the eastern portion of the Channel in early November.[4] On November 9th *U-12* became the first German submarine to make use of the Flanders bases.[5] It was roughly at this same time that serious discussions began within the navy over precisely what types of forces, if any, should be assigned to the new theatre and in what strength.

The earliest record of this debate is a letter sent from Admiral von Ingenohl to the Naval Staff on 18 November 1914 concerning a request the latter had made that several half-flotillas of submarines and torpedo-boats be sent to Flanders. Von Ingenohl agreed to send the 1st Submarine Half-Flotilla but only if the ships remained under his command. He was strongly opposed to sending torpedo-boats for any reason. He believed they would be ineffective because of the greater speed and gunpower of their British opposites. They therefore were not sent.[6] Four days later Admiral von Schröder recorded in his war diary a conversation with the Chief of the Naval Staff, Hugo von Pohl, in which he was promised both a submarine and torpedo-boat half-flotilla.[7] These were the opening salvos in a debate which continued throughout December 1914 and into 1915.

At the beginning of December a proposal was sent to the High Seas Fleet that an additional five submarines be sent to Flanders as 'Coastal Defense Force Flanders.'[8] Unaware of this suggestion von Schröder had begun a campaign of his own to win forces away from the High Seas Fleet. He had just completed a study of Ostend and Zeebrugge in which he recommended that a minimum of three submarines, a half-flotilla of torpedo-boats and a small cruiser be sent to

Flanders. He argued that the presence of such a force would require the British to implement a close blockade of the Belgian harbours and this in turn would provide the High Seas Fleet with an opportunity to strike a serious blow at the Royal Navy.[9] He repeated this argument in a letter to Ingenohl on 4 December. In it he argued that there were numerous opportunities for action by German torpedo-boats in the Channel. As just one example he cited the possibility of bombarding the allied positions around Nieuport in retaliation for the English bombardments of his positions. The torpedo-boats could also be used as reconnaissance to guide German submarines to British warships. He argued that the risks of the journey were acceptable because Heligoland was only 220 nautical miles from Flanders and the trip could be completed in one night. Furthermore the risks of the journey were worth running because the new, fast torpedo-boats could do much more damage operating from Flanders. Operating from the Bight they were essentially useless unless the British attacked the Bight directly. Geographically his bases were much better situated and from there the Germans could put tremendous pressure on the British. He also argued that submarines were essential for the defence of the coast. He believed that the mere threat that German submarines might be operating in the area would prevent future British bombardments of the coastline. As evidence he pointed to the fact that the presence of German submarines in the eastern Channel in November had forced the British to abandon their coastal bombardments.[10]

On 5 December von Schröder was informed by von Pohl of a tentative plan to create a 'Coastal Defence Force Flanders' consisting of a half-flotilla of submarines. It would be under his command and was to operate in the Channel and the southern North Sea. If necessary it would assist the High Seas Fleet.[11] On the 8th von Ingenohl weighed in on this idea. He agreed that the 1st Half-Flotilla would be assigned to Flanders once the boats finished refitting. (They were apparently receiving new batteries.)[12] However, on the 11th von Ingenohl replied in a different vein to von Schröder, arguing that because of the need for repairs and maintenance it would be impossible to send an entire half-flotilla to Flanders. Instead he would send three submarines and the loss of boats could be made up by the UB and UC boats which were being constructed specially for use in Flanders.[13] He went on to state that although he agreed with von Schröder that Belgium provided an opportunity to apply heavy pressure on Britain he believed that for the moment that pressure could only be applied by submarines. Any cruisers and torpedo-boats assigned to the area would only be destroyed by superior allied forces. The only purpose he saw the torpedo-boats fulfilling was to provide early warning of a British attack and this could just as easily be done by the auxiliary forces already in Flanders. The torpedo-boats were too valuable to waste on such an operation.[14]

Despite his reluctance pressure continued to be placed on von Ingenohl to send forces west. On the 12th von Pohl urged him to dispatch a half-flotilla of well-armed torpedo-boats to Flanders in addition to the submarines. These boats would attack British ships on submarine patrol. Von Pohl was willing though to delay the transfer of the torpedo-boats until the coastal batteries in Flanders were sufficiently powerful to deter any British attacks on the Belgian coast.[15] Both he and von Ingenohl agreed though that no small cruisers would be sent to Flanders.[16]

Throughout the rest of December von Ingenohl continued to oppose any attempt to reinforce the Flanders front. On the 14th he wrote to von Pohl that because of losses and the assignment of forces to the Baltic the High Seas Fleet only had twenty-one submarines available. Three of these had been earmarked for Flanders. Of the remaining eighteen only nine were usually available for use due to refits and maintenance and six of those were needed in the Bight. That only left three for operations overseas. As a result no additional submarines could be spared for Flanders. He also noted that he did not see this changing in the future.[17]

Part of von Ingenohl's reluctance to send submarines to Flanders can be explained by his lack of confidence in their ability to successfully attack British transports. He felt that the defences of the British troop convoys were simply too strong.[18] He was also reluctant to allow any of the High Seas Fleets' submarines to pass out of his command.[19] In none of his letters was von Ingenohl particularly open about the reasons for his decisions. It appears that they stemmed both from fear of a British attack on the Bight, a repeat of the battle of 28 August 1914, and from a reluctance to see his command lessened in any way. Despite his continual refusals the Naval Staff and the MarineKorps refused to leave the matter alone.

On the 18th von Schröder once again called for the allocation of a half-flotilla of fast well-armed torpedo-boats to his naval station. His reasons were twofold: first, the boats were currently sitting idle in the Bight and having no impact on the war, and secondly, they were needed to defend the coast while the artillery defences were being completed. He also envisioned them playing an offensive role. He proposed using them in night attacks against British patrols and against the northern French harbours. They could also be pressed into use as minelayers.[20] This request got the usual response from von Ingenohl; that allied ships were faster and better armed and therefore the German torpedo-boats could do nothing against them and any assignment of torpedo-boats to Flanders was foolish at best.[21]

Finally, on 23 December von Ingenohl wrote a thorough reply to von Schröder precisely explaining his position. He agreed with von Schröder that the geographic position of Ostend and Zeebrugge was favourable and that the bases there presented an opportunity to put significant pressure on Britain. He went on to state though that, in the immediate future, the MarineKorps should concentrate on the completion of the coastal defences because, until those were finished, the danger of a surprise attack catching the ships in harbour was too great. Therefore he was reluctant to send any more forces to the Flanders bases until the defences were complete. He also still believed that German torpedo-boats and small cruisers were too inferior to their British counterparts to be of any use. For the same reason he rejected a plan von Schröder had proposed to launch night attacks on enemy patrol craft. He even agreed that significant activity in the Flanders area would almost certainly force the British to draw ships from other theatres to strengthen the southern North Sea but he did not see this as presenting a target of opportunity for the High Seas Fleet. Rather he feared it would only force the British to attack the Flanders bases and therefore any forces based there would be lost. He did not even have much faith in mining operations since they would have to be carried out at night in unfamiliar waters. He concluded his letter by saying that once the fortifications were complete Ostend and Zeebrugge would be important submarine bases but that no effective purpose would be served by sending torpedo-boats or light cruisers to these ports. The use of such forces would only force the British to block the harbours and therefore end their usefulness as submarine bases. He believed that because Germany possessed the weaker fleet she had to maintain all of her forces in a concentrated area and could not weaken herself by assigning forces to minor theatres; therefore any dispatch of light cruisers and torpedo-boats to Flanders was categorically ruled out.[22]

Since he often referred to the dangers of the journey to Flanders Ingenohl probably feared that any group of torpedo-boats sent to Flanders would suffer the same fate as the IV Half-Flotilla, which had been totally destroyed in the North Sea in October 1914 while on a mine-laying mission.[23] His main concern though seemed to be that a British attack on the Bight, a repetition of the attack of 28 August that had caught the Germans unawares and caused the loss of one destroyer and three light cruisers, was imminent. In light of this fear he was reluctant to release any forces to additional theatres. He also appears to have been affected with an extreme pessimism that bordered on defeatism. Whether this stemmed from the shock he received on 28 August or was simply inherent in him is unknown. He was certainly not the forceful leader the German fleet required in war time. This was recognised in early 1915 following the loss of the armoured cruiser *Blücher* in the Battle of the Dogger Bank and von Ingenohl was removed from command. Up until that point he remained intransigent regarding the assignment of forces to Flanders.

In contrast, the head of the Naval Staff, Hugo von Pohl, had remained a consistent supporter of the plan to send both a torpedo-boat and a submarine half-flotilla to Flanders. On 2 January 1915 he had reported to von Schröder that he continued to support his requests for the assignment of a half-flotilla of torpedo-boats to Flanders. Von Pohl believed that this was essential if successful mine-laying operations in and around the British harbours, especially the Thames estuary, were to be carried out. However, he did state that von Schröder would have to wait until the artillery defences along the coast were completed.[24]

The continual delays and bickering began to take their toll on von Schröder by January 1915. On 7 of January he recorded in an addendum to his war diary that despite the supposed recognition of the value of the Flanders bases he was unable to persuade the Highs Seas Fleet to send out more than three submarines and was continually told that he would have to wait for the arrival of the small submarines. He however, had great doubts as to whether those submarines would actually be seaworthy enough to operate in the Channel. He had proposed, to no avail, that they be sent to the Baltic and that the Baltic submarine force be transferred to Flanders. Given the intransigence of the naval authorities at home he began to doubt whether the time and expense of building the Flanders bases had even been worthwhile. He complained that the fleet command seemed more preoccupied with maintaining the safety of the fleet than with winning the war.[25] In addition, the German army was placing increasing pressure on him to devote more resources to the land war and his inability to act aggressively at sea weakened his ability to resist their demands. He felt trapped and wanted to know what naval forces he could reasonably expect to receive.[26] No answer was forthcoming.

When von Ingenohl was finally replaced by von Pohl in early February it appears to have rekindled confidence in von Schröder. He immediately renewed his calls for the dispatch of submarines and torpedo-boats to Flanders. If he expected von Pohl to continue to support his requests however, he was mistaken. The change in fleet command meant only more of the same for the Marine-Korps Flandern.

On 30 January von Schröder renewed his requests. He complained that his command was restricted to a purely defensive role because of its limited resources. Even in the submarine war he was limited to a coastal defence role due to his shortage of submarines. He urged von Pohl to rapidly dispatch the torpedo-boats the latter had promised him in December. He also requested that two old *Siegfried*-class ships be assigned to Flanders for both coast defence and for use against the allied positions along the French coast. He suggested that the transfer be covered by the High Seas Fleet which could sortie for an attack against the British coast.[27] These opinions were seconded by Kapitän zur See Friedrich Boedicker, who later served in the battle cruisers under Hipper, when he was sent to Flanders to examine the positions there.[28] These new requests though received the old reply; namely that the forces would be sent only when the defences of the Flanders bases were complete.[29]

It was at this same time that the German navy was beginning to consider a radical new strategy; unrestricted submarine warfare. They hoped that an unlimited submarine campaign against British shipping would force the British to sue for peace.[30] Von Schröder expected the new strategy to lead to an increase in his forces and at first that was the plan. On 22 January von Ingenohl (yet to be dismissed from his command) informed von Pohl that the MarineKorps was to receive five submarines for the duration of the blockade against England and France and that these vessels were to be stationed off of Dunkirk, Calais, and Boulogne.[31] On 4 February von Pohl responded, stating that, if the MarineKorps was to carry out their part of the blockade, specifically mine laying off of the Thames, they would require the use of a half-flotilla of torpedo-boats as well.[32] Von Schröder received a telegram from the RMA on 22 January as well which informed him that he was to receive twenty large and twenty-eight small submarines as well as twenty-four torpedo-boats and a half-flotilla of large torpedo-boats![33] Things soon changed though and most of these were never sent.

A note in von Schröder's war diary from 11 February records that the navy had decided that his submarine reinforcements were not to be sent because the danger of enemy attack while in port was too great.[34] This is corroborated by two other documents. The first is from the Führer der U-Boote Hermann Bauer. In his general regulations for the submarine blockade he stated that Zeebrugge was not to be used as a base during the upcoming submarine campaign because of the dangers of attack while in port and also because of the strong British forces keeping watch on the coast.[35] The second was a letter from von Pohl to von Schröder explaining that the general insecurity of Ostend and Zeebrugge ruled out their use as bases during the upcoming submarine campaign. At best they could be used as occasional rest and resupply points. Von Pohl also pointed out that the dispatch of units to Flanders was impossible because it would weaken the High Seas Fleet's control over the submarine force. Pohl now considered it essential that he maintain centralized control over the submarines.[36] This was something of a departure from his earlier stance.

Von Schröder's case was injured further by the events of 12 February. The British air raid of that evening[37] which so badly damaged *U-14* convinced von Pohl that the danger from air attack was too great. He refused to risk further forces there.[38]

Von Pohl, who had supported the assignment of submarines to Flanders while head of the Naval Staff, had now taken up his predecessor's stance and opposed the transfer of further forces from the High Seas Fleet to Flanders. He explained his reasons in a letter to the Kaiser on 14 February. First of all he referred to the danger of air attack while alluding specifically to the British raid that damaged *U-14*. He also stated though that the coastal defences were not yet strong enough to prevent an enemy bombardment of the harbours. These arguments were consistent with those he had maintained while at the Naval Staff but he now added von Ingenohl's old argument that any torpedo-boats sent would sit uselessly in port and that the potential gains could not equal the risks involved. Furthermore he stated that von Schröder's plan to cover the transfer of torpedo-boats with a fleet operation wouldn't work. A major move by the High Seas Fleet would only serve to put the British forces on alert and hence would make the transfer virtually impossible. He believed that the half-flotilla would likely be lost in the transfer and that he would then be attacked for having thrown away a half-flotilla of good torpedo-boats in an attempt to carry out a mission (mine-laying) which could later have been carried out by the UC submarines. He was therefore firmly opposed to sending any torpedo-boats to Flanders at this time.[39] Again one can see the spectre of the lost VII Half-Flotilla in these objections. Despite von Pohl's views his successor at the Naval Staff, Admiral Gustav Bachmann, recommended on 18 February that a half-flotilla of torpedo-boats be sent to Flanders at the next favorable opportunity.[40]

At the same time Bachmann requested from von Schröder an outline of the defensive measures put in place to prevent a repetition of the events of the 12th.[41] Von Schröder replied in a letter to Tirpitz that all possible measures for air defence had been taken. He included an outline of the defensive arrangements at each of the ports.[42] Von Schröder also stated that in his opinion the chief of the High Seas Fleet was overestimating the dangers. He argued that any force in such proximity to the enemy was inevitably going to be in some danger; there could never be a guarantee of absolute security against air attack and he urged Tirpitz to support him and to consider the tremendous possibilities that the Flanders position offered. He furthermore complained that the seemingly endless debate between he and the High Seas Fleet had already cost them three valuable months in which operations could have been carried out against the British coast. He pressed for a rapid decision.[43] His views were supported by

Kapitän zur See Albert Hopman when he travelled to Flanders in late February to examine the ports.[44] By the end of February it appeared as if von Schröder had finally won his point. On 24 February Bachmann wrote to von Pohl that the Kaiser had approved the defensive measures in Flanders and had ordered the immediate dispatch of a half-flotilla of torpedo-boats to the MarineKorps.[45] The transfer though, did not take place. The reasons for the sudden reconsideration were the dangers from mines in the Channel and, still, the danger of aerial attack while in port.[46] At any rate, von Schröder did not receive his torpedo-boats. There the matter rested until April.

On 12 April von Schröder once more laid out his views on the war, this time in a letter directly to the Kaiser. In it he explained that the arrival of the UB and UC boats, which had begun in March, had led the British to tighten their watch on the Belgian coast and that he did not possess sufficient force to drive them away. As a result it was becoming increasingly difficult for the Flanders submarines to get to sea. To alleviate the problem, he required a small cruiser and two *Siegfried*s or, at the very least, a full flotilla of large well-armed torpedo-boats which could attack the British patrols and free the exits from the harbours. This force could also be used to attack British shipping along the south and east coasts of England. This would in turn force the British either to reinforce or give up the patrols off the Belgian coast. If they reinforced they would have to pull ships from other theatres and this in turn would provide the High Seas Fleet with an opportunity to attack and destroy a large group of British warships.[47] The response, however, was the same. On the 18th he was informed by Bachmann that his request was denied because the ships were needed by the High Seas Fleet.[48]

In the end, not surprisingly, the High Seas Fleet won this round of discussions. The MarineKorps Flandern would be forced to rely, for both torpedo-boats and submarines, on small, specially built units while the best forces remained with the High Seas Fleet and were mostly inactive.

The High Seas Fleet commanders, both von Ingenohl and von Pohl, had in some cases very valid objections to sending units to Flanders. Any force based there certainly faced a wide array of dangers. The southern North Sea, as was demonstrated by the fate of the 7th Flotilla in October, could be extremely hazardous and even once the ships arrived in port there were dangers from enemy gunfire, enemy air attacks, and possible attempts to block them in to contend with. There were also, however, as von Schröder pointed out time and again, significant opportunities to damage the British war effort. It certainly appears, with hindsight, that the highest levels of the German navy were more concerned with preventing the loss of ships than they were with winning the war. The German navy was not only overprotective of the High Seas Fleet but of its light forces as well.[49]

Von Schröder's claim that the presence of active light forces in the Channel would have forced the British to strengthen their forces in the southern North Sea, and that therefore the High Seas Fleet might have been able to engage and hopefully destroy a sizeable force of British ships, seems reasonable. It is doubtful that an active campaign by purely light forces would have moved Jellicoe out of Scotland but other forces, Beatty's cruisers for example, might have moved south. With Jellicoe still at Scapa Flow his timely intervention in a battle in the southern portion of the North Sea would have been nearly impossible. Of course, whether or not he could have intercepted the High Seas Fleet on its return to Germany is another issue entirely. Regardless, whether or not one accepts von Schröder's hypothesis, the campaign he suggested was the essence of the *Kleinkrieg* and should have been attempted. With hindsight, it appears that von Schröder was right and that the German fleet missed a major opportunity to damage the British war effort. This was precisely why Tirpitz had created the MarineDivision in the first place and it was deprived of the resources it needed to prosecute an active *Kleinkrieg*. To attempt to fight a war without taking risks, as the German navy did, is at best foolish and, in this case, was a disastrous endeavour. That said it is highly unlikely that a vigorous campaign in the Channel, in late 1914 and early 1915, would have altered the outcome of the war. The problem though was that this extreme caution was not an isolated event but rather continued throughout the war. It's exact source remains debatable though the defeats of August and October 1914 loom very large.

The final result of the debates within the navy meant that the MarineKorps Flandern was forced to rely upon small A-class torpedo-boats and the *UB* and *UC*-class submarines,[50] all of which were smaller and less well-equipped versions of their larger brethren. It was these vessels which initially made up the Flanders Flotillas.

CREATION OF THE FLANDERS FLOTILLAS

Despite the reluctance of the High Seas Fleet to assign more than three U-boats to the Flanders station plans went ahead to create a Flanders submarine flotilla made up of smaller, coastal submarines. On 25th February Tirpitz informed all the major commands that he intended to create a new submarine flotilla in Flanders as soon as four boats each of the *UB* and *UC*-classes were in service. In addition, a torpedo-boat flotilla would be created in Flanders once four of the new A-boats were in service.[51]

Both flotillas were to be under the command of Admiral Ludwig von Schröder and the MarineKorps Flandern.

The UB boats which made up the bulk of the Flanders U–Boat Flotilla were designed almost immediately after the outbreak of the war. Planning for the creation of these small coastal submarines began on 18 August and a second class of small mine laying submarines began to be designed in September. These craft were specifically designed for use in narrower, shallower, seas and hence were perfect for Flanders. The first orders for the *UB*-class boats were placed on 15 October and on 23 November the first of the UC boats were ordered.[52] On 5 November 1914 Admiral von Schröder was informed that fifteen of these boats were in production.[53] They were 120 ton ships armed with two 45cm torpedo tubes and 1 deck mounted machine gun. They had a radius of action of 800 nautical miles on the surface and 80 nautical miles submerged with top speeds of six knots and five knots respectively.[54] The design of the UC boats was completed in November 1914. They displaced 150 tons and carried twelve mines each, packing anywhere from 120 to 200 kilograms of explosive. They were also equipped with a small deck mounted machine gun. Their top speeds were six knots on the surface and five knots submerged with a radius of action of just under 800 nautical miles on the surface and fifty nautical miles submerged.[55]

By the end of the war both types had undergone significant changes. Two additional classes of UC boats were developed and by the end of the war the last of these, the UC III boats, were carrying fourteen mines and mounting three torpedo tubes with an 8.8cm deck gun.[56] This latter version of the UC was capable of eleven knots on the surface and six and-a-half knots submerged.[57] By the end of the war the *UB*-class had been enlarged to 500 tons and mounted four bow torpedo tubes in addition to one in the stern. They carried ten torpedoes and possessed an 8.8cm deck gun. Their top speed had been increased to thirteen knots on the surface and seven and-a-half knots submerged. These changes increased their radius of action to 9,000 nautical miles.[58]

The only UB-I or UC-I which travelled to Flanders by sea was *UB-2*; all the others were sent out in pieces by train and assembled in Antwerp.[59] The hope was that these ships would free the larger submarines from coastal defence duties and allow them to be used in the commerce war. There were serious doubts though as to how effective the new craft would prove to be.[60]

The submarines were shipped out in roughly fifteen different pieces and it required eight railway cars to transport one submarine.[61] The assembly in Antwerp took between two and three weeks and was followed by a five day journey through the inland canals of Belgium to Bruges. During the course of this journey they were towed by barges.[62] The prototypes of the classes were tested in home waters but the remaining ships of each class underwent their trials in their operational area.[63] The entire process took roughly six weeks from the time the trains left Germany until the submarines were ready to go to sea.[64] As their initial complement the MarineKorps was due to receive eight UBs and eleven UCs. The remainder of the classes were split between Germany, Constantinople, and Pola.[65]

The first of the UBs arrived on 27 March and the flotilla was formed two days later when the second arrived.[66] The flotilla was placed under the command of KorvettenKapitän Karl Bartenbach, the former head of the Bartenbach Commission and a member of the U-boat arm since its inception in 1906.[67] The initial operational area of the flotilla included the English Channel and the British east coast up to Flamborough Head, though by the end of the war it had been expanded to include the French west coast and the Bay of Biscay as well as the southernmost parts of the Irish Sea.[68] The flotilla remained an integral part of the German submarine force for the balance of the war.

The largest number of submarines under Bartenbach's control at any one time was thirty-four at the beginning of the unrestricted campaign in early 1917; his strength generally hovered between twenty and thirty boats at any one time.[69] According to Scheer, the MarineKorps at one time or another had under their command roughly one-fourth of the entire German submarine force and were responsible for roughly 23 percent of all the German submarine successes; sinking a total of 3,342,000 tons of allied and neutral shipping.[70] This force played a significant role in the war at sea, especially in the English Channel where their efforts were supplemented by those of the Flanders Torpedo-boat flotilla.

The Flanders Torpedo-Boat Flotilla was officially formed on 28 April, 1915 and was placed under the command of Kapitänleutnant Kurt Shoemann. This unit, like the submarine flotilla, consisted of a special class of ship specifically designed for Flanders. In the case of the torpedo-boats it was the A-class.[71] These were very small boats that displaced just over 100 tons and mounted two torpedo tubes with a 5cm deck gun. They could also be used as minelayers since each boat had space for four mines. They were shipped out and assembled in the same way as the submarines and it was hoped, in November 1914, that fifty such boats would be available by May 1915.[72] This proved to be an overly optimistic estimate and the flotilla was brought into service with fifteen boats.[73] Nonetheless, by the end of April the MarineKorps possessed sufficient forces to begin naval operations.

The UB boats began their activities on 9 April with the initial sortie of *UB-4*. Their primary assignment was to attack commercial traffic between Britain and the Netherlands and their initial forays proved to be successful. On its first journey *UB-4* sank four steamers and demonstrated, by fighting through some heavy weather, that the UBs were much more seaworthy than had been expected.[74] These successes against commercial shipping were followed on 1 May with a military success when *UB-6* sank the old British destroyer *Recruit*.[75] The UC boats also proved to be a pleasant surprise when they began their operations in late May, by laying a minefield off the southeastern British coast. By the middle of June 1915 the UBs and the UCs had extended their radius of action to the western mouth of the Channel and as far north as the Thames. In this entire two month period only a single boat was lost. The submarines exceeded all expectations.[76] The German navy had found a new weapon in the struggle against England.

With the creation of the Flanders flotillas and the construction of the naval bases in Ostend and Zeebrugge the second phase of the MarineKorps' existence began. While they were not free of involvement with the army von Schröder and his staff were able to devote the bulk of their efforts towards the naval war. They were aided significantly by the fact that their sector of the Western Front was generally quiet during 1915. The major allied offensives of that year occurred further to the south and the main German drive was directed against the Russians on the Eastern Front. This meant that there was little pressure from the German army for assistance and hence the MarineKorps was free to concentrate on the naval war.

THE SUBMARINE WAR MARCH 1915 – MARCH 1916

The Flanders U-Boat Flotilla was just beginning its operations when the sinking of the *Lusitania* caused a severe crisis in the relations between Germany and the United States of America. This crisis raised the spectre of war with the United States and drove the German chancellor, Theobald von Bethmann-Hollweg, to push for an end to the unrestricted submarine campaign. This was not popular within the fleet. Admiral von Schröder wrote to the Naval Staff on 3 May to register his objections, arguing that if his submarines were prevented from attacking neutral ships it would be impossible for him to continue the submarine war since the traffic in his operational area consisted mainly of Dutch vessels.[77] Von Schröder's objections, like those of Tirpitz and von Pohl, were outweighed by the Chancellor's argument that it was simply too dangerous to risk adding the United States to Germany's list of enemies.[78] In the end Bethmann-Hollweg won the day. On 1 June the MarineKorps received official notification to exercise greater caution in the submarine war and cease attacking neutral ships.[79] Von Schröder believed that this would reduce the UB boats to merely a coastal defence force[80], however, KorvettenKapitän Bartenbach had other ideas.

Back in April the commander of the German submarine force, Lieutenant Commander Hermann Bauer, had ended the passage of German submarines through the Dover-Calais straits for fear that the British patrols, minefields and net barriers in that area made it too dangerous to traverse. This meant that the German submarines, in order to reach their operational areas to the west of Britain, had to travel around the north coast of Scotland. In late April Bauer asked Bartenbach to determine if the straits could safely be passed. Based upon intelligence reports acquired by the UB boats Bartenbach believed that it would be possible to pass west directly along the French coastline and avoid most of the obstacles. If that proved impossible, he believed that the German submarines could probably pass under the various net barriers in the Channel.[81] To test his theories Bartenbach sent *UB-6* west to Boulogne on 21 June. The submarine's only mission was to pass through the Channel defences and return to Belgium. If it succeeded Bartenbach planned to send an additional three or four UB boats west to raid in the Channel.[82] *UB-6*'s journey proved to be a success. It left Zeebrugge late on the 21st, passed by Dunkirk on the surface, being forced to dive once when an enemy destroyer approached, and arrived off Boulogne on the early morning of the 22nd. That evening it made the return voyage to Zeebrugge without incident.[83]

Having demonstrated that the barriers could be breached Bartenbach then sent *UB-2*, *UB-5* and *UB-10* into the Channel to attack British shipping, all without success. They all returned however, demonstrating that the Dover barriers could be beaten.[84] They discovered that a passage along the French coast was essentially unblocked and that all the British net barriers were clearly marked by buoys which the submarines could use as navigational aids. Bartenbach put this knowledge to good use once the UC minelayers became operational.[85] The end result was that on 28 June von Schröder received authorisation from the High Seas Fleet to extend the operational area of the submarine flotilla west to a line from Portland to Cap de la Hogue.[86] The journeys through the barrage were the peak of what was otherwise a relatively uneventful two months. Over the course of May and June 1915 the UB boats undertook twenty-nine voyages and sank five enemy steamers, one armed steamer and nine smaller vessels.[87]

Despite the limited successes of the UBs May was a notable month for the Flanders U-boat flotilla for it saw the entrance into service of the vessels which became the workhorses of the flotilla, the UC minelayers. In early May von Schröder was informed that the mine laying mechanism for the submarines had been tested successfully and that they could be deployed. When he received this news he requested that the prototype, *UC-11*, be sent to Flanders immediately so that mine-laying operations could begin.[88] *UC-11* arrived in Zeebrugge on 26 May[89] and was soon joined by *UC-1*, *UC-2*, *UC-12* and *UC-13*, recently arrived from Antwerp.[90] Five days later, on 31 May, these submarines laid their first minefield, just off the southeast coast of Britain.[91]

The UC and UB boats continued their activity into July, undertaking twenty-six missions that month, seven of which consisted strictly of mine-laying. They accounted for a total of forty-one vessels sunk and laid over 100 mines in the areas of Calais and the Downs. The minefields were credited with severely disrupting commercial traffic in those areas.[92]

In August and September the UBs carried out an additional twenty-two missions sinking thirty-six British vessels. It was also in August that the flotilla suffered its first loss when *UB-4* was sunk by an armed steamer.[93] In the meantime the UCs continued mine-laying; among their missions were their first forays past the Dover-Calais Straits following the paths mapped out by the earlier UB missions. In August and September the seven UCs undertook forty-two missions. Their minefields were credited with sinking seventeen enemy and six neutral steamers as well as sixteen vessels of the British auxiliary patrol and two British torpedo boats.[94] These missions also provided evidence of the hazards peculiar to mine-laying by submarine. The first loss of a UC came not from enemy action but from a malfunctioning mine which exploded upon release and destroyed *UC-2* in late July.[95] Despite the dangers, by the end of September the submarines of the Flanders flotilla had accounted for 142 enemy vessels at the cost of only one UB and one UC.[96]

In October they carried out an additional eighteen missions, laying another 150 mines and accounting for another twenty-nine enemy vessels without loss to themselves.[97] In November the UBs were given orders to begin working in the Channel against traffic between Britain and France; this remained their area of operations until February 1916. In that span of time they accounted for another seventeen British steamers.[98] In the meantime, starting in November and continuing until February 1916, the UCs laid a series of 109 minefields around the Thames, Flamborough Head, the Isle of Wight and Le Havre. These fields accounted for 112 enemy vessels totaling 167,702 tons at the cost of two UC boats lost and one interred in the Netherlands.[99] Clearly the UCs were proving to be the more effective of the two types and consequently they became the workhorses of the flotilla. By March 1916 it was clear that the UCs, and to a lesser extent the UBs, were exceeding all expectations and had become a valuable part of the German war effort.

THE WAR ON THE SURFACE MARCH 1915 – MARCH 1916

While the Flanders U-boats were beginning their operations and proving their usefulness the Flanders torpedo-boats were also beginning their activity, though with much less success. The first encounter between the German A-boats and British destroyers occurred on 1 May, just three days after the creation of the flotilla.

Early on the morning of the 1st two German seaplanes left Zeebrugge on a reconnaissance flight to the Thames. While enroute one of the planes developed serious engine trouble and was forced to make an emergency landing. In the meantime the other plane spotted four British minesweepers (*Columbia*, *Barbados*, *Miura* and *Chirsit*) north of Ostend. In response the commander of the Flanders flotilla, Kapitänleutnant Shoemann, took *A-2* and *A-6* to sea to attack the minesweepers and rescue the crew of the downed aircraft.[100] The German torpedo-boats encountered the four British mine-sweepers shortly thereafter and a battle ensued during which the Germans fired four torpedoes at the British vessels. One torpedo struck the *Columbia*, which sank. The tide of the battle turned however with the arrival of four British destroyers, the *Laforey*, *Lawford*, *Leonidas* and *Lark*. With their inferior speed and inferior guns the German torpedo-boats were quickly overwhelmed. Both were destroyed and Kapitänleutnant Shoemann was killed.[101] The crewmen of the downed German seaplane were eventually discovered by a Dutch steamer and were taken to the North Hinder Light Ship from which they were eventually rescued by a German submarine.[102] This first encounter between the German A-boats and their British opposition only served to confirm von Schröder's conviction that his existing vessels were only useful for patrols along the coast.

For most of June and July the surface campaign was very quiet. The German vessels held to the coastline and avoided the larger British vessels which, for their part, occasionally engaged in gunnery duels with the long-range artillery along the coast. These bombardments were ineffective but served to keep the German's attention focused on the Flanders coastline.[103] This changed in August.

At the beginning of August the British began planning a new series of bombardments of the Flanders bases. They intended to convince the Germans that a landing in Flanders was imminent so that reinforcements would not be sent from the coast to the Artois sector of the front where the French were planning a major offensive.[104] The bombardment was planned for the night of 21 August but had to be postponed due to weather.[105] The bombarding force, ten destroyers and three monitors as well as more than forty auxiliary patrol vessels to keep watch for German submarines, sailed on the night of 22 August.[106]

That same night one of the German patrol vessels, *A-15*, encountered the two French destroyers *Oriflamme* and *Branlebas* west of Ostend; they were not part of the bombarding force. A battle ensued and *A-15* reportedly acquitted itself very well, scoring the first hits of the battle and reportedly knocking one of the French destroyers out of the fight. The other destroyer however soon scored a hit which destroyed the rudder of *A-15* and left her circling aimlessly while the destroyer continued to shell her. The French destroyer broke off the battle at 12.20am after doing serious damage to *A-15* and returned to its crippled comrade, taking it in tow. Ten minutes later *A-15* sank. Eventually twelve men of the vessel's twenty-seven man crew were rescued.[107] The minor skirmish did not affect the bombardment.

At 5.30am on the morning of the 23rd the British force arrived off Zeebrugge and opened fire on the port. The vessels were accompanied by a large number of aerial observers and an air battle took place over the harbour when German aircraft rose to oppose the British. An artillery duel commenced between the coastal batteries *Kaiserin*, *Hertha*, and *Freya* and the British monitors. The bombardment continued from long range for two hours until the British force withdrew at 7.30am. Only minimal materiel damage was done; one man was killed and six others were wounded, though phone connections to Bruges were interrupted. There was, however, no damage to the vessels in the harbour or to the harbour facilities themselves.[108]

The British followed the Zeebrugge bombardment with a bombardment of Ostend on 7 September which did no damage and was broken off after half an hour due to heavy fire from the *Tirpitz* battery.[109] The results were similar on 19 September when the British once again attempted to bombard Ostend and were driven off by *Tirpitz* and *Aachen*.[110] A third bombardment took place on the 25th but again did only minimal damage. These bombardments continued into October without doing any significant damage. The German coastal batteries proved their worth. They were simply too powerful and the British, to maintain their own safety, had to work from such extreme ranges that they were almost wholly ineffective.[111] These bombardments, aside from pinning down German soldiers, demonstrated the power of the German coastal artillery and the value of aircraft as artillery spotters. In fact, as a direct result of the bombardments, a section of Albatross C-Is was assigned to the MarineKorps as artillery observers.[112]

As the year came to a close the bombardments of Ostend and Zeebrugge tapered off and were replaced by bombing raids. Like the bombardments these were generally ineffective.[113] They were a reflection of the growing importance of air power however. That importance was recognised by the Germans as well and, consequently, the Flanders air station became an increasingly important part of the MarineKorps' operations.

In June the RMA created a second naval air station in Zeebrugge.[114] It became active in August.[115] Additional reinforcements followed in September when the 2nd MarineLandFlieger section was created to assist the Marine-Korps by carrying out coastal air patrols.[116] This unit arrived on 20 September and it gave the MarineKorps eight airplanes to supplement their seaplanes.[117] The number of the latter had reached twenty by the end of October, while the number of airplanes gradually increased to twelve.[118] By the end of 1915 the MarineKorps had at its disposal a force of over thirty aircraft used primarily for reconnaissance and spotting duties for the coastal artillery. In addition, they received reconnaissance reports from airships enroute to Britain.[119] The air arm was clearly growing in importance; this trend continued as the war progressed.

The year 1915 ended with the Germans firmly entrenched along the coast and effectively protected from bombardments and landings by their coastal artillery. The air section of the MarineKorps continued to expand and the submarine flotilla continued to increase its activity. The torpedo-boat flotilla, however, was still limited to essentially coastal patrols. The A-boats could only play a defensive role. Events going on behind the scenes however would soon allow the torpedo-boat flotilla to play a larger role.

THE DEVELOPMENT OF THE TORPEDO-BOAT FLOTILLA

The loss of *A-2* and *A-6* at the start of May convinced both von Schröder and Tirpitz that the flotilla needed additional A-boats as a materiel reserve to replace future losses.[120] On the 22nd the RMA requested that an additional six boats be sent from Wilhelmshaven to Flanders.[121] This would bring the number of vessels in the Flanders torpedo-boat flotilla up to sixteen. At the same time the former head of the Flanders mine-sweepers, Kapitänleutnant Kurt Assmann, was named to replace Shoemann as commander of the flotilla.[122] The force was now broken into two half-flotillas, one stationed in Ostend and one in Zeebrugge with two boats held back as a materiel reserve.[123] Their missions remained primarily defensive in nature. They were to keep the entrances to Ostend and Zeebrugge free from mines; guide submarines into port and occasionally sortie to rescue downed pilots and tow in damaged submarines. On rare occasions during the winter months they might be allowed to launch raids on enemy commerce but in general they were to serve as auxiliaries to the submarines.[124] To emphasise that point, Kapitänleutnant Assmann was allowed independent command only in an area fifteen nautical miles from the coast; any operations that would exceed that distance required the sanction of Admiral von Schröder.[125]

Of much greater importance for the course of the war was the fact that, following the ineffective showing of the A-boats in their clashes with the British and French, sentiment for the assignment of large torpedo-boats to the Flanders theatre began to grow within the fleet. In early August von Schröder received a message from Admiral Bachmann informing him that it was possible that the MarineKorps might receive three or four larger torpedo-boats in October.[126] However, it might prove necessary to pull crews from the A-boats to man the new vessels since there was a severe shortage of capable crews in the fleet.[127] At the end of August von Schröder responded, stating that he would be able to free sufficient personnel to man three V-class torpedo-boats by taking six of the A-boats out of service. At the same time he emphasised that he required a minimum of three of the larger boats if he was to have any effect on the war at sea.[128] This time there was little opposition.

At the start of November Rear-Admiral Ernst Ritter von Mann, head of the Torpedo Inspectorate, reported that in the upcoming months the MarineKorps would receive three large torpedo-boats from the III Torpedo-Boat Flotilla. These ships would be made available once several new torpedo-boats that were being built were finished and could take their place in the III Flotilla.[129]

In order to bring the new ships into service as soon as possible von Mann recommended that experienced crews be assigned to them. He suggested that, rather than have the large torpedo-boats manned by A-boat crews, the High Seas Fleet should send the ships' crews along with the torpedo-boats in exchange for A-boat crews from Flanders.[130] This prompted Tirpitz to write to the Kaiser's brother Prince Heinrich, the commander of the Baltic forces, asking that he provide replacement crews for the High Seas Fleet so that the Torpedo-boat Flotilla Flandern would not have to take six A-boats out of service.[131]

Von Schröder was informed on 12 November that von Mann had requested first-class crews from the High Seas Fleet for the new boats but that he would have to find the commanders for the new ships from his current staff. He was to select his three best A-boat commanders and assign them to the new vessels.[132] The new ships were *V-47*, *V-67* and *V-68*. They were large torpedo-boats of the *V-25* class and displaced just under 1,200 tons with a radius of action of 2,050 nautical miles. *V-47* was capable of a top speed of thirty-four knots while *V-67* and *V-68* could reach thirty-six knots. They carried a complement of twenty-four mines and were also equipped for minesweeping. Their main armament, in addition to their torpedoes, was three 10.5cm deck guns.[133] Von Schröder was told to expect their arrival in late December.[134]

Discussions continued throughout November over the question of crews for the new ships and a decision was eventually late in the month. The MarineKorps would surrender about seventy individuals to the High Seas Fleet as replacements for the crews of the V-boats.[135] The ships themselves were placed into a new destroyer half-flotilla and were placed under the command of Korvettenkapitän Paul Cleve. They were a completely separate organisation from the A-boat Flotilla under Assmann.[136]

The Torpedo Inspectorate in fact was not able to meet its December 1915 deadline and von Schröder was forced to wait until March 1916 for the arrival of the new half-flotilla. The flotilla left Heligoland on 2 March and made an uneventful journey across the North Sea arriving in Zeebrugge in the early morning hours of 3 March 1916.[137]

1915 ended on a mixed note for von Schröder and the MarineKorps. On the one hand they had rapidly constructed a series of naval bases on the Belgian coast and had created such a belt of artillery around those bases as to make any invasion by sea very costly. On the other hand they had been unable to seriously damage allied commerce. Only the UC boats were able to act effectively against the British. The torpedo-boats and the *UB*-class submarines were too slow and poorly armed to make anything more than limited forays into the Channel. On the surface the MarineKorps was too weak to oppose the Entente with any hope of success.

The German official history of the war at sea concludes that the Germans wasted their opportunities in Flanders both in 1914 and in 1915. It points out the concerns that the British had over possible German landings along the French coast as well as their fears that the Germans would attempt to block Calais or Dunkirk. In addition, the British were very worried that a powerful striking force of torpedo-boats based in Flanders could launch a surprise raid into the Channel or against their southeastern coast. Such raids would not only disrupt British commerce but might even threaten the critical supply line to France that ran through the Channel. That the Germans did none of these things was allegedly a great relief to the British.[138] In reality, it was only after the Germans launched a major attack against the Channel patrols in October 1916 that the British became truly concerned about the German position in Belgium.

Nonetheless, the Germans did miss an opportunity to inflict serious damage on British commercial traffic by being overly concerned with the security of the Heligoland Bight. The defensive mindset which pervaded the German fleet in 1915 prevented them from taking full advantage of the possibilities presented by the Flanders bases. Even given the dangers of the journey to Flanders, the dangers from aerial attack while in Ostend and Zeebrugge and the danger from minefields, the possibilities available to the Germans were, as Admiral von Schröder pointed out, worth the risk. It was only at the very end of the war's first full year that the decision was finally taken to send capable forces to Flanders. Even then the force sent was very small. Yet, as we will see, even this limited force was sufficient to alter the nature of the war in the southern North Sea.

One week after the arrival in Flanders of the Destroyer Half-Flotilla the creator and staunch supporter of the MarineKorps, Admiral von Tirpitz, resigned from his post as head of the RMA due to the Kaiser's refusal to restart unrestricted submarine warfare. His place was taken by his former assistant, Eduard von Capelle. This was one of a series of personnel changes that took place at the top of the German navy as 1915 gave way to 1916. A seriously ill Admiral von Pohl gave up his post as commander of the High Seas Fleet and his place was taken by Admiral Reinhard Scheer. These moves came on top of Admiral Henning von Holtzendorff's supersession of Admiral Bachmann at the Naval Staff in September. These changes presaged a new and more aggressive stance for the German navy, one that culminated in the Battle of Jutland on 31 May 1916. This new stance, combined with the arrival of the larger torpedo-boats, opened up new possibilities for the MarineKorps and signaled the onset of a more active German campaign in the southern North Sea.

Table 2: German Submarines

	Patrol Submarines	UB-1 Class	UC-1 Class
Displacement	650 tons surfaced/ 837 tons submerged	127 tons surfaced/ 142 tons submerged	168 tons surfaced/ 183 submerged
No of Torpedoes	4 x 20in	2 x 18in	None
No of guns	1 x 3.4in	1 x 2in	1 machine gun
Speed	15kts surfaced/ 10kts submerged	6.5kts surfaced/ 5.5 kts submerged	6kts surfaced/ 5kts submerged

Ludwig von Schröder. *(Johan R Ryheul)*

German soldiers entering Bruges. *(J Mannering)*

Kaiser Wilhelm visiting Bruges. *(J Mannering)*

Admiral von Schröder meeting with officers and troops. *(Johan R Ryheul)*

Admiral von Schröder
mit dem früheren Chef des Admiralstabes Behnke.

A view of Ostend from the air. *(Johan R Ryheul)*

Zeebrugge mole as seen from above. *(Johan R Ryheul)*

Constructing the Pommern battery. *(Johan R Ryheul)*

The Pommern battery upon completion. *(Johan R Ryheul)*

German defences in Flanders. *(Johan R Ryheul)*

The German trenches in Flanders. *(Johan R Ryheul)*

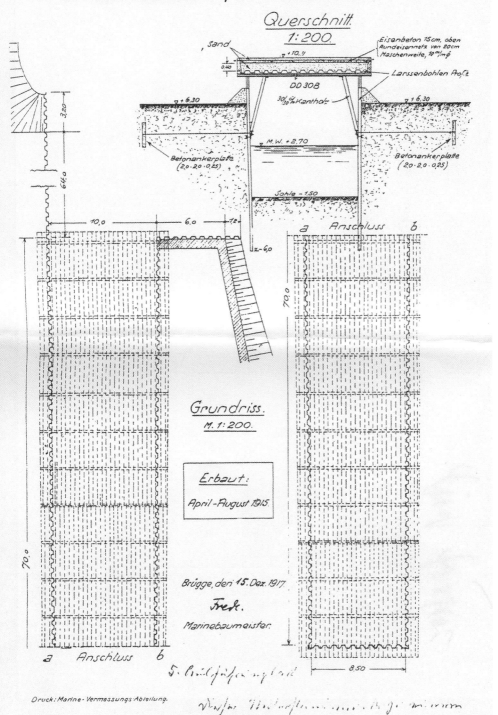

Diagram of a submarine pen. *(Johan R Ryheul)*

A submarine pen under construction. *(Johan R Ryheul)*

The completion of a submarine pen. *(Johan R Ryheul)*

The interior of a submarine pen. *(Johan R Ryheul)*

A U-boat docked in a submarine pen.
(Johan R Ryheul)

A U-boat lying exposed in a drydock in Ostend. *(J Mannering)*

A U-boat destroyed by air attack in Ostend.
(J Mannering)

Loading torpedoes into a U-boat.
(Johan R Ryheul)

A German destroyer moored in the canal at Bruges. *(J Mannering)*

A German destroyer at Ostend. *(J Mannering)*

German destroyers alongside the mole at Zeebrugge. *(Johan R Ryheul)*

Another view of German destroyers alongside the Zeebrugge mole. *(J Mannering)*

German destroyers on patrol off the Flanders coast. *(J Mannering)*

The gun crew onboard a German destroyer. *(J Mannering)*

A German seaplane squadron. *(Johan R Ryheul)*

German Albatros W4 (Marine No 747) single-seat station defence seaplane. *(Johan R Ryheul)*

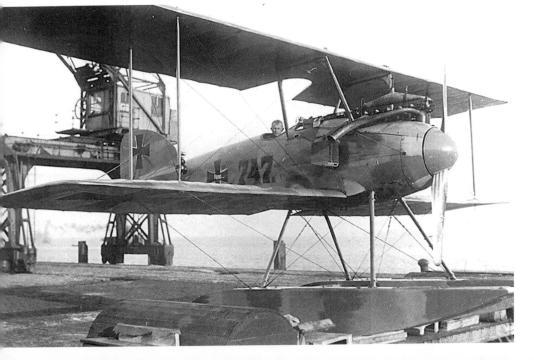

The Zeebrugge mole where British Marines landed during the 1918 raid. *(Johan R Ryheul)*

The sunken British block ships *Intrepid* and *Iphigenia* in the canal entrance at Zeebrugge. *(J Mannering)*

Table 3: German Torpedo-boats

	German A- class
Displacement	137 tons
No of guns	1 x 5cm
No of torpedoes	2 x 45cm
Speed	19kts

Table 4: German and British Destroyers

	German V-25-class	British Tribal-class
Displacement	1188 tons	1090 tons
No of guns	3 x 10.5cm/2 MGs	2 x 4in (10.2cm)/ 1 MG
No of torpedoes	6 x 50cm	2 x 18in (45.7cm)
Speed	36.6kts	34kts

NOTE: No two Tribals were exactly the same. The numbers above are from the Viking, the largest of the class.

The information in the previous three tables is from Gröner, Warships, vol II: pp22,30; vol I: pp161, 178–81; Rössler, U-boat, pp39–44; and Randal Gray, ed. Conway's All the World's Fighting Ships, 1906–21, (London: Conway Maritime Press, 1985), pp71–85, 167–73.

Table 5: British Shipping Losses from March 1915 – February 1916

Month	Tonnage Lost
March 1915	80,775
April 1915	55,725
May 1915	120,058
June 1915	131,428
July 1915	109,640
August 1915	185,866
September 1915	151,884
October 1915	88,534
November 1915	153,043
December 1915	123,141
January 1916	81,259
February 1916	117,547

The information for this table is from: C. Ernest Fayle, Seaborne Trade, III vols (London: John Murray, 1920–24), vol III: p465; Archibald Hurd, The Merchant Navy, III vols (London: John Murray, 1920–29), vol III: pp.378–79.

4

The Year of Transition

1916 PROVED TO BE A YEAR OF transition for the MarineKorps Flandern. The appointment of Admiral Reinhard Scheer as the new commander of the High Seas Fleet initially led to a new and more aggressive stance for the German battle fleet however that did not carry over to the MarineKorps. It remained a secondary command, the primary purpose of which was to carry out submarine attacks on British shipping and lay mines along the British coast. This role was occasionally expanded in early 1916 when the UBs were sometimes used as support craft during Scheer's forays into the North Sea. Then, following the indecisive Battle of Jutland on 31 May, the German navy turned once again to the submarine as their best hope for victory. With that change in strategy, the bases of the MarineKorps took on new importance and both sides began to focus more attention on the Flanders theatre. On the German side the change was demonstrated by the dispatch of entire torpedo-boat flotillas to the Flanders front late in the year.

1916 can be broken down into three distinct phases during each of which the role of the MarineKorps changed: a period from early March to 1 June, wherein the MarineKorps remained an auxiliary force; a period from June to October which saw a gradual increase in importance for the Flanders theatre while important decisions were made regarding the submarine war; and a third period from October 1916 to 9 January 1917 during which the Germans began to launch destroyer raids into the Channel. On the latter date the Germans took the fateful decision to renew the unrestricted submarine campaign and ushered in the decisive phase of the war. The MarineKorps played a critical role from that point on.

THE FLANDERS SIDESHOW: MARCH – 1 JUNE 1916

During the first six months of the year most of the MarineKorps' activity revolved around the submarine flotilla, which was strengthened considerably in early 1916 by the arrival of a new type of submarine, the UB-II. These boats displaced more than 270 tons and had a top speed of just over nine knots on the surface and five and-a-half knots submerged. Like the UB-Is they were armed with two torpedo tubes, but unlike their predecessors the UB-IIs were also equipped with one 5cm deck gun.[1] The UB-IIs were designed for greater endurance, speed and durability and it was hoped that they would be able to carry the commerce war as far as the Irish Sea and the Bay of Biscay.[2]

The first of the UB-IIs, *UB-18*, arrived in Zeebrugge on 16 February. It was followed in March by three additional boats. In order to make the new vessels effective as quickly as possible their crews were drawn from the crews of the UB-Is and fresh crews were assigned to the latter, which now became, in effect, training vessels.[3] The arrival of the UB-IIs gave the flotilla an active strength of twenty boats at the end of March 1916. Eight of these were UB-Is, eight were UCs and four were the new workhorses of the flotilla, the UB-IIs.[4]

The arrival of the UB-IIs coincided with the beginning of what the Germans called the 'sharpened' submarine war. What this meant was that all allied non-passenger vessels in the war zone were liable to be attacked without warning. During this campaign the Flanders flotilla was reasonably successful. The UB-IIs alone accounted for twelve ships totaling 26,782 tons while losing only one of their number, *UB-26*.[5] The rest of the flotilla accounted for a further nineteen ships totaling 22,289 tons.[6] Many of the latter were sunk by mines laid by the UCs, among them was the cruiser *Arethusa*, the flagship of Commodore Tyrwhitt, commander of the Harwich force.[7] The most important of the vessels attacked by the flotilla however was one that did not sink and would have been better left alone; it was the packet steamer *Sussex*.

This is not the place for a detailed discussion of the famous *Sussex* incident. The essentials of the situation were as follows. On 24 March 1916 *UB-26*, a UB-II under the command of Oberleutnant zur See Pustkuchen, spotted a British vessel that Pustkuchen claimed was traveling outside of the areas designated for passenger vessels. He therefore assumed that the ship was a British minelayer and closed to attack. In actuality the ship was the regular steamer between Folkestone and Dieppe and was carrying 380 passengers. Pustkuchen torpedoed the vessel without warning and caused severe damage. The ship did not sink and was eventually towed to Boulogne, however fifty passengers were killed, including some American citizens.[8]

The diplomatic implications of the incident were serious in the extreme and nearly resulted in a rupture of relations between Germany and the United States. As a result of pressure from President Woodrow Wilson the German Chancellor, Theobald von Bethmann-Hollweg, persuaded Kaiser Wilhelm II to order an end to the 'sharpened' campaign. On 24 April German submarines outside of the Mediterranean were ordered to proceed according to prize regulations. They could no longer attack unarmed merchant vessels without warning.[9] This measure was vehemently opposed by the new commander of the High Seas Fleet, Reinhard Scheer, who ordered the recall of all submarines from the commerce war. The only vessels which continued the trade war in the North Sea were the UCs of the Flanders Flotilla. All others were brought home for use with the battle fleet.

The implications of the *Sussex* incident were far-reaching. Not only did it nearly lead to a break with the United States, it also led to a change in Germany's naval strategy. Scheer, now that the submarines were available to support operations by the High Seas Fleet, embarked on a new and risky course that would eventually result in the Battle of Jutland. This change affected both the fleet's submarines and the UBs of the Flanders Flotilla.

After the *Sussex* incident the Flanders Submarine Flotilla was used primarily as support for the High Seas Fleet. Co-operation between the two forces had already begun. Shortly after Scheer took command, on 5 March, he took the fleet out for operations in the Hoofden, the area of the North Sea between Great Britain and the Netherlands, and the UBs of the Flanders flotilla were dispatched to watch for British warships that might sortie. They were partly a reconnaissance force but were also to attack if they found a favourable opportunity.[10] This was the most obvious form of assistance rendered to the High Seas Fleet by the MarineKorps but was by no means the only one. Scheer received other forms of aid as well. These ranged from reconnaissance reports to information on minefields and the best ways to approach the British coast.[11]

During the raid by the High Seas Fleet on Yarmouth and Lowestoft on 24 April the submarines of the Flanders Flotilla were once again present to assist the German battle fleet. The UB-IIs were assigned to a patrol line to watch for and attack British vessels and two UB-Is were sent to help the German battle cruisers navigate through the various minefields in the Hoofden. The MarineKorps was also supposed to provide seven UC minelayers to lay minefields around Harwich and the Thames but because of a series of new minefields and net barrages that had been laid off the Flanders coast by the Dover Patrol, the so–called Belgian Coast Barrage, only one of them was able to leave harbour.[12] In addition to the submarines the MarineKorps provided aerial reconnaissance for the Fleet.[13] In this instance none of the UBs achieved any noteworthy success, but this did not prevent Scheer from using the Flanders submarines in similar situations in the future.

During the planning for the operation that resulted in the Battle of Jutland, Scheer once again turned to the MarineKorps for assistance. On 12 May he sent a memorandum to von Schröder asking for UBs from the Flanders flotilla to take up positions outside the major British harbours and intercept allied warships that sortied when Scheer made his planned advance at the end of May. Two were to be sent to Scapa Flow, two to the Humber, seven to the Firth of Forth and one to the Moray Firth. He also requested frequent aerial reconnaissance reports from the Zeebrugge air station. In exchange he promised to send both a destroyer flotilla and additional fighters to Flanders.[14] As a result von Schröder sent seven UBs and two UC minelayers to assist the High Seas Fleet.[15] None of them had any success intercepting British vessels. Following the Battle of Jutland and the resulting curtailment of activity by the High Seas Fleet, the period of co-operation with the submarines of the Flanders flotilla came to an end.

The Flanders submarines therefore saw only limited action in the first part of the year. The commerce war was effectively ended by the government's decree of 24 April ending the 'sharpened' campaign. After that date the flotilla's submarines were limited to mine-laying and the occasional foray in support of the High Seas Fleet. Things were nearly as quiet for the surface forces.

The War on the Surface March – June 1916

The surface war was quiet as well in the early part of 1916. In March the Flanders Destroyer Half-Flotilla arrived. Von Schröder hoped that these new craft would make it possible for the MarineKorps to take a more active role in the naval war. The new vessels made their first journey on 16 March but encountered no enemy vessels.[16] Their first action came on 20 March.

Just after 7am on the morning of the 20th seaplane 547[17] reported two enemy destroyers[18] around the West Hinder Lightship apparently engaged in an attack against a submarine. As a result the German destroyers sortied and were led to the British vessels by seaplane 547. The British destroyers were spotted at 8.38am and an artillery duel began at 8.56am on a running course to the west. At 9.07am two additional British destroyers appeared and joined the battle. At that same moment *V-68* took a hit to her bow. The resulting list left her unable to fire her forward guns. Shortly afterward the Germans recorded two hits on the British destroyer *Lance* before *V-47* took a hit in the bow as well and the Germans broke off the battle, retreating under the protection of their coastal guns.[19]

This minor skirmish had no effect on the balance of forces, yet von Schröder was very pleased at the way the German craft handled themselves and at the co-operation between the aircraft and the naval forces. He soon began to plan operations farther afield for the Destroyer Half-Flotilla while relegating the

Torpedo-Boat Flotilla strictly to mine-sweeping.[20] After eight days in dry-dock the damaged German vessels were once again ready for battle.[21]

The only noteworthy activity carried out by the Flanders Torpedo-Boat Flotilla during this period was a brief bombardment of the Allied positions around Nieuport on 19 April. This mission was carried out by four of the small German A-boats and was designed to reconnoitre the area in preparation for a larger raid by the destroyers. The torpedo-boats were also to damage allied installations in the harbour if possible.[22] Surprisingly the German craft were relatively unmolested. As they approached the harbour they were briefly illuminated by a spotlight which was immediately taken under fire and knocked out of service at which point a second light came on and was also immediately fired upon. No fire was returned from shore. After firing sixty-seven shells the German vessels retreated and regrouped before making a second approach to within 800 meters of the harbour mole. Still no fire was returned and, after examining the shore batteries as best as possible, the vessels returned to Zeebrugge.[23] The conclusion drawn by Commander Assmann was that the defences were apparently unmanned at night, making the port a perfect target for a raid by the destroyers.[24] Before that operation could go forward however, the Royal Navy intervened.

On 24 April, while von Schröder and his staff were preparing to support Admiral Scheer during his advance against Yarmouth and Lowestoft, von Schröder received a report of a large British armada gathering at Deal and Ramsgate. He was concerned that this portended some action against his coastline. He was correct.[2]

Von Schröder's opposite number, Admiral Reginald Bacon of the Dover Patrol, did indeed have an operation planned for that day. Bacon's forces consisted of the obsolete battleship *Redoubtable* armed with four 12-inch guns, four monitors with 15-inch guns, an additional five monitors with 12-inch guns, seven monitors with 9.2-inch guns, three light cruisers, three large flotilla leaders, twenty-four destroyers (mostly of the *Tribal*-class), several small craft (called P-boats), and numerous motor launches. These were joined by a large number of auxiliary vessels, primarily drifters and trawlers that were used for patrols, minesweeping and mine-laying.[26] Bacon's forces were augmented when necessary by those of Admiral Reginald Tyrwhitt at Harwich. His force consisted of thirty-six destroyers and several light cruisers. The total British force available for use against the Flanders position in 1916 was: eight light cruisers, five flotilla leaders, sixty destroyers or torpedo-boats and sixteen monitors.[27] There was, in addition, a minor French force of thirteen small destroyers.[28] On 24 April Bacon put this formidable force to work laying what he called the 'Belgian Coast Barrage.'

Bacon sent the bulk of his auxiliary vessels, six divisions of drifters, six mine laying trawlers, four large minelayers and the monitors *Prince Eugene* and *General Wolfe* along with an entire division of destroyers to the Flanders coastline to lay the Barrage.[29] The Barrage itself consisted of interlocking nets and mines designed first to snare a submarine attempting to pass through and then destroy it. The Barrage was combined with indicator nets. These nets were attached to light buoys which would give away the locations of submarines ensnared in the nets. The entire system was designed to destroy or at least make it easier to hunt German submarines coming in and out of the Flanders bases.[30] The barrier extended from the Thornton Bank to the Belgian coast and consisted of two rows of deep mines connected with an intermediate line of mine nets. A total of fifteen miles of mines and thirteen miles of nets were laid from 24 April until 5 May 1916 and the whole Barrage was covered by a daily patrol of drifters and trawlers.[31]

While the British were laying the Barrage the Destroyer Half-Flotilla was ordered to attack the British trawlers. At 4pm on the 24th the Germans sortied, only to immediately be met by four British destroyers rushing to the aid of the trawlers. A gunfight developed which was relatively inconclusive until one of the British 12-inch monitors joined in. At that point the German destroyers, deciding that discretion was the better part of valour, retreated under the protection of their coastal artillery. The British destroyers, *Melpomene*, *Medea*, *Milne* and *Murray*, pursued the Germans and in their eagerness to come to grips with their enemy, moved into the range of the German coastal guns. The *Melpomene* took a hit from one of the coastal batteries in her engine room and was left dead in the water. She was taken under tow by *Milne* and *Medea* and the British fell back. The Germans then tried to close once again to finish off the *Melpomene* but were prevented from doing so by the heavy gunfire of the British monitors. The action was once again inconclusive.[32]

Once the Barrage had been laid the British instituted a daytime patrol to ensure that the Germans were unable to sweep up the fields or take in the nets. The patrol was discontinued at night though and within two days the Germans were able to sweep open a large enough gap to allow submarines once again to pass through the barrier.[33] The Germans did make one abortive attempt to drive off the British patrol and allow minesweeping during the day but it was a dismal failure. On 7 May the Destroyer Half-Flotilla was ordered to sortie against the patrol to determine its strength. The Germans turned back however when they were attacked by 5 British destroyers.[34]

On that same day von Schröder wrote to von Holtzendorff stating that the coastline had been placed under a close patrol by the British and that he did not have sufficient forces available to drive off the patrols and sweep for mines.

He renewed his requests for additional forces.[35] Von Holtzendorff responded by asking Scheer to send a flotilla of destroyers west to attack the patrol lines. He also suggested to Scheer that from time to time the submarines of the High Seas Fleet should attack the forces of the patrol.[36] This did not satisfy von Schröder, who again, on 29 May, requested that a full destroyer flotilla be sent to Flanders. This time, as we shall see, his call was heeded.[37] In the meantime, all that the MarineKorps could do was send out UB-Is to destroy the light buoys which appeared to be assisting the navigation of the British patrol vessels.[38]

The Belgian Coast Barrage, though a nuisance, did not stop German naval activity in Flanders. Since the British withdrew their patrols at night the Torpedo-Boat Flotilla was able to sweep the minefields and clear away parts of the Barrage. In addition, the Germans occasionally attacked the British patrols. Immediately after the Barrage was laid, on 25 April three German A-boats raided the drifters on patrol and attacked a division of British trawlers, capturing the drifter *Au Fait*.[39] On 5 and 6 May the Destroyer Half-Flotilla raided the Barrage and destroyed several light buoys before being driven off by two British light cruisers.[40] On 16 May there was a brief gun battle at long range between the entire torpedo-boat and destroyer force in Flanders and the British Barrage patrol. It was indecisive with little or no damage done to either side.[41] In general however, the MarineKorps' existing naval forces were too few and too weak to completely break the patrol or even drive it off for an extended period of time. While the British were limited in their activity by the German coastal guns, the Barrage limited the activity of the German forces as well. At sea as on land, the war had stalemated. In an effort to alleviate this situation von Schröder once again appealed to the Naval Staff to send larger and more capable vessels to Flanders.

On 26 May von Schröder received from Assmann, the commander of the Torpedo-Boat Flotilla, a memorandum complaining that the A-boats were too slow and too weak to work under the threat of the British patrol line and requesting that all the A-boats be replaced by the larger S-boats coming into service that fall. He would retain the crews of the A-boats and transfer them to the new ships so as not to lose their experience.[42] Three days later von Schröder forwarded this appeal to the Naval Staff. Von Holtzendorff, though not agreeing to Assmann's request, did decide to send the II Torpedo-Boat Flotilla from Wilhelmshaven to Flanders once the upcoming fleet operation was completed.[43] Von Schröder immediately began to plan an operation for the newly assigned unit. On 7 June, six days after the return of the High Seas Fleet following Jutland, the II Flotilla left for Flanders and inaugurated a new stage in the surface war off the Flanders coast.[44]

THE FLANDERS NAVAL AIR STATION, MARCH – JUNE 1916

What little success the MarineKorps' forces did enjoy in the first part of 1916 owed a great deal to the Zeebrugge air station and the air forces that were attached to the MarineKorps. During 1916 the I and II MarineLandFlieger Abteilungen were combined into the I MarineLandFlieger Abteilung and a new II section was created, giving the MarineKorps a force of 18 Albatross D-IIIs.[45] These craft performed three primary functions: 1) reconnaissance flights from the Flanders coastline out to the Thames estuary; 2) the bombing of enemy facilities, primarily the French coastal harbours; and 3) the protection of the German naval forces in Flanders from enemy air attack.[46]

The reconnaissance flights proved to be particularly important for the minesweeping efforts of the Torpedo-Boat Flotilla which, because of aerial reconnaissance, was able in several instances to break off its minesweeping and return to port before being attacked by British destroyers.[47]

During 1916 the planes of the MarineKorps expanded their operations by bombing enemy installations along the French coast. These new operations became increasingly important as the year went on.

In March the MarineLandFlieger Abteilungen began a series of training courses for the pilots and observers of the MarineKorps in order to better acquaint them with their new role. Three training schools were set up to teach the students how to properly handle and load bombs and also how to aim and drop them. Bombing was practiced at these schools from several different heights ranging from 200 to 1,200 metres.[48] Shortly thereafter the Marine-Korps' aircraft carried out a bombing raid on Dover, Deal and Ramsgate. One plane was lost to heavy anti-aircraft fire but several hits were reported on all three towns.[49] Several other raids were carried out but they had little success.

In May the MarineLandFlieger Abteilung began equipping all the planes of the MarineKorps with bombsights. This involved cutting away part of the floor of the plane and installing a sight infront of the observer's seat. In addition, the bombs were now attached to the undercarriage of the plane from where they could be mechanically released.[50]

Despite these advances the Germans encountered a serious problem with their bombing missions. When their planes, which were not designed for the purpose, were loaded with bombs, they lost a significant amount of speed and maneuverability. This made them easier targets for defending allied fighters and anti-aircraft fire. As a result the Germans, beginning in May, restricted their bombing runs to the hours of darkness. This made it almost impossible to accurately drop bombs and, as a result only minor damage was done to allied facilities. To help alleviate the problem the MarineKorps requested newer and more powerful planes.[51] This request was eventually granted in July when several new Rumpler fighters were temporarily assigned to the MarineKorps.[52] In the meantime they had to make do with the inferior craft they already possessed. For that reason the bombing campaigns were temporarily stopped. For the remainder of this period, with the exception of one unsuccessful raid on Dunkirk,[53] the air arm of the MarineKorps was restricted to defending the Flanders bases and carrying out reconnaissance.

The reconnaissance provided by the Zeebrugge air station was important for the coastal artillery as well. The coastal defences were augmented in March 1916 when the new 30.5cm coastal battery *Kaiser Wilhelm II* was completed. It was designed to supplement the *Tirpitz* battery.[54] Furthermore, steps were taken in April and May to improve the efficiency of the coastal defences by appointing an *Oberbefehlshaber der Kustenverteidigung* (Supreme Commander for Coastal Defences) for all the coastal defences throughout Germany.

The Oberbefehlshaber was to control those forces which were dedicated to coastal defence, whether they belonged to one of the naval stations, the MarineKorps or even the High Seas Fleet. These included all coastal fortifications. The plan came from the Chief of the General Staff, General Erich von Falkenhayn, who proposed that the post be given to General Ludwig von Falkenhausen, the current commander of the German Sixth Army.[55] The new commander was to have his headquarters in Hamburg and was to command the garrisons of all coastal fortifications as well as all naval forces assigned to coastal defence when and if the General Staff decided that an allied landing was imminent. In short, he was to have complete authority over all measures relating to coastal defence.[56]

The response of the navy was not surprising. On 20 April von Holtzendorff wrote to von Falkenhayn saying that he was opposed to the army taking command of the coastal fortifications. He argued that the 'fleet and bases are a military whole'[57] and that this was nothing more than an attempt by the army to take control of the High Seas Fleet. He stated unequivocally that he would not turn control of any portion of the fleet over to the army. He was not opposed to the creation of a Commander-in-Chief for coastal defence but wanted the commander's authority to be limited to the land forces that would repel an invasion and also wanted a naval officer on the commander's staff to advise him.[58]

Von Falkenhayn responded by explaining that the purpose of the Commander-in-Chief was to bring all the available forces that might be needed to repel an invasion under a united command, nothing more. He was willing to limit the naval forces that would fall under the new command to just the garrisons of the coastal fortifications.[59] Following the dispatch of this letter von Falkenhayn and von Holtzendorff met face-to-face to settle the issue. At this meeting von Falkenhayn denied that he was attempting to gain influence over the use of the fleet and accepted von Holtzendorff's demand that a naval officer sit on the staff of the Commander-in-Chief. This apparently satisfied von Holtzendorff who then accepted the appointment of von Falkenhausen and wrote to the naval station commanders that in the event of any disputes with the Commander-in-Chief they should send their complaints to the Naval Staff so that the navy could maintain a united front against the army in this matter.[60]

This affair demonstrated that the old rivalry between the German armed forces that was partly responsible for the creation of the MarineKorps had not vanished. During 1915, when the attention of the army was focused primarily on the Eastern Front, there was little friction between the two services. The affair of the Oberbefehlshaber der Kustenverteidigung demonstrated that, with the continuance of the stalemate in the west and the return of von Falkenhayn's attention to the Western Front, the divisions between the two services were resurfacing. Their relations were to deteriorate steadily as the year went forward and the army was ground to a pulp in the death mills of Verdun and the Somme while the navy did little to further the German cause.

GROWING IN IMPORTANCE: JUNE– OCTOBER 1916

On 21 June 1916 Admiral Scheer sent a memorandum to von Holtzendorff stating that, even though the High Seas Fleet did more damage to the British Grand Fleet than it received during the Battle of Jutland, such battles could not defeat England because of its superior geographic position. Therefore, to attain victory it would be necessary to unleash the submarines once again in an unrestricted campaign.[611] This decision marked an important turning point. From this point on Scheer pressed for the employment of the submarines against British commerce and gradually reduced the use of the battle fleet. As the submarines came to play the central role in the plans of the German navy the Flanders bases grew in importance. The second stage of 1916 lasted from early June, following the denouement of Jutland, until the decision was taken, in October, to send two full flotillas of destroyers to Flanders. It was a period during which the MarineKorps expanded its field of activity.

The Submarine Flotilla

During the early summer of 1916 the Flanders submarine flotilla concentrated on mine-laying. It continued to lay minefields from the mouth of the Thames to Flamborough Head as well as in the Channel and along the French coast, especially between Nieuport and Calais.[62] The MarineKorps placed special emphasis on the mining of the French harbours in order to prevent or at least slow down the transfer of British troops and materiel to the Somme where, beginning in July, the German and British armies were engaged in a bloody battle.[63] Most of this work from June until September was carried out by only six boats; three of which were lost.[64]

Beginning in September a newer, larger version of the UC began to come into service. This was the *UC-II*-class. The newer boats could carry eighteen instead of twelve mines; displaced over 400 tons and had a radius of action reaching 7–9000 nautical miles. In addition, they were armed with three torpedo tubes and up to seven torpedoes each as well as an 8.8cm deck gun.[65] These were obviously valuable craft since they could be used for multiple purposes.

During the early months of the summer (June and July) the UBs[66] were relatively quiet. They were still required to operate according to prize rules and were therefore held back by both Scheer and von Schröder while the navy pressured Bethmann-Hollweg to reopen the unrestricted submarine campaign. Then, at the end of July, the Flanders submarine flotilla was once again made a guinea pig thanks to the ambitions of its commander, Korvettenkapitän Karl Bartenbach.

At the end of July Bartenbach tried to determine whether a submarine campaign carried out under prize rules could do significant damage to the British.[67] The pressure which the British were placing on the German army at the Somme was a decisive factor leading him to try and experiment. The navy had to try to do something to disrupt the British supplies flowing to the Somme battlefield. Bartenbach therefore sent one submarine into the Channel on an experimental basis to attack Entente commercial shipping while following prize rules. The mission was given to one of the Flanders 'aces', Oberleutnant zur See Otto Steinbrinck and the *UB-18*, one of the UB-IIs.[68] His orders were to attack commercial shipping under strict prize rules. Only military transports were to be attacked without warning.[69]

Steinbrinck began his mission on 31 July and returned to Zeebrugge on 12 August. During the course of the voyage he sank seventeen enemy vessels totaling 6,461 tons but was unable to do any damage to the British transports because the latter were always escorted by destroyers or at least auxiliary vessels.[70] Bartenbach drew two conclusions from the mission. First of all, it was apparent that the submarines alone could not effectively strike against the allied transports to France.[71] However, the limited success Steinbrinck did have against commercial shipping convinced Bartenbach that it would be possible, even obeying prize rules, to damage the British economy. With von Schröder's backing he immediately initiated a renewed commercial war in the Channel and southern North Sea. The Flanders submarines sank a total of thirty-nine vessels totaling 21,768 tons in August.[72] This was despite the fact that the main prey of the Flanders submarines, the traffic between Britain and the Netherlands, began to be escorted by British warships in July.[73] In fact, the UB-IIs were even able to sink one of the escorts of these convoys, the British destroyer *Lassoo* on 13 August.[74]

The submarines continued to have success in September. On their first three cruises the Flanders submarines were able to destroy 67,511 tons of shipping, primarily Dutch and British.[75] By the end of the month they had sunk fifty-three vessels of 74,695 tons[76] and in October they caused a brief but total interruption of Dutch traffic to Britain.[77]

Bartenbach spent the remainder of September and the first part of October trying to convince Scheer and Bauer to unleash the submarines of the High Seas Fleet. His main argument was that even though the restricted campaign could not be decisive any damage done still reduce Britain's reserve of merchant ships.[78] Bartenbach's efforts culminated in a journey to Berlin on 6 October to meet von Holtzendorff and attempt to convince him that the restricted campaign had value. Despite the opposition of Scheer, Bauer and even von Schröder he was successful and von Holtzendorff ordered the resumption of the commercial war under prize rules.[79] The restricted campaign would continue until February 1917.

During this period the Flanders flotilla still took part in the occasional sortie by the High Seas Fleet but their primary purpose was once again to attack enemy commerce. Over the summer months they acquired experience that would prove very valuable once the unrestricted campaign began.[80]

The War on the Surface, June – October 1916

Over these months the leadership of the German navy belatedly began to recognise the value of the Flanders bases. This was made clear at the start of June when the II Torpedo-Boat Flotilla was sent to Flanders. It was continued in October by the decision to send two full flotillas of large torpedo-boats (destroyers) to Flanders. Finally, in October 1916, von Schröder was given the forces he had appealed for in late 1914.

In late May von Schröder received word that the II Flotilla was to be sent to Flanders in early June. He immediately began to plan for its arrival. On 31 May he issued orders for an attack on the British Barrage patrol for the night of 8 June, the same night the II Flotilla was scheduled to leave Germany.[81] The British had just recently begun patrolling the Barrage at night and von Schröder hoped to catch the night patrol by surprise.

At the same time that the II Flotilla was due to pass the North Hinder Light Ship the Destroyer Half-Flotilla and the Torpedo-Boat Flotilla were to sail from Zeebrugge. The torpedo-boats were to concentrate on mine-and net-sweeping and were to remain under the protection of the large coastal guns while the destroyers would move out to the far end of the Barrage and attempt to draw the British patrol vessels into a chase to the east where they would come under the guns of the II Flotilla. Once the destroyers, in conjunction with the II Flotilla, had defeated the British patrols they were to assist the torpedo-boats with mine-sweeping. Radio silence was to be maintained until the II Flotilla reached the North Hinder Light Ship at which point they were to transmit a signal to Bruges to inform the MarineKorps that they were in position and that the operation could begin.[82] However, things did not go quite as smoothly as von Schröder had planned.

The II Flotilla left Wilhelmshaven at 3am on 8 June and arrived at the North Hinder Light Ship at around 5.40am at which point they received aerial reports of two British monitors and six destroyers leaving the area of the Barrage. Due to the number of enemy vessels the commander of the Flotilla decided not to try and intercept them but merely to make directly for Zeebrugge.[83] That decision was not communicated to Bruges and the Flanders destroyers and torpedo-boats sailed as planned.

At 6.25am the Destroyer Half-Flotilla came into contact with five British destroyers and proceeded to run east to where they believed the II Flotilla would be. When the report of the battle was received by the commander of the II Flotilla he changed course to bring assistance, but, due to his earlier change in course he arrived late. In the meantime V-67 was hit between her boiler rooms and had to be taken in tow by V-47.[84] The II Flotilla arrived shortly after 7am at which point the British destroyers broke contact and retreated to the north.[85] The arrival of the II Flotilla, late though it was, probably saved the Destroyer Half-Flotilla. Given time, V-67 eventually recovered power and was able to make it back to Zeebrugge on her own. The remaining ships stayed out to cover the minesweeping of the A-boats until the arrival of a second group of British destroyers and monitors forced the Germans to head to Zeebrugge.[86]

The initial operation of the II Flotilla, instead of the brilliant success von Schröder had envisioned, was nearly a total disaster. Slight damage was done to a few British destroyers and the torpedo-boats, under the protection of the

II Flotilla, were able to sweep up 3,000 meters of nets from the Barrage but the Destroyer Half-Flotilla was nearly destroyed.[87] The skirmish did have important long-term effects. On the British side it resulted in a strengthening of the patrols off Flanders and the reinforcing of the Dover Patrol by eight destroyers and two light cruisers.[88] There were also important effects on the German side. The safe arrival of the II Flotilla demonstrated once again that the hazards of the journey from Wilhelmshaven to Zeebrugge were manageable. It also demonstrated that the presence of a large force protecting the torpedo-boats allowed the latter to sweep much more effectively. These were important factors in the later decision to send two full flotillas of destroyers to Flanders.[89]

While the II Flotilla was in Flanders von Schröder had at his command a total force of thirteen A-boats and thirteen destroyers along with his sixteen submarines and miscellaneous patrol vessels.[90] With this force the main task of the Flanders flotillas, minesweeping, was made much easier.

The main goal of the torpedo-boats and destroyers was still to keep channels through the British mine and net barriers open for the submarines. The actual work of sweeping belonged to the A-boats while the Destroyer Half-Flotilla and II Flotilla were to provide protection. At the same time planes from the Zeebrugge air station provided reconnaissance and advance warning of the approach of British vessels.[91] Most of the German sweeping efforts concentrated on the eastern end of the mine and net fields for the simple reason that this end was farthest from the British harbours and less well protected. Over the course of the summer they were able to open a gap in the Barrage in this area which, with frequent sweeping, was kept open despite occasional efforts by the British to re-lay mines.[92] As long as the II Flotilla remained in Flanders the Germans were able to sweep relatively unopposed and maintain open channels for the egress and ingress of German submarines. Von Schröder however, had other plans for his destroyers besides shepherding the small German torpedo-boats.

The II Flotilla, during its time in Flanders, carried out several other small operations, usually raids on Anglo-Dutch commercial shipping.[93] On one of these missions three of the German destroyers ran into trouble when one of their number, *G-102*, struck a mine while fleeing five British destroyers.[94] Fortunately for the Germans they were close to the protection of their shore batteries and the British were unable to pursue. *G-102* remained in dry-dock for four weeks.[95] On 23 July one of these sorties resulted in another destroyer duel.

At 9.40pm in the evening of 22 July eight destroyers of the II Flotilla left Zeebrugge on a mine-laying mission to the North Hinder Light Ship. Unknown to the Germans, Commodore Tyrwhitt was at sea with two groups,

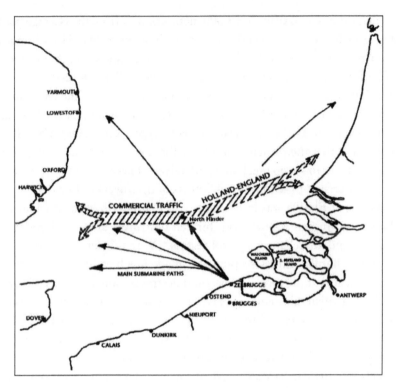

The main routes of the Flanders submarines.

each consisting of four destroyers and a light cruiser, to cover an Anglo–Dutch convoy.[96] At around 10pm one of the British forces spotted the German vessels and opened fire. The Germans, whose normal commander was ill and had remained in Zeebrugge, were thrown into initial confusion. Their temporary commander, Kapitänleutnant Dithmar, slowly realised the perilous position he was in and ordered a turn to the south to run from the British. Due to extremely poor visibility and heavy fog the Germans managed to disappear into the mists. At that point Tyrwhitt turned to the northeast to cut them off from Germany and ordered his second group to proceed south to the area of the Schouwenbank to try and cut the Germans off from Zeebrugge. At 2.45am the second group spotted the Germans and opened fire. This time the Germans were better prepared and promptly responded. Two of the British destroyers attached to this second group were unable to maintain sufficient speed to keep up with the Germans and fell behind. The remaining cruiser and destroyers continued the chase until the Germans reached the protection of their coastal batteries, at which point the British turned back to the north.[97]

Very little damage was done to either side, though for the Germans that was due mainly to the atrocious weather conditions rather than to exemplary skill. The British in this action missed a golden opportunity to severely damage von Schröder's credibility within the German navy. After his continued protestations during the first two years of the war that he could undertake an active naval campaign if only the navy would give him the forces he needed he was finally given a flotilla of destroyers and nearly had them annihilated in one evening. Since the navy had not yet committed itself to sending large forces to Flanders such a defeat may have been devastating and might have prevented further reinforcement of the flotillas. Unfortunately, for the British the weather was against them and the poor visibility allowed the Germans to escape from their better armed foes. The events of the 23rd did not dissuade von Schröder from further activity but on 30 July the II Flotilla returned to Germany, once again leaving the MarineKorps with only the small A-boats and three destroyers.[98]

Between 1 August and the middle of October when two new flotillas arrived in Flanders, the MarineKorps was once again limited to minesweeping. The torpedo-boats were restricted to minesweeping and the destroyers were once again relegated to guarding the torpedo-boats while they worked. For their part the minesweepers spent most of their time keeping the small channels they had opened in the eastern end of the Barrage open.[99] During August and September they swept up over 170 mines and over twenty miles of netting.[100]

Of critical importance to the success of the minesweepers from June to October, just as it had been in the early part of the year, was co-operation with the seaplanes of the Zeebrugge naval air station. Their reconnaissance efforts frequently made it possible for the torpedo-boats of the flotilla to escape oncoming British war ships.[101] This however, was only one of the many ways in which the air arm of the MarineKorps was becoming more important.

The Naval Air Station, June – October 1916

The missions of the MarineKorps' air arm remained the same from June to August. Their first and, now, most important task was the protection of the Flanders bases against enemy air attack. To bolster this defensive assignment the MarineKorps was assigned an additional twenty fighters in September. These craft were divided into two sections, one of which was responsible for defending the coast and the harbours while the other was assigned to assist the IV army.[102]

The MarineKorps aircraft expanded their bombing role in September and October also. During those two months the planes of the MarineKorps launched several attacks against the British Barrage patrols. They had only minimal success but, on occasion, they were able to drive off the British patrols and create an opening so that the minesweepers could go to work.[103]

Reconnaissance remained the third and final duty of the MarineKorps' aircraft. Their objective was still to warn the minesweepers of the approach of enemy warships. In October von Schröder began to order these planes to undertake more long-distance reconnaissance flights to watch for the approach of a possible enemy invasion force. By that point he had become convinced that the British could not let the stalemate in the west continue much longer and felt certain that they would soon make a major move against the Belgian coast.

This fear resulted from the general increase of British activity aimed against the Belgian coast that had been taking place since June. In particular, between July and September the British began trying to destroy the main obstacle to an attack on the coast, the *Tirpitz* battery. In July the British and French placed large batteries (one 30cm and two 23cm) at Coxyde and Adinkerke to bombard the *Tirpitz* battery and hopefully take it out of action.[104] The allied batteries were ineffective, but by the fall the British had added an additional three 30cm and one 23cm, the net effect of which was to bring about continual artillery duels between *Tirpitz* and the allied batteries with neither side having much success. The bombardments were significant enough though to convince von Schröder that the Allies intended to invade the Belgian coast.[105] His concern was shared by von Holtzendorff who wanted to know whether or not the MarineKorps could keep the Flanders harbours open in the event of a British invasion.[106] The Germans' fears seemed to be validated in September when the forces of the Dover Patrol began renewed bombardments of the Flanders coastline.

Starting on 8 and 9 September the Dover Patrol began bombarding the Flanders positions in the hopes of aiding the attack at the Somme. Their intent was once again to convince the Germans that an attack in Flanders was imminent and thereby prevent the Germans shifting forces south to the Somme.[107] The bombardments themselves had little materiel effect but were significant because they did tie down German forces. Admiral von Schröder at least was convinced that the Allies intended to invade.[108] Although no landing had taken place, even in October von Schröder was still reluctant to release any of his forces. His fears were aggravated on 5 October when the Germans received a warning from their naval attaché in the Netherlands that the Allies were planning a major offensive along the coast to turn the German flank, possibly by invading the Netherlands. This attack was expected to come sometime in the fall of 1916 or, at the latest, in the spring of 1917.[109] This warning led to the preparation of 'Fall K', a plan to be implemented in the event that the British violated Dutch neutrality or the Dutch declared war.[110] Fears of a British invasion also gave extra support to von Schröder's continuing calls for additional resources, calls that were finally answered in October with the dispatch of the III and IXth Flotillas to Flanders.

Force Allocation, June – October

Von Schröder's demands for reinforcements took two forms: a continuing call for the dispatch of destroyers so that he could take a more aggressive stance in the surface war; and calls for newer and more powerful replacements for the small and essentially useless A-boats. Following Jutland his calls began to receive a more favourable hearing in the higher levels of the navy, a fact which was reflected by the assignment of the II Flotilla to Flanders in June and July. This new willingness to support an active campaign from Flanders was due partly to a growing conviction on the part of Scheer that the Bight was relatively safe from British attack and partly to the increasing inactivity of the High Seas Fleet.[111] Under the existing conditions it made sense to make fuller use of the Flanders bases. Therefore von Schröder was more successful in getting reinforcements during this period than he had been earlier in the war.

In early June he wrote to the Naval Staff requesting replacements for the A-boats. His reasons were that the vessels were too slow and weak to be used in the frontline. With the continual development of newer and heavier guns as well as faster ships, these slow old ships would only become increasingly obsolete. Already, he reported, he was unable to carry out many operations of 'tremendous military importance.'[112] The A-boats were simply incapable of keeping the much larger and faster British destroyers from closing the harbours. They were, in fact, a drain on other resources because larger vessels had to protect them while they worked.[113] He requested that his boats be replaced with the *S-90*-class boats that were currently under construction for the Baltic. These were 300–350-ton ships with a top speed of twenty-five knots that were armed with 8.8cm guns.[114]

On 16 June a meeting was held at the headquarters of the Naval Staff to discuss the construction and assignment of the *S-90*-class boats.[115] At this meeting the Naval Staff consented to the requests of the MarineKorps and ordered the construction of eighteen boats of a new class, the *A-56*, which were to be finished sometime between January and June of 1917.[116] In the meantime the needs of the MarineKorps were to be met by the transfer of six of the *S-90* boats from the Baltic after it froze.[117] The representative of the MarineKorps at the meeting, Kapitän zur See Titus Türk, opposed the suggestion because it would take too long for the Korps to receive any ships. As a result of his protests the Torpedo Inspectorate asked that, due to the decline of activity in the Baltic, the X Destroyer Flotilla be transferred partly to Flanders and partly to the High Seas Fleet. The Naval Staff objected though. In the end a compromise was reached and it was decided that the first six of a new class of torpedo-boat, the A-II, which had also been meant for the Baltic, would be sent to Flanders instead.[118]

These ships were 210-ton vessels that, like the original A-boats, were to be assembled in Antwerp and moved to Bruges through the inland canals. All of the boats were to be in Antwerp and ready for construction by the start of November at the latest.[119] It was hoped that these ships would be ready for service in February 1917.[120] They were armed with two 8.8cm guns as well as two 45cm torpedoes and were capable of a top speed of twenty-four to twenty-six knots. They were better than the original A-boats but still not competitive with the British forces they were most likely to meet, the *Tribal*-class destroyers.[121]

In the middle of July the MarineKorps was given further good news when they received word that an additional six A-IIs were to be sent to Flanders by the end of December, giving them twelve of the new ships.[122] In early August the MarineKorps requested several modifications to the design of the new boats in order to make them more effective in Flanders, where the conditions were very different from the Baltic. For example, because of the greater danger of air attack they requested that the main armament be capable of serving also as an anti-aircraft gun. For further anti-aircraft defence two machine guns were requested as a secondary armament. In addition, it was hoped that the forward gun could be moved aft to make it less susceptible to heavy seas. An additional six men were also requested for each ship; one officer and five men to man the anti-aircraft guns.[123] The Torpedo Inspectorate responded favourably to these requests with one exception: it was not possible, due to the small size of the ships, to move the gun.[124] The new boats began to come into service in December, augmenting and updating the forces of the Torpedo-Boat Flotilla, but they were not sufficient to shift the balance of forces in the Flanders theatre. That would require full destroyer-flotillas.

On the same day that he wrote to von Capelle and von Holtzendorff requesting replacements for the A-boats, von Schröder had also requested that five destroyers be permanently assigned to Flanders.[125] He did not get a favourable response. On 21 June he was informed that, due to losses at Jutland and the needs of the other fronts, it would not be possible to increase his destroyer force at this time. He would have to continue to make due with those flotillas that could be temporarily spared from the High Seas Fleet.[126]

In July he renewed his pleas, arguing that only with strong forces could he fully utilise his geographic position and launch offensive strikes into the Channel. In the event that his request could not be granted he asked for his A-boats to be refitted for 10.5cm guns, a practical impossibility due to the small size and displacement of these ships. He also asked for six fast motorboats.[127] Before he could receive an answer to his last request his problems were aggravated by the recall of the II Flotilla,[128] which, minus the damaged *G-102*, returned to Wilhelmshaven on 31 July.[129] On that same day von Schröder sent yet another missive to the High Seas Fleet pointing out that the II Flotilla, while in Flanders, had been crucial to the torpedo-boats' ability to maintain channels through the Barrage. He also pointed out their 'successes' against the British; the ostensible damaging of a destroyer and a small cruiser and used this to argue that tremendous results could be expected if the navy made full use of the Flanders bases. Therefore it was urgent that a new flotilla be sent west as soon as possible.[130]

Von Schröder's arguments apparently had some effect. In August he was informed that he would be receiving one of the destroyers from the XXI Half-Flotilla to serve in Flanders while *G-102* was under repair.[131] However the request for small motor boats to assist in patrolling was denied because the navy lacked appropriate vessels.[132]

Further reinforcements soon followed. In early September von Holtzendorff wrote to von Capelle asking that the Flanders Destroyer Half-Flotilla be expanded into a full flotilla of eleven ships (thereby expanding it by eight destroyers). In the meantime von Schröder would have to make-do with what he had and what Scheer could spare for him.[133] Shortly thereafter the decision was made to send two full flotillas of destroyers, the III and the IX, to Flanders. The arrival of these two flotillas temporarily changed the ratio of forces in the theatre and made it possible for the MarineKorps to take a much more aggressive stance in the war at sea.

EXPANSION AND SUCCESS: OCTOBER 1916 – JANUARY 1917

The final quarter of 1916 saw a dramatic increase in activity by the Marine-Korps. The period began with the transfer of the III and IX Destroyer Flotillas to Flanders and ended with the decision of 9 January 1917 to 'play the last card' and declare the resumption of unrestricted submarine warfare. Due to that decision the MarineKorps found itself playing a crucial role in one of the war's most important theatres during 1917 and 1918. From January 1917 to November 1918 it was involved in some of the most critical events of the war.

There was also a resurgence of the dormant controversy between the army and navy over personnel issues and over matters of coast defence during the final months of 1916. As a hybrid military/naval unit the MarineKorps was vitally affected by these disputes and its position at times became extremely uncomfortable.

Naval Operations

The naval war heated up considerably in the latter part of 1916. For a change it was not the submarines that bore the brunt of the war effort but the surface forces. The latter were reinforced by the III and IX Flotillas on 19 October. The submarines however, were still critically important. It was, after all, to ensure their freedom of action that the two flotillas were sent to Flanders.

The Flanders U–Boat -Flotilla remained busy during the latter part of the year despite the restrictions placed on it by the need to observe prize rules. Between June and October the UC-Is had laid a total of sixty-seven minefields covering an area from the mouth of the Thames as far north as Yarmouth and Flamborough Head and south to the French Channel harbours. These fields accounted for a total of forty-one ships worth 62,347 tons. Three submarines were lost.[134] Between October 1916 and February 1917 the UC-Is laid an additional forty-eight minefields covering the same areas. These fields accounted for an additional twenty-four ships totaling 35,052 tons.[135] The UC-IIs laid their own series of fields. They laid sixty-four barriers that claimed thirty-four ships worth 77,190 tons. Only two submarines were lost.[136]

The UC-IIs were not limited to mine-laying though. Several of the newer vessels claimed allied ships through gunfire and torpedoes. An additional 146 enemy ships totaling 141,805 tons were sunk by the UC-IIs through these methods.[137] There was clearly an increase in activity for the mine-laying submarines late in the year. There appear to be three reasons for this. First of all, the presence of the UC-IIs with their increased capabilities simply opened a larger field of opportunity to the submarines. Secondly, the submarines were no longer tied down by fleet operations. After Holtzendorff's order of 5 October to resume a restricted submarine war the submarines of the flotillas were turned loose against the commerce of the Allies. Finally, the Flanders-Flotilla as a whole was operating with a new and aggressive attitude. That attitude was reflected in increased activity by the UB-IIs.

From October to January the UB-IIs renewed their attacks against allied commerce, especially against the traffic from Britain to Holland. They accounted for 149 enemy ships and 151,990 tons. In return they lost three submarines.[138]

By the end of 1916 the older UB and UC-Is were being taken out of service. They were simply too small to act effectively in the heavily patrolled waters off the Belgian coast. Their effectiveness had been greatly reduced by the Anglo-Dutch trade treaty of July 1916.[139] The trade treaty radically revised the export policies of the Netherlands. Food supplies that had previously been exported to Germany were now redirected to Great Britain. The problem for the submarines though was that part of the treaty called for the British to begin escorting Dutch ships carrying goods to Britain.[140] The presence of the escorts forced the UB-Is to attack while submerged and their limited torpedo armament meant they only had two shots before they had to return to port to rearm. The larger armament of the UB-IIs made them much more effective. As a result the remaining UB-Is (of which only five were left) were removed from service and in some instances converted into minesweepers.[141] Their crews, as well as those of the original UCs, were needed to take over the newer vessels.

Though the submarines remained busy throughout the latter part of the year, the true change in the MarineKorps' fortunes occurred in the war on the surface, with the arrival of the III and IX Flotillas from Germany allowed Admiral von Schröder to finally launch an aggressive attack against the forces of the Dover Patrol.

On 19 October Admiral von Holtzendorff, in conjunction with Admiral Scheer, decided to send two destroyer flotillas (a total of 20 destroyers) to Flanders to reinforce the MarineKorps on a temporary basis.[142] They were led by the Commander of the Torpedo-boats, Kapitän zur See Andreas Michelsen, and were sent specifically to disrupt the British patrols along the Barrage and, if possible, to attack Allied transports en route to France. The Germans hoped that a surprise destroyer attack might catch several British troop convoys in the Channel and destroy them.[143]

The two flotillas left Wilhelmshaven on the night of 23 October and arrived in Flanders on the morning of the 24th, along the way avoiding the forces of Commodore Tyrwhitt, who was at sea with the Harwich destroyers around the North Hinder Light Ship.[144] Their arrival meant that von Schröder now had twenty-three destroyers available for operations; ten from each flotilla and the three that belonged to the Destroyer Half-Flotilla.[145]

Von Schröder and Michelsen planned to launch a quick raid into the Channel on the night of 26 October before the British discovered that the Germans had significantly reinforced Flanders. They planned to attack the patrol craft and hoped to find and destroy British troop convoys. It was assumed that they would face only light resistance from a few destroyers. Von Schröder was certain that the Germans would be able to achieve surprise against the patrols and would then have one or two hours in which to do as much damage as possible before the British were able to assemble superior forces for a counter-attack. He wanted the destroyers to hit and run and be able to return to Flanders without being cut off by the British.[146]

There were two groups singled out for attack: the patrol craft in the straits and the shipping in the Downs.[147] According to the original plan, following the attack on the patrols the second flotilla would join with the first for a major attack on the northern exits of the Downs. An advance by the High Seas Fleet to attack the English east coast and force the British to split their responding groups between the two areas was also included as part of the plan.[148] In the actual event these plans were significantly altered. The attack by the High Seas Fleet was dropped and the attack on the Downs was changed to a drive into the English Channel in search of enemy transports.[149]

The constant inactivity of the Germans had lulled the British into a state of complacency. By October the patrol line was nearly devoid of actual warships. The bulk of the forces on patrol were auxiliary vessels, mainly drifters. These were slow and essentially unarmed with the exception of the rifle each ship kept on board to use against enemy aircraft. They were nothing short of defenceless against a concerted attack by enemy warships. Furthermore only two destroyers were on patrol in the threatened sector when the Germans left harbour on the night of the 26th. The sheepdogs were gone and the wolves were coming.

There was, however, one way in which Admiral Bacon, the commander of the Dover Patrol, was ready for a night-time torpedo-boat attack; he had previously ordered that no transports were to sail at night due to the dangers of a possible German advance. Due to this decision the Germans found very few targets for their guns when they entered the Channel.

Contrary to what the Germans believed, the British were not ignorant of the reinforcement of Flanders. The British knew of the transfer of the destroyers and, as a result, had sent one light cruiser and four destroyers from the Harwich force to Bacon and the Dover Patrol.[150] However, Bacon assumed that the Germans were planning a destroyer attack along the French coast in support of a landing against Nieuport. His main concern therefore was the protection of the French coast, not the protection of the patrols. He arranged his forces for the evening of 26 October accordingly. They were as follows: in Dunkirk, five destroyers, four torpedo-boats, and five monitors plus the cruiser and destroyers detached from Harwich; in the Downs, four additional destroyers; on patrol, one destroyer and two patrol boats with one torpedo-boat to support the drifters; and at Dover, six additional destroyers.[151]

The German plan was simple. The III Flotilla and the Flanders Half-Flotilla were to raid the patrols and then strike at British shipping in the Dover-Calais straits. In the meantime the IX Flotilla was to try and avoid detection and enter through the straits to attack the Pas de Calais and the Varne, an area in the central Channel between Folkestone and Gris Nez. Each half-flotilla was assigned a strict geographical area where they were to operate and they were not to wander into the areas assigned to the other half-flotillas. This was so they would know that any shipping they encountered was hostile. This provided them with a tremendous advantage during the battle; since they knew all the ships they encountered were hostile they were able, in nearly all instances, to get in the first blow; the British on the other hand needed to ascertain whether or not any approaching vessels were friendly before opening fire. This advantage proved critical.

The evening of the 26th was exceptionally clear with visibility out to two-to-three nautical miles and all went well for the Germans as they left port around 9.30pm.[152] The IX Flotilla was able to avoid the British patrols and pass through the straits though they did have a bad moment when they were spotted by a small British torpedo-boat, the *Flirt*, which flashed a recognition signal at the destroyers. The Germans returned the signal and that apparently satisfied the British captain who went on his way without reporting the contact. In the meantime the III Flotilla had arrived on the patrol line and commenced its attack.

At 10pm the 5th Half-Flotilla opened fire on the 10th Drifter Division and quickly sank three of the five vessels. Another was severely damaged and left burning on the water. One, however, did manage to escape.

At roughly 10.30pm the torpedo-boat *Flirt*, which had spotted and not reported the IX Flotilla, after seeing the flashes of gunfire, arrived on the scene of the attack. Her captain, seeing the burning drifters and several destroyers milling about, assumed that the destroyers were French and were hunting a submarine that had attacked the drifters. He had lowered his boat and sent several men to rescue the crew of the drifters when the destroyers suddenly opened fire on his ship. The gallant little ship went down trying to ram one of the larger German vessels. She never reached her target. The *Flirt* was sunk and all hands on board were lost. The only survivors were those who had left to rescue the crew of the drifters. The *Flirt*, which was no match for the Germans in the best of conditions, was done in by her captain's complacency and the previous inactivity of the Germans. It must have seemed almost inconceivable that a large force of German destroyers could be loose among the patrols. He and his crew discovered their mistake too late.

At 10.50pm word reached Dover of the German attack on the 10th division and Bacon ordered the six destroyers stationed there to attack the Germans. However, Bacon's orders became garbled and set the stage for a larger disaster to come. The destroyers were supposed to leave harbour and form up on the *Viking* as the command ship. The commander of the *Viking* however never ordered the *Nubian*, *Cossack* and *Amazon* to follow him; consequently they left harbour on their own and became separated from one another.[153] In addition, the destroyers that were supposed to be covering the Downs mistakenly received orders to attack as well and hence the Downs was left completely unprotected. Luckily for the British the Germans had altered their original plan.

In the meantime the 5th Half-Flotilla had moved on and attacked the 8th Drifter Division at 11.10pm. Two of these vessels were sunk as well. Moving on from there they attacked the 16th Division at 11.25pm and sank an additional two drifters while leaving another severely damaged. Following that attack they turned for home. On their return the III Flotilla engaged three large enemy destroyers,[154] most likely the *Viking* group.

While the III Flotilla enjoyed success the IX Flotilla found very few targets. They sank one non-military transport at about 11.30 and later, in the vicinity of Boulogne, sank one French and damaged one British patrol ship. It was on its return home that the IX Flotilla did most of its damage.

The 18th Half-Flotilla, on its way back to Zeebrugge, ran into the *Viking*, *Mohawk*, and *Tartar* and opened fire, gaining surprise while the British tried to determine the nationality of the approaching destroyers. The *Mohawk* was severely damaged but no vessel on either side was sunk. The 18th Half-Flotilla returned without further incident though they were pursued by the *Viking*.

The 17th Half-Flotilla had a more interesting journey. They first encountered the lone destroyer *Nubian* which had gotten separated from her fellows after leaving Dover. The *Nubian* spotted the Germans and flashed a recognition signal at them to determine if they were friendly. The Germans responded with a burst of gunfire at which point the *Nubian*, outgunned, as had been the *Flirt*, turned to ram the nearest German destroyer. The *Nubian* was hit several times by shellfire and once amidships by a torpedo.[155] She never reached her target and the Germans left her dead in the water and on fire, assuming she would sink. She was however eventually towed into harbour. Shortly thereafter the Germans encountered the *Amazon* and another brief gun battle ensued in which the *Amazon* was heavily damaged but managed to escape. As they continued on their course to Zeebrugge the 17th Half-Flotilla then encountered the *Viking*, which had been unable to bring the XVIII Half-Flotilla to battle. The *Viking* though was able to escape with only minimal damage. After that encounter the XVII Half-Flotilla completed its return to Zeebrugge without further incident.

The operation was, tactically, nearly a total success. The casualty reports differed, with the Germans reporting that they had sunk eleven enemy drifters as well as two destroyers and a steamer without loss to themselves.[156] The British claimed that only six drifters and one trawler were sunk, while three drifters were heavily damaged. Forty-five men were killed, four wounded and ten taken prisoner. None of the British destroyers were sunk though *Nubian* and *Amazon* were both severely damaged.[157] The British account leaves out the fate of the *Flirt*, which was also sunk. The proper count would appear to be seven auxiliary vessels, one empty transport and one torpedo-boat sunk, several more auxiliaries damaged, and two destroyers badly damaged.[158] On the German side only the destroyer *G-91* took any damage and that was minimal. Von Schröder and Michelsen both were very pleased with their results and planned a new attack to follow shortly. They still believed the British had not known of the reinforcement of Flanders, so they took pains to stress in their press release that the attack was launched from the Bight.[159] It appeared as if everything von Schröder had said about the potential of the Flanders bases was true. However, the Germans' success was somewhat illusory. It was aided tremendously by their own previous inactivity, which helped to create the required atmosphere of surprise without which the attack could hardly have succeeded. The truth of this was proven by the results of future raids.

The raid had important results for the British. Bacon, like von Schröder, had been struggling to get the importance of his command recognised. The changing nature of the war at sea, in particular the growing importance of the struggle against the German submarines, had led him to conclude that his command was vital to Britain's survival but he had so far been unable to convince the Admiralty. That changed after the raid of 26 October. Following the raid there was a redistribution of British destroyers. Three divisions of destroyers were transferred from Harwich to Dover and an additional five destroyers were moved from the Humber and sent to Dover.[160] To make up this shortfall destroyers were taken from the Grand Fleet. This led Admiral Beatty to reduce the latter's radius of action because he feared that he would not have sufficient destroyers to protect the fleet in the event of a meeting with the Germans.[161] Interestingly, enough this paralleled what was happening on the German side since Scheer was sending new forces to Flanders. The Dover-Flanders area, with the growing importance of the submarine and the war against it, was becoming central to the war effort of both nations. Von

Schröder's arguments of 1915[162] seemed to have been justified.

Strategically, however, this battle changed nothing. The German position now was no stronger than it had been previously and in some ways was weaker given the reinforcements sent to Bacon. This battle also demonstrated a major weakness of the Flanders positions. It took two and-a-half hours for four vessels to move from Bruges to Zeebrugge via the inland canals.[163] This, along with the prevalence of aerial reconnaissance, meant that it would be nearly impossible to achieve a second surprise attack if the German vessels were ever forced to leave Zeebrugge and shelter in Bruges. This had a negative impact on Scheer's willingness to assign large forces to Flanders in 1918.[164] Strictly in terms of morale though, the battle was a major boost to the MarineKorps and plans were immediately made to follow up the raid with new attacks.

The first of these new operations was planned for 28 October but had to be postponed due to poor weather. As a result the next attack came on the evening of 1 November.[165] In this operation the III Flotilla and the Destroyer Half-Flotilla were to attack the patrol lines once again while the IX Flotilla attacked the Downs.[166] However, just as the vessels were leaving harbour, the Germans received an aerial reconnaissance report of a large force of battleships, destroyers and cruisers gathering at Gravelines. Due to the threat this force posed to the III Flotilla they were ordered to proceed against the Downs with the IX Flotilla. The British however appeared to be aware of the advance this time since all British traffic had been pulled out of the Channel and into the Downs where large numbers of destroyers were reported to be gathering.[167] Having discovered what appeared to be a British trap[168] the MarineKorps ordered both flotillas to attack the commerce between the Netherlands and Britain instead.[169] In this attack the Germans took three prizes before they were attacked by five British cruisers and forced to flee, leaving one of the prizes behind. This vessel fell into British hands and the prize crew was taken prisoner.[170] After the success of the raid on the 26th the meager results of this second endeavour were disappointing. Nonetheless, the raid at least temporarily disrupted commerce between Britain and the Netherlands.

For the Germans there was also an indirect benefit to having a large force of destroyers in Flanders. They made it less likely that the torpedo-boats would be attacked while they were minesweeping. This also meant that it was easier for German submarines to enter and leave their bases.[171] Unfortunately this situation did not last long. On the day after the second attack, 3 November, Michelsen and the III Flotilla returned to the High Seas Fleet, leaving the IX Flotilla in Flanders to keep pressure on the British.[172] Further operations were planned during the middle of the month but in each instance they had to be canceled due to heavy seas and storms.[173] Finally, on 21 November the weather cleared sufficiently to allow another operation to take place. As a result von Schröder issued orders for an attack against the commercial shipping in the Downs to take place on the night of the 23rd.[174]

On the 23rd the Germans left Zeebrugge without incident and proceeded to the Downs without spotting or being spotted by any British vessels, however, when they arrived they found no ships to attack. The Germans assumed that the British had pulled their forces back to avoid a repeat of the events of 26 October,[175] but Admiral Bacon later claimed that he had been alerted by the Admiralty of the coming German raid and because of that warning had pulled the shipping out of the Downs.[176] That is certainly plausible given what we now know about the British ability to read the German naval codes;[177] however, since there was no attempt by the British to intercept the Germans on their return to Zeebrugge it seems unlikely. Had he known of the raid Bacon most likely would have tried to intercept the German destroyers. That he did not do so would seem to indicate that the emptiness of the Downs on this particular evening was a fortuitous circumstance. At any rate, the Germans returned to Zeebrugge on the 24th without having accomplished anything.[178]

A final operation was carried out on the evening of the 26th when the IXth Flotilla and the Destroyer Half-Flotilla sortied once more but they had only minimal success, finding and sinking one British patrol vessel.[179] In fact the Germans did more damage to themselves that night, when *V-30* and *S-34* collided on their way back to Zeebrugge and were both heavily damaged.[180] On the 30th the IX Flotilla, minus the two damaged destroyers which remained in Flanders until the turn of the year, returned to Germany, thus ending what was to date the most successful period in the brief history of the Flanders flotillas and the MarineKorps.[181] The remaining German destroyers continued to launch the occasional foray into the Channel but they enjoyed no success.[182] Without a larger force there was little the five remaining ships could accomplish. This situation was not rectified until 22 January 1917 when another flotilla, the VI, was sent from Germany to Flanders.[183] Until that point the naval war on the Flanders front settled back into an uneasy silence.

The activity of the III and IX Flotillas did have some important effects. First of all, their presence greatly eased the conditions under which the A-boats had to work. Since any British move against the A-boats would have run the risk of encountering the destroyer flotillas it was no longer possible to interrupt the German minesweeping measures with only one or two destroyers. Hence the A-boats were much more successful. By the end of November they had cleared two wide channels through the Belgian Coast

Barrage and the submarines were able to enter and exit Ostend and Zeebrugge without serious complications.[184] The lack of strong British countermeasures allowed the A-boats to complete the sweeping of the Barrage by January 1917, hence making it possible to pull the experienced A-boat crews out of the line and train them with the new A-IIs that were just coming into service.[185] The respite gained by the presence of the destroyer flotillas was of great value to both the Torpedo-Boat Flotilla and the U-Boat-Flotilla.

There were effects on the British side as well. The German attacks forced Bacon to revise his patrols, concentrating the majority of his forces in two areas, between Calais and the Goodwin Light Ship and in the Downs. In addition, a force of two cruisers, two flotilla leaders and an entire division of destroyers was kept in reserve to counter any German move against the patrol lines. The British were, for the first time, limited in what they could do along the Flanders coast.[186] This freed the German torpedo-boats and submarines from coastal defence duties and meant that the coastal bombardments ceased, at least temporarily. Despite its small scale, the battle of 26 October did alter the conditions of the naval war to the benefit of the Germans. They now held the initiative. This situation continued for as long as the British believed that large forces were present in Flanders. Once it became evident that was no longer the case, the British once again tightened their patrol lines. At least some of von Schröder's arguments for employing larger forces in Flanders were proven, by this brief period's activities, to be correct. Now all he needed were additional forces so that he could keep the pressure on and maintain the initiative.

Reinforcements for Flanders, October 1916 – January 1917

By the end of October 1916 the question over whether or not naval forces should be sent to Flanders had essentially been settled in favour of the MarineKorps. True, von Schröder still did not have the force he had originally argued for; a flotilla of destroyers stationed permanently in Flanders, but he did have the agreement of Scheer and von Holtzendorff that they would send additional flotillas to Flanders periodically. With the beginning of the unrestricted submarine campaign in February 1917 those periodic visits became increasingly common. In the meantime von Schröder's insistent calls for additional ships ceased. That, however, is not to say that there were not issues of force allocation to be resolved during the final part of 1916; for the most part they revolved around the use of air power.

In terms of naval forces the only reinforcements the MarineKorps received in the last few months of 1916 were the A-IIs. They were scheduled to come into service during December and were to become the backbone of the

Flanders Torpedo-Boat Flotilla. The plan was for six to eight of them to be assigned to patrol duties while the remainder were kept with half crews as a material reserve.[187] Unfortunately problems arose with the construction of the vessels in Germany and the first A-II would not reach Antwerp until February 1917 while the second was not due to arrive until July.[188] Von Schröder was irate and demanded that he receive his full quota of these ships by the spring of 1917 when he expected the British to once again begin laying mines off the coast.[189] He asked that, if the craft he had been promised could not arrive before July, he be sent four of the already completed A-IIs that were intended for the High Seas Fleet, suggesting that the yet to be completed boats be given to Scheer.[190] It was a measure of the growing importance of the Flanders theatre that his request was granted without serious opposition.[191] The change meant that the MarineKorps would receive their first A-II on 18 December and that the other three would arrive during January. This would give von Schröder four large, modern torpedo-boats with which he could conduct patrols and mining operations.[192]

Von Schröder also succeeded in getting reinforcements for the Flanders air stations. Most of his concerns were over land-based aeroplanes, not seaplanes. At the start of November the MarineKorps had a total of twenty-two aeroplanes of varying makes available.[193] Unfortunately only seven of them were equipped as fighters; the remainder were used as observers for the coastal artillery and for tracking enemy naval movements. On very rare occasions they were used for bombing raids. Even the fighters of the air stations had problems. They were generally older and slower than their allied counterparts and most were in dire need of maintenance and refitting.[194]

On 1 November von Schröder was informed that the aircraft of the MarineKorps were no longer able to protect the naval bases or even spot for the artillery. There were simply not enough fighters. It was impossible to make up the shortfall with seaplanes because they were not as maneuverable or as fast as allied aircraft. In the final analysis it was necessary, if the air arm was to fulfill its duties, that they receive at least an additional four fighters, though eight would be preferable.[195] This report led von Schröder to request additional planes for the MarineKorps.

Representatives of the MarineKorps, the Naval Staff and the RMA met in Berlin on 11 November. At that meeting the representatives of the Marine-Korps requested that eight first-class Albatross fighters be sent to Flanders. In making the request they emphasised the fact that only the MarineKorps, of all the units on the Western Front, had to guard three sectors; the coast, their portion of the Western Front and the border with the Netherlands. They also pointed out that any fighters assigned to the MarineKorps would serve a dual purpose; they would protect both the Flanders flotillas and the right flank of the German army. After some discussion a decision was made to equip the MarineKorps with twenty new aircraft. In order to implement the decision it would be necessary to transfer an additional 100 men to the MarineKorps.[196] The navy hoped that these additional men could be taken from the army since the MarineKorps would also be receiving thirty new seaplanes in the spring and the men to man those planes had already been taken from the older destroyers and torpedo-boats, some of which had to be taken out of service as a result.[197] Surprisingly, there was very little opposition by the army. This was probably due to the fact that the MarineKorps had just taken over an additional sector of front stretching from Ypres to Poperinghe.[198] The air service though, was reluctant to assign additional personnel to the MarineKorps.

A compromise was struck in December when, at the urging of von Holtzendorff, von Schröder agreed to take some of the MarineKorps' observation craft out of service to make personnel available for the new fighters. If all went as planned the MarineKorps would have twenty-four aeroplanes available by February; fourteen of which would be fighters.[199] This proposal was accepted by the air service at the end of December with the caveat that the planes would be delayed briefly since the army needed newer craft as well.[200]

In both of these instances von Schröder was able to achieve his aims relatively easily; certainly without all the trouble he experienced earlier in the war. The reason for this is simple. As it became increasingly apparent to the Germans that it was vital for them to defeat Britain if they were to win the war, and as the submarine gained credence as *the* war winning weapon, the forward bases of the MarineKorps became vitally important, as did the efforts of the Korps to ensure that the Channel passage remained open and available to all German submarines. For this reason the requests of the MarineKorps met a warmer reception in Berlin. The fullness of this change was demonstrated once again in late January when another flotilla of destroyers was sent to Flanders to reinforce the MarineKorps.[201] All was not roses though, the final phase of 1916 did see one old problem reemerge; relations with the army cooled. The problem, once again, was over which service was to have control over the defences along the coast.

Defence of the Coast and Harbours
During the Battle of the Somme British air attacks against German positions in northern France and Belgium increased dramatically. These attacks were one of the major reasons for von Schröder's request for additional aircraft.

They also led to changes in the air-defence system of the MarineKorps.

Towards the end of October the air arm of the MarineKorps completed a study of enemy air activity and proposed a series of changes to the air-defences along the coast. One change, of course, was an increase in the fighter force. They also recognised a need for newer and larger anti-aircraft guns and for more spotlights, especially along the coast.[202] The spotlights were of particular importance since they could be used both to illuminate targets for the anti-aircraft guns and to try and blind enemy pilots. The MarineKorps staff also requested that the entire system be linked by telephone so that the spotlights and anti-aircraft guns could communicate with one another. Then, to create a truly efficient system it would be necessary to equip every fighter with a radio so that they could communicate directly with the other defences.[203] Unfortunately for the Germans it proved impossible to implement these changes in a timely fashion and, while steps were taken to try and create a united defensive network, for the immediate future the MarineKorps had to rely on their existing defences.

Following a series of ineffective British air attacks in November, von Schröder and his staff decided to remove control of the aerial defences from the individual MarineDivisions and concentrate it in Bruges. In addition, they decided to move the anti-aircraft training school from Bruges to Zeebrugge to provide extra air defence for that harbour.[204] The two decisions met with opposition from Vice-Admiral Jacobsen, the commander of the 1st Marine-Division. He believed that having gunners still in training defending Zeebrugge and conducting gunnery practice there would create a serious hazard to German aircraft.[205] He also doubted the efficacy of the move. However, since von Schröder had already been forced to restrict large vessels from using the harbour at Ostend due to enemy air activity, it was imperative to maintain the defences of Zeebrugge; therefore all possible steps were taken to defend the latter harbour.[206] The anti-aircraft school therefore was moved in December. The adjustments appear to have been successful since no serious damage was done by air attack to either Zeebrugge or the vessels using the harbour during the remainder of 1916.

Of greater importance were the concerns of von Schröder and his staff that a British landing on the coast was imminent. These concerns began with the reports from the naval attaché in the Hague that were alluded to earlier and grew during the latter part of the year as the Germans suffered reverses at the Somme. The claim has been advanced that the MarineKorps was never seriously concerned about the possibility of a British landing simply because of the difficulties involved in such an operation.[207] In truth however, beginning in 1916 and continuing into 1918, concern over an imminent British attack along the coast grew.

In the middle of November Vice-Admiral Jacobsen sent a memorandum to Admiral von Schröder outlining new measures that he wished to implement in preparation for a British landing.[208] This memorandum began a flurry of activity at both the divisional and Korps headquarters as the MarineKorps began examining their existing defences, looking primarily for ways to improve them.

The initial memorandum called for a constant state of readiness by the coastal artillery and the torpedo-boats (this generally already existed) and the maintenance of a torpedo net outside of the canal locks in Zeebrugge. In addition, a series of recognition signals were to be created for any vessel approaching the coast during the hours of darkness.[209] With the exception of the torpedo net most of these measures were already in place. However, other changes were rapidly made.

Shortly after sending the memorandum to von Schröder Jacobsen began to implement changes on his own. They were as follows:

1. All signal stations along the coast were connected by telephone and were equipped with an electronic alarm system that was to be triggered upon spotting enemy vessels. If that alarm malfunctioned, a signal rocket was to be launched.

2. Each station was equipped with a series of flares that were to be used to illuminate the threatened sector of the coast for artillery fire.

3. Machine gun nests were set up every 1,000 meters along the beach to act as supplements to the coastal artillery. It was hoped that they would be able to keep any attacking force on the beaches.

4. Strongpoints equipped with two machine guns, a spotlight and two-to-four quick-firing light artillery pieces were created.

5. Extra artillery pieces of smaller calibre were added to the major coastal batteries for use solely against an invading force. These ranged from 5 to 12cm.

. All of the strongpoints and machine gun nests were covered with barbed wire.

7. All strongpoints and machine gun nests were connected to each other by trench lines.

Implementation of these measures began in late November.[210]

At the MarineKorps' headquarters in Bruges there was also new activity devoted to trying to stop an allied invasion. In late December, after considerable deliberation, von Schröder issued a new series of orders detailing what measures were to be taken in the event of an enemy landing.[221] The orders obviously varied for each force. Those for the U–Boat Flotilla were that one submarine was to be on patrol at all times along the approaches from Dunkirk. It was only to report on the advance of enemy forces and was not to attack. Any other submarines in harbour, upon receiving such a report, were immediately to prepare to go to sea. Once at sea they were to try and group together for a joint attack.

The Torpedo–Boat Flotilla and Destroyer Half-Flotilla were also to maintain a coastal patrol at night. Upon spotting enemy forces they were to immediately report to Bruges. After that it was left to the discretion of the commander on the scene whether or not to attack. In the meantime all the vessels in harbour were to raise steam and prepare to go to sea. If the possibility of a favourable attack arose the ships were to take it; otherwise they were to leave the harbour and scatter.

The air stations were responsible for patrols during the daylight hours. If an attack came during the day the planes were to spot for the artillery and control what were called *Fernlenkboote*. These were small radio-controlled boats filled with explosives. They were operated by an observing aircraft and were used to try and ram enemy ships. In essence they were radio-controlled torpedoes. In an attack at night the planes and the Fernlenkboote were not to be used.

Preparations were also made to lay an emergency minefield off the coast. In the event of an invasion all the available forces were to come under the command of the 1st MarineDivision, which was responsible for coastal defence.

In conclusion, von Schröder pointed out that any attack would most likely come in the spring but that it could come either during the day or at night, and if it were a night attack it would probably come during the longer nights of January and February. Therefore the highest level of alertness was to be maintained for the immediate future.[212] Von Schröder's concerns were echoed by Admiral Scheer who sent a letter to von Schröder on 26 December warning him of a possible British attack. Scheer also explained that the High Seas Fleet would probably not be able to intervene.[213]

On 28 December von Schröder wrote to von Holtzendorff to inform him that he believed a British landing on the coast would soon be launched in conjunction with a major land offensive in the west and strong political pressure on the Netherlands.[214] In this letter von Schröder pointed out that even a minor allied advance in the west would bring Ostend within range of enemy artillery and make it useless as a submarine base. Furthermore, should the Netherlands join the war, the German position on the coast would become untenable. He therefore ordered the planning of an appropriate German response should the Dutch join the war or be invaded by Britain. This 'Fall K' was obviously never implemented but, briefly, involved a rapid seizure of the south bank of the Scheldt to ensure, at the minimum, that enemy artillery could not reach Zeebrugge.[215] In conclusion von Schröder demanded that the importance of holding every inch of ground in Flanders be brought to the attention of the new leaders of the German army, Generals Paul von Hindenburg and Erich Ludendorff.[216] Von Schröder was especially concerned that the latter's plan to withdraw forces on the Western Front to the so-called Hindenburg line would expose his position along the coast. This concern was a symptom of a rift that had been growing between the army and the navy since the start of the year. Once again, due to their unique position, the MarineKorps was drawn into the argument.

The central problem remained the relative lack of activity by the fleet while the army was engaged in a bitter struggle on several fronts. The military successes of 1915 kept the problem under control but when the war turned sour in 1916 the problems and divisiveness resurfaced. We have already seen one symptom of this in the arguments over the creation of the commander-in-chief for coast defence. A second problem arose from Germany's dwindling supply of manpower. This shortage of vital personnel created disputes between the services.

Von Schröder and his staff were hit in several ways by the personnel shortage. In June von Holtzendorff ordered the MarineKorps to return several of its artillery specialists to the forts in Germany as replacements for men that had been sent to the frontlines.[217] Despite several protests there was little that von Schröder could do but release the men.[218] This was only the beginning. In September von Schröder came into conflict with the IV army when they ordered one of his infantry brigades to the Somme. He tried to get an additional 2,000 men sent out from Germany to replace those he had lost but was not successful.[219]

Following the institution of the Hindenburg Plan industries in Germany were also drawing trained personnel away from the MarineKorps.[220] In September the Korps was forced to return several thousand men to Germany for work in war related industries.[221] Von Schröder demanded that they be replaced. Von Capelle responded by claiming that the navy could not provide replacements but would try to get the army to do so.[222] The army was not accommodating and suggested that the navy provide its own reinforcements, if necessary drawing new personnel from the large number of men that were employed in non-combatant roles.[223] Von Schröder was not pleased and responded by writing a new letter to von Capelle bitterly attacking the government for its short-sighted policies and for taking trained men away from the armed forces when they could simply requisition workers from the conquered territories.[224] He was willing to return the men but wanted a promise from the War Ministry that it would provide the Korps with an additional 4–5,000 men to take their place. He also proposed that a certain portion of each year's recruits should in the future be set aside specifically for the MarineKorps.[225] In fairness to von Schröder it should be pointed out that he was also being pressured by his subordinates, particularly Rear-Admiral Gisberth Jasper, Commander of the Second MarineDivision, who wanted replacements for the men he was losing.[226] In the end the MarineKorps was forced to surrender the troops and received only 450 men from the naval forts in Wilhelmshaven and Kiel in return.[227] This acrimonious little dispute was a sign of larger problems to come.

While these discussions were taking place the general personnel shortage was causing problems in other areas as well. For example, the Torpedo-Boat Inspectorate reported to the North Sea and Baltic naval stations in October that, due to losses of personnel, all larger destroyers would have to reduce their crews by 40 percent in order to free men for industry and the burgeoning submarine arm.[228] The situation within Germany was reaching a critical point and this was a major factor pushing the German government to play their famous 'last card', unrestricted submarine warfare, the following January. Before that point arrived though, the army and navy engaged in a new battle over which service was to control the Flanders coast.

This new problem began with questions concerning the anti-aircraft school which had been moved to Zeebrugge. In theory all of the anti-aircraft guns on the Western Front were under army command, including those of the naval anti-aircraft school; therefore, when von Schröder ordered the school to be moved to Zeebrugge he was technically exceeding his purview. As a result the Kommandierenden General der Luftstreitkräfte requested confirmation from von Holtzendorff over whether or not the guns should be moved.[229] Otto Kranzbühler, the Naval Staff liaison officer to the Oberste Heeres Leitung, the German High Command (hereafter written as OHL), replied that since von Schröder was effectively the chief of a naval station he had the same powers as the head of either the Baltic or North Sea stations and this included control over those anti-aircraft guns in his area of command.[230] Von Hindenburg did not agree.

This minor matter soon developed into a discussion over who was in control in Flanders. Von Hindenburg argued that the army was in command of all occupied territories including Belgium and Flanders and that the navy was

responsible only for purely naval affairs.[231] Von Holtzendorff was actually
willing to accept von Hindenburg's verdict in order to prevent a crisis in which
the Emperor, in all likelihood, would side with the army.[232] Von Schröder was
not interested in such a settlement. He argued that it was essential that the
power relationship between the army and navy in his sector be clarified. His
main point, in a letter written in early January, was that, in his command, it was
not possible to have a 'mathematical' separation of land and naval affairs. They
were too inextricably intertwined. He also argued that it was vital for the
MarineKorps' commander to have the same rights as a station commander in
the homeland so that the Korps could concentrate on the naval war with only
minimal interference from the army. He wanted a statement clarifying, once
again, his equal status with the commanders of the Baltic and North Sea
stations.[233] The matter, at that point, was taken before the Kaiser.

On 18 January Kaiser Wilhelm issued a telegram explaining the new
relationship between the MarineKorps and the army. Von Schröder would
have been better served to have taken Holtzendorff's advice. The land forces
of the MarineKorps were placed under the command of the OHL as were the
coastal batteries but the naval forces remained under the command of the
MarineKorps. Nonetheless even those were subject to interference by the IV
army. In the event of an enemy landing the IV army would assume command
over the entire coastal sector, including the Flanders flotillas. In that instance
von Schröder and his staff would be reduced to subordinates of von Arnim
and the IV army. Despite the disappointing response von Schröder did retain
his right of *ImmediatStellung*.[234] This put the matter to rest for the short-term,
though there were still other areas where the two forces conflicted; one of these
was over the question of war aims.

THE MARINEKORPS AND GERMAN WAR AIMS, 1914 – 1916

Germany's war aims regarding Belgium were consistently annexationist. This
was true from the creation of Bethmann-Hollweg's September Programme
until the end of the war. Not only was the government interested in annexing
Belgium or controlling it in some veiled form, so were most of the powerful
organisations within Germany, including the military. Both the army and navy
wanted to maintain their control over Belgium, especially Flanders, in order
to prepare for a coming 'Second Punic War' with Great Britain. Admiral von
Schröder and the MarineKorps shared these annexationist goals.[235]

On 9 September 1914 Bethmann-Hollweg announced his 'September
Programme.' Several of his demands concerned Belgium. Liege was to be
transferred to Germany and a frontier strip was to be granted to Luxembourg,

which would remain under German control. Belgium itself, including French Flanders, was to become a German 'vassal state.' The Germans intended to occupy all militarily important ports and rail lines and the Belgian economy was to be tied to and dominated by the German economy.[236] The September Programme, though modified slightly as the war went on, remained the basis of all later German plans for Belgium.

Bethmann-Hollweg was not alone in his demands. Heinrich Class and the Pan-German League also demanded that Germany maintain its control over Belgium. In addition, they called for the annexation of the entire Franco-Belgian coastline as far as the mouth of the Somme.[237] They, however, went one step further than Bethmann-Hollweg and demanded the deportation of the Belgians so that the country could be 'colonised' by Germans.[238] The call for annexations spread even beyond the Pan-Germans. For example, the 'moderate' Centre Party leader Matthias Erzberger and the leading figures of German industry, including men like August Thyssen and Gustav Krupp, argued for the military control of Belgium after the war or even its incorporation into Germany.[239] Some of the minor German princes had their own aims as well. For example, Crown Prince Rupprecht of Bavaria wanted Prussia to keep Belgium and large areas of France as well as parts of the Netherlands and then give Alsace-Lorraine to Bavaria.[240] Clearly the retention of Belgium was popular within Germany.

While this is not the place to go into a full discussion of the evolution of German war aims concerning Belgium a few points are worthy of discussion due to their direct bearing on the German navy and the MarineKorps. One of these was the notion, developed by Bethmann-Hollweg in late 1914, of not annexing Belgium outright but instead controlling it economically and militarily while leaving it some limited 'independence' as window dressing.[241] As part of this scheme Bethmann intended to encourage the Flemish separatist movement within Belgium. What Bethmann intended to create was a Belgian state that would not be allowed any independent foreign or colonial policies and whose army would be trained and commanded by German officers. Germany would also retain the right to veto any domestic policies that were deemed detrimental to herself. Economically Belgium would be forced to join the customs union which was to cover all of central Europe (*MittelEuropa*). In addition, the Deutschmark would be adopted as the Belgian currency and German social legislation would be incorporated into Belgian law. Finally, the Germans would take control of the Belgian railways and the port of Antwerp.[242]

Bethmann circulated this memorandum to both the civilian government and the military. One of the responses he received was a lengthy denkschrift written by Admiral Tirpitz which expressed the views of the RMA.[243] In short, the navy desired the complete annexation of the Flanders coastline. This was, after all, one of the reasons for the creation of the MarineKorps in the first place. Some members of the navy also wanted to annex the French coastline as far as Boulogne and the Dutch coast to the mouth of the Scheldt.[244] Admiral Tirpitz started a discussion over war aims within the navy in March of 1915 when he requested a list from each of the major commands outlining what they thought were the minimum gains needed to assure German security.

In late March 1915 Admiral von Schröder responded by arguing for the complete annexation of Belgium following the war. His reasons reflected the dominant view that this war was only the first round against Great Britain and that it would be followed by a 'Second Punic War.' In that case, von Schröder wrote, it would be beneficial to Germany to retain Belgium, especially the coastline, so that the work being done by his men would not be wasted and the Germans would be able to utilise the new harbours and their defences in the next war without having to rebuild them.[245] Retaining these facilities would be beneficial in another way as well; the navy would have the time to continue developing them during peacetime. In addition, von Schröder argued that since the Belgian people were indifferent to politics, they would not mind being governed by the Germans as long as the economy was returned to its pre-war state! He also mentioned that it was necessary to retain and develop Antwerp as a major naval base, though this would require the acquisition of the south bank of the Scheldt from the Dutch. He does not mention how that was to be accomplished.[246]

According to von Schröder direct control over Belgium would provide the Germans with several advantages. First of all, it would allow them to expand the port facilities of Ostend, Zeebrugge and Bruges. They would also be able to widen the canals connecting the harbours so that they could accommodate larger warships. Furthermore, direct control would limit the opportunities for Britain to cause trouble in Belgium. He argued that a Belgium that was merely economically dependent on Germany would serve as a continual source of friction and unrest and would inevitably cause another war. If, on the other hand, Germany controlled Belgium then Britain's risks in a future war with Germany would be so great that the British would have to step aside and allow Germany to 'properly assert its world position.'[247] Some of these ideas became fixtures in the war aims of the German navy. For example, as late as 1917 Admiral von Holtzendorff was still basing the navy's aims on the retention of the Flanders coastline.[248]

Von Schröder's views concerning Antwerp were seconded by the harbour master of Antwerp, Oberbaurat von Eich, in November 1915 when, in a report on the affairs of the harbour, he argued that the Germans should retain Antwerp after the war so that they could make alterations to the port facilities and turn the port into their major western naval base. He was concerned that if Germany surrendered Antwerp in a peace treaty that it would become a 'beachhead' allowing the British to reassert their interest in continental affairs.[249]

In order to make Antwerp into an effective naval base it would be necessary to acquire the south bank of the Scheldt from the Dutch, who had their own place in German war aims. According to the September Programme the Dutch were to be brought into the greater German customs union and were to be made economically dependent upon Germany.[250] How that was to be brought about was left unsaid, though, as the war dragged on, the position of the Netherlands became increasingly difficult.

CONCLUSION

Overall, 1916 proved to be a critical year in the war. With the apparent defeat of the Russians in the east in 1915 von Falkenhayn turned his eyes back to the west and launched the ill-conceived and worse fated Battle of Verdun which, combined with the defeat on the Somme and the collapse of Austria during the Brusilov offensive, left Germany in a difficult and desperate position. It appeared as if the only way out of that position, and the only road to a 'German peace' was the full and unrestricted use of the submarines. This was the famous 'last card' that would either bring victory or, by bringing the United States into the war as an enemy of Germany, defeat.

As the Germans moved closer to tying their fate to the submarines the Flanders position became increasingly important. This importance was recognised by Admiral Scheer who began to send destroyer flotillas to Flanders on a temporary basis beginning in October 1916. The success of the flotillas on the night of 26 October had far-reaching implications and demonstrated a new willingness by the Germans to take advantage of the Flanders harbours. Then, with the famous decision at Pless on 9 January 1917 to begin unrestricted submarine warfare, the importance of keeping the Channel passage open for German submarines became a task of the first magnitude. This placed the MarineKorps in a new and prominent position. For them, and for Germany as a whole, 1917 would be the year of decision.

5

'Fall K': The MarineKorps and Dutch Neutrality

WHEN BRITAIN AND GERMANY WENT to war in August 1914 the Netherlands was left in a very difficult and delicate situation. The Dutch had significant economic ties to both belligerents and were also strategically vulnerable to both nations. The Dutch had a long border with Germany; one that became even more difficult to defend once the Germans occupied Belgium. That fact alone was sufficient to force the Dutch to tread lightly when dealing with the Germans but they had an additional incentive for caution; their connections with various German industries in the Rhineland were vital to their economy and were very vulnerable. The Dutch could not afford to incur the wrath of their powerful neighbor.[1]

They could not afford to incur the wrath of Great Britain either. Though Britain did not present the same spectre of invasion that Germany did there were other ways in which the Dutch were vulnerable to the British. First and most obviously, the large Dutch empire in the Far East was hostage to British seapower. If, for example, the Dutch were to side with the Central Powers their empire would have been forfeit. The British could also have threatened the Dutch with the annihilation of their overseas trade and their navy, which was quite small. It consisted of eight cruisers built during the latter portion of the 1890s, nine coastal defence ships, twenty-eight first-class torpedo-boats, and ten second-class torpedo-boats. They also owned eight submarines and various minelayers and minesweepers. The fleet was supplemented by ten small gunboats but was dispersed between the Netherlands and the Dutch colonial empire. Just before and during the war the Dutch added to the fleet by building an additional twenty-eight torpedo-boats of various classes but even that addition left the Dutch fleet no match for the British. The Dutch might have been able to defend their coast from a British attack but they certainly would have lost the merchant marine and their overseas trade.[2] Clearly the Dutch were faced with a serious dilemma.

They attempted to solve the problem by declaring neutrality in August 1914. According to a scholar of Dutch foreign policy the people of the Netherlands as a whole tended to be pro-allied; largely due to Germany's violation of Belgium. The major exception was the city of Rotterdam which remained strongly pro-German.[3] Sentiment aside, the Dutch remained neutral throughout the war; though not without struggling. Both coalitions put pressure on them to try and win trade concessions; the British were especially interested in winning Dutch food imports away from Germany and toward themselves. They accomplished this with the trade treaty of 1916. The pressure the British applied was generally economic in nature; the Germans, however, used political as well as economic leverage in their struggles with the Dutch government. Despite the difficulty of their situation, the Dutch managed to maintain their neutrality and they may have played a key role in easing the pressures of the blockade on Germany. The fact that they were able to survive the war as a neutral in a very vulnerable situation is a testament to Dutch patience and diplomacy. Despite all their efforts to stay out of the war their situation almost underwent a radical change in 1916 and 1917. It was during those two years that the MarineKorps Flandern was ordered to prepare what was called 'Fall K': a plan for intervention in the Netherlands. This chapter is an examination of that plan: how it came to be; what it was; the circumstances under which it was to be implemented; and the reasons why it was eventually shelved.

GERMAN-DUTCH RELATIONS, 1914 – 1918

During the war relations between Germany and the Netherlands were usually strained. The Germans were dependent upon the loophole in the British blockade that was provided by the Netherlands, yet the weight of the German submarine campaigns and the raids by the destroyers and torpedo-boats stationed in Flanders fell very heavily upon the Dutch. There were a number of areas of controversy between the two nations over the course of the war. They ranged from questions over the transit of military materials across Dutch territory to questions over the treatment of belligerent warships, prize regulations, contraband, and questions over the use of Dutch airspace.[4] No matter how acrimonious negotiations became over these issues none of them were as damaging to German-Dutch relations as the submarine war.

The renewal of the unrestricted submarine campaign in 1917 was the most serious blow that was dealt to German-Dutch relations during the war. It led to the growth of anti-German sentiment in most of the country and by August 1917, German military intelligence was reporting that, due to the campaign the Dutch nation had become thoroughly anti-German.[5] According to this report there was growing sentiment within the Netherlands for a stronger stance against Germany; specifically there were calls for a trade embargo and even, in some circles, calls for military action. As a result the army suggested that the fleet avoid attacking Dutch shipping for the foreseeable future.[6]

At the same time the British were pressuring the Dutch to cut-off trade with Germany. In October 1917 newspapers in Britain and the Netherlands began reporting that the British and American governments were threatening to extend the blockade to the Netherlands unless the Dutch cut-off all trade with the Germans.[7] Probably the only thing restraining the Dutch in 1917 was fear of the German army. The German victories in the east had convinced some members of the Dutch military that the Central Powers were going to win the war and that they needed to join them to make sure that they were not left out in the cold after the peace. These views appear to have been largely ignored in the Dutch government, fortunately for the Netherlands.[8]

Still, Germany remained the greatest danger to the independence of the Netherlands. Dutch ships remained very vulnerable to the German submarine campaign due to the Netherlands' geographical location and the vital trade that the Dutch carried on with the British. In fact, as we have seen, Dutch ships were frequently specifically targeted by the forces of the Flanders Flotillas. By March 1916 the Dutch had lodged several protests with the German Government. At the same time Admiral von Schröder was becoming convinced that Britain intended to invade the Netherlands and that the Dutch were not willing or able to defend themselves. This eventually became an obsession for him as 1916 wore on[9] and was the direct impetus for the creation of 'Fall K.' In fact, while the Germans were still in the initial phase of planning this operation, the MarineKorps ordered three submarines to maintain a patrol off the Dutch coast.[10] These submarines involved the Germans in a minor diplomatic crisis when one of them fired on a Dutch submarine in December 1916, apparently thinking the Dutch vessel was British. Fortunately for both sides no damage was done and the crisis was smoothed over.[11]

The delicate nature of the Netherlands' position was pointed out again in the summer of 1917. On the evening of 15 June two British air attacks were launched on the German positions in Belgium, allegedly from Dutch airspace. According to the German reports the British aircraft approached Belgium through Dutch airspace without the Dutch taking any steps to defend themselves and then proceeded to bomb German installations in northern Belgium.[12] Von Schröder was incensed but the German government limited itself to mild protests. They did not want to antagonise the Netherlands at a very delicate juncture in the war.[13]

The situation between the two nations did not improve in 1918. During the final great German offensive that spring the Germans demanded transit rights through the Netherlands for troops and weapons. This problem was defused by Dutch agreement to ship military supplies if the troops themselves did not enter the country.[14]

Unease continued to grow during 1918. After the British attempted to block Ostend and Zeebrugge, on 22 April 22 1918 German agents in the Netherlands reported a general feeling of nervousness in the country due to a fear that, if the German bases in Belgium were destroyed, the Germans would invade the Netherlands to gain control of the Scheldt so that they could use Antwerp as a naval base.[15]

As the summer of 1918 continued it appeared to the Germans as if the Netherlands was beginning to lean increasingly toward the Allies. In May the German military attaché warned the government that *under no circumstances*[16] should they risk a violation of Dutch airspace, even if future allied air attacks took advantage of Dutch neutrality. He warned that such an action might rupture relations completely.[17] The naval attaché attributed the hardening of Dutch attitudes to a growing realisation by the Dutch Government that if Germany won the war they would, in all likelihood, demand that the Dutch turn over both banks of the Scheldt.[18]

This very brief survey of German-Dutch relations makes one thing clear; the Germans were concerned over the position of the Netherlands. Their concerns began in 1916 with the failure of the Verdun offensive, the allied successes on the Somme and the entry of Romania into the war. At that point the German military was acutely conscious of their vulnerability. In fact, the major reason for the initial opposition of Hindenburg and Ludendorff to a renewal of unrestricted submarine warfare was fear that the Netherlands might join the Allies and destroy Germany's position on the Western Front.[19] This fear gradually solidified into a belief that the British were planning to invade the Netherlands and turn the German flank. The Germans feared the Dutch would not actively resist such an invasion.[20]

FEARS OF A BRITISH LANDING IN THE NETHERLANDS

The Germans first became concerned about the possibility of a British invasion of the Netherlands in 1915. That summer the MarineKorps was ordered to prepare a study examining the chances of success for an allied invasion of the Scheldt (this was apparently motivated by the Gallipoli campaign). The report was finished in September and became the basis for the creation of 'Fall K.'

Von Schröder began by examining the three main channels leading into the western Scheldt estuary; the Wielingen, Deurloo, and Oostgat. Each of them was studied to determine depth and suitability for use by large warships. Of the three the least useful was the Oostgat which, with a maximum width of 200 metres, was deemed too narrow for large warships, though it could be used if the invading force only intended to occupy Walcheren Island. The Deurloo Channel, which had sufficient depth at high tide to be used by large warships and was not within range of any German coastal guns, was the more suitable of these three channels.[21] The primary channel though, and the one most likely to be used in any landing, was the Wielingen. Even at low tide its depth of 8.3 meters was sufficient to allow the passage of most warships and it was wide enough that vessels would not need to pass through the Channel in single file.[22]

The eastern Scheldt estuary was also briefly considered but at that time it was seen as an unlikely place for a landing. The reasons why were the changing depth of the estuary and the greater distance that troops landing there would have to traverse before they could reach the major river crossings. The implication was that any attack would come in the western Scheldt; most likely in the Wielingen or Deurloo channels.[23]

From there he went on to list the Dutch defencein the Scheldt. These consisted primarily of light guns; generally 7.5cm. There was no heavy artillery to speak of and only older fortifications that were largely obsolete. In addition, there were no anti-air defences along the coast and no defences of any kind in the eastern Scheldt. Only along the banks of the western Scheldt were there any new gun emplacements and these were judged to be insufficient to prevent a landing.[24] The only effective defences were the minefields that the Dutch had laid in the western Scheldt and the supplemental fields that the Germans had laid off the Dutch coast. This led to the conclusion that either the British were pressuring the Dutch to leave their coast relatively undefended or the Dutch had no intentions of defending their neutrality should the British land in the Scheldt.[25]

Von Schröder then posited the likely outcome of a landing attempt in two different scenarios; first with the Netherlands on the allied side or simply not resisting the landing and the second with the Dutch joining the Germans and offering strong resistance to the British. In the first instance the Germans expected that the attack would come at night down the Oostgat channel. The Wielingen would not be used because it could be covered by the German coastal artillery and the German minefields north of Zeebrugge would make navigation difficult. Consequently they believed the British would follow the Oostgat as far as Walcheren Island and Vlissingen. They would seize those two locations and use Vlissingen as their major base while they brought in additional troops and supplies. Von Schröder argued that the British would move very rapidly to reinforce the Dutch positions in Flanders. He expected that the British could land 50,000 men in twelve hours without opposition. With artillery support an additional 15,000 could be landed directly on the southern bank of the river. This would present the Germans essentially with a devastating *fait accompli* that would turn their flank in the west and force them out of Belgium. To prevent naval interference from the German harbours in Flanders the British were expected to lay several mine and net barriers in the vicinity of Zeebrugge.[26] This was the MarineKorps' worst nightmare.

The alternative was more palatable but was also deemed less likely. In the event that the Dutch actively defended themselves the landing would of course be much more difficult. The mere presence of Dutch mines and artillery, no matter how weak, would require the British to move with greater caution. In addition, the Dutch would, in all likelihood, be able to completely block the Oostgat with mines and force the British to use one of the other, more exposed channels. In that scenario von Schröder believed that the British would land in the eastern Scheldt and content themselves with seizing Walcheren and South Beveland islands as their major bases. This would allow the Germans to seize the vital south bank of the river before the British could reach it.

In either case it would be vitally important for the MarineKorps to seize strong defensive positions as soon as possible along the line of the Scheldt. If this could be achieved von Schröder believed that the enemy attack could be defeated. The British could be allowed to retain Walcheren; the island itself was hardly decisive though long-range artillery constructed there could become a nuisance. In order to be ready for the landing he suggested that the Germans keep three to four artillery batteries along the Dutch border at constant readiness. He also intimated that it might be necessary for Germany to move first if they suspected that the Dutch would not resist the British. He stated that: 'political considerations should not keep us from gaining the south bank.'[27]

Von Schröder concluded by suggesting several actions that the Germans should take to prepare for any such landing attempt. Regular patrols of the Dutch coast were recommended to ensure that there would be no surprise attacks, at least during the day. (The patrols would be withdrawn at night because of the risks to the ships.) Also, a new minefield was to be laid north of Knocke and, if they were given sufficient warning of the attack, the UCs were to lay mines to block the Oostgat and Deurloo as well as the eastern Scheldt. Proper and effective air reconnaissance would therefore be of vital importance. The Germans could not move too soon and violate Dutch neutrality but they needed to move in time to get the minefields laid before the British arrived. To make this possible the torpedo-boats and submarines of the Flanders flotillas were to be maintained in a state of constant readiness once word went out that a British move was expected.[28]

On land the main goal was to keep the British north of the Scheldt and to create strong defensive positions complete with artillery and machine guns on the south bank. This was to be done by maintaining the aforementioned three or four artillery batteries at readiness along the Dutch frontier. Von Schröder made no mention of additional forces being drawn from the army. He apparently intended this to be a purely naval endeavour.[29]

This document gained considerable attention within the navy in 1916 when the British began to apply heavy economic pressure on the Dutch to restrict food exports to Germany. The Germans feared that this was the first step to Britain forcing the Netherlands into the war on the side of their side. The study also became the basis for the plan designed by Admiral von Schröder and the MarineKorps to deal with such an event.

Due to their military problems in 1916 the Germans became increasingly concerned over the position of the Netherlands. On 3 February the army asked the MarineKorps to begin patrolling the Scheldt to ensure that no surprise British landing took place. Von Schröder replied that since this could only be done with aircraft and that they could not fly in bad weather or search at night he could not guarantee success.[30] On the following day von Schröder met with the commander of the IV army, von Arnim, and informed him that his current forces were incapable of preventing a surprise British attack on the Netherlands and that, even if he had a full flotilla of destroyers available, he still could not give any guarantee to the army.[31]

During March rumours that a British attack was imminent began to circulate; because of these rumours von Schröder decided to strengthen the nightly submarine patrols off the Dutch coast and to begin a patrol of the Scheldt with three A-boats.[32] On 30 March word was sent from the Naval Staff to the attaché in the Netherlands that a large flotilla was gathering in Britain; apparently to launch an invasion of the Netherlands. The attaché was asked to inform the Dutch of this because the Naval Staff feared that the Dutch would not be able to resist a British attack. He was also instructed to offer military assistance and to inform the Dutch government that Germany would take whatever steps were necessary to maintain their position in Belgium. The Dutch apparently understood this to mean that if they were unable to enforce their neutrality on their own, they would receive German help whether they desired it or not.[33] When the Dutch responded by cancelling military leaves and strengthening their forces along the coast the Germans replied that they

were grateful for the sign that the Dutch intended to defend their neutrality.[34]
Nonetheless, it was at that point that the MarineKorps began actively planning
for 'Fall K'.

Even though the expected British attack never materialised concern over
the position of the Netherlands continued into 1917. The Germans considered
it inconceivable that the British would not take advantage of what appeared to
be a golden opportunity to break the stalemate on the Western Front. On 7
January 1917 the General Staff reported to the Naval Staff that they believed
the eastern Scheldt was now the most seriously threatened area. The eastern
mouth of the river had two entrances and weaker artillery defences than did the
western mouth. In addition, the northernmost entrance to the eastern Scheldt
was also free of mines and Dutch warships. The problem, of course, was that,
for the British to seize the southern bank of the river they would have to first
cross the western Scheldt either before German forces arrived to oppose them
or, failing that, in the face of enemy fire. At the same time they made this
report, the General Staff also pointed out that German preparations should
not exclude the western Scheldt, which was protected by only three modern
artillery emplacements and several obsolete guns that were very low on
ammunition. Furthermore there was still no significant anti-aircraft defence
in either area.[35]

Hermann Nordmann, the head of the operations section of the Naval Staff,
replied that he generally agreed though he argued that the army was
discounting the difficulties of a landing in the western Scheldt because the
army's list of defences for this branch of the river did not include the German
coastal artillery. These included new 30.5cm guns installed at Knocke in late
1916 that were able to reach the western Scheldt.[36] The navy estimated the
total number of Dutch guns around the western Scheldt at: seven heavy guns
ranging from 21.7cm to 30.5cm; thirty-two medium-calibre guns ranging
from 10.5 to 15.7cm; and twelve light guns of 7.5cm. Nordmann also stressed
the dangers of mines in the western Scheldt. According to him, the navy had
come to believe that the main allied landing would occur in the eastern
Scheldt and that only small forces would be sent to the western branch of the
river, mainly to try and take a series of beachheads that could be used for a
crossing of the river.[37]

The navy expected that the allied attack, when it came, would come at night
since they believed that no landing in the western estuary could succeed
without surprise. Any large scale invasion would have to land much further
east, say at Rotterdam or Amsterdam, in order to capture a poorly defended
major port.[38]

On 24 January the naval attaché in the Hague reported to von Holtzendorff that the Allies were planning a major landing in either the Netherlands or Belgium to coincide with an upcoming allied attack on the Western Front.[39] The attaché was personally convinced, after speaking with the Chief of the Dutch Naval Staff, that the Dutch would defend themselves to the best of their ability. That being the case it was most likely that the Allies would try and land in the lightly defended eastern Scheldt rather than risk the defences of the western channel.[40] The Germans expected the attack to come that spring once the anticipated allied land offensive had begun to push the Germans back.

By May the allied offensive had still not materialised and, that month, the Germans intercepted British communications stating that the Foreign Office was now totally opposed to a landing in the Netherlands because it would not turn the German flank but would only bog down and create another Salonika.[41] The Germans apparently did not believe this. In August the IV army prepared its own study of the possibility of a British landing in the Netherlands and argued that, due to the general stalemate, public pressure in Britain would force the government to make some kind of move to acquire tangible gains, if for no other reason than to boost morale. That being the case, the Dutch coast was a logical target since the British would be able to make full use of their fleet there. There was also historical precedent, the most famous case of course being the ill-fated Walcheren expedition of 1809 (though why the British would want to repeat that disaster is not explained.) Militarily, an occupation of Walcheren Island would allow the British to base long-range artillery there that could reach as far as Zeebrugge. The British would then be able to bring both Ostend and Zeebrugge within range of their guns.[42] This could have a potentially disastrous effect on the German submarine campaign.

The army also feared that Walcheren could be converted into a base for British light forces. This would allow them to patrol the Flanders coast more effectively. Together, it was feared, these measures would make it impossible to continue the naval war from Flanders. On the other hand, if Germany was to move first and grab the Scheldt the Germans would then be able to make full use of Antwerp as a naval base and could move cruisers and battleships to Belgium. This would of course force the British to bring heavier forces south and would present the German submarines with more valuable targets.

The army expected that the initial British attack would consist only of a landing on South Beveland Island. A small force would fortify the island and hold it until reinforcements arrived, at which time they would begin the push overland toward Belgium. The main force would then land and secure Walcheren. The army did not believe that the Dutch could hold off the British and argued that the navy should seize these islands as well as the southern bank of the Scheldt in the event that 'Fall K' had to be implemented.[43] The navy disagreed.

For the remainder of the year the MarineKorps was convinced that a major British landing in the Netherlands was imminent and they remained ready to implement 'Fall K' at a moment's notice. Only in 1918 did these worries abate. Clearly the Germans were very concerned over the possibility of a British landing in the Netherlands that would make their position in the west untenable. Just what they intended to do about it remains to be seen.

'FALL K'

In October 1916 von Schröder was ordered to prepare operational plans for intervention in the Netherlands if the British did actually invade. On 15 October he was informed that the Naval Staff expected the British to 'make use' of the Netherlands in the near future.[44] What they meant by this was that the British would either apply strong economic pressure on the Dutch to force them into the war or, at the very least, force them to allow the Allies to use Dutch territory in a fashion similar to what the Allies had done in Greece in 1915.[45] Another possibility was that the British would simply invade the Netherlands. If that occurred and the Dutch proved to be willing and able to protect their own neutrality then Germany could stand aside; if not, Germany would have to intervene to protect their position in Belgium. To prepare for the worst the MarineKorps was ordered to begin immediate reconnaissance flights along the Dutch frontier to try and locate Dutch strongpoints that would have to be overcome if Germany decided to intervene. This was to be done, as best as was possible, without actually entering Dutch airspace.[46]

At the same time the Naval Staff issued the first orders for what they now termed 'Fall K.' These were issued to the MarineKorps, the High Seas Fleet, and the North Sea naval station. They stated that any British attempt to land in the Netherlands must be opposed by German air and naval forces. The initial response to any landing was to be the laying of several minefields throughout an area extending from the Hook of Holland to Ymuiden.[47] In the event that the Netherlands joined the Entente voluntarily all major harbours, industrial areas, and military facilities were to immediately be attacked by the air forces of the MarineKorps. Areas listed as being of particular importance were: Amsterdam, Rotterdam, Ymuiden, Utrecht, Arnhem, the Hague and Vlissingen. Also the Flanders flotillas were to immediately commence mine-laying within Dutch waters and all Dutch coastal shipping was to be attacked and destroyed.[48]

Von Schröder was very enthusiastic about the possibilities such an operation presented. On 15 January 1917 Nordmann wrote to Scheer to tell him that von Schröder was urging the Naval Staff to authorise an immediate occupation of the south bank of the Scheldt so that cruisers could be dispatched to Flanders. By taking the south bank of the river the Germans would be able to use Antwerp as a naval base and its larger facilities would in turn allow them to base larger warships in Flanders. Nordmann wanted to know Scheer's opinion on the matter.[49]

Scheer responded on the 19th. He replied that he was in favour of the occupation of the south bank of the Scheldt. He believed it was critical for the future course of the war. The ability to use Antwerp as a naval base would allow him to send cruisers and larger numbers of destroyers to the Flanders front. He currently could not do so because of the space limitations in Ostend and Zeebrugge and what he saw as the inadequate defences of those two harbours. The use of Antwerp though could radically affect the course of the war at sea. He wholeheartedly agreed with Admiral von Schröder.[50]

Taking these opinions into consideration, von Holtzendorff then wrote to von Hindenburg explaining the advantages that would accrue to Germany if the army provided the MarineKorps with enough troops to seize the Scheldt. He explained what Scheer had told him; that the use of Antwerp as a naval base would allow the Germans to send larger forces to Flanders and that this would allow the navy to seriously threaten British communications to France. The presence of numerous destroyers and cruisers in the Flanders area, along with extensive new minefields, would make it nearly impossible for the British to adequately patrol the Flanders coastline, therefore the submarines would be able to move in and out of port more easily and would be able to pass through the Channel without much difficulty. This would dramatically increase the threat to British commerce and would force the British to station larger forces in the southern North Sea. These ships would make appealing targets for German submarines and torpedo-boats operating out of Antwerp. Finally, the need for destroyers to escort warships in the southern North Sea would take those vessels away from other fronts and again, would make the work of the submarines easier.[51] Shortly thereafter they detached a small number of troops from the army specifically for use against the Netherlands. These units were formed into a unit known as *Gruppe Ghent* which eventually encompassed two battalions of artillery, several anti-aircraft batteries, two companies of *Pioniere*, six companies of infantry taken from the XVIII and X ReserveKorps, four squadrons of cavalry and one section of aircraft. These units were pulled primarily from the IV army and were left as a standing force to guard the Dutch border.[52]

On 19 February von Holtzendorff issued more detailed orders. Once it appeared that a British attack was imminent the cables between the Netherlands and Britain were to be cut by submarines and mines were to be laid by the UCs along the main approaches to the Dutch harbours though, as long as the British were not in Dutch waters, Dutch neutrality was to be respected. Once a condition of war existed with the Netherlands mine laying of the major Dutch harbours was to begin and air attacks were to commence against the major industrial and military bases. The targets were, in order of importance: the industrial areas of Rotterdam, Amsterdam, Ymuiden, Vlissingen, Helder and the Hook of Holland; the rail yards at Arnhem, Utrecht, Amersford, and Herzogenbusch; Fort Pannerden; the wireless stations at Ameland, Terschelling, Scheveningen, Schiermonnikoog, Walcheren and Schouwen. The main targets for the minelayers were, again in order of importance: the Scheldt, Ymuiden, the Hook of Holland, Texel, Terschelling, Rotterdam and Amsterdam. In addition to the mine-laying and air attacks all Dutch vessels in Germany were to be seized or destroyed.[53]

There was a military component to the plans as well. Gruppe Ghent was to seize the banks and crossings of the Scheldt in order to protect the German position in Belgium. The Gruppe was broken into two smaller groups (Division Lokeren and Division Bruges respectively) which were to remain on alert along the frontier. In the event that the Netherlands appeared to be wavering in their neutrality, these two groups were to cross the frontier and seize the south bank of the river. They would then proceed to seize the main bridges and crossing points with the support of two torpedo-boats from the Flanders- Flotilla.[54] The naval orders were revised in March. In conditions where a British landing appeared likely (alert status) the UCs were to begin mine-laying before Ymuiden and Den Helder and the cables connecting the Netherlands and Britain were to be cut. Again, Dutch territorial waters were not to be violated unless it was absolutely necessary. At the same time aerial reconnaissance of the approach routes was to begin and the torpedo-boats of the Flanders-flotilla were to be kept at readiness to attack British forces approaching the coast.[55]

Once a condition of war with the Netherlands existed the destruction of Dutch as well as British shipping by submarines, aeroplanes and surface forces was to commence. The war zone for the unrestricted submarine campaign, which began on 1 February 1917, would be extended up to the Dutch border though for the first twenty-four days of the war with the Netherlands neutral vessels would only be attacked according to prize regulations. After that period had expired the unrestricted campaign would begin. Air attacks were to commence immediately against the same targets (there were no changes in priority from February) as well as against the bridges over the Maas and Waal rivers to the north and west of Herzogenbusch. All surface action was to be undertaken by the Flanders flotillas; the High Seas Fleet would remain in port.[56]

These measures were war gamed by Gruppe Ghent later that year. The premise for the game was that the Allies had launched a major offensive in the area of the IV army and, in preparation for a landing in the Netherlands, had destroyed the coastal batteries around Zeebrugge. The game resulted in a draw. Gruppe Ghent's two component divisions were able to seize the Scheldt and the coastline of Dutch Flanders but the British party seized Walcheren and South Beveland islands.[57] This outcome was considered acceptable but planning for the operation continued.

Beginning in May 1917 the Germans became increasingly concerned that the Dutch defences along the coast were inadequate and they accordingly sent spies into the country to report on their condition.. This move was sparked by a report from the German naval attaché in the Hague stating that he was utterly unable to convince the Dutch navy minister of the threat from Great Britain.[58] The Germans therefore doubted whether the Dutch truly intended to defend themselves. The reports they received reassured them though. The spies reported that there was a battery of nine 7.5cm guns hidden on the northern coastline of Walcheren Island near the coastal patrol station at Vrouwenpalder. Just to the north, an additional artillery emplacement was under construction and it appeared that the entire area was being linked by telephone cables. More fortifications and troops were noted around Domburg where a second coastal patrol station existed. There were also a series of pillboxes under construction from Domburg to West Kapelle. These were linked to a series of concrete buildings just behind the dunes. West Kapelle was further fortified by various infantry strongpoints and three 12cm guns. Vlissingen, however, was protected only by two 7.5cm guns though two battalions of infantry were stationed in that area. The agents concluded that the Dutch seemed to be taking the threat seriously and were quietly preparing for any attempted invasion.[59] This eased von Schröder's mind but planning for both versions of 'Fall K' continued.

More changes were made to the plan in the summer of 1917. A second group equal in strength to Gruppe Ghent was created. This was *Gruppe Antwerp* and their primary mission in the event of war was to cross the South Beveland Canal to the northern bank of the Scheldt and hold that side of the river.[60] In the meantime both they and Gruppe Ghent remained behind the frontier essentially as border guards. In addition, von Schröder now issued orders for the MarineKorps to occupy the entirety of Dutch Flanders in the event of war.[61]

The naval plans were also modified. The primary goal was now to win and maintain naval superiority in the western Scheldt so that any allied positions on Walcheren or South Beveland island could be assaulted and any southern British landing attempt could be disrupted. Control of the estuary would also allow the Flanders flotillas to support any German attempts to cross the river. Von Schröder's ultimate goal was for the Germans to cross the Scheldt and seize Walcheren for themselves.[62] To assist in this two A-Is were to be sent to the Scheldt as a reconnaissance force. Their mission was primarily to determine the type and number of enemy forces in the area. If possible they were also to determine what the enemy's defences were and the extent of territory they occupied. Only once that was achieved, and only if their chances looked favorable, could they attack enemy vessels or bombard allied positions. Finally, they were to lay minefields in both channels of the river and maintain a swept channel from Zeebrugge to Terneuzen in the Netherlands.[63]

The submarines had their own role to play. They were to patrol the mouth of the river and lay minefields before the eastern estuary of the Scheldt. Finally, the air command was to maintain aerial reconnaissance over the river as well as the Hoofden and was to attack the enemy with *Fernlenkboote* and bombers. If possible, they were to bomb Vlissingen, Veere and other harbours. Reconnaissance remained their main task though.[64] These were the final changes made to 'Fall K'.

The MarineKorps spent the remainder of the year studying Dutch defences along the islands. In late August the German navy intercepted a message from the Dutch commander in the Scheldt area which stated that Walcheren could not withstand an assault for more than two weeks unless its defences were upgraded, especially with more artillery. He doubted if Dutch Flanders could be held at all.[65] Later that month von Holtzendorff reported that the only significant Dutch defences in the eastern Scheldt were a series of minefields. There was very little artillery and no serious naval presence. The fleet, consisting of one battleship, one armoured cruiser, eight torpedo-boats and three submarines was located in the western Scheldt.[66] This was disheartening but the Germans did receive encouraging news at the start of September when the Dutch called up an additional 800,000 men in expectation of a British attack.[67]

From that point until the end of the year the Germans continued to receive periodic reports regarding the Dutch positions. For example, they were able to ascertain the specific strength of the artillery on South Beveland Island.[68] They also intercepted Dutch orders to their forces in the Scheldt estuary. These flotillas had similar orders regardless of whether they were attacked by Germany or Britain. In either case the flotillas were simply to patrol and give the alarm when enemy forces were spotted. Most of the fighting was expected to be done by the shore emplacements while the flotillas served as decoys and tried to lure enemy forces over a series of minefields.[69]

They also received reports on the Dutch air force. The Dutch allegedly had about sixty-five aeroplanes[70] and 100 trained pilots available. An additional 120 aeroplanes were on order from Sweden but no arrival date had been set. In the meantime the Dutch were attempting to make up the shortfall with several 3.7cm anti-aircraft batteries.[71]

The planning and studying that went into 'Fall K' obviously came to nothing. The expected British attack never occurred. The planning for the operation went forward briefly into 1918 when the bridges around Dordrecht were added to the list of targets to be bombed[72] but by April the Germans were convinced that no attack was coming. On 28 April Gruppe Ghent was disbanded, its components were returned to the IV army[73] and the naval forces that had been assigned to the operation were also returned to their normal duties. 'Fall K' went into the archives and was forgotten.

In retrospect it appears that German concerns were exaggerated. A British landing in the Netherlands could only have been devastating to Germany if the Dutch had openly joined the Entente; from the reports the Germans received it seems as if this was not seriously contemplated. As long as the Dutch resisted it is most likely that such a move by Britain would have ended in either disaster or stalemate. Without landing in the western Scheldt the British would not have been able to beat the Germans to the banks of the river and therefore they would probably have been restricted to the islands. That would have significantly harmed the German war effort. The venture would in all likelihood have ended up as another Salonika. The British understood this and never seriously contemplated adding the Dutch to their list of enemies.[74] Had the British been able to gain Dutch adherence, however, an allied landing in the Netherlands might have broken open the war and spelled doom for the Central Powers. An additional 500,000 men striking the German army in the flank in correlation with an offensive on the Western Front would have been devastating. In the end Dutch neutrality proved to be more of an assistance to the Germans than a hindrance and 'Fall K' was shelved and left merely as a interesting side note and another of the many 'what ifs' of the First World War.

6

The Decisive Year

As 1916 GAVE WAY TO 1917 CONDITIONS in Germany rapidly deteriorated. Within Germany the winter of 1916–17 was popularly known as the 'Turnip Winter' due to the failure of roughly half of the potato crop of 1916; this left the bulk of the population, those who could not afford the prices of the black market, to rely upon turnips as their staple food. By the end of 1916 the weekly ration of food staples had dropped to: 160–220 grams of flour; 120 grams of fish; 100–250 grams of meat; 60–75 grams of fat; 200 grams of sugar; 270 grams of jam; seven litres of milk; and one egg.[1] In addition, prices for most goods on the black market had reached ten times their pre-war level. The British blockade and German economic mismanagement were beginning to take their toll on German society.[2] The first major food riots and strikes also took place that winter. The strikers' main demand was for higher wages and better food, though in some rare instances they also called for an end to the war.[3] It was against this backdrop that the fateful conference took place at Pless on 8 January.

At that conference Chancellor Bethmann-Hollweg finally acquiesced in the resumption of the unrestricted submarine campaign. His earlier attempts to float peace proposals in order to garner the goodwill of the United States had come to naught and he no longer felt able to resist the calls of the navy, backed by the new OHL, to resume the campaign.[4] Thus it was that the leaders of Germany came to the decision to play the famous 'last card.' That this decision would likely add the United States to the ranks of Germany's enemies was unfortunate but not a major consideration. In the words of the new Quartermaster-General Erich Ludendorff, 'It has to be. We expect war with America and have made all preparations [for it]. *Things cannot get worse.*'[5] The Germans felt compelled to make this decision because they could see no other way to strike effectively at their *Hauptfeind*, Great Britain. This meant that Germany was embarking on an all-or-nothing gamble for final victory. If Admiral Holtzendorff's predictions proved to be accurate and the submarines could sink 600,000 tons of shipping per month the war would be won by the end of the summer, if not, Germany would be defeated. The fate of the nation now rested on the shoulders of the German navy. The MarineKorps Flandern and the Belgian naval bases would play a key role in the new campaign.

THE PRELUDE: JANUARY 1917

The activity in Flanders increased immediately following the Pless Conference in order to prepare the bases for the beginning of the submarine campaign. These preparations included: additions and modifications to the defences of the bases; an increase in the air strength of the MarineKorps; and an increase in the destroyer strength of the Flanders flotillas.

The Naval Staff was aware that when the new submarine campaign began the Flanders coast would become a primary target for a British attack. As a result on 12 January Admiral von Holtzendorff sent a memorandum to the General Staff warning them that the British would probably attempt a landing on the Flanders coast in order to destroy or capture the submarine bases. As evidence of British intentions he pointed to the expansion of enemy rail yards, the construction of new airfields and the increase in the number of heavy guns on the MarineKorps' sector of the frontline. What he expected was an enemy move by land against Flanders coupled with a landing in the Netherlands, and he wanted to make the General Staff aware that the MarineKorps believed that *any* enemy advance to the east would prove disastrous to the upcoming campaign, since it would allow the enemy to bring the Belgian bases under fire by heavy artillery. This would effectively end the usefulness of these bases and this in turn would have a disastrous effect on the submarine campaign by making the UBs and UCs of the Flanders flotilla virtually useless. The point of the memorandum was to bring about joint military/naval planning for the defence of the coast. It had the desired effect.[6]

A similar memorandum was sent from von Holtzendorff to von Schröder on 20 January. In it von Holtzendorff mentioned the likelihood of an allied attack in Flanders and stated that he had discussed such an eventuality with the OHL and they agreed that it was vitally important to hold every inch of ground on that front. Preparations were under way to repel any such attack whether it came by land or sea.[7] As a result of the Holtzendorff memorandums the MarineKorps was placed under the tactical command of the IV army and General Sixt von Arnim, even though von Schröder retained his *ImmediatStellung*.[8]

Also, as a result of the greater threat to Flanders, the MarineKorps renewed its calls for additional aircraft. In late 1916 Vice-Admiral Jacobsen of the 1st

MarineDivision had commissioned a study examining the efficacy of aerial observation for the coastal guns and had determined that the aerial resources currently available were insufficient. According to him, for truly accurate spotting it would be necessary for each of the major batteries (*Tirpitz*, *Hertha*, *Freya*, *Deutschland*, and *Kaiser Wilhelm II*) to have their own reconnaissance aircraft equipped with radios. These aircraft would work exclusively with their assigned battery so that the gunners and observers could develop a familiarity and comfort level with one another. Each battery would also be equipped with radios and would be assigned its own particular band in order to eliminate irrelevant traffic. In addition, each observer would require its own fighter escort.[9] These measures would of course require that additional aircraft be assigned to the Flanders air station. The study reaffirmed the fact that the air forces of the MarineKorps had come to play an increasingly important role in the war.

Despite the reinforcements they received in 1916, MarineKorps' air forces remained numerically inferior to their allied counterparts. The MarineKorps had two separate naval air squadrons made up of seaplanes; one was based in Zeebrugge and the other in Ostend. They combined to form the Naval Air Service with its headquarters in Zeebrugge. In addition to those squadrons there was a fighter squadron headquartered in Neumünster and two sections of land-based observers stationed in Ghistel and Jabbeke. Each section of land-based observers consisted of twelve aeroplanes, while the seaplane sections had six planes each and the fighter squadron consisted of fourteen planes.[10] These figures give the MarineKorps a strength at the start of 1917 of fourteen fighters and forty-eight observers; twenty-four seaplanes and twenty-four aeroplanes. If the air arm of the MarineKorps was to fend off the expected allied air attacks against the harbours, these would not be sufficient. The MarineKorps would have to be reinforced, especially with fighters. Accordingly, the Naval Air Service requested an additional seventy planes, preferably all fighters. They also pointed out that it would be necessary to construct new airfields out of the range of enemy artillery and that these fields would have to be connected by both radio and underground telephone cables.[11] Von Schröder concurred and ordered the Air Service to begin making preparations for the arrival of two new sections of observers. These planes were to be placed along the land front with the 2nd MarineDivision and an additional fighter squadron. He hoped to eventually have three fighter squadrons along the land front and one strictly for use along the coast.[12]

Von Schröder brought these requests to the attention of Admiral von Holtzendorff in a meeting between the two men in January 1917. He reported that the Allies had 'crushing superiority in the air' and that he needed urgent reinforcements for his air station. He suggested that units from the North Sea or Baltic air stations be sent to Flanders. In particular he requested the assignment of numerous new fighters; preferably either the 37th or 38th Jagdstaffel. These two units had been equipped with the newest German fighters.[12] He also asked for more spotlights for the anti-aircraft batteries and additional kite and balloon defences. He believed that these were necessary to protect the bases against the extremely heavy air attacks that he expected would take place once the submarine campaign began.[14] The air campaign though was only one of the issues he took up with von Holtzendorff at this mid-January meeting.

Von Schröder understood that the resumption of the unrestricted submarine campaign would place even heavier demands on his limited surface forces, so at this meeting with Holtzendorff he once again requested reinforcements from the High Seas Fleet. In particular he requested additional torpedo-boats and destroyers as well as small motorboats that would be able to work in the Scheldt and along the coast. He hoped that the latter could be equipped with torpedoes and also used as fast attack craft.[15]

Though there was no longer serious opposition within the fleet regarding the dispatch of additional forces to Flanders there were still problems basing large numbers of vessels there permanently. These problems had to do with the harbour facilities in Ostend, Bruges and Zeebrugge. In late December 1916 von Schröder had been informed by Michelsen that the current harbours lacked sufficient mooring places for more than one flotilla each and that there were also insufficient air raid shelters for the ships' crews. Michelsen also pointed out that Ostend was not an effective harbour because it was too close to the enemy lines, furthermore ships based there had a tendency to become stranded at high tide. If these problems were not corrected he would oppose the permanent basing of large numbers of destroyers in Flanders.[16] As a direct result of this letter von Schröder ordered the expansion of the harbour facilities in Bruges so that the forces currently using Ostend could base there instead.[17] These minor problems though did not keep Scheer from sending an additional destroyer flotilla to Flanders at the end of January.

Scheer had originally intended to send the II Flotilla back to Flanders at the end of December but their journey was delayed due to inclement weather and eventually cancelled.[18] Instead, Scheer decided to assign the VI Flotilla to Flanders on a temporary basis, starting on 22 January. On that date the force, consisting of ten destroyers and one destroyer leader, left Helgoland and began its journey to Flanders.[19] Unfortunately for the Germans Commodore

Tyrwhitt and the Harwich force were alerted in advance by Room 40 and Tyrwhitt set to sea to ambush the Germans.[20]

Tyrwhitt's total force for this operation consisted of sixteen destroyers, two flotilla leaders, and six light cruisers. Tyrwhitt split his destroyers into two equal sections and stationed one by the Maas lightship and the other by the Schouwen Bank while his cruisers took up positions to the east of the North Hinder lightship. They were in position by midnight.

In the meantime the VI Flotilla passed the Terschelling lightship at 9.45pm on a course for the Schouwen Bank and from there to Zeebrugge. At 3.45am the Germans sighted a series of what appeared to be light cruisers or destroyers on a converging course at a range of about 2,000 metres. KorvettenKapitän Max Schultz ordered an attack with torpedoes. The group they had spotted consisted of the light cruisers *Aurora*, *Conquest*, and *Centaur* under the command of Tyrwhitt. The Germans closed the range and *V-69* fired her torpedoes[21] while the British returned a withering fire on the Germans. Tyrwhitt managed to avoid the torpedoes by turning away from the Germans who took that opportunity to make smoke and retreat to the south. Tyrwhitt then pursued.

The chase continued to the south and things began to go very wrong for the Germans. *V-69* received three hits in rapid succession, the first of which destroyed her rudder. The second hit destroyed the port magazine and a third destroyed the bridge and killed KorvettenKapitän Schultz. The leaderless and rudderless ship was left moving in circles. The smoke being made by the German destroyers and the smoke from fires on *V-69* combined to make visibility very poor. While the crew of *V-69* attempted to repair their rudder, a ship suddenly appeared out of the smoke in front of them and rammed them in the port side. This was the German destroyer *G-41*, which apparently did not recognise who she had hit and disappeared once again into the smoke only to reappear on the starboard side and ram *V-69* once again; this time causing one of *V-69*'s remaining torpedoes to explode and start new fires on the damaged ship. *G-41* was also heavily damaged by the two collisions and was lost to sight in the smoke.

In the confusion *S-50* became separated from the rest of the flotilla and her captain decided to continue along the previous course to Zeebrugge; a course that brought him into contact with the British destroyers at the Schouwen Bank. *S-50* and the British destroyers stumbled into each other and a gunfight developed between the two units. *S-50*, despite being severely outgunned, managed to launch a torpedo attack which hit and severely damaged the British destroyer *Simoom*. *S-50* herself took several hits, one of which destroyed her radio and her captain wisely decided to retreat to the east. She was able to escape and returned to the Ems estuary at 2pm the next day.

In the meantime *G-41* left the site of the crippled *V-69* and attempted to rejoin the remainder of the flotilla which had continued to the south. Tyrwhitt continued the chase and scored two hits on *G-41* destroying the latter's aft gun and the forward torpedo launcher. This, added to the damage she had done to herself ramming *V-69*, convinced her captain to head for Dutch territorial waters from where he might crawl into Zeebrugge. *G-41* managed to lose contact with Tyrwhitt in the smoke and confusion. She was found the next day by planes from the Zeebrugge naval air station and was guided into Zeebrugge by the remainder of the flotilla, which had managed to escape from the encounter unharmed.

Only *V-69* remained. Tyrwhitt had left her behind while he pursued the rest of the flotilla to the southwest. She was found shortly afterward by the second group of British cruisers which fired additional shells into her before steaming off convinced that she was sinking. The crew of *V-69*, however, managed to keep her afloat and repair the rudder enough to make it to the Netherlands where they were allowed to make repairs and return to Germany on 12 February. Amazingly none of the Germans were sunk. Despite advance warning and successfully finding the Germans Tyrwhitt was unable to destroy the VI Flotilla which arrived in Flanders battered but ready for further action on 23 January.[22]

On the morning of the 23rd Admiral von Schröder reported to Scheer and von Holtzendorff that the flotilla had arrived without *V-69*, *S-50* or *G-41*. Initial aerial reconnaissance had not spotted them though they did spot one British destroyer that appeared to be sinking (apparently the *Simoom*). Von Schröder believed that *V-69* and *S-50* had to be considered lost.[23] He had received word from *G-41* (apparently the radio had been repaired) of the battle and knew that the ship was badly damaged but trying to make Zeebrugge. The rest of the flotilla was sent out to assist.[24] Later that day word arrived that *S-50* had returned to Germany and that *V-69* was in the Netherlands. The Germans believed that the exit of the flotilla from Germany must have been witnessed by a British submarine and reported. There was no inkling that their codes had been compromised.[25]

Von Schröder and Scheer actually considered the outcome of the encounter to be a good omen. An entire flotilla could have easily been destroyed. Visibility had been fairly good and yet the Germans had managed to escape, albeit with heavy damage. Even the most heavily damaged vessel, *V-69*, managed to survive. Surely this boded well for the campaign to come.

Further good omens came from the restricted submarine campaign during January. That month the Flanders flotilla, now consisting of four UB-Is, five UC-Is, six UB-IIs, and seven UC-IIs, carried out a total of twenty-eight missions and accounted for the destruction of ninety-nine enemy vessels totaling 119,357 tons. This brought their total since the start of the war to 995 vessels totaling 1,211,960 tons. In addition, the minefields laid by the UCs disrupted traffic around Calais, Dunkirk, Boulogne, Le Havre, Brest and St. Nazaire as well as Portland and Weymouth.[26] That month the submarines as a whole accounted for 195 ships totaling 328,391 tons.[27] 1917 had indeed begun promisingly; it remained to be seen if that promise would bear out.

THE FIRST PHASE: FEBRUARY – MAY 1917

The Submarine Campaign

The latest German bid for victory began on 1 February. On that day the Germans announced the resumption of the unrestricted submarine campaign. The campaign went through two distinct phases during 1917; an initial phase from February to May when the submarines enjoyed even greater success than Holtzendorff had envisioned, and a second phase that followed the introduction of convoy by the Royal Navy. During the second phase it became evident to the Germans that the submarine campaign would not fulfill the hopes they had placed in it and that the war would indeed continue into 1918.

When the unrestricted campaign began the Flanders submarine flotilla had twenty-three submarines available for immediate use.[28] They soon received reinforcements that brought their strength up to thirty-two submarines.[29] This number would fluctuate throughout the submarine campaign; dropping to thirty-one in March, then rising to thirty-three in April and to thirty-four in May.[30] The strength of the flotilla peaked in May, from then on it gradually declined over the rest of the year though it never fell below twenty-nine submarines.[31] To put these numbers into perspective it may be useful to briefly list the numbers of submarines assigned to the other major German commands, the High Seas Fleet and the flotillas at Pola in the Mediterranean. The High Seas Fleet had forty-six submarines under its command in February, fifty-two in March, fifty-four in April and fifty-six in May. The fleet reached its peak strength in June and July when it had fifty-nine submarines under its command.[32] At the same time the Pola flotilla had twenty-three submarines available in February, twenty-four in March, twenty-five in April, and twenty-six in May. Its peak strength came during November and December of 1917 when it controlled thirty-one submarines.[33]

The Flanders flotilla consisted of four separate types of submarines: the nearly obsolete UB-Is; the mine laying UC-Is; the UB-IIs; and the UC-IIs. Each type had its own particular area of operations based upon its capabilities. The weakest of the types, the old UB-Is, were restricted to limited patrols in the Hoofden and purely defensive patrols along the coast. By February and March of 1917 only four of these vessels were still in service and that number dropped to three in April and May. They carried out twelve missions in February but their role was gradually reduced as they were slowly lost and not replaced. By May the number of missions undertaken by the UB-Is had dropped to ten. Due to the limitations of the class they were slowly phased out and were replaced later in the year by the UB-IIIs.

The UC-Is, though also an older design, proved to be of greater value than the UB-Is due simply to the fact that their mission was not to attack surface craft but rather to lay mines. The UC-Is remained active throughout the year, concentrating their efforts along the French and British coasts. The Flanders flotilla had five UC-Is during the first phase of the submarine campaign. They carried out varying numbers of missions from a low of eighteen in February to a high of twenty-three in May.

The third type of submarine, the UB-II class, concentrated their efforts in the Hoofden but, unlike the UB-Is, they also worked in the much more hazardous confines of the English Channel. In February there were only five UB-IIs assigned to the Flanders flotilla but that number gradually increased to a high of nine in May. The number of missions carried out by the UB-IIs ranged from a low of five in March to a peak of eighteen in April.

The final type of submarine employed by the Flanders flotilla during the first phase of the campaign was the very versatile UC-II. These vessels were capable of attacking with torpedoes or gunfire and could also lay mines. In addition, they had the greatest range of any of the Flanders submarines and made up the bulk of the flotilla. There were twelve UC-IIs assigned to Flanders in February and that number gradually rose to fifteen in March and to a peak of seventeen in April and May. With their greater range the UC-IIs were able to operate as far afield as the Irish Sea and the Bay of Biscay. They remained the workhorses of the flotilla until the development of the UB-III.[34]

The exact details of how much shipping was sunk by the Germans vary from source to source, but they all agree that the submarine campaign began very favourably. According to the submarine activity report for February, the Flanders flotilla destroyed 115 ships totaling 164,568 tons.[35] These figures roughly correlate to those given in the German official history. The latter credits the Flanders flotilla with 163,455 tons, slightly more than 25 percent of the total of 520,412 tons for the fleet as a whole.[36] The German official history though also includes 111,855 tons of damaged shipping and puts the total loss to the Allies in February at 632,267 tons in exchange for three submarines lost, a brilliant beginning.[37] The only real negative for the campaign that month was the expected break with the United States which came on 3 February. That was far overshadowed though by the great successes of the submarines.

Von Schröder though was not pleased with the performance of the Flanders flotilla in February. He sent a letter to von Holtzendorff on 10 March apologising for the poor showing of the Flanders submarines. He attributed the disappointing results to four factors: a week of poor weather with very thick fog; a late start to the campaign, since the Flanders flotilla did not begin operations until 13 February; a virtual disappearance of neutral traffic in the Hoofden; and finally, greater protection for allied shipping in the Channel, in particular the use of escorts for some merchant vessels. (This most likely refers to the introduction of convoy for the Anglo-French coal trade.) He concluded his letter optimistically, by stating that the prospects for March appeared to be very favourable and that the submarines were having no difficulty passing through the allied Barrage.[38]

March did indeed turn out to be a favorable month for the Germans and the number of sinkings continued to escalate. The Flanders flotilla reported sinking an additional 195 ships totaling 234,871 tons.[39] This was just under half of the 564,497 ton total for the entire fleet.[40] If damaged vessels are included the latter total rises to 655,326 tons. The Germans lost only two submarines in exchange.[41] That month the Flanders flotilla reported that, despite the British patrols of the Dover Strait, the submarines were able to pass through easily and the entire Flanders coast itself remained free of nets and mines. The only problem reported was the increasing number of air attacks against Bruges.[42]

In April the total number of German sinkings sky-rocketed to its peak of 860,334 tons.[43] With damaged vessels included, the total loss of shipping was an amazing 963,872 tons; well in excess of Holtzendorff's predictions.[44] The Flanders flotilla's share of this total was a respectable 117 vessels and 253,840 tons.[45] Only one submarine was lost.[46] The only dark spot for the month was the United States' declaration of war on Germany; even that, however, could not dampen the enthusiasm of the navy's leadership. Their predictions appeared to be coming true. There was only one dissenting voice.

Von Schröder sent another note to von Holtzendorff at the end of April expressing his concern that the British, despite the high level of shipping losses, did not appear to be on the brink of defeat. He argued that if the campaign was to succeed it would be necessary to exceed even these brilliant numbers. In order to accomplish this he wanted all available resources to be flung into the submarine campaign over the course of the following three months. In particular, he wanted the submarines that remained in the Baltic sent to other theatres where they could be more useful. He argued that every available submarine, including ones used for training, should be thrown into a massive effort to try and win the war within the next three months.[47] However, von Schröder's concerns were not shared by von Holtzendorff who confidently awaited the victorious conclusion of the campaign.

May witnessed the first setback of the campaign as the number of sinkings dropped from the astronomical totals of April down to the more realistic figure of 616,316 tons; albeit still devastating losses for allied shipping.[48] With damaged vessels included the total increased to 655,131 tons.[49] Out of that total the Flanders flotilla accounted for 146 ships and 217,743 tons.[50] That month the flotilla reported that both enemy patrol activity and air attacks against the naval bases were increasing. The British even undertook, for the first time in a year, a bombardment of Zeebrugge. This attack took place on 12 May and did no significant damage but it did demonstrate a continued willingness to fight on the part of the British. Aside from some small difficulties in navigating through the Channel and passing though British countermeasures, the actions of the flotilla were not significantly hindered, [51] One disquieting note did appear in the May activity report though; the submarines were beginning to spring numerous leaks and were experiencing increasing engine trouble as well. These problems were attributed to the increased strains being placed on the machines and von Schröder feared that their effectiveness would be reduced in the coming critical months.[52]

One of the keys to the success of the German submarine campaign was the inability of the British to effectively stop the passage of German submarines through the Dover Strait. During the first phase of the campaign German submarines passed through the Dover Strait 122 times and only two boats were lost, both to destroyers. The mine and net barrage was singularly ineffective.[53] In the Royal Navy's defence however, it should be pointed out that they not only had to contend with the Flanders submarines but also with the increasingly active torpedo-boat and destroyer flotillas. The primary mission of the latter was to protect the German submarines and they accomplished this mainly by attacking British patrol craft.

Force Allocation and the War on the Surface

The Flanders torpedo-boat and destroyer flotillas carried on a very active war in the Channel and the Hoofden during the first phase of the submarine campaign. In addition to protecting the submarines they were trying to disrupt communications between Britain and France by attacking the Channel patrols and, if possible, the cross-channel transports. The raids that had begun late in 1916 continued unabated into 1917 despite the near destruction of the VI Flotilla on its way to Flanders. In fact, shortly after its arrival the VI Flotilla and the Destroyer Half-Flotilla undertook a new operation. On the evening of 25 January they raided the Channel patrols but had no success. Since they were unable to find any patrol craft they settled for a desultory bombardment of Southwold. A further raid was launched on 29 January to try and catch a large Anglo-Dutch convoy but that mission also came to naught. Two additional advances followed on the 30 January and on 11 February but were equally fruitless.[54]

Early in February von Schröder was informed that he was to receive additional reinforcements. On the 6th word came from von Holtzendorff that six new destroyers had been cleared for transfer from the Baltic to Flanders. The new ships were expected to leave Germany sometime around the new moon though the exact details of the transfer were left to the High Seas Fleet.[55] Three days later von Schröder received word from Scheer that the six destroyers would leave for Flanders around the 17th and would be accompanied by four A-IIs, also from the Baltic. The MarineKorps was to provide aerial reconnaissance to ensure that this group was not intercepted.[56] The ships; destroyers S-15, S-18, S-20, S-24, G-95 and G-96; torpedo-boats A-39, A-40, A-42 and A-45 arrived as planned on 18 February.[57] The S destroyers were actually V-1-class ships displacing over 650 tons and the G-type destroyers were even larger, displacing over 1,100 tons. The S-boats were armed with two 10.5cm guns in addition to their torpedo and mine armament. The G-boats were slightly more powerful since they mounted three 10.5cm guns.[58]

With these new forces en route von Schröder planned two attacks for 14 and 20 February and a major operation for the night of 25 February.[59] On the latter evening the German forces put to sea in three separate groups. The first group, consisting of S-49, V-46, V-45, G-37, V-44 and G-86 was to attack the Channel patrols and bombard Dover. The second group, consisting of G-95, V-67, V-68, V-47 and G-96, was to advance in the direction of the North-Foreland lightship to attack commercial shipping in that area and, if possible, bombard Margate. The third group, (S-18, S-20 and S-24) was to attack commercial shipping between Britain and the Netherlands. This operation was designed to coincide with a major advance by the High Seas Fleet into the Hoofden, though the latter move was cancelled at the last moment due to 'unfavorable light conditions.'[60] The main goal of the operation was to facilitate the passage of German submarines through the Channel by disrupting the British patrols. The destruction of merchant shipping was purely a secondary goal.[61]

The British forces available that evening consisted of the light cruisers *Conquest* and *Active*; the monitors *Erebus* and *Terror*; eighteen destroyers and two destroyer leaders (the *Faulknor* and the *Broke*.) The cruisers, the monitors and four destroyers were in the Downs with an additional nine destroyers at Dover and five destroyers on patrol in the Channel.[62]

The Germans left Zeebrugge at 7pm and the first group passed through the Channel Barrage at 11:30pm. Almost immediately they made contact with the destroyer *Laverock* and opened fire. After closing to within 400 yards the Germans launched a torpedo attack which forced the *Laverock* to turn into the German gunfire. Due to the overcast conditions visibility was poor and little damage was done to either side before the Germans broke contact. They believed that numerous allied destroyers were closing on their position.[63] Once the *Laverock* was out of sight the Germans returned to hunting along the Barrage. Finding no other allied vessels they returned to harbour.[64]

The other German forces had equally dismal evenings. Two destroyers did carry out a bombardment of Margate but did very little damage. Other than that the evening turned out to be another disappointment; on both sides. For the Germans the night was a disappointing attempt to repeat their success of October 1916, while for the British, the evening proved that they were unable to prevent the Germans from raiding the Channel at will. What was even worse was that they could not catch the Germans on their return to the Flanders harbours. Von Schröder, though, considered the evening a success. Although his forces did not win any major victories, he considered it very important to constantly remind the British that the Germans had a large force of destroyers in Flanders. His numerous raids served that purpose. Furthermore, he considered that any destroyer raid was beneficial because every raid served as an additional deterrent to neutral commerce. He maintained the opinion he had voiced earlier in the war, namely that a vigorous destroyer campaign based out of Flanders would eventually force the British to concentrate increasing strength in the southern theatre. This would reduce the danger faced by German forces in other theatres.[65] Consequently, despite the lack of success during January and February, the German destroyer raids continued.

The next major effort came on 17 March. The main objective once again was to destroy enemy patrol craft, though this time the Germans hoped to be able to bombard Dover as well. Once again they divided their force into three operational groups. The VI Flotilla and a half-flotilla of destroyers, a total of fourteen ships, were to raid the Channel patrols while a second half-flotilla of four destroyers attacked enemy shipping in the Downs.[66]

Early on the 17th the British received word that a German operation was planned for that evening and Bacon sent four destroyers to patrol the Barrage while other forces were held ready in Dover and the Downs. The British reserve forces consisted of: four destroyers, one light cruiser and one destroyer leader in the Downs; an additional two monitors just to the north of the Downs and five destroyers and one leader at Dover.[67]

The German forces left port once again at 7pm. At 11.47pm the destroyer *S-49* made the first contact of the evening when it encountered the British destroyer *Paragon*. *S-49* quickly launched two torpedoes and opened fire while the British once again, as in October, waited for the German to respond to a recognition signal. *G-86* then joined the fray and fired two additional torpedoes at *Paragon* which was hit by three of the four torpedoes. The impact caused some of the depth charges stored on the deck of the British destroyer to explode. As a result the *Paragon* broke in half and sank. The German commander, KorvettenKapitän Tillesen, then saw a flash of light which he took to be a signal of some kind and moved in that direction. This led him to the destroyer *Llewellyn* which was also attacked by torpedo. The *Llewellyn* received a hit to her bow which tore off the front section of the ship and she appeared to be sinking. The Germans did not finish her off but instead moved on. The *Llewellyn* never saw her attackers and believed that she had been torpedoed by a submarine. No further enemy forces were sighted and the Germans returned to Zeebrugge. The *Llewellyn*, miraculously, did not sink and was later towed into port.[68]

In the meantime the second German force found and torpedoed a small steamer outside of the Margate Roads at 1.30am and then attacked a group of British auxiliary patrol vessels, sinking two of them. The British forces in the Downs did sail out but were unable to intercept the Germans who returned to Zeebrugge undamaged. The British were very confused throughout the entire action. Bacon received conflicting reports that seemed at one point to indicate submarine attacks in the Channel and at other times seemed to point to another German destroyer raid. Unable to find any hard and fast information the British commander at first ordered his Dover destroyers to sea, then recalled them when the reports came in of submarine attacks and then ordered them out again. The Germans had raided the British patrols and sunk British vessels, without damage to themselves, for a second time.[69]

This led Bacon to conclude that the Germans could continue these raids indefinitely and that there was very little that he could do about them. He was correct, the Germans definitely held the initiative in the Channel. The attack of 17 March did lead Bacon to make some changes to his dispositions however. The patrol area was now broken into two sections, each of which would be patrolled by a leader and a destroyer division. In addition, one week after the raid, six more destroyers were detached from the Grand Fleet and sent to Dover.[70] As von Schröder had predicted, even without further stunning victories, the German raids were slowly leading to an increased concentration of British forces in the southern theatre.

The Germans quickly followed up this raid with another on 22 March against the Anglo-Dutch trade route but, though one merchant vessel was sunk, that raid was uneventful.[71] It was also the last raid undertaken by the VI Flotilla from Flanders. On 29 March the flotilla returned to Germany as scheduled.[72] Von Schröder was compensated, however, by the transfer of the III Flotilla to Flanders to take its place. This time, however, the transfer was not temporary. The III Flotilla was permanently assigned to the MarineKorps.[73]

According to a copy of a telegram from Scheer to von Schröder preserved in von Schröder's war diary, the flotilla was assigned to Flanders because it could be most useful there. Scheer assigned it to the MarineKorps with the caveat that he might need to recall it if the High Seas Fleet suffered major losses. Von Schröder was ecstatic, especially since at the same time the Destroyer Half-Flotilla was also being increased to full flotilla strength.[74] The new forces arrived in Zeebrugge on the morning of 24 March.[75]

The new disposition of forces gave the MarineKorps a total of twenty-five destroyers and fifteen torpedo-boats. This force was under the command of FregattenKapitän Kahle, the commander of the III Flotilla.[76] The new forces were arranged as follows:

Führer der Torpedoboote Flandern:	FregattenKapitän Kahle
Destroyer Flotilla:	KorvettenKapitän Albrecht

– eight active destroyers with one leader and one destroyer under repair.

III Flotilla:	FregattenKapitän Kahle

– ten active destroyers and one leader.

Torpedo-boat Flotilla:	Kapitänleutnant Assmann

– ten active torpedo-boats with one leader and two reserve boats.

Motorboat Division

– six fast motorboats used exclusively for minesweeping and close coastal patrol work.

During the early months of the year the torpedo-boat flotilla continued to concentrate on minesweeping and coastal patrols. One half-flotilla was on patrol during the evening hours while the other remained in port. Two of the ships in port were kept ready to respond to any enemy movement; the remainder were left at four hours preparedness. There were no daytime patrols.[78] These regulations remained in force throughout the first phase of the submarine campaign. Between February and May though the Torpedo-Boat Flotilla received significant reinforcements that allowed it to be used offensively for the first time. The major change was the presence of the A-IIs. The four that arrived in February were the first installment of this new series. Additional A-IIs were due to arrive in February, though due to bottlenecks in production they were delayed.[79] Attempts by von Schröder to get units from the Baltic reassigned to Flanders to take their place failed and the MarineKorps was forced to make do with the few A-IIs they had. Those four though allowed Assmann to begin offensive operations.[80]

As a direct result of his inability to acquire additional A-IIs von Schröder decided to keep the A-Is active.[81] In March von Holtzendorff agreed to a plan of von Schröder's to place eight of the A-Is into a special third half-flotilla of the Torpedo-Boat Flotilla. They were to be based in Bruges (Ostend was considered too dangerous to use because of enemy airpower) and used as a materiel reserve.[82] In April this unit became the Minesweeper Flotilla Flandern. Its primary mission was to maintain swept channels through the enemy minefields though it was also occasionally used for mine-laying.[83] For example, in early January they laid a minefield just off the mouth of the Scheldt.[84] With its reinforcement by the A-IIs and the creation of the Minesweeper Flotilla the Torpedo-Boat Flotilla was now able to take a more aggressive stance in the war at sea.

Starting in March, once the new A-IIs were fully operational, Kapitän-leutnant Assmann planned his first offensive operations. The first occurred on 24 March when he led the A-IIs on an attack against Dunkirk. The Germans bombarded the harbour and dockyards for six minutes, sinking two old colliers. They appear to have achieved total surprise since the Allies did not return fire.[85] Additional raids were carried out in April and May.

On the night of 24 April the Torpedo-Boat Flotilla returned to Dunkirk for another bombardment. En route the four A-IIs had a brief encounter with several small allied motorboats but no damage was done to either side and the Germans continued on course. They bombarded the port from 2.15am until 2.22am, firing roughly 350 shells. On their return to Zeebrugge the Germans encountered the French torpedo-boat *Etendard* and sank it in a massed torpedo attack. Shortly afterward they were intercepted by a second French torpedo-boat, the *Notre Dame des Lourdes*, which was heavily damaged in an exchange of gunfire. After sinking an auxiliary patrol vessel the Germans returned to port unharmed and were commended by Admiral von Schröder.[86]

Another minor engagement followed on 2 May. On that afternoon two of the A-IIs left port to search for a downed German pilot and were attacked by four small enemy motorboats. The Germans took no damage and reportedly sank two of the small allied craft.[87]

The Torpedo-Boat Flotilla remained active throughout May. On the evening of the 10th they undertook a joint-operation with the destroyer flotillas. The destroyers made another sweep toward the Channel to try and destroy British patrol craft and the torpedo-boats patrolled the lanes the destroyers would use to return from their sweep. As a result the torpedo-boats nearly wound up in a gun battle with several British cruisers and destroyers.[88] On the 19th they carried out their final offensive operation of the first phase when they were sent on a patrol into the Channel. Assmann was unable to lead this mission and his place was taken by a young Oberleutant zur See named Günther Lütjens, who gained fame in the Second World War as the commander of the German battleship *Bismarck* on its ill-fated journey. Lütjens and the Torpedo-Boat Flotilla encountered four enemy destroyers, apparently French, and engaged them in a running battle. The Germans were seriously outgunned and launched a desperation torpedo attack before retiring to the east.[89] Following this near escape the Torpedo-Boat Flotilla was once again relegated to a purely defensive role.[90]

While the Torpedo-Boat Flotilla was experimenting with offensive operations, the destroyer flotillas did not sit idle. They launched a series of raids on 10, 13 and 18 April, none of which had any effect. It was not until they undertook yet another sweep on the evening of 20 April that they once again encountered enemy forces.

For that evening's mission the Germans divided their force into three groups: *Gruppe Gautier*, consisting of the 5th Half-Flotilla with one leader and one boat from the 6th Half-Flotilla; *Gruppe Albrecht*, with the 1st Destroyer Half-Flotilla and two boats from the 6th Half-Flotilla and one leader; and *Gruppe Zander*, made up of only three destroyers. The first two groups were assigned to attack the Barrage patrols and bombard Calais and Dover. The third group was to operate against the traffic around the Downs. That evening the British had four destroyers and the two leaders *Swift* and *Broke* on patrol in the Channel while an additional two destroyers patrolled the waters around the Downs. There was also one monitor stationed off of

Ramsgate and three destroyers with one leader and one light cruiser actually in the Downs. In addition, Bacon had his usual reserve of six destroyers at Dover.[91]

The night's action began with a bombardment of Calais by Gruppe Albrecht around 11.10pm. Roughly one half-hour later Gruppe Gautier, after shelling a small British patrol boat and leaving it in what was believed to be sinking condition, attacked Dover. Heavy fire was returned by the coastal batteries. Due to the exchange of fire between the Germans and the coastal batteries Bacon elected to keep his destroyers in harbour to protect them from the shells of their own guns. Once they finished the bombardment, the Germans moved off into the Channel to attack the patrols. The British reserves from Dover then left harbour in pursuit but they returned around 1.25am after being unable to find the Germans. They were convinced that the Germans had returned to Zeebrugge. In reality the night's action was only beginning.

At 1.38am Gruppe Gautier sighted the two British leaders *Swift* and *Broke* and moved to attack. Firing on both sides commenced at 1.44am and both British vessels began ramming attempts against their smaller German foes. The *Swift*'s initial attempt failed and the British settled for firing a torpedo which hit one of the German destroyers, *G-85*. The *Broke* also missed on its first ramming attempt and had to fire torpedoes as well. The Germans then attempted to break contact and retreat to the east but both British ships, though heavily damaged, were able to pursue the Germans.

At that point the *Broke* made a second ramming attempt and succeeded in severely damaging *G-42*. In fact the two vessels were locked together for a brief period of time. Both ships were heavily damaged and while they were attached to one another, the crew of *G-42*, which was sinking, tried to board the *Broke* and seize the ship. The crew of the *Broke* was able to defeat the German boarding party and separate their ship from the doomed German destroyer but the damage they had sustained made it impossible to continue the pursuit. Instead both the *Broke* and the *Swift* disengaged and concentrated their fire upon the two damaged German ships. *G-85* was soon engulfed in flames and *G-42* sank. It looked for a time as if the *Broke* might go down as well since its engines had been badly damaged and it slowly drifted toward the burning *G-85* which could have exploded at any time. Fortunately for the British several of their destroyers arrived on the scene and the latter were able to tow both leaders back to port after finishing off *G-85*. The two remaining German groups returned safely to their bases in Flanders. The Germans managed to sink one sailing ship and do some minor damage to the two cities of Dover and Calais but they had no tangible success with which to offset the loss of two destroyers.[92]

This was the first major defeat for the Germans in their new campaign. In their previous operations they had always escaped destruction but on this evening they suffered serious losses. The two lost destroyers represented nearly 10 percent of the total strength of the Flanders destroyer flotillas and could not be replaced; the losses of 20 April forced von Schröder to change the focus of his efforts. After 20 April the Channel patrols were no longer molested and the Flanders destroyers turned their attention to the convoys between Britain and the Netherlands.

On 26 April the III Flotilla and the Destroyer Flotilla took to sea once again. This time their mission was to attack shipping at the mouth of the Thames. Finding no naval targets the Germans contented themselves with a bombardment of Margate.[93] This operation was followed up on the 30th with another attack but it was also unsuccessful.[94]

Another sweep followed on 10 May. This was supposed to be a raid against the convoys between the Netherlands and Great Britain but it became instead a running gun battle between the III Flotilla, the 1st Destroyer Half-Flotilla and three British light cruisers accompanied by four destroyers. The Germans had left port on the 10th after receiving word that a large convoy was due to leave the Netherlands that evening, however, before they could find the convoy, they were discovered by the British. At 4.40am the British ships opened fire. The German commanders, recognising that they were seriously outgunned, quickly made smoke and ran to the south where they were able to link up with the remaining destroyer half-flotilla and the Torpedo-boat flotilla at 5.30am. At that point the British broke off their pursuit and retreated to the north. The Germans then pursued the British until 6.30am at which point they returned to Zeebrugge. Neither side suffered serious damage in the battle but the British accomplished their objective, the Germans were unable to raid the convoy.[95]

One week later, on the 17th, yet another raid was carried out against the Dutch convoys. This time one small Dutch steamer was sunk. The only other contact was a brief encounter with an enemy destroyer which appeared out of the fog and rammed *S-55* before vanishing back into the mists. No serious damage was done to either side.[96] The attempt was repeated on the 23rd, once again without success,[97] and again on the 26th. On the latter evening the Germans briefly encountered two monitors and two French torpedo-boats which engaged them in a fifteen minute gun duel before breaking contact and retreating to the north.[98] That was the final German attack of the first phase.

As the preceding survey shows, both the surface forces and the submarines were quite active during the initial stage of the 1917 campaign and the Flanders bases were rapidly becoming a major thorn in the side of the British. The

British had already tried to destroy or at least neutralise the German bases in Flanders by bombardment or by blocking them with mines, but they had not succeeded. During the first phase of the submarine campaign, it became increasingly clear to the Royal Navy that the time had come to do something definitive about the Flanders bases. They were uncertain, however, as to what the best course of action would be.

British Countermeasures

The Flanders bases posed a very serious threat to British commerce. There were several reasons for this. First of all, by using the bases in Flanders, German submarines could extend both their radius of action and the time they were able to spend on station. Secondly, the Flanders bases allowed the Germans to make extensive use of the smaller and cheaper (in terms of production cost) submarines of the *UB* and *UC*-classes. Finally, as we have seen, the ports provided a sally point for the destroyers of the Flanders flotillas. The Flanders harbours therefore were a chink in Great Britain's armour, but until late 1916 they were not fully exploited by the Germans. When that changed in 1917 it became necessary for the British to do something about the Flanders bases.

Though the Flanders positions posed difficult problems to the British they also provided unique opportunities. The same proximity to major traffic lanes and naval bases that made the Flanders ports so dangerous also made them a good deal more vulnerable than the distant and essentially inaccessible German bases at Wilhelmshaven. Operations that were simply too difficult to implement against the major bases in Germany could be considered for use against the 'Triangle'. During 1917 the British tried to take advantage of this in several ways: they stepped up their bombing attacks in Flanders; they once again began to bombard the coast; they started to plan blocking attacks against Zeebrugge and Ostend; and they created a plan for a combined land and naval assault to clear the Germans out of Flanders. During the first phase of the unrestricted submarine campaign they concentrated on air and sea attacks against the harbours. For example, they launched a new series of air raids and recommenced bombarding the coast. The potential blocking operation and the combined offensive were still in the planning stages during the early part of the year.

On 1 February von Schröder recorded in his war diary that he expected the British to soon begin launching new and aggressive campaigns to dislodge the Germans from Flanders. He did not expect them to allow the Germans to continue to use the Flanders bases essentially unopposed.[99] His prediction soon proved to be correct. On the very next day the British resumed their air attacks against Bruges, albeit without doing any serious damage.[100] This was the precursor to a full scale air war against the Flanders harbours that lasted throughout the entire first part of the year. The Germans responded by launching increasing air attacks of their own against allied airfields at St Pol and Coxyde, the harbours at Dunkirk and the shipping collected in the Downs.[101] In the early years of the war the air raids on the Flanders harbours had only a minimal effect; that was not the case in 1917. The first success for the British air campaign came on 7 February when some of the munitions stored at Bruges were destroyed. This led Admiral von Schröder to order the removal of all munitions from the harbour, thus hampering the ability of the artillery around the harbour to repel any future assault.[102] Then, on 4 April the British scored another success when they managed to destroy two German aircraft during a raid on the Zeebrugge air station.[103] That was followed by a more significant success on 8 April.

During the course of the air raids in February and March the Germans began sending their destroyers and torpedo-boats out of Zeebrugge when the air raid alarm was sounded. Instead of basing them in the harbour they had them tie up to the outside of the mole, presumably this provided them with additional protection against the bombers. The British became aware of this through aerial reconnaissance and on the early morning of 8 April they launched an air raid in conjunction with an attack by their small coastal motorboats. The plan was to use the motorboats to strike at the German craft lying alongside the mole. The motorboats were to run in with surprise and launch torpedoes at the German ships. Given their speed, the British believed that the motorboats would be able to escape before the surviving German destroyers could take any action. The attack went forward as planned and was a brilliant success. When the raid began the Germans, as usual, sent their destroyers to lie alongside the mole. Shortly thereafter the motorboats attacked. They fired their torpedoes and escaped before the Germans even realised what had happened. *G-88* was hit and sunk by one of the torpedoes which, and this clearly demonstrates their confusion, the Germans believed had been fired by a British submarine. It was only two days later that they realised what had happened.[104] Aside from the loss of *G-88* the net result of the raid was that the III Flotilla was no longer allowed to leave the harbour during air raids.[105]

The British raids continued throughout April and into May, steadily increasing in intensity but without attaining another major success. Several times the raiding planes were accompanied by the coastal motorboats but in every instance the Germans were behind the protection of the mole. There were, however, a few brief skirmishes between the motorboats and the patrolling German torpedo-boats.[106] Though there were no further dramatic successes, the perpetual British raids gradually took a toll on both the dockyard facilities and the air stations in Belgium. There were several instances where aircraft were destroyed on the ground and the repair of damaged ships was delayed. No further damage was done to German shipping though.[107]

In addition to attacking the German ports, the British used their aircraft to begin the so-called 'spider-web' patrols. These were flights undertaken in an octagonal pattern centered on the North Hinder lightship. They covered roughly 4,000 square kilometres of sea and took about five hours to complete. Their purpose was twofold; at the very least the British hoped to force German submarines in that area to submerge. Their real hope though was that they would be able to attack and destroy them from the air. Unfortunately for the British the patrols were not very successful and they destroyed only one submarine during the remainder of the war.[108] Clearly the air force alone could not yet provide an answer to the submarines, therefore the British needed to augment their attacks. In May they began to do so.

On the 12th the British once again began bombarding the Flanders coast. Their goal was to cut Zeebrugge off from Bruges by destroying the locks of the canal that linked the two cities. This particular bombardment was carried out by three monitors armed with 15-inch guns. Several destroyers accompanied them to provide protection against submarines. The morning was especially foggy and the normal German reconnaissance did not spot the approaching British force. Therefore they first became aware of the bombardment when the shells began falling in the city and harbour. The bombardment began at 5.30am; due to confusion on the part of the Germans and to the foggy conditions the coastal batteries did not return fire until 6.45am. Shortly thereafter the British broke off the bombardment and returned home. They succeeded in killing one German and destroying the rail lines that connected Zeebrugge to the rest of Belgium. The lock gates though were undamaged.[109] This was the only bombardment attempted by the British during the early months of 1917.

As the submarine war intensified and the British position became increasingly serious, it became obvious that something more needed to be done about the Flanders bases. Therefore Admiral Bacon began to plan an operation that he hoped would result in the blocking of the German harbours. His initial plan consisted of four steps. First of all there would be a diversionary bombardment of the area around Knocke. The second part of the operation would be an advance to the Zeebrugge mole by several monitors which had been specially modified through the attachment of a collapsible bow. This would allow the monitors to ram themselves bow first into the mole. At that point a secondary modification would come into play; a large bridge would be attached to the bow of the ships and would drop down over the outer wall of the mole, thus allowing British troops to cross from the monitors to the mole. Once the monitors were in position three separate groups of 300 men each were to attack the mole. One group was to attack and destroy any German destroyers tied up to the inside of the mole while the second group captured the mole's defensive guns and the third group held the mole against reinforcements from shore. The entire attack was to be concealed by a smokescreen and protected by a division of destroyers.

While the raid was underway an additional monitor would pull alongside the mole and fire at the gates to the canal connecting Zeebrugge to Bruges. Then, once the landing parties had secured the mole, they would fire a signal rocket to alert block ships to move into the harbour. (The fighting was expected to take about fifteen minutes.) Once in the harbour the block ships were to be taken to the canal entrance and sunk at which point the British landing parties would return to their monitors and leave.[110]

The plan was never carried out, but it is interesting since it was the precursor to the plan developed and eventually implemented by Bacon's successor as commander of the Dover Patrol, Admiral Roger Keyes. Bacon claimed that he was very eager to attempt the blocking attack even though he doubted that it would have any long-term significance.[111] He never received the opportunity. The blocking operation was shelved and its place was taken by a much more ambitious plan put forward by the commander of the BEF, Douglas Haig. Haig intended to seize the entire Belgian coastline and he believed that he would need the German harbours intact in order to supply his army. It was only when that attack failed, in late 1917, that the British once again began to consider a blocking attack on the Belgian ports.

While all of these efforts to neutralise the 'Triangle' were underway the British actually found the answer to the submarine menace, though it was not apparent until later in the year. On 27 April a reluctant Admiral Jellicoe, virtually in desperation, ordered the implementation of several trial convoys from both North America and Gibraltar to see if they could protect British shipping from the depredations of the submarines. Convoy had been resisted for most of the war for several reasons, chief among them being concerns over the slow speed of the convoys, the congestion that would be caused in British harbours, the suspected inability of merchant captains to keep formation in a convoy and a conviction that the Royal Navy did not possess enough resources to protect all the shipping coming into and out of Britain. It was only in the dark days of April that a desperate Admiralty decided to try convoying merchant shipping, not in any expectation of great success, but for lack of other options.[112]

On 10 May the first homeward bound convoy sailed out from Gibraltar. It arrived in Britain without loss. On 24 May the first transatlantic convoy sailed. It lost one ship, a vessel that had dropped out of the convoy along the way. Though no regular system of convoy was created until later in the year and they did not yet realise it, the British had found the answer to the submarine. The first phase of the submarine war came to an end with the beginning of the convoy system. The Germans still enjoyed several months of success while the British slowly implemented the convoy system but they would never again experience the same success that they had in April.[113] At the time, though, that was not apparent to either side and planning went forward on both the British and German ends for a major offensive in Flanders.

Coast Defence

Beginning in April both the OHL and the MarineKorps began to pay increasing attention to the defence of the Flanders coastline. They were aware that, with the desperate straits the Russians were in and the failure of the French offensive of that spring, the British would soon launch some kind of attack on the Western Front to bolster their allies. The logical area for such an offensive was Flanders. In this region the Germans could not afford to surrender any ground. If they did they would lose, at the very least, the ability to utilise Ostend as a naval base. In fact their entire network of bases was very vulnerable. Ostend could already be reached by long-range allied artillery and any loss of territory in Flanders could bring these guns within range of both Zeebrugge and Bruges. Since Flanders had become such a vital sector of the Western Front the navy and the OHL decided to expand the MarineKorps once again. On 11 April the Kaiser ordered the creation of a third Marine-Division. The new division was to consist of eight regiments of naval infantry and was to take over the southern portion of the land front assigned to the MarineKorps. The 2nd MarineDivision, which had been holding that area, was now given coastal responsibilities. They took over the defence of the coastline west of Ostend and retained control over the northernmost sector of the land front. The 1st MarineDivision was freed to concentrate its attention on the cities of Ostend and Zeebrugge and the intervening beaches.[114] The reinforcement of the MarineKorps came at an opportune time, for by April 1917 von Schröder and his staff had several concerns regarding the defence of the coast.

Admiral Jacobsen, the commander of the 1st MarineDivision, was very worried about whether or not Ostend could be defended at all. It was obviously the most vulnerable of the harbours. After studying the defences of the area in late April, Jacobsen found discovered that they consisted of only one coastal battery, *Eylau*, which was only equipped with 8.8cm guns, and several machine guns.[115] He considered these to be far too weak and as a result proposed several changes. First, a 6cm battery was to be constructed around the town as soon as possible and a 3.7cm was to be added later in the year. Jacobsen also suggested that a net barrier be laid across the entrance to the harbour to protect against enemy torpedo attacks. To provide further protection all vessels in the harbour should also be equipped with protective nets.[116] Von Schröder responded to these suggestions on 30 April. The extra net around the harbour entrance was rejected as superfluous but the installment of the additional guns was approved. As a result one 3.7cm and one 8.8cm battery were to be added as soon as possible. The Korps would also attempt to make a 10.5cm gun available later in the year.[117]

The remainder of the coast's defences were arranged as follows. The 1st MarineDivision had two strong groups centered on each of the two main harbours, Ostend and Zeebrugge. Additionally five strongpoints were created on the western Flanders coast between Ostend and Knocke. Inbetween the various strongpoints and the harbours were thirty-three individual machine gun nests, each of which contained two machine guns. Older artillery pieces were also set up behind the machine guns. Together the machine guns and the artillery covered the entire coast. To further tighten the defences each strongpoint and gun emplacement was surrounded by barbed wire. Additional wire barriers were strewn about the beaches to deter landings.

The 2nd MarineDivision contributed to the defence of the coast by building an additional eighteen gun emplacements between Knocke and the land front. These emplacements contained a total of twenty-five guns ranging in calibre from 3.7 to 8.8cm. Additionally, the division created seven separate strongpoints along the coast with the intervening terrain blocked by an unbroken array of electrified wire.

The strength in each sector broke down as follows:

Dutch border to Blankenberg:	two battalions with one in reserve.
Blankenberg to Raversyde:	one battalion with one in reserve.
Raversyde to the land front:	one company with one in reserve

As a general reserve the 1st MarineDivision maintained seven bicycle companies (picked for their maneuverability) and one artillery company. The reserve for the entire MarineKorps consisted of one battalion with a regiment of infantry and a section of artillery detached from the IV army. The latter force was kept in Bruges.

For purposes of air defence there were five 8.8cm anti-aircraft batteries scattered along the coast. Within the ports themselves there were a large number of 3.7cm and one 10.5cm battery. In order to ensure that the defences were alerted of the enemy's approach in time, the entire coast was patrolled by torpedo-boats at a distance of three-to-five kilometres. The Germans fully expected that their defensive arrangements would soon be put to the test.[118]

On 20 May Crown Prince Rupprecht sent a warning to the IV army that the British were expected to launch an attack against the Flanders submarine bases in the upcoming months. The OHL believed that this might include a large scale landing on either the German or Dutch coastlines. A second possibility, which was seen as less likely, was that the British would initiate further naval and air bombardments aimed at destroying the ports. In either case the OHL believed that the British attack would be accompanied by an assault against the German line running from Ypres to the coast. The IV army was empowered to take all measures that were deemed necessary to prepare for such an eventuality. In addition, the Crown Prince requested that the army draw up a set of general regulations governing coastal defence and submit them to him.[119]

Word of this was passed down to the MarineKorps. In his diary for 21 May von Schröder noted that the OHL had received from 'secure sources' (his quotes) that the British Government had decided to destroy the Flanders submarine bases and that a major offensive was expected against the Belgian coast.[120] As a result von Schröder took two steps. He first ordered his staff to begin a new study that would consider possible enemy operations against the Flanders bases and he then requested that the MarineDivisions send him additional reports detailing the existing defences.

The study undertaken by the MarineKorps' staff was completed very quickly and was received by von Schröder the next day. It outlined the possible goals of any enemy operation against the coast and the likely ways in which the Allies might try to attain their objectives. The enemy's primary goal was believed to be the paralysis of the submarine war. That could be achieved in one of three ways: by blocking the exits to the ports with mines and nets; by destroying the bases through coastal bombardments or by conquering the coast. Each of these options was considered in turn.

Mine and net barriers were considered to be, at best, a nuisance. They could be laid at night close in to the coast but could not be constantly patrolled and therefore could be swept up relatively easily. The report did point out, however, that if the enemy were to lay an effective barrier farther out in the Channel, it would be very difficult for the Germans to do anything about it. Such a barrier would form a much more serious obstacle. However, seeing as how such a barrier had not been laid, it was logical to assume that the British intended to pursue one of their other two options.

The main goal of the British bombardments to this point had been the destruction of the canal locks linking Zeebrugge with Bruges. The Germans expected that these bombardments would continue with even heavier complements of aircraft in support for spotting purposes. Therefore, it would be essential for the MarineKorps to take and hold air superiority so that they would be able to drive off enemy observers and provide reconnaissance for their own guns. There was also concern that the enemy might be able to approach close enough at night to even bombard Bruges which lay only ten kilometres from the coast. There was no real defence against such a bombardment except for the coastal artillery. Destroyers and submarines would be unable to get close enough to the enemy monitors to launch an attack and the flat-bottomed monitors were also very difficult to stop with minefields. Therefore the only real defence against a bombardment was the coastal artillery, but to be truly effective those guns needed aerial spotters. Therefore air superiority was crucial.

They also examined the possibility of a large scale enemy landing and concluded that it was highly unlikely that any such landing could succeed as long as the artillery defences of the coast remained operable. Before a landing could proceed with any hope of success, the British would have to destroy the German coastal guns. This they had so far been unable to do. However, a small landing undertaken with complete surprise was not deemed out of the question. It would be unable to attain a lasting victory, but could do significant damage to the coast or the harbours before being defeated. However, the only way that the Allies could conquer the Belgian coast was by breaking through on the land front.[121]

On the 26th the 1st MarineDivision confirmed this when they reported to the MarineKorps on their defensive plans. Since their main goal was to prevent an enemy landing on the coast and to keep enemy warships as far out to sea as possible the artillery would obviously be the key to the defence of the coast. Along the coast from Raversyde to the Dutch border (a total frontage of forty-two kilometres) there were a total of twenty-four batteries, mostly concentrated around Ostend and Zeebrugge. Most of these ranged from 8.8 to 15cm (a total of sixteen batteries) with eight larger-calibre batteries; the largest of course being *Tirpitz*, *Kaiser Wilhelm II*, and *Deutschland*. These were supplemented by a series of anti-aircraft batteries. All of the batteries were connected by a telephone network that was backed up by light signaling stations. In addition, the major batteries all had their own sets of wireless receivers and transmitters.[122]

Infantry defences were much weaker. The division had the equivalent of three battalions in place immediately along the coast. Most of these troops manned the thirty-three concrete machine gun nests which were scattered along the Flanders beaches. Their job was to sweep the beaches with machine gun fire and, if possible, throw any enemy forces that managed to reach the beach back into the sea.[123]

Due to the coastal artillery, any landing attempt would run into tremendous difficulties because enemy vessels could be brought under attack by the German guns from as far as thirty kilometres away. Therefore a landing could really only be attempted after the coastal artillery was destroyed. Even at night an approach would be difficult. Due to the lack of visibility at night the guns were automatically set to fire salvoes at ranges of one, two and three kilometres. Jacobsen considered it highly unlikely that any landing could succeed and that the British therefore would probably not attempt one. He thought it was much more likely that they would launch a small raid against one of the ports in an effort to destroy valuable materials. He believed that even that type of operation had only a minimal chance of success.

In the unlikely event that an enemy landing did succeed the beach was to be immediately assaulted with heavy artillery to try and prevent reinforcement while the reserve bicycle brigades moved into position for a counter-attack. These reserves consisted of varying numbers of bicycle battalions and companies based around Ostend, Blankenberg, and Zeebrugge. Due to 'Fall K' most of the 1st Division's reserves were allocated to the eastern sector of the front, therefore they received assistance from the 2nd Division which provided the reserves for the area around Ostend.[124] These defences were supplemented by the coastal patrols. During the day, these were carried out by long-range aircraft equipped with radios and at night by the A-I torpedo-boats.

The renewed emphasis on the defence of the coast also impacted the disposition of the Flanders flotillas. On 24 May von Schröder recorded in his war diary that German observation of British signal traffic indicated that the British forces at Harwich and Dover had recently been reinforced. This led him to conclude that an enemy operation against his position was imminent. As a direct result of these reports, he ordered that henceforth the destroyers and torpedo-boats in Flanders would concentrate on defensive patrols and there would be no further offensive sweeps.[125] This order remained in effect until 1918.

On the following day von Schröder received confirmation for his conclusions from Admiral Scheer, who sent a memorandum to the fleet, the MarineKorps and the Naval Staff noting that he expected an allied attack against Flanders to come in late May or early June. Once word of such an attack was confirmed he intended to assemble the entire High Seas Fleet in the Jade and prepare for a sweep into the North Sea in the hopes of catching and destroying a portion of the Grand Fleet, which he expected would cover the operation.[126] Further word came in from the 1st MarineDivision on the 26th. Since allied air activity had increased all along the coast the entire defence network was now to be kept at a high state of alert around the clock.[127]

As a result of the increased state of preparedness, in June, more artillery was transferred to the coastal sector between Ostend and the land front. A new row of batteries made up of field howitzers and equipped with light signals were built three to four kilometres from the coast and connected with communication trenches.

While the intelligence received by the MarineKorps was not strictly accurate, the steps taken to improve the defence of the coast and raise the alertness of the troops were wise moves; the British had just such an operation under discussion in the War Council at that time. That operation was launched on 31 July and became immortalised as the Passchendaele campaign.

THE SECOND PHASE: JUNE – JULY 1917

The second phase of the year ran from the introduction of convoy in May to the beginning of the Third Battle of Ypres at the end of July. For the British it was a period of planning and preparation for their major offensive, while for the MarineKorps it was a period of defence. The submarines continued their depredations but the activities of the surface flotillas were greatly curtailed by von Schröder's order of 24 May. During this period the staff of the MarineKorps expected a large allied offensive and expended most of their effort on modifying and improving their coastal defences.

The Naval War

The German submarines were never able to repeat their dramatic success of April but throughout the second part of the year they continued to deal heavy blows to the world's merchant shipping. During June the total tonnage lost by the allied and neutral nations reached 696,725 tons, still in excess of the 600,000 per month that Holtzendorff promised would force Britain to surrender. In fact, when the number of damaged vessels is added in, the totals reach 800,755 tons.[127] The Flanders flotilla's portion came to

117 ships and 246,436 tons. In exchange they lost one submarine, *UC-66*.[129]

Despite the campaign's successes there was growing concern in the Naval Staff. The British were not showing signs of imminent collapse nor had the submarines been able to hinder the cross-channel transports from Britain to France. Furthermore, in June submarines passing through the Channel reported that allied defences were much stronger than they had been earlier in the year and that even unescorted vessels were much better armed than they had been previously.[130] It certainly did not appear as if the British were on their last legs. This was despite the fact that the submarines had usually reached, and in some months even exceeded, the goals set for them by von Holtzendorff. Hoping to increase the effectiveness of the submarines von Holtzendorff sent out new directives for the campaign in June. In general the new regulations ordered the submarines to focus on the British iron traffic with Spain and their food shipments from Denmark and the Netherlands.

To bring this about the Naval Staff ordered additional submarines to the Bay of Biscay where the submarines of the MarineKorps had already had some success. Since February they had sunk a total of eighty-nine steamers totaling roughly 200,800 tons in that area.[131] Their success led the Naval Staff to expect that even greater results could be gained by the assignment of larger fleet submarines in the area. Additionally the Naval Staff decided to assign two large submarines to patrol the route between Britain and the Netherlands at all times. As an additional measure the UCs were ordered to lay a series of new minefields in the Firth of Forth, between the Orkney and Shetland islands and in the Hebrides.[132] Finally, in order to strike at the Anglo-Dutch convoys and the troop convoys in the Channel, work was begun on new mines equipped with timers that would automatically trigger the mine within three or four days of its laying. The intent was to spread uncertainty in the minds of the British and force them to continuously sweep in front of their convoys.[131] This would slow down the convoys and make them more vulnerable to submarine attack. Fields of these new mines were to be laid around the North Hinder lightship and the Hook of Holland.[134]

The Naval Staff also suggested a new method of attacking convoys, namely sending groups of submarines to launch a joint attack on a single convoy. They hoped that by using groups of submarines the Germans could alleviate the biggest problem posed by the British convoys, which was the fact that an individual submarine generally only had one shot at a convoy before it was attacked by the escorts. This meant that the majority of the ships in the convoy, even if the convoy was attacked, would be untouched. Fortunately for the Entente the Germans were unable to effectively implement this tactic.[135]

Despite the German's best efforts, the submarines saw their tonnage score drop again in July. The totals for that month came to 555,514 tons sunk and 43,736 damaged for a total of 599,250 tons removed from service.[136] Out of this total the Flanders flotilla, which brought two more UB-IIs and UC-IIs each into service in July, accounted for eighty-five ships of 203,066 tons.[137]

Of additional concern to the Germans was the fact that seven submarines were lost in July. The Flanders flotilla lost five of those seven.[138] Due to the heavy losses provision was made in July to send an additional six UCs to Flanders once the dockyards there had the capacity to maintain them. Four were sent immediately and the other two followed later in the year. Eventually von Holtzendorff decided to raise the strength of the Flanders flotilla to forty-six submarines.[139] Despite the losses and the drop in sinkings von Schröder remained optimistic and continued to believe that the campaign would eventually result in the strangulation of Great Britain. He saw the drop-off as purely temporary.

For the war on the surface the summer of 1917 was relatively uneventful. The British continued their air attacks on the Flanders harbours but had only one notable success; they damaged the destroyer S-53 on 3 July and the ship was out of service until January 1918. In general, the air attacks, though heavy, were inconsequential.[140] Of greater importance was a bombardment of Ostend carried out by the Dover Patrol on 4 June. This bombardment, the only one carried out by the Dover Patrol during June and July, resulted in the only surface action of the summer months. That evening, while the British force was enroute to Ostend, S-15 and S-20 were returning from an ineffectual sweep out to the Thornton Bank and encountered the enemy force at 4.20am. Being heavily outgunned, two destroyers against twelve destroyers and one leader, the Germans promptly retreated under the protection of their coastal artillery. The British, however, promptly opened fire and hit S-20 directly in the boiler room before the latter could escape. The hit killed the commander of the destroyer and left S-20 dead in the water. S-15 received two hits as well, one damaged her rudder and the other destroyed one of her turbines, dropping the ship's speed to seventeen knots. Nonetheless she was able to reach the protection of the coastal artillery at which point the British vessels broke off their pursuit. S-20 was lost and four crewmen were killed on the badly damaged S-15 which was towed back to port. Shortly thereafter the bombardment of Ostend began.[141]

The bombardment, which was carried out by two monitors accompanied by six destroyers, and a separate force of two destroyer leaders, four light cruisers, eight destroyers and one leader from Harwich,[142] lasted forty minutes and did serious damage to *G-41* which was in dry-dock at the time. It also lightly damaged *S-55* and *UC-16*. The main British objective, the canal locks, were not seriously damaged though they did take one direct hit. The major result of the bombardment was the sinking of *UC-70* and two barges.[143]

The bombardment had two effects on the Germans. First of all it convinced von Schröder that Ostend was now too vulnerable to remain a useful base. To take its place he ordered that plans be developed to expand the canals to Ghent and to create harbour facilities there that would be capable of handling destroyers and submarines. In order to do this it would be necessary to expand the canals from Antwerp to Ghent as well so that the ships could be assembled in Antwerp and then towed to their new base. He expected that it would take four to five weeks before Ghent would be useable by anything larger than the A-boats. In the end most of the materials from Ostend were towed to Ghent and the expansion of the harbour there was begun.[144]

Furthermore, the bombardment convinced Jacobsen that the gunnery commanders, who he felt had reacted too slowly during the bombardment, needed additional training. As a result he implemented a new training programme for them.[145] The bombardment therefore brought the coastal defences to an increased level of alertness and might, had the planned British coastal landing intended for August gone forward, have had a detrimental effect on its chances for success.[146]

The bulk of the activity of the Flanders destroyer and torpedo-boat flotillas over those two months consisted of defensive patrols and minesweeping. A new British minefield was found by the minesweeper flotilla at the very beginning of June and this field, which was well patrolled by the British, kept the flotillas busy for most of the month. It also proved to be very hazardous. On 25 June *G-96*, which was detailed as an escort for the minesweeping flotilla, ran onto a mine and was lost with all hands.[147]

An additional barrier was laid by the Dover Patrol on 25 July in order to limit any possible interference by the Flanders flotillas against the landing which was expected to begin in two weeks.[148] The day the barrage was laid was thick with fog but the British forces were still spotted by the coastal batteries and were engaged. Later that afternoon the III Flotilla put to sea to search the area and they discovered the new mine and net barriers; before sweeping could begin, however, they were attacked by eight destroyers and one light cruiser and were driven back to the coast. Eventually the Germans were able to begin sweeping this new field and over the course of the next several weeks the Dover Patrol and the Flanders flotillas engaged in a new round of heavy mine-laying by the former and frequent sweeping by the latter.[149]

The minesweeping of the flotillas also led to several minor skirmishes between German and British forces; none of which had any serious impact on the war. An example of one such skirmish took place on 19 June when four German destroyers that were attempting to rescue a downed German plane were attacked by a British motorboat. No damage was done to the Germans and the motorboat was reportedly sunk.[150] The flotillas did plan for the occasional attack on Nieuport and Dunkirk; none of them were actually carried out though.[151] In general the second phase of the year was a quiet interlude for the surface forces of the MarineKorps. Despite that fact they remained a high priority for reinforcements.

On 21 June KorvettenKapitän Kahle, the new Führer der Torpedostreitkräfte Flandern, sent a memorandum to von Schröder pointing out that, in the previous few months, the flotillas had lost five vessels and had two others severely damaged. At the current time he had only twelve functioning ships and he pointed out that without further reinforcements his force would not be ready for action again until August. As a result he requested four new ships for the Destroyer Flotilla and one for the III Flotilla. He hoped that these would be oil-burning vessels rather than the older ships which relied on coal.[152] He got his wish.

On 7 July von Schröder replied to Kahle stating that the Naval Staff had decided to assign eight new destroyers to the MarineKorps as soon as possible.[153] Furthermore von Schröder informed Kahle that the needs of the MarineKorps were now considered by the Naval Staff to be equal to those of the High Seas Fleet. The Naval Staff's plan was for the first eight boats of a new class, the S-113s, to be sent to Flanders between August 1917 and April 1918. Scheer intervened though, by volunteering to send another half-flotilla of destroyers to Flanders in exchange for the return of the three boats from the II Flotilla that had remained in Flanders for repairs. As part of the bargain though von Schröder had to agree that the first eleven of the new destroyers would go to the High Seas Fleet. Von Schröder agreed to Scheer's proposal in order to raise the strength of the Flanders flotillas immediately.[154] The new ships, five V-25-class destroyers, arrived in early August[155] and the Marine-Korps promised to return the three boats of the II Flotilla to the High Seas Fleet by the middle of September.[156]

Later that month, in a letter to von Capelle, von Holtzendorff explained that he intended to raise the strength of the Flanders flotillas by an additional two destroyers as soon as possible and hoped to have a total of four destroyers sent west by the end of the year.[157] Clearly the priorities of the German naval leadership had changed and the Flanders theatre was now seen as critical to the war effort. However, this did not mean that von Schröder and the

MarineKorps always received what they demanded. For example, in June von Schröder asked that several torpedo-boats of a new class, the A-III, be sent to Flanders immediately. Back in February the Naval Staff had ordered the North Sea station to make available for immediate transfer to Flanders an additional 1,500 men to man these boats since they were much better suited to work in the Channel than the A-IIs.[158] Von Schröder intended to use the A-IIIs as a powerful group of minesweepers that could work beyond the protection of the coastal artillery.[159] The first of these new craft were supposed to come into service on 31 March.[160] June arrived and the A-IIIs had still not appeared in Flanders so, at the start of the month, von Schröder wrote to von Holtzendorff renewing his request for at least twelve of these ships.[161] Von Holtzendorff replied on 5 June stating that it was not possible at the present time to transfer any A-IIIs to Flanders because they were needed as minesweepers in the Bight, however, he expected that to change in fall when more ships became available and he hoped that some could then be assigned to Flanders.[162] His decision was confirmed in early July and the MarineKorps was forced to make do until fall with the A-Is and A-IIs they already had.[163]

Despite the growing recognition of the importance of the Flanders theatre it never received the same resources as the High Seas Fleet. To an extent this was only natural since so much money, time and attention had been focused on the latter but the Flanders theatre provided the Germans with opportunities that did not exist anywhere else. Certainly it was important for the High Seas Fleet to have sufficient minesweepers, but by the summer of 1917 the Flanders theatre had become vital to the course of the war. The British recognised this more clearly than the Germans did. They were painfully aware that the Grand Fleet needed to maintain its destroyer strength to meet any possible advance by the High Seas Fleet but that the same was not true for the Germans since they knew when they would and would not sortie the fleet. Therefore they could easily detach forces for other missions (as they did with the destroyers sent to Flanders in the fall and winter of 1916–17). Hence they could transfer large numbers of destroyers to Flanders for a concerted raid against the British convoys and transports whenever they saw fit. The fact that the Germans never did so hardly mattered; the threat was always there. In June and July 1917 the British continued planning measures that they hoped would permanently end to this threat.

The Land War
On land the MarineKorps remained primarily on the defensive during the second phase of 1917 as the MarineDivisions continued their preparations for

the expected allied invasion. They were not completely passive, however, and in July the MarineKorps launched only its second offensive of the war, 'Operation Strandfest.'

Operation Strandfest

Starting in early July, the newly created 3rd MarineDivision began making plans to retake the eastern bank of the Yser river. The operation was christened 'Strandfest' and eventually involved several units from the MarineKorps. The goal of the operation was to liberate the eastern bank of the Yser and bring the western bank of the river under the fire of German guns. It was launched because the Germans expected the British to make a push along the coast and they wanted to have the benefit of the riverbank as a defensive bulwark.[164] The attack was to begin at 8pm on the evening of 9 July with a nine-hour preparatory barrage followed immediately by a diversionary attack from the flamethrower companies of the 2nd MarineDivision. It was to be supported by gunfire from the destroyer and torpedo-boat flotillas.[165] The attack was to include most of the 2nd and 3rd MarineDivisions; a total of six battalions, four companies of engineers plus one flamethrower company, two sections of aircraft, and fifty-eight artillery batteries.[166]

The attack was launched one day later then planned, on 10 July, and took the British completely by surprise. In one day of fighting the Germans destroyed two battalions of British troops and recaptured the eastern bank of the Yser.[167] The battle itself, though very minor, was significant for two reasons. First of all, by retaking the eastern bank of the river the 3rd MarineDivision disrupted the planning of Sir Henry Rawlinson, the British general who was to command the coastal advance in Douglas Haig's master plan for the Third Battle of Ypres. The additional defence supplied by the river bank meant that not only would Rawlinson's men have to advance further to attain their goals but they would also have to cross over the Yser which at that point had only four useable bridges remaining. Secondly, the German victory demonstrated to the German IV army that the units of the MarineKorps were fully capable not only of defending the Channel harbours but also of launching limited offensives.[168] The victory though did not change the strategic posture of the MarineKorps, which remained on the defensive and devoted the bulk of its energy to preparing for an allied invasion.

On 6 June von Schröder sent a copy of the defensive plans for the Flanders coast to Crown Prince Rupprecht. In his letter he reiterated that any serious invasion would, in all likelihood, fail. The only vulnerable spot was the area immediately behind the frontline around Middelkerke. This section was now held by the 3rd MarineDivision but was only weakly supported by coastal artillery. Security against a surprise raid was provided by aerial reconnaissance and defensive patrols by the UB-Is during the day. At night the patrols by the submarines were continued but the air patrols were taken over by the A-Is. The defences were also equipped with numerous spotlights and flares to illuminate any night attack and the coastal batteries were always set to lay down a heavy barrage at fixed distances from the coast and the harbour entrances. The backbone of the infantry defence remained the series of machine gun emplacements that overlooked the beaches. To supplement those the MarineKorps was in the process of constructing a second defensive line.[169] The Crown Prince expressed satisfaction with the defensive measures but asked von Schröder to send him a capable staff officer who could provide advice on naval affairs. He was primarily concerned with the possible locations for enemy landings.[170]

The Germans continued to make adjustments to their defensive plans. One consideration that was given great attention in June was the belief that the attack would probably not come during the day, or, if it did, that it would be protected by a heavy smokescreen. As a result the 1st MarineDivision, which remained in overall command of the defence of the coast, sent new regulations to each of the battery commanders. In the event of the enemy using a smokescreen the guns were to try and target on muzzle flashes or rely on aerial spotters for guidance. Furthermore, each commander was warned to expect a collapse of communications and was told to be prepared for independent decision-making when the attack began.[171]

On 26 June the MarineKorps received further word concerning the expected attack. On that day von Schröder was told that all available information pointed to an imminent allied attack against the German right flank with the intent of destroying the Flanders naval bases. The major attack was expected to come along the coast, just to the south of Nieuport. In all likelihood this attack was to be accompanied by an amphibious landing just behind the main German lines. The IV army ordered that immediate preparations be made for a counter-attack to throw the enemy off the beaches should the landing be initially successful. In particular the 1st MarineDivision was to begin placing additional artillery around the threatened area. Furthermore, von Arnim, the commander of the IV army, planned to send an additional division to the coast once the attack began. Therefore Jacobsen was ordered to send him, as soon as possible, a detailed map of the area showing all the artillery positions for the planned counter-attack, a complete listing of all reserves, and proposals for where the reinforcing division could be put to the best use.[172]

On the following day von Schröder took special note in his war diary of the fact that the 32nd British Division had just replaced the 29th French Division along the coast. He suspected that this was a preliminary move to the upcoming offensive.[173] As a result another feasibility study of an enemy attack on the coast was done in July. It reinforced the earlier conclusion that any coastal landing would face extreme difficulties. If the enemy chose to attack along a beach it would be difficult to land heavy weapons but if they tried to directly attack one of the ports they would run into much heavier defences. For an attack to be successful it would be necessary for the Allies to first destroy the coastal artillery. Given that fact the most likely place for a landing was in the general vicinity of Knocke where the coastal artillery was weakest. Von Schröder concluded that additional heavy artillery was needed to support a counterattack and that approach trenches should be dug to the second defensive line to facilitate the transfer of the four reserve battalions to the front. He also decided that additional defences were needed around Ostend and Zeebrugge.[174] The IV army agreed with his assessment.[175]

The defences of the harbours themselves were far from insignificant. At Zeebrugge for example the defences consisted of, in addition to the coastal batteries, five strongpoints set up at varying distances around the perimeter of the city and an additional three strongpoints on the harbour mole. The strongpoints consisted of concrete pillboxes surrounded by barbed wire and equipped with two-to-four machine guns. One of the strongpoints, which doubled as the main signal station and headquarters for the commander of the defences, also had a battery of 3.7cm guns. In addition each strongpoint was arranged in such a way that it could provide supporting fire for every other strongpoint. Finally, each one constantly had a full garrison. The strongpoint at the head of the mole was the most heavily armed. It had, in addition to its machine guns, two 3.7cm, three 9cm, and four 8.8cm guns. The entire system was eventually surrounded by a single wall of barbed wire.[176]

On 25 July the MarineKorps conducted a table exercise to test their coastal defences. The 'blue' side in the war-game represented the forces of Great Britain which, for purposes of the game, landed around Knocke after several days of heavy naval bombardments. The coastal artillery was assumed to have been reduced to 50 percent effectiveness by the bombardments and all the auxiliary guns along the dunes destroyed. Also, a second British landing was underway at Den Han. The assignment of the blue team was to break out of the beachhead at Knocke. The 'red' team was to contain them and muster reinforcements to throw both landings into the sea.[177]

The game justified the defensive measures of the MarineKorps. The red forces were able to contain the Knocke landing while mustering reinforcements to counter-attack the landing at Den Han. It took just over five hours for the reserves to arrive and begin the counter-attack. Both landings were beaten back. The only negative result for the red team was that the phone lines of the two MarineDivisions were unable to handle the necessary traffic.[178]

The war-game vindicated the preparations that von Schröder and his men had made. As a result they were confident in their ability to throw back any attempted landing. The one area of concern was that they lacked sufficient fighters to maintain control of the air; as a result, more aircraft were requested from the IV army on 29 July.[179] Before that request could be answered the long awaited allied attack began, though not along the coast. It was launched to the south and became known as Passchendaele.

Planning Passchendaele[180]

Ever since the Belgian coast fell into German hands in October of 1914 the Royal Navy had been very concerned about the Belgian ports and the possible use the Germans might make of them. From that early stage, the navy, which had originally left the ports intact at the request of the BEF, urged the British army to recapture the coast. When it became apparent late in 1914 that the war in the west had stalemated and that there would be no rapid reconquest of the coast the navy began to discuss other ways of dealing with the harbours, including bombardments and blocking schemes. No blocking attempt was carried out however and the bombardments, as we have seen, were essentially ineffective. Therefore the navy returned to the idea of a coastal offensive.

There were varying reasons for why such an offensive had not been launched earlier. In 1914 the British simply did not have the necessary manpower. Their only force was the small BEF. Secondly, and this was largely the result of their lack of forces, they were tied, for all intents and purposes, to the decisions of the French High Command and the latter was more interested, understandably, in throwing the Germans out of occupied France. This meant that there was to be no Flanders offensive for the Allies in 1914. By 1915 the factors of the equation had begun to change.

The British created various plans early in 1915 for the liberation of the Belgian coast, several of them sprang from the fertile mind of Winston Churchill. One such plan, dated from January 1915, posited an advance down the coast by the British army with the support of the Royal Navy and a landing of additional troops in Zeebrugge. The French, however, refused to participate and wanted the major allied effort in 1915 to be directed against occupied

France.[181] By the middle of 1915 British attention had been diverted from Flanders to the Near East with the beginning of the Gallipoli campaign.

In November, in the aftermath of the failure at the Dardanelles, a new plan was created to seize the Flanders coast. This time a diversionary attack was planned around Ypres and the main advance was once again to be directed from Nieuport toward Ostend and was to be supplemented by an amphibious landing near Middelkerke.[182] Once again, however, the attack was postponed due to French resistance.

In 1916, the change in the strategic position in the Channel caused by the dispatch of significant numbers of German destroyers to Flanders made the reconquest of the coast seem all the more necessary. Beginning in January of that year Sir Douglas Haig, the newly appointed Commander of the British Army in France, began discussions with Admiral Bacon concerning the feasibility of an attack in Flanders. Haig also consulted with Joffre and won his consent, finally, to a British attack along the coast provided that the British also participated in the joint attack Joffre had planned at the Somme.[183] The Flanders attack though never took place, mainly because of the German attack at Verdun. That attack so badly damaged the French army that the British were forced to carry out the attack on the Somme virtually on their own.

The key event that pushed the Royal Navy to lobby heavily for an attack in Flanders in late 1916 or 1917 was the German destroyer raid of 26 October. That raid, and its immediate successors, convinced the British that the Germans now held the initiative in the Channel. This was a very dangerous state of affairs that could not be allowed to continue. The only way to remove the threat was to remove the bases.[184] To that end Jellicoe, Bacon and Haig began lobbying the government to make the seizure of Ostend and Zeebrugge one of the army's main goals for 1917. By the end of 1916 these efforts had paid off and both the French and the British governments lent their support to an attack in Flanders.[185] However, the attack encountered new difficulties before the turn of the year.

With the fall of Asquith and the rise of David Lloyd-George as the new prime minister Haig's plans were put in jeopardy. Lloyd-George preferred an offensive from Italy against the Austrians rather than a repeat of the Somme and opposed Haig's plans for a Flanders offensive.[186] This forced Haig once again to lobby for his plan. Initially Lloyd-George supported an alternate plan proposed by Joffre's successor as commander of the French army, General Nivelle. This plan proposed an allied attack further south near Artois that would be carried out primarily by the French army. This attack failed and resulted in the famous mutiny of the French army. This left the Entente back at square one, so to speak. There was very little support, either in the government or among the Allies for Lloyd-George's Italian scheme and once again Haig was allowed to plead his case for an attack in Flanders. He was strongly supported by the new First Sea Lord, Admiral Jellicoe, who by April was convinced that if the army did not seize the German bases in Flanders the British could not continue the war into 1918.

In March Jellicoe explained:

> 'The occupation and fortification of Zeebrugge and Ostend by the Germans has greatly added to the difficulties of the navy. These ports . . . are a constant menace to our cross-channel communications and to our south-eastern coasts. Their fortifications are very strong and they are quite invulnerable to purely naval attack.'[187]

Jellicoe was not primarily concerned with the submarines, but rather with the destroyers and torpedo-boats. He believed that there were twelve German submarines working out of Flanders, a figure which was little more than one third of the actual number in the flotilla.[188] That small a number of submarines did not pose a serious threat; what was serious was the presence of German destroyers in Flanders.

Starting with the raid of 26 October and continuing up until von Schröder's decision in May to restrict the destroyers and torpedo-boats to defensive patrols, the Germans had continually harassed British patrols in the Channel area. While none of their raids had caused catastrophic damage that was not due to British counter-measures but rather to the lack of sufficient force in the Flanders flotillas. Von Schröder simply did not have enough strength to deal a really decisive blow. Admiral Bacon admitted that he had lost the initiative in the Channel and really could do nothing to prevent the German raids. Bombardments of the coast were ineffective because the German coastal batteries forced any bombardment to be undertaken at extreme range and the German ships could simply leave their harbours and proceed to Bruges that was out of range of the British guns. Any damage that was done to the ports was easily repaired. Similar problems attended any attempt at blocking the harbours since it would be relatively easy for the Germans to dredge around block ships or even blast holes into the middle of them. These were the means of striking at Flanders that were preferred by the Prime Minister but it was apparent to the responsible naval leadership that only a land assault could permanently remove the threat of the destroyers.[189]

By June Jellicoe's predictions had turned very dire. It was then that he made his oft-quoted prediction that the British need not plan for the summer of

1918 because they would lose the war before then if they did not retake the Flanders coast. It was Jellicoe's predictions that eventually turned the tide and led the War Policy Committee to accept the plans for an attack in Flanders.

In short, the British feared that at some point the Germans might realise the advantage the Flanders positions gave them and might decide to strike with serious force into the Channel. The implications of such an attack, which could not be prevented, were truly frightening to the Royal Navy. So the planning went forward.[190]

The plan which Haig and Bacon eventually settled on was a modified version of the one first proposed in late 1915. It included an amphibious landing at Middelkerke, which, incidentally, several members of the Royal Navy thought did not stand a chance,[191] and a large push east out of Nieuport. In Haig's plan, however, the coastal advance became secondary and what had been originally intended as a feint attack at Ypres now became the heart of the assault.

Haig's plan was to proceed in very deliberate stages. The first phase would involve the capture of the ridgelines around Ypres in preparation for a major assault to break out of the salient there and drive towards the coast.[192] Once the British army reached the vicinity of Roulers then the advance from Nieuport was to begin. For the coastal portion of the offensive, the original plan of which was thrown off by 'Operation Strandfest', two British divisions were to push east from Nieuport while two other divisions were held in reserve to exploit any breakthroughs. A fifth division was to be landed by the Royal Navy behind German lines at Middelkerke.[193] If the coastal advance had sufficient success it would then become the new axis for the advance. Haig hoped he could sweep all the way to the Dutch frontier and win a decisive victory that would break the German army and throw them completely out of Belgium, hopefully winning the war in 1917.

The most difficult part of the entire operation was the coastal landing. The plans worked out by Bacon and Haig called for the landing of 13,750 men as well as three tanks and twelve artillery pieces along the beaches before Middelkerke. The force would have to move in at night or else be covered by a thick smokescreen in order to be protected from the German coastal guns. The fleet was to move in as three separate columns, each with 4,500 men, one tank and four guns, carried on specially constructed pontoons which were to be towed between monitors and dragged right up to the beach.[194] The 1st Division, which was assigned the task, was secreted away in a specially built camp in France where they built replicas of the coastline and spent months practicing the assault. Bacon was convinced the attack would be a success, as was Sir Henry Rawlinson, who was slated to command the advance from Nieuport. Haig himself had few doubts but was determined that the landing would only take place after his troops had reached Roulers and could provide support. With their plan in place the British began their prepatory bombardment of the German positions around Ypres on 21 July. Ten days later the major attack began. The war quite literally hung in the balance.[195]

THE FINAL PHASE: AUGUST - DECEMBER 1917

The second phase of 1917 came to an end when the British troops went over the top at Ypres on 31 July. At that point the most critical stage of the entire year began. It was not just the Third Battle of Ypres that made this a critical period in the war, there were also things going on within Germany in July 1917 that would have tremendous consequences for the future. In early July Matthias Erzberger, the leader of the Catholic Centre Party, presented his own study of the submarine campaign and demonstrated that the claims put forward by the Naval Staff at Pless were faulty and that the submarines were not having the desired effect. His arguments were bolstered by the fact that Holtzendorff's original prediction that Britain would surrender within six months of the start of the unrestricted campaign had been proven incorrect. That original six month period ended in July and there was as yet no sign that Britain was prepared to drop out of the war. This precipitated a major crisis within Germany and led to the famous war aims debate of 2–7 July and the 'Peace Resolution' of the 19th. This crisis led directly to the fall from power of the German Chancellor, Theobold von Bethmann-Hollweg. He was replaced by a non-entity, Georg Michaelis, who was essentially the servant of the commanders of the OHL, Paul von Hindenburg and Erich Ludendorff. From July 1917 on Germany was essentially a military dictatorship ruled by the OHL.[196]

Shortly afterward, right at the beginning of August, there were major disturbances in the German fleet. These were essentially hunger strikes by the lower ratings who were protesting against the poor food on the ships. The strikes eventually resulted in five sailors being executed for treason.[197] Though these initial disturbances were successfully repressed they were a sign of things to come.

While these crises raged within Germany the MarineKorps was preoccupied with the declining results of the submarine campaign and the progress of the allied attack at Ypres.

The Land War: August – December

The British assault from Ypres began on 31 July and the left wing of the advance was able to achieve its initial goals even though the right wing quickly bogged down. This set a pattern that continued for the entire first month of the battle, which quickly deteriorated into a typical Western Front slogging match. The campaign consisted of eight separate battles stretching from August into November:

The Battle of Pilckem Ridge	(July 31–August 2)
The Battle of Langemarck	(August 16–18)
The Battle of Menin Road Ridge	(September 20–25)
The Battle of Polygon Wood	(September 26–Oct 3)
The Battle of Broodseinde	(October 4)
The Battle of Poelcappelle	(October 9)
The 1st Battle of Passchendaele	(October 12)
The 2nd Battle of Passchendaele	(Oct. 26–Nov 10)[198]

The MarineKorps was not directly involved in the fighting at Ypres; their sector of the line was further north. However, von Schröder and his officers were very concerned about the fighting to their south.

Von Schröder and his staff first felt the impact of the Passchendaele campaign when the German army attempted to take over some of the duties of the MarineKorps. In late July the IV army proposed that the Guard Korps take over both the sector of the land front that was currently held by the MarineKorps and the coastal defences from Nieuport to Ostend. As part of this arrangement the coastal artillery from Ostend to the frontline would be placed under the direct control of the IV army.[199]

This led to a vehement protest from von Schröder who believed that it was essential for the entire coastal area to be kept under a united command. This would facilitate the defender's ability to turn back any assault from either land or sea. In addition, he argued that the portion of the land front controlled by the MarineKorps was an integral part of the entire reconnaissance and communications network that the Korps had created. If this sector was taken over by another unit it would create tremendous confusion. His main concern though was that the MarineKorps retain control over the coastal artillery. He concluded his protest by asserting that if the IV army went forward with this plan it would destroy the MarineKorps and ruin three years of effort by the German navy.[200] Apparently von Schröder was convincing; nothing further was heard from the IV army about the scheme.

Von Schröder and his staff were also busy continually improving the defences along the coast. On 4 August the 1st MarineDivision sent a report to the IV army concerning these defences. They reported that Ostend was now covered by three large batteries; *Eylau*, *Hindenburg* and *Irene*. The harbour itself was protected by five machine gun emplacements each of which was equipped with two guns. There were also machine guns set up in the houses along the western side of the town. As for Zeebrugge, a battery that was designed so that it could cover the entire town was under construction in the center of the mole. To provide additional defence the *Friedrichsort* battery had been resighted so that it now also covered the town. Furthermore an additional line of defensive works was being built behind the beaches. It consisted of isolated machine gun emplacements that would supplement the main defences if the Entente forces actually made it off the beaches.[201]

As additional security the MarineKorps reconnoitered the area east of Zeebrugge to check for possible landing sites. None were found. The MarineKorps considered all the terrain from Zeebrugge to the Dutch border to be unsuitable for a rapid advance from the beaches. They believed that any landing in this area would be relatively easy to contain. The major concern on the eastern end of the front was to prevent a successful allied landing in Zeebrugge itself. Such a landing, if it succeeded, would immediately give the enemy a working harbour and good roads which they could use to spread out quickly into the countryside.[202] Though any such landing would be very difficult that didn't mean the Entente wouldn't attempt it.

As the battle around Ypres continued additional defences were built along the coast. By 17 August the 1st MarineDivision had erected a new series of guns ranging in calibre from 3.7 to 12cm all along the coast. These were intended as supplements to the larger emplacements and were intended strictly for use against an enemy that had already landed on the beach. The Germans hoped that the presence of these guns would allow them to use the larger batteries to attack any enemy ships that accompanied a landing. By the end of August Jacobsen finally felt confident that the beach defences were ready to turn back any allied invasion.[203]

On 22 August General Ludendorff issued a statement on the state of the war to all the major commands. In it he mentioned that the forces around Ypres were holding and that the situation there was satisfactory; however, further attacks were to be expected during the remainder of the year. He claimed that the British attack, which he believed was aimed at throwing Germany out of Belgium, was a sign that the German submarines were taking their toll on Britain. He did admit that there were serious problems within Germany, especially with regard to rationing, but in general, the German position was stable and the outlook for the war remained favourable.[204]

This certainly seemed to be true along the MarineKorps' front, which remained quiet until the British successes at Menin Road Ridge and Polygon Wood at the end of September. At that point von Arnim became convinced that the expected invasion was imminent. He was particularly concerned that the British would win air superiority over the beaches and would thus be able to hinder the effectiveness of the coastal artillery. He hoped that the aircraft of the MarineKorps would be able to maintain control of the air over the coast on their own since he could not spare any reinforcements. To ease his mind he wrote to von Schröder to find out precisely what measures had been taken to prepare the air services for their role in a battle along the coast.[205]

He received an answer on 30 September. The MarineKorps' air commander reported that three observers accompanied by three fighters carried out reconnaissance flights at dawn each day and that an additional six fighters were held at ten minutes readiness to give aid should it be necessary. Once the initial planes returned to base, an additional three observers set out to patrol the barrage. They were to look for enemy naval forces and prevent the enemy from carrying out aerial reconnaissance along the coast. Additionally, in the afternoon long-range reconnaissance flights were carried out. The planes assigned to these missions generally travelled out to the mouth of the Thames. If enemy aircraft were sighted the air forces of the Korps had standing orders to immediately engage and drive off the enemy.[206]

Despite the concern of von Arnim all remained quiet along the Marine-Korps' front until late October when the coast was suddenly put on alert. In late October the MarineKorps received a report from a German agent informing them that a major British action would be launched against the Belgian coast on either 20 or 21 October. As a direct result of that warning all aerial reconnaissance was extended as far as the Thames and the daily patrols were reinforced with extra fighters. The torpedo-boat patrols were also extended further out to sea and all ships were ordered to leave Ostend.[207] The expected attack never materialised and, aside from the usual British coastal bombardments, nothing occurred. The alert though did launch a fresh effort by the MarineKorps to improve the coastal defences yet again.[208]

In November, even as it became apparent to the British that the Third Battle of Ypres was not going to be a success, the MarineKorps continued their build up. They did so not only because of the scare they received in October but also because Ludendorff, on 1 November, issued a new statement on the condition of the war in which he called attention to the defences along the coast. In that statement, he reiterated that the heavy allied attacks in Flanders were certain evidence that the submarine campaign was having the desired effect in Great Britain. He also pointed out that German armies were now occupying the Ukraine and that Russia was about to leave the war. Aside from a small coal shortage the war was going extremely well and if the army could defeat the allied campaign in the autumn Germany should be in a good position come the following spring. Since it was necessary to defeat the current allied offensive, Ludendorff called particular attention to the state of the defences along the coast and urged that they be expanded.[209]

Also on the 1st the IV army sent a scathing memorandum to the 1st MarineDivision complaining that the planned second line of defence was not yet complete. General von Arnim wanted it to be finished immediately.[210] To make an early completion possible the army assigned an additional engineer company to the task.[211] Von Arnim's concern briefly turned to panic following the British capture of Passchendaele on 10 November. After the fall of the city he met with von Schröder personally to determine what the effect on the submarine war would be if the German army was forced to abandon the Belgian coast. This alarmed von Schröder, who immediately wrote to the Naval Staff to find out whether or not this was being seriously considered. He then ordered the 1st MarineDivision to reassess their defences to find out if an enemy landing was a serious threat.[212]

The 1st MarineDivision finished its assessment one week later. Jacobsen once again reiterated that a large invasion could not succeed though he did point out that there was a vulnerable sector between Ostend and the land front in the vicinity of Middelkerke. The defences there were relatively light and based entirely on coastal artillery. If that artillery was destroyed, for example by a coastal bombardment, then a landing in that area was possible. (This is essentially what the British intended to do.) Jacobsen ruled out the possibility of a successful surprise landing in either Zeebrugge or Ostend because he believed that the defences of the two cities were too strong. As for other possibilities, he believed that it might be possible to land a small force of roughly 100 or so men on one of the open beaches along the coast, though he believed that any such force would be unable to establish any kind of beachhead, rendering any major invasion unlikely. If the British were to attempt a landing he believed it would most likely be a surprise attack against the Netherlands whose defences were not nearly so formidable as the German's in Belgium.[213] This report apparently put both von Arnim's and von Schröder's minds at ease.

Though both the army and the navy were agreed on the importance of retaining Belgium, the latter part of 1917 saw the two organisations once again at loggerheads; this time over the use of the coastal artillery. Once again the MarineKorps was at the centre of their dispute.

In early August the Guard Korps inquired as to whether or not it was possible for the coastal artillery to be used against the land front as well as against naval targets. The MarineKorps replied that yes it was possible, but not recommended since frequent firing would quickly wear out the barrels of the guns and that any weakening of the coastal artillery would weaken the entire coastal defence system. The issue rested there until 16 November. On that day the OHL wrote to the Naval Staff requesting the permanent transfer of two 28cm guns from the MarineKorps to the IV army. Furthermore, Ludendorff wanted all the artillery in the area of the IV army to be placed directly under the command of von Arnim. This meant that *all* the German coastal guns would be removed from von Schröder's command. Ludendorff stated that the heavy fighting currently underway in Flanders made it imperative for the IV army to have as much artillery support as possible.[214]

These demands were forwarded from von Holtzendorff to von Schröder who replied to them on 17 November. He argued in very strong terms that if the navy acquiesced in this move it would greatly hinder his ability to defend the coast since the coastal guns were the backbone of his entire system. He could spare four mobile 28cm guns and possibly the battery *Pommern* on a temporary basis but he was completely opposed to turning over the entirety of the coastal artillery to the IV army.[215]

This response was sent, verbatim, to the OHL by von Holtzendorff who added his own comments on a separate memorandum. He argued that the IV army did not require direct control over all of the coastal artillery since the navy was willing to support the IV army in any way possible as long as the coast was not threatened. He added that the MarineKorps had the most experience with the coastal guns and that it should be the 'responsible authority' where the batteries were concerned. He also mentioned that the IV army had recently returned to the MarineKorps two 28cm batteries that had been temporarily assigned to the land front. The guns of both batteries had such severe wear on their barrels that they were no longer accurate enough to be useful against naval targets. He wanted to be certain that this would not occur in the future. He concluded by arguing that if the war was to end in an acceptable peace the MarineKorps to have sufficient weapons with which to defend the coast.[216]

In the end a compromise was reached. The MarineKorps received replacements for the guns worn out by the IV army and, on 19 December, two 28cm and twelve 17cm guns were transferred from the coast to the land front. The

MarineKorps also turned over control of the battery *Pommern* to the IV army so that it could be used to bombard allied positions in Flanders.[217]

Despite the fears of the IV army and the MarineKorps, 1917 ended quietly on the land front. The major British attack at Ypres died out without ever reaching Roulers. As a result the coastal advance and the amphibious landing at Middelkerke never took place. What might have happened had they been carried out will obviously never be known but given the existing information a reasonable hypothesis can be created.

Even after the war Admiral Bacon remained convinced that his plan would have worked and that the Germans would at the very least have been driven from Ostend. Few historians, however, have looked closely at the plan. Most have simply dismissed it as part of the failure at Passchendaele. The one exception is Andrew Wiest. Wiest, in his study of the intended landing, also seems convinced that the landing would have succeeded. However, he does not consult any of the German records. Given the advanced state of the Flanders defences it seems highly unlikely that the British landing would have been anything other than a disaster. Even at night the attack could not have proceeded with a reasonable chance of success as long as the German coastal artillery was intact. The pre-requisite to any successful British attack on Flanders was the destruction of the coastal guns. Admiral Bacon had been trying to destroy those with coastal bombardments since 1915 and had not succeeded. In fact, since the completion of the batteries the German forces in Flanders had possessed a safe zone near the shore where the British fleet dared not tread. The destruction of these guns would have required the Royal Navy to move into close range and carry out a series of artillery duels the most likely would have been disastrous for the fleet. As the British had learned at Gallipoli it was very difficult to use relatively vulnerable naval vessels to assault fortifications along the shore. In any such artillery duel the Germans possessed many advantages. Yes, the batteries could have been destroyed but the cost in ships and lives would have been prohibitive. This was something that Bacon and Rawlinson preferred not to risk. Bacon instead intended to advance right under the eyes of the coastal guns behind the protection of a smokescreen. This would no doubt have hampered the German gunnery but it seems unlikely that it would have crippled the artillery to such an extent that a major landing would have become possible.

Furthermore, getting ashore was not the end result. At that point the mission of any landing force was only beginning. Bacon and Rawlinson mistakenly assumed that there were only two brigades stationed along the coast. They believed that these could be relatively quickly and easily overwhelmed by an entire British division. What they did not realise was that the Germans actually had nearly a division and a half worth of troops both stationed along the coast and held back as reserves. While the British troops were trying to get over the sea wall they would have come under fire from the machine gun emplacements along the beach and, if they did manage to gain a foothold, they would have had to hold it against heavy counter-attacks. The latter, if the coastal guns were still in operation, most likely could not have been effectively hindered by naval fire. Given the strength of the defences prepared by the MarineKorps and the fact that the element of surprise, which both Rawlinson and Bacon saw as essential, was absent, the landing would most likely have ended in a disaster that would have dwarfed the failure at the Dardanelles. The inability of the British army to reach Roulers may, ironically, have prevented the destruction of the British 1st Division. It can only be guessed what kind of impact a major disaster like that might have had on the course of the war. Passchendaele may be considered a dismal affair by the British but it could have been much worse. As it was, the failure of the British at Ypres guaranteed that the war would continue into 1918.

The Naval War: August – December

What of the naval war during the latter part of 1917? For the most part the trends outlined in the first half of the year continued. The successes of the submarines continued to decline and the destroyers and torpedo-boats were still limited to a purely defensive role.

The Submarine Campaign

During the latter half of 1917, the strength of the Flanders submarine flotilla remained fairly constant at around thirty submarines. These were still predominantly UB-IIs and UC-IIs. From August to December the flotilla contained three UB-Is and, generally, seven UB-IIs (one was lost in November and not replaced). These vessels continued to work primarily in the Hoofden and on coastal patrols. As a result they suffered very few losses; just one in the entire five-month period. The UCs were not so fortunate.

The number of UC-Is started at four in August but by December two of those had been lost. The UC-IIs, the flotilla workhorses, suffered the worst losses. In August there were seventeen of these craft assigned to Flanders and their numbers steadily dropped; to sixteen in September, fifteen in October, eleven in November, and to just eight by December. The losses were not replaced.[218] The flotillas did receive new submarines during the latter half of the year but they were of a new type, the UB-III.

The UB-III was a new and improved version of the UB-II. These boats displaced about 500 tons and were more maneuverable than their predecessors. They were able to dive more quickly than the older ships and were equipped with 8.8cm deck guns that were upgraded to 10.5cm in 1918. In addition, each UB-III was equipped with five torpedo tubes, four of them in the bow. They had a range of 4,220 nautical miles at a surface speed of six knots and fifty-five nautical miles submerged. Their top speed was thirteen knots on the surface and eight submerged.[219] They were a significant improvement over the UB-IIs. These new subs, which were put into production in late 1916, began to arrive in Flanders in August 1917. Two were activated in August and by December there were seven serving in the flotilla. They were initially restricted to the Hoofden, until November, when they were sent into the English Channel for the first time. Each UB-III was limited to one operation per month during the remainder of 1917. They did not become a truly active part of the flotilla until 1918.[220]

The success which the submarines had been enjoying over the course of the year drastically tapered off during August and September. In August the Germans destroyed 472,372 tons of neutral and allied shipping. This was down from 555,514 tons in July and the total dropped even further in September, to 353,602 tons.[221] With the addition of damaged vessels the numbers came to 538,779 tons in August and 450,187 in September.[222] Out of those totals the Flanders flotilla accounted for seventy-seven vessels, equaling 203,598 tons in August and eighty-six ships of 167,610 tons in September.[223]

The declining numbers of sinkings were largely due to improvements in the Entente's defences. By August the British were making increased use of aircraft and towed balloons in anti-submarine patrols. With these measures the British could spot German submarines before the latter could spot enemy ships. This meant that the submarines could either be avoided or attacked at a safe distance from any convoys. In short, it robbed the submarines of initiative and surprise.

At the same time the British stepped up their bombardments of the Channel ports. Some of these were serious. For example, in September the constant bombardments of Ostend did serious damage to the port facilities.[224] The Germans did not have solutions for these problems but hoped that the arrival of large numbers of UB-IIIs in 1918 would slowly reverse the trends.[225] They also understood that their primary problem was the introduction of a convoy system by the British and in September they began casting about for new ways of dealing with that.

By that point it had become clear to von Holtzendorff that the British had permanently adopted the convoy system and that it was the primary reason why the submarines were having so many difficulties. As he explained in a letter to Scheer and von Schröder on 21 September, even if a submarine was able to find a convoy, which was a difficult task in itself, it would most likely only get one or possibly two shots at the convoy before the escorts either drove it off or sunk it. The logical response, according to von Holtzendorff, but one which was difficult to implement, was to have multiple submarines attack individual convoys. To try and accomplish this he wanted to send submarines to sea in pairs. They would then patrol in tandem and listen for word that a convoy was approaching their area. Then they could launch a joint attack on it.[226]

Von Holtzendorff had other ideas as well. For example he returned to his idea of sowing mines with timed fuses in the Channel. The hope was that these would sow confusion amongst the British and, if they discharged at the correct time, could possibly force a convoy to scatter so that it could be attacked by submarines waiting in the general vicinity.[227] However, the Germans were unable to put either of these schemes into practice before the end of the war. Defeating the convoys remained an insurmountable task.

Despite their problems, the submarine campaign experienced a brief resurgence in October 1917. Sinkings for that month climbed back to 466,542 tons or, with damaged vessels included, 528,033 tons.[228] The Flanders flotilla accounted for sixty ships and 155,039 tons but lost five UC-IIs. This was the highest number of submarines lost in a single month so far. Many of the losses were caused by new mine and net barriers that had been laid near the coast and were guarded by powerful enemy patrols. The new barriers led von Schröder to once again call for more torpedo-boats lest the Flanders harbours be closed entirely.[229]

The serious losses incurred by the UC-IIs in October had other repercussions as well. They had a very detrimental effect on the ability of the flotilla to continue its mine-laying operations. To make matters worse there were no UCs set to come into service in the near future. As a result von Holtzendorff urged the fleet to develop a new mine that could be launched from the torpedo-tubes of the UBs.[230] However, like the effort to plant timed mines along the convoy routes, this scheme was stillborn.

November turned out to be the worst month of the year for the German submarines. The tonnage sunk dropped to 302,599 tons. Even with the inclusion of damaged vessels it only reached 370,828 tons.[231] The vessels of the Flanders flotillas accounted for nearly two-thirds of this total. They sank fifty-seven ships totaling 193,714 tons.[232] The reason for this was the fact that, as the convoy system became more comprehensive, the submarines were forced to hunt closer to shore and to concentrate in the coastal areas. These were the normal hunting grounds for the Flanders flotillas and therefore their activities became more important.[233]

In December the submarines enjoyed renewed success. In the last month of the year, eleven months into the campaign that was supposed to force Britain to its knees in six months, the submarines destroyed 411,766 tons and damaged another 86,389 tons for a total loss in world shipping of 498,155 tons.[234] Out of this total the Flanders flotillas accounted for 68 ships totaling 205,329 tons.[235] This was in spite of torpedo problems that the flotilla began to experience in late November,[236] perhaps the pendulum was swinging back in Germany's favour? However, the British soon proved that this was not to be the case.

From early 1915 on the British had been searching for a way to close the English Channel to German submarines. The most notable effort was the Cross-Channel Barrage, which was a dismal failure. Submarines were easily able to pass over the nets on the surface and several times even when a net was fouled the mines attached to it did not function properly. The Channel remained the major highway for German submarines going to and from their various stations until late in 1917.

In December 1917, von Schröder mentioned that the British had instituted a new patrol of the Channel and had laid new net barriers that were supplemented by what he called a 'light barrier' patrolled by British destroyers. This new development was making the Channel passage extremely hazardous.[237] He was referring to the new Channel Barrage laid in late November 1917. This Barrage had its origins in changes within the leadership of the Royal Navy.

On 17 November the Admiralty created a new committee known as the Channel Barrage Committee. It was led by Rear-Admiral Roger Keyes and its duty was to investigate ways by which German submarines could be barred from passing through the Dover Strait. The committee made a number of suggestions. First of all, a new series of deep minefields consisting of over 9,500 mines staggered in a step formation was laid from Folkestone to Cape Gris Nez. Then, to force submarines to dive into the new minefields instead of passing by on the surface, the entire area was illuminated by flares and spotlights. This created von Schröder's 'light barrier.'[238]

These changes, particularly the illumination of the entire area by spotlights mounted on ships, were opposed by Admiral Bacon who only reluctantly agreed to implement them. Unfortunately for Bacon the new barrage paid immediate dividends as *UB-56* was forced to dive into the minefield and was destroyed on the first night of the new barrage's existence.[239] Shortly afterward Bacon was removed from his post and was replaced at Dover by Keyes.[240] By forcing the Germans on to the surface and illuminating them, the new Barrage made the Channel passage too dangerous and by early 1918 the German submarines were forced to proceed around Scotland to reach their cruising areas. Von Schröder and the MarineKorps did not simply acquiesce in this, and in early 1918, the Germans renewed their destroyer raids against the British patrols.[241]

By the end of the year it was readily apparent that 'the last card' had failed. Von Holtzendorff's optimistic prediction that Britain would be forced to sue for peace by the summer of 1917 had not come true even though the submarines had performed nearly as well as had been expected and, in some instances, April for example, far beyond expectations. Over the course of the year the Germans lost sixty-three submarines[242] and destroyed well over 2 million tons of enemy and neutral shipping, yet the war went on. What had happened?

In his history of World War One, Holger Herwig lays out several reasons for the failure of the unrestricted campaign. Some were deficiencies with the submarines themselves; they were too slow and were spotted too easily by the leaking of air from the submarine or from its torpedoes. There were tactical problems as well, probably the most detrimental being that the British, through Room 40, were able to read the German codes. The real problem, however, was not a lack of effective submarines or faulty tactics. As we have seen the submarines basically did what was expected of them in terms of destroying British shipping. The real problem was that von Holtzendorff's calculations were wrong. He had clearly underestimated the ability of Britain to sustain shipping losses by adjusting their imports and implementing rationing programmes. He also overestimated the terror that the submarine campaign would induce in neutral nations. Many of these nations were initially frightened off but then returned to doing business with Great Britain. Furthermore, he clearly underestimated the British will to continue the war. He apparently believed that the British people would never be able to withstand the privations which the Germans had been experiencing since 1915 (rationing and food shortages).[243]

Hence the real problem the German submarine campaign faced was that it was based on an overly optimistic view of the situation. The German Government took their great gamble based upon faulty assumptions and despite the best efforts of the crews, of their submarines they were unable to drive Britain out of the war. In the process they added to their list of foes the world's most powerful neutral, the United States. The effect on the morale of the Entente of the promise of virtually limitless numbers of American soldiers cannot be overestimated. The war would continue until November 1918 but the failure of the submarine campaign had already sealed the fate of Imperial Germany.

The Surface Campaign

The destroyers and torpedo-boats of the Flanders flotillas remained on a defensive footing in the latter half of 1917. Their two major tasks were minesweeping and patrolling the coast.

The minesweeping flotilla had difficulty carrying out its responsibilities due to the presence of British patrols along the mine and net barriers. In order to try and alleviate this problem, the Germans began to use their destroyers and torpedo-boats as escorts for the minesweepers. This presented its own problems though; in particular it put the very valuable destroyers in grave danger. In fact, while engaged in escort duty in August, both *V-81* and *S-15* were severely damaged by mines. This led to brief discussions within the MarineKorps over the wisdom of using the destroyers this way but von Schröder decided that the work of the minesweepers was too important and that these risks would have to be run.[244] This almost inevitably led to more damage. In November *A-50*, one of the new torpedo-boats, struck a mine, broke in half and sank in about twenty seconds. Fourteen of her crew of thirty-two were saved. To make matters worse, in the midst of the rescue efforts, *S-54* struck a mine and was severely damaged herself.[245] Nonetheless the practice continued.

Despite the escorts, the minesweepers were unable to keep up with the British minelayers and by November the Germans had fallen hopelessly behind in their work. Kahle reported to von Schröder on 2 November that he was no longer able to keep the usual two channels in the fields open on a consistent basis because he simply did not have enough sweepers and escorts. He urgently requested additional ships. This led the Germans to requisition several small motorboats to augment the minesweeper flotilla. With the addition of the extra ships the torpedo-boats were able to reopen two channels through the British minefields and keep them open until the end of the year.[246]

Minesweeping was not the only matter the flotillas had to be concerned with. In an effort to make sure that the MarineKorps had adequate warning of any advancing British force the torpedo-boats carried out nightly patrols along the coast. These patrols led to several minor skirmishes.

As we have seen the British renewed their bombardments of the coast in late 1917 with Ostend as their favourite target. Ironically, the city had already been abandoned as a torpedo-boat base and was only occasionally used by submarines. On 22 and 24 September two major bombardments of the harbour and town took place and severe damage was done to the harbour installations. However, no vessels were in port at the time.[247] Another major bombardment took place in October and this time the floating dock was destroyed. This forced the one remaining destroyer in the harbour, *G-102*, which was undergoing repairs in the floating dock, to be towed to Bruges.[248]

The bombardments were usually accompanied by heavy air battles over the coast as each side tried to drive off the others' observers and ensure that their own made it through to their targets. In addition, these bombardments were supplemented by continuing allied air raids on the Flanders bases. Some of the latter did serious damage. On 16 August *A-13* was destroyed in an air raid on Ostend. Six days later *A-44* was damaged during an air raid on Zeebrugge.[249] On 3–4 September another raid on Zeebrugge damaged *A-49*, *A-39*, *UB-54*, *S-18* and *S-54*.[250] This was the most damage done by any single raid in the entire war up to this point. It did not bode well for the future.

To make matters worse, in late August the MarineKorps was ordered to release three squadrons of fighters for use in the battles around Ypres. These planes, which were badly needed on the coast, were simply turned over to the IV army.[251] Von Schröder was not pleased, especially when the commander of the Korps' air arm wrote to him in early September demanding the creation of a strong escort squadron to protect his observers. The only way this could be done was by reducing the strength of the two remaining fighter squadrons (which had ten planes each) to six planes and using the extras to create a special squadron that would only be used to escort observers for the coastal artillery.[252] This was done on 16 September.[253]

Unfortunately for the MarineKorps the squadrons were also equipped with obsolete planes and the Korps was perpetually at a serious disadvantage in the air. Therefore, the air commander requested that an additional fourteen modern fighters be assigned to the MarineKorps. If that was not possible he at least hoped to be able to exchange his twenty obsolete craft for newer and faster ones from Germany.[254] Both of his requests were denied. Things became even worse in October when the land-based plane section of the MarineKorps was completely disbanded in order to free up personnel for reassignment to Germany.[255] Von Schröder vehemently protested by citing the MarineKorps' need for experienced pilots since their area of operations was one of the busiest in the entire war. Without experienced pilots and modern land-based fighters his forces could not hope to oppose the British in the air. Unfortunately for the MarineKorps his pleas had no effect.[256] In the meantime the seaplanes of the Korps continued to carry out bombing raids against enemy patrol vessels and merchant shipping though they generally were not very successful. By the end of the year the MarineKorps was clearly losing the air war over Flanders. This of course had a negative impact on flotilla operations. From 1916 on aerial reconnaissance had been vitally important to the minesweepers. The turning of the tide in the air was a major reason for the decreasing effectiveness of the minesweepers.

Another area in which the changing tide in the air war had a negative effect was in the use of the radio-controlled boats, or *Fernlenkboote*. These craft were controlled by aircraft flying over the vicinity of the intended attack. Only two Fernlenkboote attacks were carried out in 1917, both against monitors during coastal bombardments. One was a complete failure since the boat was destroyed before it could reach its target[257] but the other did succeed in damaging one British monitor.[258] The weapon, however, was at best a minor nuisance to the British.

There were some brief encounters in this period between the Flanders flotillas and the forces of the Dover Patrol but none were of much significance. A brief duel took place on 27 September when *U-70* struck a mine in the Channel and *G-91* was sent out to search for her. The German destroyer encountered eight British destroyers but was able to escape without suffering any damage.[259] Another example took place on 27 October when the VI Half-Flotilla briefly sortied against the coastal patrol and drove it off without any damage being done to either side.[260] Most of the latter part of 1917 was filled with this type of small encounter; there is no need to list them all here. The only operation of note carried out by the flotillas in the latter half of the year was another brief bombardment of Dunkirk by the A-IIs. The latter were attacked in turn by a monitor moored outside of the harbour at Dunkirk. The Germans fired their torpedoes at the monitor and then turned for home.[261] That was the only offensive action carried out by the flotillas during the third portion of the year.

One of the main reasons why the flotillas were so quiet during this period was their lack of resources. In late 1917 von Schröder and the MarineKorps once again found themselves short of vessels with which to oppose the Entente. Von Schröder expended a vast amounts of ink trying to rectify that situation.

Force Allocation
Von Schröder's new problems began in September. Due to fresh losses from mines and the fact that several damaged vessels were still under repair, the effective force available to him was reduced to eleven destroyers. That force was reduced even further by the needs of 'Operation Albion', a German plan to seize the islands in the Gulf of Riga. Von Schröder was forced to surrender

five destroyers to the High Seas Fleet for use in that operation. This left him with only six effective destroyers by the middle of September.[262] In addition, Scheer insisted that the damaged *G-102* be returned to the High Seas Fleet as soon as its repairs were completed.[263] Von Schröder promptly wrote to the Naval Staff requesting reinforcements and was informed that all decisions on reinforcements would have to await the outcome of 'Albion'.[264]

Throughout October and November von Schröder made numerous complaints in his war diary over his lack of forces. For example, on 11 November he recorded that the forces available to the MarineKorps had been so reduced that it was not possible to provide adequate protection for the minesweeping flotilla. Furthermore, the minesweeping flotilla itself was so small that the best it could hope to accomplish was to maintain two channels through the minefields open for the use of the submarines.[265] To rectify the latter problem von Schröder requisitioned ten small motor launches as minesweepers on 28 November. This alleviated one immediate problem but did not address the larger issue, that of providing adequate protection for the minesweepers.[266]

The latter problem was partially rectified when the five destroyers that had been sent to the High Seas Fleet returned at the end of November.[267] To further supplement the forces of the MarineKorps, Scheer promised to dispatch an additional three destroyers to Flanders. These, however, were currently under repair and could not be sent until those repairs were completed.[268] The latter vessels eventually arrived in Flanders on 18 December, and Scheer actually sent four instead of the three he had promised. The fourth was a replacement for *G-102*, which had recently completed its repairs and had returned to Germany.[269]

The destroyers were not the only vessels that were in short supply in Flanders; there were also problems with the Torpedo-Boat Flotilla. In early August Kapitänleutnant Assmann had written to von Schröder requesting four of the A-IIIs as replacements for three A-IIs which had been damaged. He claimed that he needed these boats if the submarine war was going to continue to be waged from Flanders.[270] As a result of pressure from both Assmann and von Schröder this request was granted in September and Assmann was informed that the first four boats of the new class would be assigned to Flanders.[271] Von Schröder made additional requests on Assmann's behalf later in September but was told that he would have to wait for further reinforcements until 'Operation Albion' was completed.[272] Von Schröder's requests were renewed in November when one of the very valuable A-IIs was lost to a mine while escorting back to port the destroyers that were returning from 'Albion'.[273] This time his request was granted and four additional A-IIs were sent to Flanders in mid-December.[274]

By the end of the year the destroyer and torpedo-boat flotillas were beginning to recover their strength and were ready to once again become a factor in the war. The flotillas had been restricted to a purely defensive role during the latter half of 1917. Most historians have attributed this to the results of the April battle where two German destroyers were sunk by the *Swift* and the *Broke*.[275] This, however, was not the case. The destroyer raids continued into May until von Schröder issued orders for them to concentrate on defensive patrols. This move was brought about not by the losses of April but rather by the growing concern that the British would attempt to invade Flanders. By the latter part of the year, when such a landing was no longer a threat, the forces of the Flanders flotillas had been so reduced due to damage and the needs of 'Operation Albion' that it was not feasible for them to resume their aggressive raids. As a result they were forced to play a passive role in the latter part of 1917. That would soon change though.

CONCLUSION

In retrospect, 1917 was the decisive year of the war and the MarineKorps Flandern played a key role in the year's events. The year began with the fateful decision to launch unrestricted submarine warfare. The German leadership understood that this was a gamble but the results of 1916, in particular the Battle of the Somme, convinced them that it was necessary to take the risk. They called it the 'last card' because it was seen as their only chance to defeat Britain. They understood that it would likely add the United States to their roster of foes but believed it was necessary regardless. The unspoken assumption was that this was their last chance to earn a 'German peace' and that if it failed Germany would have to settle for a negotiated one. However, when the campaign failed, rather than seek a negotiated peace, the German High Command decided to continue the war, despite the growing discontent within the country. Their new rationale was that the surrender of Russia had made possible the playing of a new 'last card'; a major offensive on the Western Front that would destroy the armies of France and Britain before the United States could really make its influence felt. As a result the war continued into 1918.

1917 was also decisive for the British. The institution of the convoy system saved the remainder of the nation's shipping from the submarine menace and eventually, in 1918, with the aid of the United States, allowed ship production to finally exceed shipping losses. Before the efficacy of the convoy system was realised the submarine campaign caused tremendous concern and even convinced some members of the country's military, most notably Admiral Jellicoe, that the war would soon be lost if some remedy for the submarines could not be found. These fears led to the decision to launch a Flanders offensive in the summer of 1917. This decision has traditionally been attributed to the recognition by the British naval leaders of the dangers posed by Ostend and Zeebrugge; however, as Andrew Wiest has recently argued, very persuasively, the Admiralty's real concern was not with the submarines in Ostend and Zeebrugge but with the destroyers based there. It was the destroyer raids of October 1916 to April 1917 that convinced the Admiralty that the Germans could, if they ever realised the potential of the Flanders harbours, strike a serious blow against the communications of the British Army in France. Clearly the Germans were able to transfer forces back and forth across the North Sea. Since that was the case they possessed a great advantage. The Grand Fleet needed to maintain a relatively constant destroyer strength in case the High Seas Fleet decided to give battle; the Germans, however, knew in advance when the High Seas Fleet intended to sail and could shuffle their destroyers from position to position as necessary. In other words there was nothing that could stop them from transferring several flotillas to Flanders for a concerted strike against, for example, the troop convoys to France. That this had not yet happened meant only that it had not yet occurred to the Germans, not that it could not be done. As a result the Admiralty strongly supported the Flanders campaign.

That campaign eventually bogged down in the mud of Flanders and was only a tactical success for Great Britain, not the strategic victory Haig had been hoping for. Again, in retrospect, this may have been a blessing in disguise. It is highly unlikely, given the advanced state of the German defences in Flanders, that the planned amphibious landing would have been anything other than a major disaster. The failure of the Flanders campaign ensured that the Belgian bases would remain in German hands in 1918, a year in which the destroyer and torpedo-boat flotillas of the MarineKorps would once again become active in the Channel. Their depredations, however, never reached the level feared by the British Admiralty. In fact, though they did not yet realise it, the Central Powers had already lost the war. Only the endgame remained to be played out.

7

Endgame

THE CONVOY SYSTEM PROVED TO BE the cure for the submarine threat. By the end of 1917 submarine sinkings had plummeted from their April peak and would never again reach Holtzendorff's key figure of 600,000 tons per month. According to the logic behind the Pless decision, Germany had played its last card and failed. In theory the time had come to seek an end to the war, however there were two compelling reasons for the Germans to continue. First of all, the Bolshevik Revolution and Russia's consequent withdrawal from the war appeared to shift the balance of power in Germany's favour. To the responsible leaders within Germany, especially General Ludendorff, this seemed to make possible the playing of a new 'last card'; a final, major offensive in the west that would drive Britain and France out of the war before the rising flood of American soldiers irrevocably turned the tide.

The other reason for the continuation of the war was the desire to achieve the remainder of Germany's war aims. The Treaty of Brest-Litovsk allowed Germany to attain her aims in the east and all that now remained was to complete the reorientation of Europe toward Germany by achieving total victory in the west.[1] This was particularly important for the German navy. Germany's aims in the east were primarily those of the army; the navy's aims were concentrated in the west and remained as yet unfulfilled.[2]

THE MARINEKORPS AND GERMAN WAR AIMS, 1917–18

As Fischer has amply demonstrated, Germany's war aims remained remarkably consistent throughout the course of the war. The navy's main aim remained the acquisition of the Belgian coast, especially the naval bases. The importance of this area to the navy was reiterated by Holtzendorff in a meeting of the Crown Council on 11 September, 1917. Three days later he sent a memorandum to then Chancellor Michaelis demanding that Germany retain the 'Triangle' after the war.[3]

The navy was less concerned with the remainder of Belgium, which the

Germans still intended to convert into a German satellite state. Part of their plan revolved around a future division of the country into two parts, Flanders and Wallonia. The latter could be used as an enticement to try and get France to sign a separate peace. As part of this scheme Flanders would be occupied by Germany for ten years during which time the Flemish would not be allowed to possess their own armed forces. Afterward, presumably, Germany would retain the coastline, though that was not made explicit.[4] One of the navy's more interesting schemes was a plan to retain Antwerp as a naval base.[5] Germany could then develop all the Belgian harbours into a cohesive naval base in preparation for another war with Britain.

Where did the MarineKorps fit into all of this? War aims do not appear to have been one of von Schröder's main concerns during 1918 but he did pen a study in February that sheds some light on his views at this stage in the war. In 1915 he had argued for the complete annexation of Belgium by Germany. His reasons were essentially militaristic. He wanted the opportunity to make further improvements to the harbours and also wanted to widen the canals so that they could be used by larger ships. His views changed only slightly between 1915 and 1918. In his study he argued that the Germans could never allow Belgium to be restored to independence. He claimed that after the experiences of the war, Belgium could never again profess neutrality and that if the Germans granted them independence they would quickly gravitate into the camp of the Western powers. This could only be prevented by military force, not through contracts or treaties. Germany also *had* to retain the Belgian coast at the end of the war or they would be forced to retake it in the next war. Then, once again, they would have to build up naval bases from scratch. He feared that the next time this would be much more difficult because the British would never again make the mistake of allowing the Germans to capture the harbours intact.[6] He was also concerned that if the Germans allowed Belgium to fall into British hands, the British would be able to launch aerial attacks against the Rhenish industrial areas in any future war. Furthermore, if the British controlled Flanders they would be able to completely close the Channel to German submarines. 'The Dover Strait can only be held open from Flanders.'[7]

The retention of the bases would also provide Germany with other benefits. For example, if Germany controlled these bases at the beginning of a war with Britain and France, they would be able to intercept any British transports bringing troops or supplies to the continent. Even the mere existence of such a threat would be beneficial since it might at least force the British to bring their forces in further to the west, possibly as far afield as Brest. This would effectively prevent rapid British involvement in any future war between France and Germany.

Keeping the coastline would also provide political advantages, especially vis-à-vis the Netherlands. Von Schröder attributed Dutch neutrality to the fact that, after the fall of Belgium, the country was effectively surrounded by German-controlled territory. If, however, Belgium was held by or allied to Britain in a future war then the British would be able to put correspondingly greater pressure on the Netherlands and possibly even force it to join a war against Germany. Von Schröder even believed that if Germany retained Flanders the Germans would be able to convince the Dutch to join an anti-British alliance. For all of these reasons he considered the Flanders coast to be of the highest military value.

The German position could be enhanced even further if they could somehow acquire the mouth of the Scheldt. Then they could utilise the facilities of Antwerp and their position would become 'truly deadly to Britain.'[8] Even at this late date, despite the numerous setbacks in the submarine campaign and the fact that his flotillas had become purely defensive forces, von Schröder firmly supported the annexation of Belgium. At the very least he believed that the navy had to retain the Flanders coast. He was not alone.

On 8 April General Ludendorff and Admiral von Holtzendorff had a meeting to discuss the state of the war and Germany's war aims. During the course of the meeting Ludendorff expressed doubt over whether Germany would be able to acquire the French Channel ports or even retain the Flanders ports. In response Admiral Holtzendorff suggested that Germany offer Wallonia to France in exchange for a separate peace. As part of that peace Flanders would be made into an independent kingdom under German control. The new state would be forced into an alliance with Germany and would turn over control of its coastline to the Germans so that they could make the fullest possible use of the military harbours. Such a settlement would provide an extra benefit since it would allow the Germans to economically encircle the Netherlands. Using that leverage the Dutch could then be forced to accept German 'protection.' This would deny the British any bridgehead on the continent and allow the Germans to make use of the large Dutch colonial empire.[9]

Ludendorff objected that France would never allow the Germans to retain the Flanders coastline. Holtzendorff replied that it was absurd to believe that France would surrender the remainder of Lorraine and Longwy-Briey but would balk at surrendering Belgian territory! He concluded by arguing that Belgium was simply a British bulwark on the continent and that it would be a great mistake not to take advantage of this opportunity to destroy it. He therefore asked Ludendorff to reconsider his position.[10] Admiral von Schröder and Admiral Scheer both agreed with Holtzendorff's proposition.[11]

Clearly the defeat of the submarines had done little to dampen the German leaders' zest for conquest. Ludendorff and the army may have been content, to a degree, with their conquests in the east but clearly the navy had yet to achieve its aims. They still believed that Germany could win the war and they pinned their hopes on two things: the submarines and the great western offensive.

THE PERIOD OF CONFIDENCE: JANUARY – APRIL 1918

Despite their declining effectiveness the submarines remained the German navy's primary weapon in 1918. The submarine campaign and the continuing British efforts to defeat it provide the essential backdrop for the events of early 1918.

The Submarine Campaign

By the beginning of 1918 the Flanders submarines were divided into two flotillas under the overall command of KorvettenKapitän Karl Bartenbach. Flandern I was led by Kapitänleutnant Hans Walther and consisted of ten UB-IIIs, two UC-Is and six UC-IIs. During the latter part of the year one UB-II and several additional UB-IIIs were added to the flotilla.[12] Flandern II, commanded by Kapitänleutnant Rohrbeck, consisted of four UB-Is, one of which had been converted into a minelayer by removing its torpedo tubes, six UB-IIs, six UB-IIIs and seven UC-IIs.[13] During the first four months of 1918 the total number of submarines based in Flanders dropped from a peak of thirty in January, to twenty-nine in February, twenty-six in March and twenty-five in April.[14]

The submarines were assigned to the various theatres of war according to the following weekly plan. Three minelayers worked exclusively in the Hoofden, one UB-II or UC-II worked off the British east coast, one or two UB-IIs or UC-IIs patrolled the eastern Channel, one UB-III and either one UB-II or one UC-II patrolled the western Channel while one UC-II and one UB-II worked in the western approaches. Additionally one UC-II and one UB-III patrolled the Bay of Biscay while one UC-II and one UB-III worked in the Bristol Channel. Finally, one UC-II and one UB-III patrolled the Irish Sea.[15]

Throughout the early part of 1918 the Flanders submarines continued to be moderately successful. In January they were reportedly responsible for the destruction of sixty-three ships totaling 136,072 tons. This was at the cost of three submarines.[16] This number is probably somewhat high. The official German history credits them with sinking forty-seven ships of 57,280 tons. This seems more accurate, though again, as in 1917 the actual numbers are difficult to determine.[17] Estimates for January from all fronts vary from 183,766 tons,[18] to 295,630 tons[19] and 302,088 tons.[20] Similar discrepancies exist for the remaining months as well. The flotilla activity report for February claims that the flotillas destroyed a total of forty-nine ships worth 121,961. One submarine was reported lost.[21] Total sinkings from all theatres for that month came to 335,202 tons.[22] This brief upsurge continued into March when the total number of sinkings rose to 368,746 tons.[23] Out of this total the Flanders boats accounted for seventy-three ships totaling 186,805 tons.[24] In April though things took a downward turn as the total dropped to 300,069 tons[25] of which the Flanders boats claimed 90,606 tons.[26]

These modest successes were accompanied by ever increasing losses among the submarines. From January to March their losses remained low, only around 8 percent of their total strength; however, starting in April this figure climbed to first 33 percent and then to 40 percent by the end of the war.[27] Flandern I lost nine UB-IIIs before the summer and an additional five UB-IIIs and two UCs between June and October. Flandern II suffered even more severe losses. Over the course of the year they lost a total of twenty submarines; four during the evacuation of the Flanders bases in October.[28] The flotilla activity reports give us some clues as to why this occurred.

According to von Schröder's reports one of the factors that made the life of submarine commanders much more difficult in 1918 was the extensive use of aircraft by the Entente. During 1917 the British began using aircraft as anti-submarine patrols. This practice reached its peak with the creation of the famous 'spider-web patrols' in the North Sea. While the aircraft themselves were not very effective at destroying submarines they were able to force the submarines to dive and this limited the ability of the submarines to make daytime attacks on the surface.[29] The aircraft were not the most serious problem faced by the submarines though; that honour belonged to what the Germans called the 'Dover Light Barrage.'

By December 1917 it was becoming increasingly difficult for the submarines to pass through the Channel due to this new mine Barrage, which was also brightly illuminated and strongly patrolled. The new barrier was the brain-child of Rear-Admiral Roger Keyes, who had been appointed director of the Plans Division of the Admiralty in late 1917 and then, in November, had been made chairman of the Channel Barrage Committee.[30] While in charge of that committee Keyes developed a plan to lay a new deep minefield across the

Channel and patrol it with numerous trawlers and drifters equipped with magnesium flares. These small craft would be supported by destroyers equipped with spotlights. The plan was opposed by the current commander at Dover, Admiral Bacon, who thought the risks of an enemy surface attack against the patrols were too great. He preferred to build specially constructed light vessels that would carry the spotlights. These would be supplemented by shore-mounted spotlights.[31] Bacon dragged his heels on implementing the new defensive measures until he was ordered to do so by Jellicoe on 18 December 1917. That first night a German submarine was destroyed in the minefields and 'this sealed Bacon's fate.'[32] Shortly thereafter the Royal Navy underwent a major changing of the guard; Jellicoe was replaced as First Sea Lord by Sir Rosslyn Wemyss and Bacon was supplanted by Keyes.[33] On 1 January 1918 Admiral Keyes took up his new post at Dover, bringing with him an air of action that would eventually transform the war in the Channel.

Keyes' new Barrage was very effective in gradually closing the Channel to the German submarines. The barrier was patrolled by, on average, four old destroyers or patrol boats with searchlights, fourteen trawlers burning magnesium flares, sixty drifters, four motor-launches, and two large paddle minesweepers with searchlights. These forces were supported by one large monitor and six-to-eight destroyers that kept watch to the east of the patrol.[34] These forces were augmented by daylight patrols off the Flanders coast by one monitor and five destroyers and by a new series of coastal bombardments that began in February.[35] During January 1918 alone the Barrage accounted for four German submarines. This was twice the number of German submarines that had been lost in the Channel from 1914-1917.[36] By the end of January Bartenbach considered the Channel passage to be the most dangerous part of any submarine's journey and he urged the fleet to launch an attack against the Barrage.[37] He soon got his wish.

Surface Naval Actions, January – April

For the most part the Flanders flotillas remained on a defensive footing throughout the winter of 1917–18. This was due to the fact that their primary mission was still the protection of the minesweepers. Furthermore, they were limited in their activities because their numbers continued to dwindle. During 1918 von Schröder and his subordinate commanders once again had a very difficult time getting reinforcements.

When the Russians dropped out of the war in the winter of 1917–18 the Naval Staff decided that it was no longer necessary to keep the Baltic squadrons at full strength. Von Schröder concurred in that opinion and hoped that some of the ships currently in the Baltic would be reassigned to Flanders. In the event though, the MarineKorps received no reinforcements. Two torpedo-boat flotillas remained in the Baltic and the rest of the Baltic fleet joined the High Seas Fleet to help with minesweeping in the Bight.[38] The disappointments continued. In early January the MarineKorps was informed that they would be receiving an additional four ships from the I and II Torpedo-Boat Divisions.[39] However, they never arrived. Then, in March, von Schröder was informed in March that the High Seas Fleet was claiming these four destroyers as well as an additional eight A-IIIs that were originally intended for the MarineKorps. Scheer claimed that they were needed to escort submarines through the minefields in the Bight.[40] Von Schröder received this information right after he had sent four boats of the III Flotilla back to Germany for a major overhaul in the expectation that they were to be replaced.[41]

The latter step had to be taken because of the constant air attacks on the Flanders harbours. The MarineKorps had lost control of the air and in the first months of 1918 they were bombed incessantly by the British. These attacks did enough damage to the port facilities that lengthy repairs could no longer be completed in Flanders. The air raids had also become a very real threat to the surface forces of the flotillas. The destroyers and torpedo-boats that were not on patrol were moved out of the harbours and into the canals every night in an effort to save them from damage. This also meant that minor repairs on seaworthy craft could not be completed at night.[42]

The four destroyers from the III Flotilla were originally scheduled to return to Flanders on the evening of 17 April[43] but their trip ended up being postponed until the evening of 20 April. At 8.45am that morning the four vessels, *V-71*, *V-73*, *S-55* and *G-91*, left Heligoland to begin the return journey to Flanders. They followed the 8th Minesweeper Flotilla and were accompanied on their journey through the Bight by two armoured cruisers. At 9.25am their trip was delayed when they ran into a new and unmarked minefield. The sweeping of the minefield took too much time and it was decided that the flotilla could no longer make the trip to Flanders that day, instead they began to return to Heligoland. On their way back they ran into another new minefield and one of the minesweepers struck a mine and sank.[44] Then, at 6.17pm, smoke was sighted and the destroyers, which had been trying to rescue the crew of the sunken minesweeper, made off to the south to try and protect the other minesweepers. They closed with what they estimated were five enemy destroyers and opened fire at a range of seven kilometres while the minesweepers made smoke and moved off to the east. Several hits were reported on one enemy destroyer and the entire enemy force turned away as the cruisers of the IV Reconnaissance Group arrived. A brief German pursuit was broken off due to the presence of the minefields.[45] As a result of the battle the four destroyers remained temporarily in Heligoland.

Despite their shortage of forces the Flanders flotillas were not completely inactive. They did launch one minor expedition on the evening of 14 January. The objective of this raid was to attack shipping north of the Thames and, failing that, to bombard Yarmouth and Lowestoft. A bombardment was thought to be useful if for no other reason than to add to the growing discontent within Britain over the effort, or lack thereof, by the Royal Navy. Fourteen destroyers from the III flotilla and the Destroyer Flotilla were assigned to the raid and were divided into three groups.[46]

The British had an operation of their own planned for that same evening. They intended to lay a new minefield to the north of Zeebrugge and assigned ten destroyers to the mission. They were alerted, however, presumably by Room 40, of the intended German operation. Keyes suspected that the German advance would be aimed against his new patrol line so he put to sea in the cruiser *Attentive* with four leaders and six destroyers to try and intercept the Germans either on their way into the Channel or on their way home.[47]

The Germans left harbour at 5.15pm (4.15pm Greenwich) and proceeded to the north. Before they left harbour several radio intercepts seemed to point out that the British were expecting some kind of German attack. The Germans intercepted messages ordering all merchant traffic out of the Channel and also intercepted orders to hold all shipping in harbour. At 8pm they intercepted a message reading 'enemy torpedo-boat activity to be expected tonight' but the decision was made to go forward with the operation regardless since most of the enemy counter-measures seemed to be directed at the Dover-Calais area. Von Schröder attributed Britain's advance warning of the German move to either aerial reconnaissance that had spotted the German force while it was assembling in Zeebrugge, enemy submarines that had reported the destroyers leaving harbour, spies or simply a lucky guess on the part of the British. There was still no inkling of the fact that the British were able to read the German codes. At any rate the raid went forward as planned.[48] No British forces were encountered and the bombardment proceeded with minimal effect.

At about 12am Greenwich time, Keyes received word that Yarmouth had been bombarded and, since he was out of position, he ordered *Erebus* and *Terror* to put to sea to support the mine-laying operation.[49] However, the German forces regrouped north of the North Hinder Lightship and returned to harbour without contacting the British force. The only damage suffered by the Germans occurred when *V-67* struck a mine on her way back to port and had to be towed in by *G-95*.[50]

On 23 January, German and British destroyers had a very brief engagement off the Thornton Bank[51] and that action was followed by another minor encounter on 5 February, when a series of coastal motor boats laying a minefield off Ostend encountered a group of German torpedo-boats. Again there was no serious damage done to either side.[52] A new major encounter was about to occur however.

Bartenbach's pleas for help for his submarines finally fell upon sympathetic ears and early in February von Schröder appealed to Scheer for help in fighting the Dover Barrage. He specifically requested that the High Seas Fleet attack the British patrols since he did not feel he could spare sufficient forces to do so himself. Scheer agreed and decided to send the II Flotilla under KorvettenKapitän Heinecke directly from the Heligoland Bight. He hoped that not stopping first in Flanders would allow them to achieve complete surprise.[53]

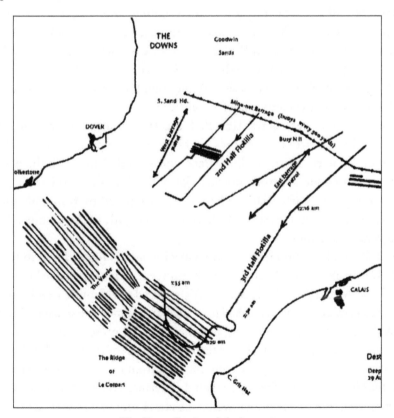

The Dover Strait and the barrage

The flotilla, consisting of eight destroyers, was due to leave Germany on 13 February but was delayed due to poor weather. It actually left on 14 February, but one of the destroyers developed condenser problems and had to drop-out of the operation. Heinecke decided to continue on with his remaining seven destroyers. The British were totally unaware of the approaching danger.[54]

Keyes had received word earlier that day that a homeward bound German submarine would attempt to pass through the Channel that evening and he accordingly sent word to the patrols to be alert but did not order any special defensive preparations. The British forces were arrayed as follows: the cruiser *Attentive* and three destroyers were based in the Downs; the western Barrage patrol was covered by the leader *Swift* and one destroyer; the eastern Barrage patrol was secured by four destroyers; and on the Barrage itself there were fifty-eight drifters, a group of trawlers burning magnesium flares, four motor-launches and two paddle-minesweepers. The entire force was supported by one monitor, one destroyer, one patrol boat and three French torpedo-boats. Most of the drifters and trawlers were essentially defenceless against modern destroyers and consequently they had standing orders that if an enemy destroyer attack took place they were to fire a green signal rocket and then scatter to either the French or British side of the Channel, depending on which was closer. While they scattered the naval forces of the patrol would try to cut the Germans off from their bases.[55] While sound in theory this plan did not work very well in the confusion of a night attack.

The German destroyers travelled together until they reached the Sandettie Bank at which point they split into two groups. Heinecke took his group to the north of the Colbart Bank and intended to attack the patrols south of Dungeness before moving down the line of patrol craft from Folkestone to the Varne Bank. The second group, led by Kapitänleutnant Kolbe, was to roll up the patrols from the southern side of the Channel. Both groups had good luck.[56]

At 1.30am (12.30am Greenwich) Heinecke and his force closed to within roughly fifty metres of a large paddle mine-sweeper and then opened fire. This vessel, the sweeper *Newbury*, was quickly reduced to a flaming wreck and the Germans pressed on. *Newbury* had been unable to launch the signal rocket that would have warned the remaining patrol craft of the presence of the German raiders. The gunfire could be heard throughout most of the patrol line but was mistaken either for artillery fire from the land front or for the expected battle with the German submarine. As a result the Germans retained their surprise.[57]

One vessel, the *Shipmate*, witnessed the attack on the *Newbury* but did not fire signal rockets either. There was apparently some confusion on the part of her captain as to what exactly his proper course of action was. Apparently he had spotted a green signal rocket in a different sector of the line (from where the southern German group was attacking) and was uncertain whether or not to repeat the signal. In the meantime Heinecke and his ships moved in and destroyed the *Shipmate*. The Germans then moved on and attacked a division of patrol craft; the alarm had still not been sounded. After continuing on and attacking a second division of patrol craft Heinecke and his half-flotilla turned for home at 2.30am.[58]

On the other end of patrol line the III Half-Flotilla ran into two of the French torpedo-boats but the French assumed that the destroyers were British and did not report them. About ten minutes later the Germans found a large group of patrol craft. They sank one armed steamer as well as three other ships. Three additional vessels were severely damaged before the Germans moved on to other targets. One of the damaged vessels did manage to finally send off the green alarm rocket. (This was apparently the signal seen by *Shipmate*.) Nonetheless the Half-Flotilla continued on, eventually sinking two more drifters and reducing two others to burning wrecks before turning for home at about 2.40am.[59]

In the meantime the gunfire of the battle was heard as far away as Dover where Keyes himself initially thought it was the sound of his patrols attacking a German submarine. When the gunfire did not abate after roughly twenty minutes he began to become concerned that something more serious might be underway; as a result he sent a signal to the monitor on patrol inquiring as to what was happening. He received no reply. At 1.35am Greenwich (in other words as the Germans were turning for home) Keyes ordered the destroyers in the Downs to rendezvous with the Dover destroyers south of the Goodwins and try to cut off what he was now certain was a group of Flanders destroyers. He was already too late.[60]

The monitor, *M-26*, which, upon seeing the alarm signal, had moved to investigate, did not arrive in time to intercept the Germans. Heinecke and his half-flotilla escaped undamaged. Kolbe and his group had one more barrier to cross. On their way to Flanders they stumbled onto the path of the eastern Barrage patrol consisting of the destroyers *Zubian*, *Amazon*, *Melpomene* and *Termagant*. The rearmost British destroyer, *Amazon*, challenged the Germans three separate times without receiving any response and still assumed that they were British! As a result Kolbe and his group also escaped undamaged.[61]

The action turned out to be a brilliant German success. The Germans initially estimated that they had completely destroyed between fifteen and twenty-five British ships.[62] According to Scheer Heinecke's group accounted for thirteen patrol craft, one torpedo-boat and two motorboats while the southern group sank an additional twelve patrol craft and two motorboats. He also claimed that the raid brought about an end to the illuminated patrols.[63] His numbers were rather high. The actual total came to one trawler and seven drifters sunk and one trawler, five drifters and a paddle minesweeper severely damaged.[64] The only German ship damaged was *G-102* which hit a mine returning to port. The destroyer was not severely damaged and made it back to harbour under its own power. It rejoined the High Seas Fleet on 19 February.[65]

Once again, as in their initial raids in 1917, the Germans were aided significantly by the confusion that their sudden attack created. The British were taken completely by surprise. Despite Keyes' precautions the British forces actually on the patrol line seem to have been lulled once again into a false sense of security by the long interval between German attacks. An angry Keyes responded by relieving the commanders of *M-26*, *Termagant*, and *Amazon*. The commander of the latter was blamed for allowing the Germans to escape and was court-martialled. He was only given a severe reprimand though; a punishment which Keyes thought was much too lenient.[66]

The Germans promptly launched another raid. On the following evening von Schröder, thinking that the British would not expect a repetition of the attack so quickly, sent the III Flotilla and the Destroyer Flotilla out once again. They moved out in two groups, one on the Dover side of the straits and one on the Calais side, but found no enemy vessels of any kind and no patrols. They briefly bombarded Dover and then returned to Flanders.[67]

There is some question as to just what the short term impact of the 14 February raid was. The German sources insist that the advance on the night of the 15th found no British forces anywhere and they therefore decided that the illuminated patrol had been withdrawn.[68] The British, on the other hand, Keyes in particular, insist that the patrol was out in full force once again on the following evening.[69] What is one to believe?

In all likelihood the truth probably lies somewhere between the claims of both sides. The most likely explanation for the discrepancy between the German and British sources is that when the German flotillas entered the Channel on the night of the 15th they did not proceed as far west as they had on the previous night; as a result they could not see the patrol vessels that were at sea since, despite Keyes' protestations, the level of light in the area was probably at a reduced level. Evidence for this can be found in the reports of German submarines from February and March. According to the Flanders submarine flotilla report for February the passage through the Channel was much easier after the raid because the Barrage was less brightly lit.[70] However, in the reports for March, von Schröder pointed out that the easier transit of the straits had been only a temporary phenomenon and that further raids were necessary to drive off the British permanently.[71] Whatever its short-term impact the long-term result of the raid was minimal since the Barrage was soon restored to its full strength.

The attack, despite being a brilliant success, turned out to be merely another pinprick by the German light forces. Why the Germans did not repeat the raid remains a mystery. Von Schröder made no additional requests for support from the High Seas Fleet until late in September. Considering the total success of the attack the failure to repeat the raid has to be rated as a major strategic blunder by the Germans. This is further evidence that they simply failed to understand the potential of the Flanders bases. For whatever reason the raid was not repeated and the British patrols were allowed to peacefully go about the business of forcing German submarines to dive into the deep minefield. By mid-summer the Barrage had succeeded in effectively barring German submarines from the Channel. While the Barrage alone did not defeat the submarines it certainly played a key role in their ultimate defeat. By forcing the Germans to travel north around Scotland to reach their cruising areas the Barrage reduced the amount of time that the submarines could spend on station and prevented them from reaching the vulnerable shipping lanes in the central Channel. The Barrage symbolised the total defeat of Germany's underwater offensive. Germany's only remaining hope for victory lay with the army and Ludendorff's grand assault. The MarineKorps would have a role to play in that as well.

THE MARINEKORPS AND THE GREAT WESTERN OFFENSIVE

In January 1918, as part of the planning for the upcoming offensive, the MarineKorps was asked to reevaluate the French Channel ports and determine whether or not their conquest would make it worth diverting forces from the main thrust of the attack. They were also asked to determine what preparations would be necessary to bring the French ports up to the same level of readiness as Ostend and Zeebrugge. The study was completed on 7 January.[72]

Admiral von Schröder began his study by pointing out that any advance to the west would be beneficial, whether or not the French ports fell into German hands, because moving the frontline would push enemy artillery further away from Ostend. He went on to argue that, if the French ports were actually to fall into German hands, this would make it vastly more difficult for the British to close the straits and would also open up greater possibilities for offensive action by the Flanders flotillas; though how valuable the harbours would be would depend to a great extent on the condition in which they were captured. He did not expect the Entente to make the same mistake it had in 1914 with Ostend and Zeebrugge. Instead von Schröder fully expected that they would try to block the harbours before surrendering them. Furthermore, even if the harbours were captured in pristine condition, he pointed out that the navy would not be able to take full advantage of them until sufficient coastal defences could be created. That said, von Schröder went on to examine how the war would be affected if the Germans were to occupy the Channel coast as far as Dunkirk. Finally he examined what the impact on the war would be if the Germans managed to get as far as Calais and Boulogne.

Dunkirk was still considered a highly desirable harbour due to its large dock facilities and the shifting sands off the coast which gave it considerable natural protection against enemy bombardments. Calais and Boulogne were less desirable because they were considered to be dangerously exposed to enemy attack. The seizure of Dunkirk would be particularly important. It would mean, first of all, that Ostend would no longer be threatened by the enemy's artillery. He also believed that the conquest of Dunkirk might force the Entente to withdraw their patrols from the Flanders coast since the vessels that carried out those patrols were currently based in Dunkirk. Seizing Dunkirk would even make it more difficult for the Entente to launch air attacks against Flanders since many of the enemy aircraft were also based at or around Dunkirk. All of this meant that the capture of Dunkirk would have a generally positive effect on the submarine war, because it would be easier for the submarines to get in and out of port. Even if Dunkirk was taken though, Bruges would still remain the primary naval base in the west since it was already fully equipped and was much safer from enemy attack.

The seizure of Dunkirk would be even more beneficial for the Flanders destroyers and torpedo-boats since they would no longer have an enemy force based out of there on their flank and, by using Dunkirk as a forward base, they could strike further into the Channel. Finally, and most importantly, Dunkirk was accessible not only by destroyers but also by cruisers. This was not the case with the Flanders bases. If the Germans were able to base cruisers out of Dunkirk they would pose a much more significant threat to Great Britain.

Of course, if Dunkirk was taken several things would have to be done before the harbour would be ready for use. Von Schröder was primarily concerned about the state of the coastal artillery around the port. Those defences would have to be significantly expanded. He envisioned bringing several mobile 28cm, 17cm, and 15cm batteries from Flanders and placing the entire coastal area under the command of the 2nd MarineDivision, which would obviously have to be pulled out of the frontline. The fast motorboats currently based in Blankenberg would have to be transferred immediately to Dunkirk along with one A-I for defensive purposes. The remaining destroyers and torpedo-boats, as well as the Flanders submarines, would remain in Flanders until the defences of Dunkirk were completed. Lastly, a new air station would also have to be built at Dunkirk as soon as possible.

The capture of Calais would be less important since von Schröder considered it to be more vulnerable to enemy attack than Dunkirk. He envisioned using it purely as a temporary harbour for forces raiding into the Channel. The most important effect of the conquest of Calais would be the fact that German artillery based there would be able to reach across most of the straits and could therefore restrict enemy shipping from using parts of the Channel, at least during daylight hours. The conquest of Calais would also be beneficial because it would force the British to retract at least a portion of the Dover Barrage. Von Schröder stated, '. . . the further to the west we push the more opportunities for contact with the enemy will our surface forces have. This will afford us the opportunity to display our military superiority.'[73]

If the MarineKorps was to make the fullest possible use of Calais, the MarineKorps itself would have to be expanded and its headquarters would have to be moved from Bruges to Dunkirk. The stretch of coast from Dunkirk to Calais would be taken over by the 3rd MarineDivision, which at this point made up the Korps' reserve. The Korps would then require two divisions from the army as a new reserve. Furthermore, the MarineKorps itself did not have sufficient artillery to defend such a large area. Additional supplies would have to come from both the army and from Germany. Long-range artillery would be especially important.

As for the naval forces of the Korps, the fast motorboats would again be moved forward but the larger craft would continue to use Dunkirk and Bruges as their main bases. Another new air station would have to built in Calais as well and material for that would also have to come from Germany.

The conquest of Boulogne would be ideal and von Schröder was convinced that a German seizure of that port would have very serious repercussions for the British. Boulogne would give the MarineKorps a naval base actually inside the English Channel and would make the Flanders flotillas a very serious threat to both the communications between Britain and France and to commercial shipping. It would also be a very useful base for the German submarines which would be in their operational area almost as soon as they left harbour.

On the other hand the acquisition of Boulogne would require a major organisational change for the MarineKorps, since the front would be far too large for them to hold on their own. In this case von Schröder proposed expanding the Korps into the *Oberkommando des Küstenschutzes und Seekriegs Flandern*. Essentially, the Korps would be doubled in size and would have two separate headquarters, one in Ostend and one in Boulogne; the former would command the eastern portion of the coast and the latter the western. A front of this size would require that three divisions be held in reserve to counter-attack any attempted enemy landing. However, he expected that most of the naval craft would continue to operate from Bruges and Dunkirk with only the submarines moving permanently to Boulogne.

Of course, all of this could only come to pass if Ludendorff's offensive enjoyed phenomenal success, and in fact, Ludendorff put the conquest of the coast on the back burner and concentrated his efforts further to the south. The MarineKorps though was still called upon to aid that offensive, by bombarding the enemy coastline to disrupt communications and by putting pressure on the coastal sector of the front.

At the end of March von Schröder issued orders to the 2nd MarineDivision to increase the number of patrols along the front. He wanted them to keep track of enemy movements; in particular they were to alert him immediately in the event that any large-scale troop transfers took place. He also ordered the 2nd MarineDivision to launch a series of small-scale harassing attacks against the enemy lines to try and keep the Entente from transferring troops to other fronts.[74] The MarineKorps though remained weak on the land front and the area where they could provide the most help was at sea.

In order to facilitate the attack on the Western Front the Flanders flotillas planned an operation for the night of 21 March. It was designed to coincide with the beginning of the offensive and was to consist of a bombardment of Dunkirk and the surrounding areas. The primary targets were the railroads running from Dunkirk to the frontline.

On the evening of 19 March, two days before the scheduled bombardment, the destroyer and torpedo-boat flotillas went on reconnaissance towards the French coast in order to place navigational aids and check on the enemy's coastal defences. Several photographs of the enemy coast were taken and studied in preparation for the attack on the 21st.[75] On that evening the Germans left harbour in three separate groups. The first group, under Assmann's command, consisted of five A-IIIs, and was to bombard the railroads running east from Dunkirk; the second group, commanded by FregattenKapitän von Stosch, consisted of three A-IIs that were to bombard the Bray Dunes area; the final group, seven destroyers led by Albrecht, was to bombard La Panne and

Adinkerke. To help guide the bombarding groups to their targets four A-Is were sent out, two to the Nieuport Bank and two to the Small Bank.[76]

The flotillas left at 3am and proceeded without incident to their bombarding positions. At 4.48am Assmann's group opened fire on the area west of Dunkirk. They broke off the bombardment after only seven minutes when the British and French forces based in Dunkirk, the leader *Botha* and four destroyers, put to sea and two monitors, the *Terror* and *M-25*, began to return the German fire. The *Botha* immediately steamed off to the northeast to try and cut the Germans off from their bases. A running gun duel developed between the two forces as the Germans tried to get back to harbour. At 5.32 Assmann and his group met up with two of the A-Is that had been serving as navigational aids, *A-19* and *A-7*. At 5.38 the enemy force was spotted to starboard and both groups opened fire. The *Botha* was hit by a torpedo and lost speed. Assmann took the opportunity to escape with his A-IIIs. Unfortunately for *A-19* and *A-7*, which were older and slower A-Is, they could not keep up the pace and fell astern. The *Botha*, even with her speed reduced, was able to keep up with the latter two Germans and succeeded in ramming *A-19*. The German vessel was torn in half. *Botha* then attempted to ram *A-7* but failed. In the course of the battle with Assmann's group the *Botha*'s recognition lights were destroyed and then, in the confusion of her battle with the A-Is, the *Botha* became turned around. When she finally emerged from the smoke of the battle with the Germans she was on a course back toward her own destroyers. When they spotted the *Botha* the latter assumed she was a German destroyer and the *Capitaine Mehl*, a French destroyer, torpedoed her. The *Botha* was left dead in the water and had to be towed back to port. In the meantime the destroyer *Morris* finished off *A-7* with gunfire but Assmann and his vessels escaped.

The second group of German A-boats carried out an uneventful bombardment of the Bray Dunes area and returned to Flanders without incident. Albrecht and his group bombarded La Panne from 5.05 to 5.13am and while on their way back to harbour received word from Assmann that he was being pursued by British destroyers. Albrecht then steamed to link up with Assmann and met the latter at 5.50am. Aside from a brief attempt by one British coastal motorboat to attack the Germans with torpedoes, no further contact was made with the enemy and both forces returned to harbour without further loss. Later that day the Germans sent out a reconnaissance mission to try and find the missing *A-19* and *A-7* but only wreckage and bodies were found. The mission was a dismal failure for the Germans. Their bombardment had very little effect and the operation had cost them two, admittedly obsolete, but still useful vessels and, more importantly, forty-one men either dead or missing.

In his memoirs Keyes castigates Assmann for leaving the two A-Is to the tender mercies of their British pursuers. Both he and Newbolt however thought that the German force consisted of five destroyers, not the smaller and less well-armed A-IIIs. Assmann was seriously outgunned even after the torpedoing of the *Botha* and had he tried to fight matters out with the British he would likely have lost his entire force. Once he linked up with Albrecht the odds were in the German's favour, but by that point the two A-boats were beyond assistance. There was little else Assmann could have done.[77]

Von Schröder, for his part, was initially convinced that the Germans had won another victory. He claimed in his war diary that the bombardment had sunk two British and three French destroyers and badly damaged another British destroyer.[78] This was simply not true. The bombardments had a minimal effect on the naval resources of the Allies; what damage was done was mainly done by the French, and the bombardments did not affect the results of the land battles in the slightest. In spite of that, the Germans repeated the bombardment on 9 April and then again on the 18th but they did not have much success on either night.[79]

As far as the OHL was concerned there was still one other way in which the fleet could assist Germany's final bid for victory. By this juncture they had lost faith in the ability of the submarines to force Britain to the peace table and they now wanted the fleet to use its submarines against the British lines of communication with France. This, however, the navy was reluctant to do.

The Naval Staff laid out its stand on this issue in late March. They agreed that the fleet had to be prepared to assist the army in what was widely considered to be the decisive hour of the war, but believed that the submarines needed to continue to attack commercial shipping. They were to concentrate their efforts against the grain traffic between Britain and the USA. All other shipping was of secondary importance and all available submarines were assigned to the western approaches to attack this trade. They were not to be thrown away in attacks against British troop convoys. Neither were the surface forces in Flanders which, instead, were to strike at the British east coast traffic south of Hull. Their attacks were to be supplemented by air raids against British commercial shipping. In short, the British were to be given no respite since the next few months would decide the war.[80]

The Naval Staff also argued that the OHL was taking a dangerous position by assuming that a victory in France would force Britain to make peace. As evidence they cited reports in the British press discussing the feasibility of Britain carrying on the war in tandem with the United States even if France was defeated. The submarines remained the only effective weapon against

Great Britain. The navy was willing to support the offensive but not if it meant throwing away their ability to carry on the commercial war. The Naval Staff feared that the policy being urged by the OHL would result in such heavy submarine losses, that Germany's ability to resume the commercial war in the future would be destroyed. Therefore any attacks against the cross-Channel transports would have to be carried out by the light forces of the fleet. To make that possible they urged Scheer to transfer all available torpedo craft to Flanders from where they could launch several concerted strikes into the Channel against the transports. Numerous such raids would certainly force the British to retaliate by redistributing their forces and that would make an advance by the entire High Seas Fleet worthwhile.[81] In the meantime, the submarines would keep up the economic pressure on Great Britain. Here again, we see the plan of action that was first urged by von Schröder as early as 1915. Unfortunately for the Germans, they still lacked the will to take such a risky course and they let this last golden opportunity to decisively influence the course of the war pass them by.

For his part, von Schröder agreed with the findings of the Naval Staff. On 30 March he met with Rear-Admiral Walter Freiherr von Keyserlingk, chief of the operations group of the Naval Staff, to discuss possible action against the British Channel transports. Von Schröder reported that he did not think submarines could be used with any effect west of the Barrage; either against troop convoys or, for that matter, against the grain trade. The enemy defences in that area were simply too strong. The best that he could do was send the remaining submarine minelayers to mine the most widely-used enemy harbours. Von Schröder suggested that he could launch additional attacks against Dunkirk with both air and sea forces, but pointed out that his forces were certainly not strong enough to successfully attack the British troop transports. If he was to do that he would once again need the assistance of flotillas from the High Seas Fleet. Keyserlingk replied by informing von Schröder that any such decision would have to be taken by Scheer. He intimated that if the fleet was to bring significant forces west, they would have to make use of Antwerp and this would require some kind of decision on the status of the mouth of the Scheldt. This obviously, since it affected German relations with the Netherlands, was a political matter and out of his purview.[82] The meeting ended with no decision being taken other than to repeat the bombardment of Dunkirk.

For the most part the fleet was unwilling to take the steps necessary to provide any meaningful aid to the army. Had a concerted raid been undertaken in early April, similar to that of 14 February, it may have had a critical impact on the course of the battles in France, even without directly attacking troop transports. The attack might have delayed the shipment of vital reserves at a critical time. However, no action was taken and the navy left the army to fight the decisive battle on its own. For the last time the Germans' unwillingness to risk losses to their fleet negatively impacted their war effort. They were running out of time and chances but did not yet realise it. In the meantime, von Schröder's opposite number at Dover was busily planning one of the most famous and courageous exploits of the entire war.

TWISTING THE DRAGON'S TAIL: THE ZEEBRUGGE AND OSTEND RAIDS[83]

By this stage of the war, Bacon's plan for a great landing on the Belgian coast to support an advance by the British army was no longer feasible and the British were searching for other ways to destroy the effectiveness of the Flanders bases. Roger Keyes believed he had the answer. He intended to sink block ships in the entrances to the canals at Zeebrugge and Ostend. If he was successful the German forces in Bruges would be cut off from the sea.

The Plan

The idea for an attack on Zeebrugge and Ostend was as old as the German occupation of the coast itself. As early as December 1914, Winston Churchill proposed a concerted landing to retake Zeebrugge.[84] During 1915 the British considered a whole series of landing operations, some of which concerned the Flanders coast, before eventually settling on the Dardanelles offensive.[85] These somewhat amorphous plans began to take on firmer shape during late 1916 when Commodore Tyrwhitt created a plan for the blocking of the harbour at Zeebrugge. He intended to sink a block ship directly between the lock gates. This plan was rejected by Admiral Bacon, however, Tyrwhitt, undaunted, revised it in May 1917 and included in the revised version a landing on the Zeebrugge mole. He hoped to capture the mole and use it as a forward base for an attack against Antwerp which, if successful, would force the Germans out of Flanders and turn their right flank. Once again however, Bacon intervened. By that point he was already planning his own landing on the coast.[86] This was roughly where things stood when Keyes took command of the Plans Division.

Following their failure in the Third Battle of Ypres the British began to seriously consider the possibility of blocking both Ostend and Zeebrugge.[87] This was during the latter days of 1917 and it was as yet far from clear that the British had already found the answer to Germany's submarine campaign. Therefore planning for a blocking operation began in the Plans Division on 13

November 1917 and an initial plan was presented to the Board of the Admiralty on 3 December.[88]

The British were convinced that the blocking of these two harbours would seriously limit Germany's ability to carry on the submarine war. They estimated that Bruges had the capacity to house over thirty-five torpedo-boats and more than thirty submarines. The loss of this base would not only greatly restrict the submarine campaign; it would also deny the Germans the forward bases they were using to launch their destroyer raids.[89] To paraphrase Keyes himself, 25 percent of all British shipping losses were due to the Flanders submarine flotillas and by blocking the Flanders harbours the Royal Navy would end the threat of the Flanders submarines. They would also remove 'the nasty threat of a large destroyer flotilla on the flank of our communications.'[90] That said, blocking these harbours would be no easy task. Even though von Schröder and his staff were pessimistic about their ability to turn aside a small raid they had created an immense ring of fortifications. Any attack against those fortifications would have to be very carefully planned and prepared.

The British, in planning the attack, had to deal with a large number of both potential and real obstacles. Captain Alfred Carpenter, the commander of the *Vindictive* during the raid on Zeebrugge, listed those that pertained to Zeebrugge: the German aircraft patrols; submarines; surface patrol craft; mines; a lack of navigational aids along the coast; the heavy German coastal artillery; the guns on the mole itself; the net barrage in the harbour; the shore batteries around the canal; and, finally, the weather.[91] With the exception of the mole guns all of these obstacles also existed at Ostend. The most serious of them were the German naval forces and the coastal artillery, both the heavy batteries and the guns on the mole.

The British believed that there were thirty-eight submarines and twenty-eight torpedo-boats based at Bruges and an additional thirty destroyers at Zeebrugge (this was an overestimation) the latter of which could intervene, possibly decisively, in the defence of the harbour.[92] There were also the numerous coastal batteries to deal with. The British estimated these as amounting to: six batteries of 5.9-inch guns (twenty-two guns total); three 4.1-inch batteries (nine guns); two 3.5-inch batteries (eight guns); one 6.7-inch battery (four guns); one 8.2-inch battery (four guns); five 11-inch batteries (twenty guns); and one 15-inch battery (four guns).[93] This list did not include the batteries on the mole which consisted of two 3.5-inch guns and four 4.1-inch guns.[94] These were serious obstacles indeed. In fact, while the British overestimated the number of submarines and torpedo-craft in Bruges and

Zeebrugge, they underestimated the number of coastal guns. The mole at Zeebrugge was formidable in itself. It was divided into four sections that together totaled over one and-a-half miles in length. The mole batteries were at the furthest end from shore on a small extension that was about 260 yards long and fifteen feet wide. They were placed so they could command the entrance to the harbour. The main body of the mole itself housed the mole garrison. (Estimated to be about 1,000 men.) This portion was 1,874 yards long and eighty-one yards wide and was also home to the Zeebrugge air station. Next to the main body of the mole was an iron viaduct that connected the mole to the shore and provided rail access to the mole itself. The main communication lines, especially the telephone wires connecting the mole garrison with the headquarters of the 1st MarineDivision, also ran along the viaduct, which was 330 yards long.[95] The outer sea wall of the mole, which would have to be scaled by any attacking force, was forty-nine feet above sea level at low tide and twenty-nine feet above sea level at high tide. That meant that an attack on the mole could only realistically be launched at high tide. This restricted the possible dates for the operation to just two weeks of every month; only one week if the attackers wanted the protection of a moonless night. Not daunted by the considerable difficulties, Keyes and his staff went to work preparing a plan of action.

For Zeebrugge the British eventually settled on a three-part plan. The first part was partially a diversion; it was an attack on the Zeebrugge mole designed to capture or destroy the mole battery so that it could not fire on the block ships as they tried to reach the canal entrance. The second part of the plan involved the destruction of the viaduct connecting the mole to the mainland and the third part of the operation was the actual attempt to sail three block ships into the canal entrance and sink them.

It would not be enough though to just block Zeebrugge. To really block the German forces into Bruges the British would also have to block the canal at Ostend. On the surface this was an easier task since there was no mole there to aid the defenders. The plan for Ostend was simply to sail two block ships into the canal entrance and sink them.[96]

Keyes first submitted his plan to the Admiralty on 3 December 1917. The original plan did not envisage an attack on the mole; that touch was added by Admiral Bacon when the plan was sent to him for approval. Bacon wanted to land troops on the mole from a monitor that would be specially modified with a collapsible bow so that it could 'ram' the mole and then drop down a large, hinged landing bridge which men could quickly cross over to get on the mole. Keyes modified Bacon's scheme. In his plan the old cruiser *Vindictive* was assigned to attack the mole. She was fitted with a series of walkways that were spaced around her port side (these replaced Bacon's large drawbridge) and would drop onto the mole thus allowing the troops on the cruiser to cross over. In addition, most of the cruiser's standard armament was removed and replaced by two flamethrowers, ten Lewis guns, three other machine guns and sixteen mortars. Finally, *Vindictive* had one 28cm and two 19cm howitzers installed for use against the mole battery and the lock gates.[97]

The force assigned to attack the mole consisted of 200 sailors and 600 marines, however, only 100 sailors and 200 marines were carried in *Vindictive*. Rather than risk the total failure of the attack should the old cruiser not reach the mole Keyes wisely chose to use three separate ships to transport his attacking force. The other two ships were ferry boats; *Iris* and *Daffodil*. The remaining men were split evenly between the two craft. The ferry boats, being considerably smaller than *Vindictive*, were equipped with scaling ladders so that their complement of men could reach the mole. *Daffodil* though, had a second duty. It was her responsibility to push *Vindictive* alongside the mole and hold her in place while her anchors were secured. This was necessary because Keyes wanted the cruiser to place its port side against the mole, not its bow. As a result the force of the water thrown against the mole might push her away. *Daffodil* was to ensure that did not happen.

The British intended to bring the *Vindictive* alongside the mole and anchor the cruiser directly across from the mole battery so that the troops could be disembarked right on top of their target. Once the mole battery had been taken or destroyed, the landing force was then to proceed down the mole and do as much damage as they possibly could by planting demolition charges. Keyes hoped that they would be able to destroy the air station and possibly some of the German destroyers moored alongside the mole. Aside from the mole battery their specific targets were: the air station; the anti-aircraft batteries; the lighthouse; and, finally, the torpedo-craft. If all else failed, Keyes hoped that the attack on the mole would at least divert the German's attention from Britain's real objective, the canal entrance.

To increase the diversionary aspect of the assault Keyes intended to destroy the viaduct connecting the mole to the mainland. If this could be done it would isolate the mole garrison since their only connection to 1st MarineDivision headquarters were the phone lines across the viaduct. The garrison was not equipped with radios. Two old C-class submarines were assigned to this mission. Both submarines had their bows packed with explosives. According to the plan the submarines were to be towed across the North Sea until they were just off the coast at which point they would be released from their tow lines and would proceed under their own power to the viaduct. Upon reaching their objective they were to ram themselves bow first into it. The hope was that they would become jammed in the steel girders supporting the railway. Once that had been accomplished the crews were to set the timers on the explosives and abandon ship. Each submarine (*C-1* and *C-3* were the two chosen) was also equipped with gyroscopic steering devices so that the crew could abandon ship prior to reaching the viaduct if they so chose. Keyes hoped this would increase the crew's chances of survival.

As for the block ships themselves, three old cruisers were selected, *Iphigenia*, *Intrepid*, and *Thetis*. Each of them was given a minimum crew. Their goals differed. *Thetis*, which was to enter the harbour first, was to steam as far as the lock gates and then scuttle herself while the two following vessels were to enter the canal, swing themselves across the breadth of the canal so that they were blocking the entirety of it and then scuttle themselves. In order to make the removal of the ships more difficult, and also to protect the ships' vital machinery on their way into the canal, they were all filled with cement. Finally, so that a lucky hit by the enemy would not totally disable a ship, each was outfitted with alternate conning and firing positions.

The block ships and submarines were to be followed by coastal motorboats which were to create artificial smoke to cover the approach of the British forces and, once the attack was completed, were to rescue the crews of the other vessels. These small craft were the key to the entire operation. It was vital for the British to attain surprise. They knew from their experiences bombarding the coast that the German coastal guns could be devastating and that advancing in the clear against those batteries, even at night, would invite disaster. For that reason it was absolutely critical that the British be able to produce an effective smokescreen that would hide the advance of their flotilla until it was too late. Unfortunately for the British, the need for the smokescreen added another variable to their plan. Since the smoke was so important they would need an onshore wind in order to launch the attack. An offshore breeze would push the smoke back into the British force and obscure their vision while giving the German gunners excellent targets; a recipe for disaster.

To create additional surprise, and hopefully convince the Germans that the operation was merely a routine attack on the coast, Keyes included bombardments by the large monitors and air raids on the harbours in the plan. The bombardments were to begin one week before the planned attack so that the Germans would have time to become accustomed to them. The air attacks, on the other hand, were to begin shortly before the scheduled arrival of the naval forces. In order to protect all of this from interference by the German navy four cruisers, two leaders and two divisions of destroyers from the Harwich force were to patrol to the northeast of the main advance. Ten additional destroyers went with the motor-launches and coastal motorboats to protect the blocking force. Finally, the monitors *Lord Clive* and *Prince Eugene*, along with three French destroyers, were to patrol along the western axis of the advance. All told, 146 British and French vessels were to take part.

The plan for Ostend was much less elaborate. The British selected two more old cruisers, the *Sirius* and the *Brilliant*, to attack Ostend. Their mission was the same as it was for the block ships at Zeebrugge; to sail into the canal and then turn roughly perpendicular to it and sink themselves. As was the case at Zeebrugge they were filled with cement to make the work of salvaging them more difficult. Also as at Zeebrugge there was to be a preliminary coastal bombardment by monitors and an air attack. Here as well a vital barrier of artificial smoke was to be created and, once the attack was complete, several small motor launches were to rescue the crews of the block ships. The plan was approved by the Admiralty in February 1918 and preparations went forward to implement it.

The attack was initially intended for March but a lack of sufficient smoke producing chemicals forced its postponement until April. The first time all the conditions would be met, high tide at roughly midnight with a new moon, would be around 11 April.

The Attack[98]

On 11 April, the first day of the period during which tidal and lunar conditions would be appropriate for the attack, the wind was also favorable. As a result Keyes ordered the armada to set sail. Unfortunately for the British the wind changed as they approached the Flanders coast and began to blow offshore. Since this would make it impossible to maintain the critical smokescreen Keyes was forced to order the force to return to harbour. The only parts of the operation that went forward were the air attacks, the coastal bombardments and a brief attack by a British coastal motorboat against the harbour at Ostend. The crew of the motorboat had not received the recall order.[99]

Keyes was not deterred and tried again on the 13th. Once again, though, the weather forced him to abandon the mission. By that point the Admiralty was concerned that after two false starts the advantage of surprise had to have been lost and that the Germans must realise what was going on. Therefore they were very reluctant to allow Keyes to wait for the next favourable weather period, which would not occur until May, however, when Keyes urged Admiral Wemyss to allow him to try again in late April when all the conditions would be right except for the moon, which would now be full, Wemyss agreed.

Were the Germans aware of what was going on? To a degree, yes. However, the events of the 11th and the 13th had little impact on them. They noted the unusually heavy air activity and the patrols reported hearing engine noises out to sea around midnight on the 11th. At around 1.15am a heavy bombardment of Ostend was noted and shortly thereafter a British coastal motorboat appeared and seemed to attack the piers. The German gunners sank the British ship and the entire crew was lost. However, upon salvaging the vessel the Germans discovered maps and orders for the planned British operation.[100] Finding these maps convinced von Schröder of two things: first of all, that the operation had been aimed only at Ostend and secondly, that the fire from the coastal artillery had been so severe that it forced the British to abandon the attack. Aerial reconnaissance on the following day showed a large force of enemy vessels assembled in both Dunkirk and Dover. As a result von Schröder placed the coast around Ostend on alert in the belief that the British would try another blocking attempt there in the near future. The strength of the nightly coastal patrols was not increased because von Schröder was convinced that, due to the poor visibility at night and his low number of available patrol craft, such a move would not be cost-effective. He also feared that if significant German naval forces were at sea the gunners of the coastal artillery would be overly cautious and as a result might not be able to effectively defend the coast.[101] Finally, von Schröder, though warned that the British had intended an operation of some type, basically remained ignorant as to that operation's main objective. Aside from raising the state of general awareness all along the coast there was little else that could be done.

The first day of Keyes' new period of favourable weather was 22 April. Since the wind was also favourable that day Keyes decided to try again. The British force left harbour at 1pm, rendezvoused with their escorting destroyers at 5pm, and then proceeded to the Flanders coast. This time the wind remained favourable and the weather gradually became rainy and drizzly which aided the British by further obscuring vision. Unfortunately the rain and drizzle did mean that the planned air attack had to be cancelled. Otherwise the operation proceeded as planned.

At 12.10am (11.10pm Greenwich) the various small craft began laying their smokescreen.[102] At 12.19am the MarineKorps Luftabwehr received word that Ostend was under bombardment from both land and sea. A few moments later, at roughly 12.30am, *Erebus* and *Terror* began their bombardment of Zeebrugge and the alarm was sent out. At this point, however, the Germans still considered this to be merely another bombardment. Therefore when the alarm was sounded the garrison and the crews of the destroyers alongside the mole took shelter.[103] Shortly after the beginning of the bombardment three British coastal motorboats launched a sudden attack on the mole and the ships of the 2nd Destroyer Half-Flotilla which were tied up alongside the mole's inner wall. The motorboats appeared out of the smoke very quickly, fired torpedoes at the German vessels and then disappeared. No damage was done but the Germans were finally alerted to the fact that this was not simply a routine bombardment.[104] This was at roughly 12.35am, the same time that the battery *Würtemberg*, having heard engine noises, began firing starshells.[105] At 12.45am the mole battery's garrison, having heard engine noises as well, returned to their battle stations, turned on their spotlights and began firing their guns.[106] At the same time the coastal batteries began to lay down their planned barrage fire just outside the entrance to the harbour. They still could not see any enemy vessels. That suddenly changed.

At about 12.50am the British had a stroke of ill-luck as the wind they had been using so effectively for protection suddenly veered and began to blow out of the south, offshore. At 12.56am the German gunners on the mole saw a large shape loom out of the artificial fog on a direct heading for the mole; this was the *Vindictive*. She was immediately taken under very heavy fire from the mole battery which reported that the deck of the cruiser was 'black with men.'[107] The deck proved to be an appealing target and the German gunners concentrated their fire on the masses of British soldiers crammed on board. Casualties were accordingly very high. When he emerged into this withering gunfire the commander of the *Vindictive*, Carpenter, increased speed and brought his ship alongside the mole as soon as possible, reaching the mole at roughly 1.01am. This increase in speed took him rapidly into a 'dead area' where the mole battery could not reach the ship; unfortunately it also took him far to the west of his intended landing area. This posed a serious problem for the troops assigned to land on the mole. They would now have to fight their way to the mole battery against stiff opposition. This made it unlikely that they would be able to destroy the mole battery before the block ships arrived. Unfortunately for them that was not their only problem. On its approach the *Vindictive* had lost all but two of the specially constructed landing bridges. As a result, the flow of men onto the mole was more of a trickle than a flood. Furthermore three of the four officers chosen to lead the assault had been killed while the cruiser was making its approach run and the fourth had been knocked unconscious. As a result there was a tremendous amount of initial confusion for the landing force; confusion that was aggravated by the inability of the *Vindictive* to stay alongside the mole. The force of water that she had thrown against the mole on her approach caused the ship to roll heavily, which in turn left the two existing bridges bouncing and sliding along the outside wall of the mole. The ship itself also had a tendency to slide away from the mole and the ferry *Daffodil* had to struggle to hold the *Vindictive* against the mole. Since the former ship was forced to stay next to *Vindictive* the troops she carried had to first cross to the *Vindictive* and then over to the mole. Very few of them made it.

The other ferry, the *Iris*, was having serious problems of her own. She was unable to secure herself to the mole despite the valiant efforts of two members of her landing party who gave their lives climbing up the scaling ladders to try to secure the ship. Eventually she was forced to give up her efforts and *Iris* too moved to the *Vindictive* to try and get her contingent of troops onto the mole by sending them over the cruiser. However, by the time they managed to reach the cruiser, the retreat had already been sounded.

The Germans initially believed that *Vindictive* was a block ship that had missed the entrance to the harbour.[108] That notion was soon dispelled when British marines began trickling on to the mole from the cruiser. Most of the mole garrison as well as the crews of the 2nd Destroyer Half-Flotilla were still in their shelters at the time and they now rushed to their battle stations. At this point the commander of the II Torpedo-Boat Half-Flotilla, Günther Lütjens, dismounted one of his machine guns and brought it onto the mole to aid the defenders.[109] The remaining ships of the flotilla soon became involved in the battle as well. *V-69*, which by chance was directly across the mole from the *Vindictive*, was able to use her deck guns to fire at the cruiser. Since the mole battery could no longer reach the *Vindictive* most of the damage sustained by the old cruiser came from the guns of *V-69*. Kapitänleutnant Konrad Zander, the commander of the II Destroyer Half-Flotilla, then ordered the crews that were still in the shelters to assist in the defence of the mole.[110] The mole battery also organised a group of men to assist the other defenders.[111]

Despite the commendable bravery of the few British marines who managed to reach the mole, this haphazard German defence was able to hold them off. The *Vindictive*'s change in speed had left them too far from their objective. They had to advance 250 yards into the face of German machine gun fire without the aid of the special weapons on the *Vindictive* such as the flamethrowers and Lewis guns, since most of those guns had been destroyed or rendered useless by the heavy fire directed at the *Vindictive*. The majority of the British troops that did manage to land were simply pinned down and were unable to accomplish any of their goals.

While this battle was getting underway the entire scene was suddenly rocked by a massive explosion to the west. The submarine *C-3* had managed to reach the viaduct and ram itself into its girders. The Germans on the viaduct let her approach, evidently believing that the submarine was trying to enter the harbour by slipping below the viaduct. It was not until the crew of *C-3* abandoned ship and attempted to escape that the Germans opened fire. As a result the British succeeded brilliantly. The explosion of *C-3* completely destroyed the viaduct severing the mole garrison from any reinforcements and also severing their communications with the 1st MarineDivision.[112]

It was in the light of the explosion of the viaduct that the gunners of the mole battery got their first glimpse of the approaching British block ships. By 1.20am *Thetis*, the first of the block ships, had already traversed the harbour entrance where the heaviest German barrage was being laid down. She was immediately fired upon by the mole battery and the batteries around the canal entrance. She was hit several times, including at least twice below the waterline and veered to port, eventually running into a net barrage the MarineKorps had laid across the entrance to the canal. In the process the net barrage was destroyed but *Thetis'* screws became so fouled that her engines stopped and her commander was forced to scuttle the vessel in the harbour itself instead of within the canal. Fortunately for the British, by destroying the barrage the *Thetis* cleared the way for the remaining two block ships.

The British were also fortunate in another regard. The attack on the mole, though tactically a failure, did divert the attention of the mole garrison and, more importantly, that of the crews of the torpedo-boats, away from the block ships. Therefore the torpedo-boats were not in a position to launch torpedoes at the block ships as they moved into the harbour. The gunfire of the coastal batteries, withering though it was, could not divert the cruisers from their objective. As a result both *Iphigenia* and *Intrepid* were able to enter the canal and sink themselves in their appointed locations by 1.45am. By the time the two vessels had been scuttled the only opening in the canal was a small gap to either side of the block ships, roughly 17m wide. Unfortunately for the British, the failure of *Thetis* to reach the lock gates would prove to be very important to the success or failure of the mission.

Seeing the block ships entering the harbour Captain Carpenter ordered the *Daffodil* to sound the recall order on her whistle since the signal whistle on the *Vindictive* had been destroyed. This happened at roughly 2am. Most of the landing force was taken off with numerous wounded men being carried off by their comrades. In total the Germans took less than twenty prisoners. However, retreating did not mean an end to the battle for *Vindictive*, *Daffodil*, and *Iris*. While they were leaving they once again came under fire from the German batteries. *Iris* was hit by twelve successive salvoes and was reduced to a flaming

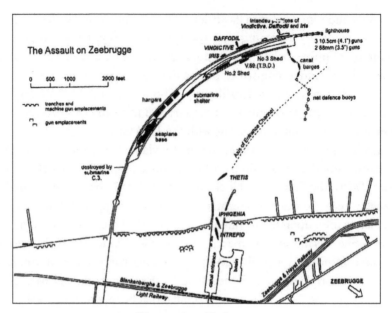

The assault on Zeebrugge

wreck.[113] She eventually had to be taken in tow in order to return to Britain.

The crews of the block ships also had a harrowing time. They were rescued by the small motor-launches and coastal motorboats but some of those were also struck by shells and damaged. As the battle was winding down the British destroyer *North Star* entered the harbour and fired torpedoes at what her commander believed to be German destroyers alongside the mole. Of the two torpedoes she fired, one missed and the other hit and sank a dredger. The attempt brought *North Star* to the attention of the mole battery which dealt a series of blows that soon left the destroyer motionless. Several attempts by her sister-ship *Phoebe* to take her in tow eventually had to be given up. The crew was taken off and the *North Star* was then sunk. The remainder of the British force was able to escape.

British losses in ships were fairly light, only two motor-launches and the *North Star* were sunk though the *Vindictive*, *Iris*, and several motor-launches were seriously damaged. They were not so fortunate in terms of manpower. The Germans estimated that 214 British were killed, 383 wounded and nineteen taken prisoner.[114] The British reported 170 killed, 400 wounded and forty-five missing.[115] Von Schröder reported the German losses as eight dead and sixteen wounded.[116] In the course of the battle *V-69* and *S-53* both took minor damage while *S-63* was heavily battered but remained seaworthy.[117] Despite the discrepancy in losses, von Schröder's initial assessment of the

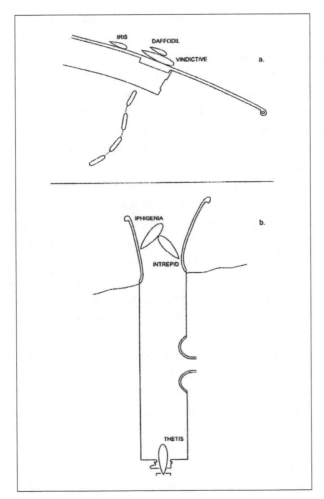

The planned positions of the block ships at Zeebrugge

battle was not positive. 'The entrance to the Zeebrugge locks is blocked at low tide,' he recorded on the evening of the 22nd, also noting that they would have to wait for high tide to determine if vessels could be passed through at all.[118] Keyes left the scene of battle confident that he had succeeded. It must be remembered, however, that the operation was a two-pronged attack aimed not only at Zeebrugge but also at Ostend. At the latter harbour the British did not have as much success.

The group assigned to block Ostend consisted of the old cruisers *Sirius* and *Brilliant*, two destroyers and once again several motor-launches and coastal motorboats to first create the smokescreen and then rescue the crews of the block ships. The British had a more difficult time here for two main reasons.

First of all, the night before the attack the Germans moved one of the light buoys that they used to mark channels along the coast one mile to the east. This was not in expectation of an attack, it was simply a defensive measure used occasionally by the MarineKorps, unfortunately the British had intended to use this buoy to mark their way into the harbour.[119] Therefore, when *Sirius* and *Brilliant* arrived they found the buoy and proceeded to the coast but ran aground about one mile east of the canal entrance. The second major problem the British had was that the fire from the German coastal batteries was much heavier at Ostend than it was at Zeebrugge. The battery commanders on this sector of the coast did not have to worry about hitting their own ships since there were no German ships in the harbour. As a result the battery commanders had a free field of fire and were able to lay down a much heavier barrage here than the commanders at Zeebrugge could. The end result of the gunfire and the moved buoy was the failure of the British attack. Keyes, however, was not willing to let matters rest there and intended to follow up the failure at Ostend with another attack as soon as possible.

He was able to convince the Admiralty to approve his plan for a second attack on Ostend because he had been successful at Zeebrugge. The second attack would follow essentially the same plan as the first except that this time he intended to proceed with only the *Vindictive* as a block ship. The old cruiser would be accompanied by eighteen French and British destroyers to prevent interference from German forces in the Bight or Zeebrugge. The attack would also be accompanied by four monitors that would provide a preliminary artillery barrage. There were also the usual motor-launches and coastal motorboats to provide a smokescreen and rescue the crew of the *Vindictive*. When it proved impossible to launch the second attack in April due to the extensive damage the *Vindictive* had taken at Zeebrugge the operation was postponed until May. As a result Keyes had time to find a second old cruiser that could accompany *Vindictive*; this was *Sappho*. The new period of favourable weather would begin on 9 May.

The weather conditions turned out to be auspicious on the 9th and Keyes decided to go ahead with the mission. *Vindictive* and *Sappho* accordingly left Dover and proceeded first to Dunkirk to pick up the monitors and several of the accompanying destroyers. They left Dunkirk for Flanders at 11.30pm (Greenwich). Shortly after leaving harbour though *Sappho* experienced boiler trouble and was unable to keep up the necessary speed. As a result she was sent back to Dunkirk and *Vindictive* proceeded alone after all.[120]

The MarineKorps was not unaware that conditions were favourable for a renewed enemy attack. As a result two A-Is were on patrol off Ostend and two

minesweepers patrolled off Zeebrugge. The two A-Is left harbour at roughly
the same time that *Vindictive* and *Sappho* were leaving Dunkirk. At 1.30pm
GMT they reported the muzzle fire of large guns off to the northwest. Shortly
afterward they spotted a small motorboat making artificial fog through which
they could just make out what appeared to be a cruiser and a destroyer. At 1.40
they fired off alarm rockets to alert the coast. Both craft then tried to escape
the area so as not to be hit by the fire of their own batteries. While trying to
escape they ran into the enemy fog bank and ended up colliding with each
other, leaving one of the vessels, *A-8*, unmaneuverable due to rudder damage.
She was eventually spotted and attacked, though without success, by an enemy
motorboat before running aground about 2.20am. Eventually *A-8* was found
by the other boat, *A-11*, and towed back to harbour.[121]

While *A-8* and *A-11* were having their misadventure the main allied attack
began. At 1.45am the monitors began a heavy bombardment of the coast that
was accompanied by air attacks against both Ostend and Zeebrugge. The
coastal batteries immediately responded, targeting on the muzzle flashes of
the British guns. Once the enemy smokescreen was sighted, the batteries
began to lay down their planned barrage fire before the entrance to the
harbour. They also fired starshells to illuminate the entire scene. Under the
cover of the bombardment several coastal motorboats raced into the harbour
to fire torpedoes as well as their machine guns at the piers jutting out from the
coastline.[122] At roughly 2.05am the *Vindictive* reached the entrance to the
harbour though her commander, no longer Carpenter, had a difficult time
finding the canal entrance and spent several minutes steaming parallel to the
coast searching for the piers. During this entire time the ship was held under
a heavy barrage by the German coastal guns and *Vindictive* suffered very
heavy losses, including the commander, who was killed when he stepped
outside the bridge just as a German shell smashed into the ship. The ship
continued on her course but ran aground just east of the entrance to the main
shipping channel. Despite efforts to get her back into the channel, the damage
she had received was too severe and the ship had to be abandoned. Once again
the attempt to block Ostend had failed. The British suffered ten men killed,
twelve wounded, and three taken prisoner while the Germans lost three killed
and eight wounded. The Germans attributed their victory to the fire of the
coastal artillery.[123] Interestingly, all the German reports refer to a second
cruiser which appeared out of the smoke at the same time as *Vindictive* but
then went back into the smoke and was not seen again. It is unknown what
vessel they are referring to, perhaps one of the British destroyers briefly
became visible. At any rate the German claims to have done serious damage

to an additional cruiser must be considered as false since the *Vindictive* was the only cruiser involved in the attack.

Von Schröder was convinced that this would not be the last attack against Ostend[124] and as a direct result of this raid a new minefield was laid before the entrance to the harbour despite the difficulties that it would pose for the few German craft still using the port. The minefield was completed on 15 May. On the 25th a similar field was laid in the harbour at Zeebrugge with only a 150-metre gap left open directly alongside the mole and under the guns of the mole battery.[125]

Keyes did suggest that he make a third attempt against Ostend but he was prevented from doing so by the Admiralty which now considered it to be too dangerous and no longer worth the risk. As a result Ostend was left open. That said, two questions remain to be answered: what effect did the raids have on the MarineKorps' prosecution of the war and were the raids themselves a success?

The Aftermath

The Germans reacted to the attack with both anger and surprise. The Zeebrugge canal was clearly impassable at low tide and it remained to be seen whether or not it could be used at high tide. Von Schröder visited Zeebrugge on the 23rd to examine the damage first hand and was not pleased.[126] In his initial report he stated that the British had made a surprise landing on the mole at Zeebrugge and had attempted to block the canal there. During the attack they destroyed the viaduct connecting the mole to the mainland and managed to sink three cruisers in the entrance to the canal. The entrance was totally blocked at low tide and, in von Schröder's initial opinion, would probably be blocked at high tide as well, though it did appear that it might be possible to remove the ships. As for the mole, the facilities there and the vessels that were moored to it were undamaged. This report was sent to both the Naval Staff and the IV army.[127] In a later supplement sent only to von Holtzendorff von Schröder elaborated on the attack.

In the latter report he mentioned that, after perusing captured documents and interrogating prisoners, he had discovered that the British had hoped to block the Zeebrugge canal. He reiterated that two enemy ships had been sunk in the canal and that the latter was at least partially blocked. He included a detailed report on *Vindictive*'s attack on the mole and claimed that one enemy destroyer and several small motorboats had been sunk by German gunfire. He believed that an additional two destroyers had been sunk but had no proof. Finally, he suggested that the press release emphasise the successful defence of the mole and the inability of the enemy to destroy the lock gates. The cruisers were to be mentioned as having 'been sunk directly off the coast.'[128] In other words, the attack was to be described as a failure. The Kaiser himself wrote to Ludendorff in this vein on the 23rd informing him that their enemies' attempt to render the Flanders bases inoperative had failed.[129]

Admiral von Holtzendorff considered the attack a serious German defeat and wanted answers to two particular questions: if the MarineKorps knew of the intended raid from the documents captured on the 11th why were they not better prepared to defend the harbours; and why were there no coastal patrol craft before Zeebrugge on the night of the 22nd? He was not the only one who wanted answers. General Ludendorff also wanted to know why the coastal defences could not stop the enemy ships from reaching the canal.[130]

Von Schröder replied by pointing out that the 1st MarineDivision had always said that they could not prevent small enemy raids. Their defences were designed to defeat full-scale enemy invasions. The reason that the usual nightly patrols were not at sea was because of the limited resources he currently had; the majority of his torpedo-boats and destroyers were involved in the daily minesweeping missions and their crews needed a respite from activity. It was 'simply not possible to maintain the minesweeping as well as an uninterrupted coastal patrol.'[131] In addition, he had not considered the weather on the 22nd to be suitable for an enemy attack.

Von Schröder took this opportunity to fling verbal darts at Germany's naval leadership, stating that the navy had made the attack possible by not sending him the forces he needed to properly defend the coast. Since he had been told that no further reinforcements were to be expected he had felt it necessary to husband his resources. He also pointed out that, on the night of the first attempt, two A-Is had been at sea but had not detected the enemy force; hence he considered it unlikely that the patrols would have been of any use. The failure of the coastal artillery to destroy the enemy vessels before they could reach the coast was attributed to the very heavy artificial fog laid down by the British. Finally, he concluded by commending the mole garrison for holding their ground in very difficult circumstances, particularly after the destruction of the viaduct. In a supplement to his report he listed a series of new defensive measures that would be implemented to better prepare the harbour for a repeat of the raid: 1) the mole garrison would be expanded by an infantry company and half a machine gun company; 2) an overall commander for the defence of the mole would be appointed; 3) a new battery would be built at the base of the mole that would be capable of covering the entire area; and 4) additional guns for close range combat would be installed around the harbour to supplement the larger coastal guns.

Even so, he pointed out that there was no way to prevent or guarantee a successful defence against future surprise raids; which he considered inevitable.[132] The Kaiser concurred and fully approved of von Schröder's proposed defensive changes. He ordered their immediate implementation.[133]

To Ludendorff's complaints von Schröder replied that, regardless of the damage done by gunfire, it still took time for a ship to sink and while it was sinking it could continue moving forward under its own momentum even if its engines had been destroyed. In other words, the coastal guns themselves could not have kept the block ships from their targets unless they scored a lucky hit and forced a ship to explode by, for example, hitting a magazine.[134]

Von Arnim supported von Schröder's conclusions. After reviewing the MarineKorps' reports on the raid, von Arnim concluded that the defenders were properly prepared and that there had been no 'omissions of duty.' He did, however, suggest placing additional machine guns and smaller calibre artillery around the harbour to provide a stronger defence in the event that the British tried again. He also suggested that the Flanders torpedo-boats be used in a continuous patrol line that would ensure advance warning of the approach of any enemy force. Finally, he suggested laying a minefield alongside the mole.[135]

While these exchanges took place, the Marinekorps was also engaged in an ongoing effort to determine how much damage had actually been done. On the 24th reports trickled in to von Schröder that one dredger had been totally destroyed during the attack and that an additional one was severely damaged (one was torpedoed by *North Star* and the other was rammed by *Intrepid* on her way into the canal). This would significantly delay the work of clearing a channel around the block ships.[136] However, there was good news. That evening four boats of the II Torpedo-Boat Half-Flotilla left Bruges at high tide and passed through the canal. These were not large destroyers, just the smaller A-IIs, but their passage seemed to indicate that it would be possible to restore the canal to full use relatively soon.[137] On the following day *UB-16* became the first submarine to pass through the canal. Despite the passage of the submarine and the torpedo-boats the canal remained closed to the larger destroyers. The latter had to use the canal to Ostend.[138] Even though that canal was still useable, von Schröder had to make a decision on what should be done with the block ships.

On 1 May he met with members of the Northern Salvage Association to discuss the best ways to remove the block ships. The salvage company presented him with three options: 1) pumping out the ships and then raising them; 2) destroying them with explosives; or 3) cutting through them and removing them piece by piece. In the end none of these were desirable. The use of explosives was ruled out because it might only aggravate the problem by creating a large mass of debris that would then have to be removed piece by piece. Pumping out the ships would most likely only result in sand taking the place of the water, thereby making the ships even heavier and more difficult to remove. That left cutting through them and removing them piece-by-piece. This, however, would be very time-consuming and the MarineKorps lacked both the personnel and the equipment for the job. Therefore, von Schröder decided to have a channel dredged through the silt around the block ships. This would clear a path roughly 3.5m deep at low tide and would be sufficient to allow any of the craft based in Bruges to use the canal.[139] The MarineKorps did eventually make plans to move *Iphigenia*. They intended to seal the holes in the ship and then pump out enough water so that the ship could be towed further into the canal and turned parallel to the canal. This was not done before the end of the war. The dredging of the channel was successful and the immediate damage to the German war effort was quickly repaired. On 4 May *UC-17* became the first UC-II to pass through the canal.[140] 14 May was the key date however. It was on that day that four destroyers from the Destroyer Flotilla moved through the canal without difficulty; though they did have to do so at high tide.[141] By 8 June a wooden walkway had been stretched across the break in the viaduct to allow foot and bicycle traffic back and forth to the mole.[142] The long-term affects of the raid on the course of the naval war therefore were minimal.

The raid did lead, however, to major changes in the defences of Zeebrugge. The most basic change was the transfer of several guns from the MarineKorps' land front to the harbours. These amounted to: two 5cm guns that were mounted on the mole; an additional four 7.7cm guns erected at the harbour entrance to lay down barrage fire; and two 17cm guns taken from the *Sachsen* battery and moved to the base of the mole where they were paired with three 15cm guns. Finally, the mole battery was expanded by adding a 10.5cm gun. In Ostend an additional three 15cm, four 7.7cm, one 8.8cm, and four 17cm guns were brought in to lay down barrage fire.[143] Furthermore an additional company of infantry was assigned to the mole garrison. Also, in the event of a future attack, the commander of the mole garrison was empowered to commandeer all air and naval forces in and around the harbour. In urgent cases the mole commander was also empowered to take command of the artillery placed around the harbour.[144] The Germans also installed hydrophones in both Ostend and Zeebrugge and their naval patrols were increased in intensity.[145]

The preparations did not end there. Von Schröder and his staff also examined methods by which the harbour entrance could be narrowed, for example, by using chain barrages that would force traffic to use one primary channel that would run directly under the mole battery.[146] Von Schröder also decided to add a specially built torpedo battery at the end of the mole extension that would theoretically be able to torpedo any enemy forces trying to break into the harbour.[147] This battery was completed on 8 June.[148] Mortars were also added to the mole itself.[149] Finally, a new series of defensive minefields were laid.

These minefields were first proposed by Admiral Schultz on 26 April and were initially opposed by von Schröder,[150] who believed that new minefields would make it much more difficult for German submarines to get in and out of the harbours. Essentially the Germans would be blocking the harbours themselves. Von Schröder, at least initially, preferred to risk a successful blocking attempt, but he was eventually converted when officials from Wilhelmshaven who came to review the harbour's defences sided with Schultz.[151] As a result a new minefield was laid in Ostend on 14 May and a similar barrier was laid down in Zeebrugge on 25 May.[152] The Zeebrugge barrier left a small gap directly adjacent to the mole so that German craft could still the harbour but enemy forces would have to face the guns of the mole battery if they wanted to avoid the mines. The laying of the field proved to be hazardous however. *V-74* was sunk by a prematurely exploding mine and ended up blocking part of the harbour.[153]

In addition to these new defensive measures, new orders were issued for the existing defences. From now on, on nights when the weather was favourable for an enemy attack, one destroyer was kept moored near the outer edge of the mole in a position where its torpedoes could be added to those of the torpedo battery.[154] Also, two large motorboats were kept ready in Zeebrugge to move information and reinforcements back and forth from the mole to the shore.[155] Finally, the 1st MarineDivision issued new orders for the defence of the mole itself. According to these new plans a total of fourteen machine guns were set up, in seven pairs, in various places along the mole, from near the mole battery and the lighthouse to the air station. These guns were supplemented by twelve captured Lewis guns that were distributed evenly along the mole. Any enemy attempting to land on the mole was to be immediately attacked with machine guns and hand grenades. If the enemy still managed to land they were to be cut off from their ships and pinned down.[156] The other regulations remained essentially the same. In the event of an enemy bombardment the garrison troops were to retreat to their shelters and prepare for battle. Machine gun crews were to remain near the entrance to their shelters so that they would be the first to reach their posts. In the event of a landing all men were to immediately take their battle stations and the crews of the ships in harbour were to go aboard. The mole itself was divided into subsections with specific numbers of troops assigned to each subsection and given individual duties. For example, the troops of subsection B, where the mole battery was located, were under the immediate command of the battery commander and were to defend the battery. The torpedo-craft and the torpedo battery were to concentrate on enemy vessels that tried to enter the harbour. Finally, explosives were kept near the batteries and sheds for use against enemy ships that pulled alongside the mole. The goal was, at the very least, to contain an enemy landing.[157] Obviously these new defences were never tested. They do indicate very clearly though that the MarineKorps was shaken by the attack on Zeebrugge and was determined to prevent its repetition.

Assessing the Raid

So, was the assault a success or a failure? What impact did it have on the war in Flanders? Both sides of course claimed victory. Keyes and the British left the coast convinced that they had achieved their aim. They had good reason to feel confident. They knew that two of the three cruisers used as block ships had reached their intended positions in the canal and then had scuttled themselves. Keyes was knighted for his efforts and lauded as a hero.[158] Yet von Schröder was honoured as well, receiving the oak leaf cluster to the *Pour le mèrite*.[159] How could both men be lauded as victors in the same operation?

The initial German press release called the battle a 'shining success' of German weapons against a well-planned and carefully executed enemy operation. The Germans claimed that their gunnery had been superb and unhampered by the poor visibility. They also claimed, and appear to have believed, that the British had intended to reach and block the lock gates themselves, not simply the canal. They also pointed to the defence of the mole and the fact that no serious damage had been done to any German installations or to German craft in the harbour. They reported that the enemy's goal of rendering the sub base useless had not been attained and that 'the U-Boat war was not interrupted for one hour.'[160] Of course the other critical point was that the attack on Ostend had failed. This meant that Bruges was not blocked since the Flanders submarines and torpedo-boats could use the Ostend canal to reach their operational areas. The report was concluded with the claim that the attack was a sure sign that the British 'felt the knife at their throat.'[161] The official statement issued by the OHL echoed these claims, stating that the enemy attack had been aimed at destroying the vessels in the harbours and at blocking the *harbour* (not canal) exits. This release made several statements that the Germans clearly knew were false. For example, they claimed that none of the British troops that reached the mole returned to the *Vindictive* alive and that none of the enemy cruisers made it to the entrance of the canal. The exaggerations for the attack at Ostend were even worse, claiming that the block ships there 'had hardly been sighted before they were sunk by German gunfire.'[162] Certainly the Germans realised that they were stretching the truth; there is little wonder Keyes was irate when he read the German dispatches.[163] The Germans were clearly attempting to put the best face possible on what was certainly a tactical defeat; the British achieved at least half of their main aim by sinking the block ships in the canal at Zeebrugge and the Germans themselves admitted, though only internally, that the canal was blocked. But was there an element of truth to the German spin-doctoring? Was the raid really a strategic success?

This has been debated ever since the raids took place. In his memoirs, Admiral Scheer claimed that the attack had been a complete failure and that the submarine traffic between Bruges and Zeebrugge was not interrupted for even one day.[164] His argument is echoed by Admiral Bacon. Bacon asserted that 'nothing material had been achieved.'[165] He continued to believe that the correct approach would have been to continue the bombardments of the lock gates. He may have been right. As for his and Scheer's claims, they simply are not true. A close study of the number of submarines that entered and exited from the Flanders harbours during 1918 clearly shows that on both 23 and 24 April no submarines left the Flanders bases.[166] Of course, this doesn't tell us *why* no submarines left harbour. In fact there were a great many days over the course of 1918 when no submarines entered or exited the bases. However, Scheer's statement is also contradicted by von Schröder's report of the 23rd which clearly stated that the canal was blocked.

The other side of the argument is put forward by Keyes and his supporters. They claim that the raid was a complete success and base much of their argument on aerial reconnaissance photos of Bruges taken in the days after the raid. These photos clearly show that the harbour, and the canals near it, were jammed with destroyers and submarines. The British official history also points out that after 22 April the German destroyer raids on the Channel patrols stopped. This is attributed to the blocking of the canal at Zeebrugge.[167] This was fairly clear British spin-doctoring, after all they knew that the Ostend canal was still open.

It is now generally accepted that the raid was only temporarily effective in reducing German naval activity.[168] The canal was blocked but only very briefly. If that is the case, however, how does one account for the visual evidence assembled by the British? There are two explanations for the apparent logjam of torpedo-craft in Bruges. First of all, the photographs were of necessity taken during the day when the Flanders flotillas were generally not active. The only forces usually at sea during the day were the small A-I minesweepers and whichever large destroyers happened to be on escort duty. The submarines tended to leave during the twilight hours or at night and the few operations that were carried out offensively by the flotillas were also launched at night. Naturally then the destroyers would be in harbour during the day. The second reason though is that the canal *was* blocked for much of the summer of 1918.

Before offering further explanation, it is pertinent at this juncture to quote Admiral Bacon at some length concerning his views on the blocking operation. He had stated:

> It may be asked, if blocking was so undesirable why did we bombard the lock-gates at Zeebrugge? The answer is a simple one. If a lock-gate were hit when shut the chances were that the canal would be efficiently blocked for some weeks for a caisson must be dead true to slide in and out of its housing position. Should, however, we require to use the canal it was not so long a job to repair the caisson as to remove a blocking-ship; especially as we had accurate plans, and, in case of necessity, could have built a new one in England. Damage to the caisson blocked the canal efficiently against small craft for some weeks; blocking-ships did not do so.[169]

In June of 1918 Admiral Bacon's faith in the bombardment of the Flanders coast was vindicated.

Shortly after the Germans had dredged enough of a channel around the block ships to allow them to use the canal the lock-gates suffered a direct hit during an air attack on the night of 28 May. As a result one of the old gates had to be removed and replaced. This closed the canal for roughly one week, until 4 June.[170] However, just as the Germans managed to repair the lock-gate it suffered a direct hit during a coastal bombardment on 9 June. The newly replaced gate was completely destroyed and once again had to be replaced. This time though it was mangled much worse and several attempts had to be made to remove it. As a result the canal was closed to all German shipping, not just the larger destroyers and submarines, for the entire month of June.[171] In a strange and ironic twist Bacon was proven right in the end. So, with the exception of a brief two week period from 14–28 May, Bruges was essentially blocked. This accounts for the photographic evidence.

This poses yet another question: what effect did the blocking of Bruges have on the war as a whole? The answer unfortunately was, not much. The submarine campaign had already been defeated and the Channel Barrage, by closing the Channel to German submarines, nullified the major advantage that the Flanders bases had provided. Since the Flanders submarines also had to take the long route around Scotland to reach their main staging areas the distance saved by basing in Flanders was no longer worth the increased risk of attack. The advantage that the Flanders position gave the German torpedo-boat and destroyer flotillas had never truly been taken advantage of and, by this stage of the war, had basically been surrendered by the Germans. The Flanders flotillas were increasingly restricted to a defensive role and the numbers of available destroyers continued to drop. The only effective destroyer forces left to the Imperial Fleet by this stage of the war were those based in Germany and the blocking of Bruges meant nothing to them. Had Scheer desired to send them west on a raid against the Dover Barrage he could have done so at any time. They had demonstrated in February that they could reach the Barrage from Germany without stopping in Flanders, and even if it became necessary to stop, Zeebrugge served as a fully functional base. True, any destroyers based there would have been unable to retreat to Bruges in the event of a coastal bombardment but their chances of being damaged while in harbour during a bombardment were exceedingly slim anyway. The likelihood of another German raid on the Barrage was very low, however, since Scheer apparently had lost interest in such operations by the middle of 1918. The actual blocking of the canal at this stage of the war really meant nothing strategically; had it occurred in 1917 it would have been devastating to the German war effort but by the summer of 1918 the German naval campaign was no longer a serious threat to the Entente.

All of this is not to say that the raid meant nothing. It was certainly one of the more gallant events of the entire war and it significantly boosted the morale of both the Royal Navy and the population of Great Britain at a time when the German armies were once again on the offensive and winning tremendous victories in France. Ofcourse it is impossible to measure the effect of a boost in morale on the outcome of the war, and it would certainly be overstating the case to say that the raid was one of the key factors in Germany's defeat, but it provided a badly needed success during what was otherwise one of the war's darker months. In the end though it must go down as a tremendously courageous but largely ineffective operation. In a way it was akin to Jutland in that it was a tactical victory without much strategic importance. The British had 'twisted the dragon's tail', but by this stage the dragon was already on its last legs.

THE FINAL MONTHS OF THE MARINEKORPS:
MAY – OCTOBER 1918

At the beginning of May 1918 the raid on Ostend and Zeebrugge did appear to be an act of desperation on the part of the Entente. Their armies were reeling under the force of Ludendorff's final offensive. On 27 May the Germans made a major breakthrough on the Chemin des Dames and renewed their push towards Paris. The advance was halted though on 9 June and then, on 18 July, the Second Battle of the Marne marked the beginning of the great retreat of the German armies; the retreat which ultimately ended with the famous loss of nerve by Ludendorff and his appeal to the government to begin peace negotiations. During this phase of the war, the MarineKorps lost its remaining offensive character and became simply a coastal garrison. The change affected every branch of the unit.

The Air War

The latter part of the war in Flanders was characterised by a dramatic increase in air activity by both the MarineKorps and the British. For most of the final months the MarineKorps was on the defensive in this struggle. In fact, by the final months of the war the Allies had total air superiority over the Flanders coast. This complicated all phases of the MarineKorps' operations. For example, the commander of the air forces in Flanders reported to von Schröder in early April that enemy air activity over the coast was becoming heavier and that this was making the work of the minesweepers much more difficult. Enemy planes had reportedly been making low-level attacks against the German torpedo-boats and the latter's anti-aircraft guns were insufficient protection. An additional problem was the fact that the enemy's aircraft were able to maintain a nearly constant presence over the German minesweepers and thus could keep records on which areas of the coast had been swept recently. It was urgent that additional fighters be assigned to the naval front to drive off these enemy planes.[172] At this point the MarineKorps only had ten fighters available and these were usually employed on the frontlines. They covered the torpedo-craft on their morning patrols, but after those patrols were completed the planes returned to their duties on the land front unless special conditions (i.e. a major enemy air attack) required their presence on the coast.[173]

The most common target of the Entente air raids were not the German patrol craft, but the Flanders harbours. In the early part of 1918 allied air attacks had succeeded in causing minor damage in Flanders, but by the end of the summer they had become a serious threat to the German forces there. The first major allied attack of 1918 had taken place on 17 February and had damaged two German torpedo-boats.[174] That attack was followed by another on 3 March which destroyed four planes of the 2nd Naval Air Station in Ostend.[175] On 23 March a daylight raid on Bruges damaged two destroyers and a raid that same night damaged *UB-30*.[176] On 1 April the destroyer *V-74* took a direct hit during a raid and was seriously damaged.[177] These raids, though minor compared to those later in the year, had important effects. First of all, they led directly to the transfer of a squad of Brandenburg seaplanes from the High Seas Fleet to Flanders and temporary permission from the IV army to use the fighters of the MarineKorps on the naval front.[178] These raids were only pinpricks though compared to what was to come.

The new, heavier raids began after the 10 May attack on Ostend and they took a serious toll on the fighting ability of the MarineKorps, especially at sea. The German destroyers and torpedo-boats suffered the worst from these raids. The first casualty was *S-53* which was seriously damaged in Bruges on the night of 17 May.[179] That was followed by an attack on the 30th which damaged four A-IIs.[180] During June *V-69*, *V-82*, and *A-49* were all damaged in separate attacks and in July *V-70* was heavily damaged.[181] In August *S-53* was damaged once again, as was *G-91* and the torpedo-boat *A-9*, which was hit while minesweeping.[182] Nor were the surface craft the only forces to suffer damage; the submarines did as well, despite the protection offered by the submarine shelters completed in March.[183] The first submarines seriously damaged while in harbour were *UB-88* and *UB-10* which were hit on 2 July.[184]

The air raids also did considerable damage to the harbour facilities and made it much more difficult for the MarineKorps to keep the flotillas up to strength. This in turn had a detrimental effect on the naval war.[185] This was all in addition to the damage done to the Zeebrugge lock gates in May and June. Clearly, despite post-war claims to the contrary, the Germans were seriously hurt by these heavy allied attacks.[186]

The MarineKorps responded to these attacks in two ways; they increased the number of anti-aircraft guns along the coast and they appealed to the German army for assistance. In 1917 they had a total of seventy anti-aircraft guns ranging in calibre from 3.7cm to 15cm centered primarily around Ostend and Zeebrugge. By the end of the war that number had been increased to 212.[187] These guns supposedly shot down 133 enemy aircraft over the course of those two years.[188] Nonetheless the guns clearly did not provide sufficient protection and they had to be supplemented by fighters but, for most of 1918, the MarineKorps' fighters were occupied on the land front and were not available for naval purposes. That changed slightly in April but even when von Schröder was able to reassign his fighter craft to the defence of the coast he did not have enough to provide adequate protection. To try and change this von Schröder met with representatives of Crown Prince Rupprecht early in June.

These meetings proved to be productive. On 6 June Crown Prince Rupprecht put forward a plan for the protection of the Flanders harbours in which the bombers of the IV army would attack allied air fields in France. The IV army would retain control over these bombers but their targets would be selected by the MarineKorps.[189] The primary target was the enemy airfield at Coudekerque and attacks against this airfield had already begun on the evening of 4 June and they continued into July and August.[190] They had moderate success, destroying five planes and damaging 48 others while also destroying eight hangars. In July the IV army expanded these attacks to include Dunkirk and managed to succeed in damaging the *Erebus*.[191] Von Schröder was very pleased by the results since, after the beginning of these raids, the attacks on his bases decreased in intensity. He attributed the change directly to the bombing campaign.[192]

The MarineKorps still needed fighters though. Von Schröder was promised assistance from the fleet on 9 June and new fighters finally arrived in Flanders on 23 June. They formed a third fighter squadron.[193] This was still not enough though. On 29 June von Schröder received a request from the commander of the Korps' air forces to expand the fighter group currently in Flanders to a fighter wing.[194] That request was passed along to the naval staff by von Schröder in July but was rejected by Scheer in August.[195] Von Schröder continued to press his case despite the rejection but the expansion never occurred and the MarineKorps was forced to rely on its existing forces.[196] By the end of the war those amounted to a total of forty-five seaplanes and seventy-five airplanes.[197]

These forces were reorganised in June 1918. They were split into two separate sections; one, called Gruppe 12, was assigned strictly to the land front and the remaining section was assigned strictly to the naval theatre.[198] The naval section was created by taking three planes each from the 1st and 2nd MarineFeldFlieger Abteilungen. By splitting the forces in this way von Schröder hoped to provide better protection for the minesweepers and the coast since these six planes would always be available for their defence.[199] In reality though the section was too small to be of much use and had little effect on the course of the war.

Overall the air forces of the MarineKorps were outnumbered and outmatched by 1918 and were hard pressed merely to defend the German installations in Flanders. Their ability to carry out offensive missions, bombing raids on the Barrage patrol for example, was negligible. They were forced firmly onto the defensive and this in turn had a detrimental effect on the ability of the MarineKorps to prosecute the war at sea.

The Naval War

During the latter half of 1918 the Flanders flotillas were relegated to almost purely defensive tasks. This had very little to do with the fact that the Zeebrugge canal was blocked for most of May and June; rather it was mainly the result of increasing losses. Despite appeals from both von Arnim and von Schröder to the Naval Staff, little was done to rectify this.

In early May both men requested that additional patrol craft be sent from Germany so that the MarineKorps could institute a permanent and continuous patrol of the coast. They hoped that such a patrol would give them ample warning of an approaching allied fleet and that they would then be able to defeat any attempted landing on the coast. Their requests were rejected by von Holtzendorff who justified his response by stating that, as von Schröder himself had previously pointed out, the small A-boats were so inferior to British craft that their use was greatly restricted and assigning more of them to Flanders would not materially aid the situation. That meant that only destroyers would be useful and, if these were to be used as a continuous patrol, the number of destroyers which would have to be sent west was prohibitively high, though he did not mention what he felt that number was. In the end von Schröder was told to do the best he could with what he had.[200] The only reinforcements he received during the last part of the war weren't strictly reinforcements at all; they were the destroyers of the III Flotilla that had been sent to Germany for refitting and had tried without success to return to Flanders earlier. These four destroyers finally arrived in Zeebrugge on 12 May.[201] They had originally left Wilhelmshaven on 4 May but were detained by bad weather at Heligoland.[202] These few reinforcements did nothing to alleviate von Schröder's problems. In fact, the only offensive operation carried out at sea by the MarineKorps during the final months of the war was a brief raid by seven small motorboats against Dunkirk on 22 August. The Germans believed that they sank one torpedo-boat and one destroyer in the raid.[203]

With the restriction of their offensive capabilities minesweeping became nearly the exclusive duty of the Flanders torpedo-craft. During 1918 the British stepped up their mine-laying efforts because, back in early January, Keyes had received a letter from Admiral Reginald Hall, the head of British naval intelligence, that suggested that heavy mine-laying off the Flanders coast would effectively immobilise the German torpedo-craft by forcing them to escort submarines through the minefields. This would prevent them from undertaking offensive actions. The same policy had already proven successful in the Bight.[204] After the raids on Ostend and Zeebrugge Keyes ordered the forces of the Dover Patrol to begin laying extensive new minefields off the coast. The results of this campaign proved Hall right; by the end of August the Flanders destroyers were not only protecting minesweepers, they were also escorting submarines in and out of harbour.[205] At times these escorts were rather large. For example, on 27 August an entire destroyer flotilla was assigned to escort a single submarine out to sea![206] These escorts did occasionally have brief clashes with the enemy, but none of them had any significant results. For example, on 30 May there was a very brief clash between the German torpedo-boats and a British monitor. Neither side suffered any damage. Another clash on 27 June was similarly indecisive.[207] The escorting of the minesweepers and the submarines eventually led to many of the German torpedo-craft being severely damaged by mines.

Even in the earlier part of the year losses to mines had been high; by April the minesweeper flotilla had suffered so many losses that the A-IIs and A-IIIs had to be converted into minesweepers.[208] In August the number of German losses increased even further. The heavier losses were the direct result of a new field of magnetic mines laid by the British on the night of 7 August.[209] These new mines claimed their first victim immediately. On the 8th *V-68*, which was protecting the minesweepers, detonated one. The destroyer suffered such serious damage that it sank within five minutes. While *G-95* was trying to rescue the crew a second mine exploded and *G-95* was heavily damaged. The latter ship did manage to get back to port under its own power.[210] Attempts to sweep the area over the following days yielded no results but on the 11th, in the same area, *G-41* set off a similar explosion and was so heavily damaged that it had to be towed back to port.[211] A final ship was claimed by this field on the 15th when *A-58* struck a mine and had to be towed back to port. Unfortunately the ship broke apart on the return and sank about one nautical mile north of Zeebrugge, right in the main shipping channel, which was now partially blocked once again.[212] Since all of the efforts to sweep that area had failed von Schröder began to suspect that the recent losses were due to a new type of mine but he was never able to confirm his suspicions. The heavy losses slowed down the flotilla's minesweeping efforts, but by the end of August not many submarines remained in Flanders to use the swept channels anyway. Their losses had also been high during this period.

The number of active submarines in Flanders consistently declined from June to October. In April there had still been twenty-five submarines operating out of 'the Triangle'; that number fell to twenty-three in May but went back to twenty-four in June. After that it steadily declined, falling to twenty-two in July, eighteen in August, thirteen in September and finally to just eight in October.[213] During this period the number of cruises that ended with the loss of the submarine rose from 8 to 40 percent.[214] Von Schröder had no more success getting replacements for the submarines than he did for the destroyers. He was told that the dangers in the Channel had become too great to risk submarines in that area and that because of this reinforcing the Flanders flotillas would not aid the submarine campaign in terms of materiel.[215] The losses eventually became so heavy that on 21 September the two submarine flotillas were recombined back into one.[216] The Channel Barrage was the major reason for the problems of the Flanders submarines.

By August the Barrage had effectively closed the English Channel to all German submarines. From then until the end of the war only one submarine managed to get through the Barrage without damage.[217] The last submarine to head to the Dover Strait from Flanders left on 19 August. From that date on all submarines of the Flanders flotillas were ordered to use the northern route around Scotland.[218]

The air forces of the MarineKorps kept a close watch on the Barrage patrols, which they discovered normally consisted of two monitors and eight to twelve destroyers accompanied by several auxiliaries.[219] Despite the size of the force, von Schröder called several times for a repetition of the February raid on the patrol, a raid which he felt the MarineKorps was too weak to launch.[220] He had no success. In fact, Scheer replied to von Schröder's requests by suggesting that von Schröder should send his remaining forces against the Barrage on their own. Von Schröder believed that was essentially suicide.[221] As a result the British were able to seal the Channel and deny the German submarines passage without having to face the opposition of the German surface fleet.

The success rate of the submarines dropped accordingly during this period. In May von Schröder reported that the Flanders submarines had destroyed forty-one ships totaling 113,772 tons.[222] This was most likely an overly optimistic estimate. The official German history records the total for the Flanders boats as being 39,277 tons.[223] Von Schröder attributed the lower losses of that month to two factors; the increased use of aerial reconnaissance by the British and the fact that the Zeebrugge canal was closed for much of the month, penning in the larger and more effective submarines.[224] Things did improve for the Flanders forces in June when they sank 58,931 tons of enemy shipping.[225] Most of their successes came on the British east coast which was now becoming the primary hunting ground for the Flanders submarines. That month von Schröder finally admitted that the submarines most likely would never regain their earlier levels of success. The allied defences had simply become too thorough. Especially problematic were the increased air attacks on Flanders and the decreasing numbers of available submarines.[226] July did not bring any improvement as the amount of tonnage sunk dropped to 53,612 tons.[227] The numbers continued to decline after that point with the totals dropping respectively to 48,658 tons destroyed in August, 35,725 tons in September and 9,815 tons in October.[228] This drop off in results affected all the theatres. The total amount of tonnage sunk by the German submarines in the latter half of 1918, on a month by month basis, is listed below:

May	296,558 tons
June	268,505 tons
July	280,820 tons
August	310,180 tons
September	171,972 tons
October	116,237 tons
November	10,233 tons[229]

Despite the brief upsurge in August, the submarines were fighting a losing battle throughout this entire period. In May of 1918 new allied shipping construction finally surpassed the amount being sunk by the submarines.[230] Both the great submarine campaign and the naval efforts of the MarineKorps had ended in failure. During these months the MarineKorps' presence at sea was negligible. The German navy had staked victory or defeat on the submarines and had failed; the fate of the nation now depended on Ludendorff's western offensive.

The Land War

The MarineKorps did not play a large role in the western offensive. The units of the Korps on the frontline (the 2nd and 3rd MarineDivisions) remained on the strategic defensive only making small localised attacks. Had there been a major breakthrough forcing the British to abandon the coast they would have been able to move forward and occupy the Channel harbours but there were no plans for a strategic offensive from the MarineKorps' front. The duties of the MarineKorps were very limited; they were to attack allied shipping in the Channel and protect the flank of the army by guarding against enemy counterattacks or landings along the coast.

The MarineKorps' first mission was to use the submarine flotillas to strike at military transports and supply ships. This was not something that von Schröder was eager to do but the situation left him with little choice. As a result, between three and four submarines worked in the eastern part of the Channel off the major French harbours and supposedly destroyed around 97,000 tons of enemy shipping in the earliest days of the offensive. The UCs operated almost exclusively off the major harbours in northern France and claimed another 9,000 tons with their minefields.[231] In May these attacks became increasingly important.

On 3 May von Holtzendorff sent a message to both Scheer and von Schröder, informing them that Ludendorff anticipated making such large gains in the near future that the British would either be forced to evacuate or rush large numbers of reinforcements and supplies to the front. If the British opted for the latter, the navy was to concentrate on destroying the transports. That mission was left to the submarines, especially the mine-laying UC-class, the ships least able to carry it out. The submarine campaign was to be supplemented by air attacks against the allied harbours but attacks by surface forces were ruled out as too risky. The air of unreality that governed the German fleet at this stage of the war is demonstrated by the fact that the two commanders were ordered to increase their attacks against the convoys *without* increasing the risks to the submarines, so that after France was beaten they could resume the commercial war. Just how that was to be done was left unsaid. Von Holtzendorff was convinced that this was the decisive moment of the war and he wanted to ensure that the navy played its part. He also insisted that the commanders send him weekly reports on the progress of the campaign so he could document 'the role played by the navy in deciding the war.'[232] Clearly von Holtzendorff was looking to preserve the position of the navy in post-war Germany despite the navy's clear lack of success during the war. He did not want all the credit for a German victory to go to the army.

To assist the MarineKorps in its efforts to attack the military convoys in the Channel the High Seas Fleet was to send its UC boats to the Flanders theatre. According to von Holtzendorff this would give 'the MarineKorps more submarines than they could use.'[233] In his marginal notes von Schröder simply put a question mark next to the last phrase.[234] One has to wonder just what von Holtzendorff was thinking. The submarines simply were not capable of meeting these demands. Nonetheless they were dutifully sent. Von Schröder, however, decided not to bother sending weekly reports.[235] Apparently the post-war status of the navy was not a primary concern of his.

As favourable reports continued to come in from Ludendorff during May and June, von Holtzendorff prepared an elaborate memorandum for the Kaiser which precisely detailed the degree of support provided by the navy during the campaign. This memorandum, which was never completed, was simply titled 'Naval Support for Operation Michael.' It laid down von Holtzendorff's plans for the naval campaign, namely that it would be carried out primarily by aircraft and submarines and that the High Seas Fleet would remain in port to protect the Bight from a British attack. Destroyer attacks on the Channel were only to be carried out under favourable conditions. According to this memorandum the MarineKorps' main role in the western campaign was to attack traffic in the eastern Channel and, at the very least, force the British to send their supplies and reinforcements to ports further to the west, away from the decisive sector. The risk to the submarines was recognised as being very great but was made necessary by Germany's overall position. Von Holtzendorff included von Schröder's figures for sinkings in the early part of the campaign (97,000 tons in April with an additional 45,500 supposedly accounted for in May.) In a clear effort to inflate the numbers he argued that since most of the ships sunk by the MarineKorps were probably fully loaded a further 33,000 tons could be added to this total.[236] Clearly, the effort to whitewash the navy, an effort that culminated in the aborted sortie of October 1918 that sparked the revolution, was already beginning.

Despite the losses to the Germans (sixteen submarines in May)[237] the flotillas continued their efforts into June without notable success.[238] The campaign went on into June and July until, following the Second Battle of the Marne and the obvious failure of the offensive, von Holtzendorff sent a new memorandum to von Schröder with a new and urgent task for the Flanders submarines. Now they were to concentrate their efforts against the harbours on the French west coast and attack transports from the United States. Despite the fact that no submarine sent to the Bay of Biscay since March had safely returned to Germany, the difficulties of the journey were made necessary by what von Holtzendorff called the 'dire situation' of the army.[239] Clearly desperation and unreality were settling in at the Naval Staff.

Von Schröder wrote back to von Holtzendorff, warning him not to expect many successes in this latest endeavour. The increase in the defensive strength of the enemy and the loss of experienced submarine commanders meant that relatively green officers would have to be sent into these highly dangerous waters. Furthermore, the Flanders flotillas only had eight submarines left that could reach the Bay of Biscay. He agreed to send two submarines to that area in the coming days but warned that great successes were very unlikely.[240]

By July the MarineKorps' flotillas were so weak that they could hardly have any impact on the war. Due to damage, losses and the inability to make sufficient repairs (due to the constant allied air attacks) by August the flotilla was down to only eleven operational submarines. Their losses in the Channel had been especially heavy. Despite all of their difficulties they still managed to destroy 250,000 tons of shipping between March and August.[241] Nonetheless, the submarines were unable to alter the course of the battles on the Western Front.

The naval high command was simply asking the submarine commanders to do the impossible. They had never been able to successfully attack troop convoys yet, during the most critical period of the war since 1914, they were asked to destroy the British reinforcements and supplies that were being sent to France while the torpedo-craft and the High Seas Fleet, the only forces truly capable of accomplishing von Holtzendorff's goals, stayed safely in harbour. One cannot escape the conclusion that the German navy, despite von Holtzendorff's concern for the future of the service, gave up its final chance to affect the course of the war. An aggressive sortie by the High Seas Fleet or even large numbers of destroyers might have been able to destroy or at least delay the arrival at the front of critical British reserves. Unfortunately for the Germans the overcautiousness that governed their conduct of the entire war at sea was still dominant and such operations were considered to be 'too risky.' In her moment of need Germany was let down once again by her navy.

Aside from trying to run the futile submarine campaign in the Channel, the MarineKorps also had the important task of protecting the right flank of the army. After the Zeebrugge and Ostend raids von Schröder and his staff reexamined the defences of the coast at the request of Hindenburg and Ludendorff, who were concerned that the British might launch a major invasion to try and turn the German flank. Von Schröder and his staff came to the usual conclusion, that it was virtually impossible for any large landing to succeed as long as the coastal artillery was intact. They stated that the gaps that had previously existed in the defences that had been exploited by the British in April had now been closed and that a successful invasion was, for all intents and purposes, impossible.[242]

The reinforcing of the coast had begun immediately after the raids when the MarineKorps reinforced the defences of the entire coast, not just the harbours. On 25 April Vice-Admiral Schultz recommended to von Schröder that a second regiment of infantry be sent to the coast and that small units of assault troops be stationed near the main harbours to act as a quick strike force which could try and repel enemy landings.[243] On 3 May von Schröder replied that two additional regiments of sailors, along with an additional artillery battery, were to be made available, not for front line use, but as a coastal reserve force. They would serve as a supplement to the current Korps reserve which consisted of one regiment of infantry headquartered in Bruges.[244] While the great offensive was progressing well this was as far as matters went. Starting in July, though, even the MarineKorps became increasingly concerned that an allied landing was in the works.

They received word over the summer that the Allies were planning a new landing supported by amphibious tanks. Von Schröder feared that these weapons might make a successful landing on the coast possible, especially near Nieuport where they could be adequately supported by allied artillery. In order to meet the threat three new mobile batteries were placed near Westende and the 1st and 2nd MarineDivisions were ordered to begin testing methods by which these tanks could be destroyed.[245] On 9 July von Schröder heard from 'reliable sources' that the British were planning to make a major landing on the coast in the autumn. These reports were confirmed by agents later in July[246] and also by the OHL which reported, on 20 July, that another allied attack against the coast was to be expected; this one would most likely be accompanied by amphibious tanks. The OHL's reports came from an agent in the British embassy in Amsterdam who had reported that the British had a new class of tanks that they had designed especially for amphibious operations in Flanders. Supposedly they intended to test them in an attack in the near future.[247] The attack never took place.

More reports of a possible landing flooded in from German agents in the middle of August.[248] These reports became even more numerous in September.[249] The newest reports pointed out that the Allies were gathering together large amounts of shipping in the Channel harbours. These were supposedly intended for an attack on the Flanders coast. The IV army put little stock in the reports. Von Arnim believed that they were deliberately being put out by the British to mislead the Germans and distract them from the fighting on the land front.[250] Nonetheless von Schröder took them seriously and made arrangements to prepare for the enemy landing. The IV army assigned one division as a coastal support force which the MarineKorps could call upon in the event of a landing. It was kept at three-hours readiness.[251] Eleven mobile guns of 15 and 17cm calibre were also moved into the Korps reserve[252] and new regulations were issued to the Flanders patrol craft.[253] The reports also led von Schröder to pen another denkschrift in which he reevaluated the coastal defences.

This study confirmed the conclusions he had reached in 1917.[254] He considered three possible enemy actions. They were: continued bombardments in an effort to destroy Ostend and Zeebrugge; surprise landings similar to that of 22 April; and a major invasion, most likely in conjunction with a push on the land front. The latter was still considered to be the least likely due to the strength of the German defences and the navigational difficulties inherent in any such attempt. If such an invasion was to occur it would most likely strike the coastline between Ostend and Wenduyne. Von Schröder maintained his stance from earlier in the war; without the prior destruction of the coastal artillery such a landing could not succeed even if the attacking ships were protected by a heavy smokescreen. The coastal defences remained strong, consisting of two 5cm, five 8.8cm, four 10.5cm, ten 15cm, five 17cm, two 21cm, six 28cm, one 30.5cm and two 38cm batteries. In addition to the coastal artillery, any invasion would also have to contend with multiple machine gun emplacements and the fortified infantry positions that were spaced along the beach. This frontal zone was reinforced by concrete pillboxes at varying depths behind the beach reaching as far back as 1 kilometre inland. Each pillbox was equipped with two machine guns. The plan was to hold the enemy on the beach. Fire was to be directed into the heavily loaded landing craft to try and cause as many casualties as possible before the enemy reached the beach. If, inspite of everything, the landing succeeded, it was to be immediately counter-attacked by assault troops that had been held back as local reserves. If that failed then it would be up to the Korps' reserve to hold the front while the IV army prepared a counter-attacking force.[255] Von Schröder believed that a successful landing in the face of these defences would be nothing short of a miracle. He was much more concerned about a possible British invasion of Holland.[256]

Up until October von Schröder remained confident that the MarineKorps could repel any attempted enemy landing. It was only on 12 October that Schultz wrote to von Schröder warning him that, due to the general deterioration in the German position, an enemy landing now had a relatively good chance of success. For this reason the entire coast was put on alert status from 3am to 7am daily since these were considered to be the most likely hours for an enemy attack. Schultz also requested additional reserves to help him secure the coastline.[257] By this time, however, the Germans had no reserves available.[258]

The expected enemy landing never took place, but by October it was also no longer necessary. The defences of the MarineKorps were indeed formidable but the British never had to challenge them directly. By October the Allies had already beaten the German army on the land front. The great retreat had begun and the occupation of Flanders was nearing its end.

THE EVACUATION OF FLANDERS

By the end of August 1918 the fortunes of the Central Powers were clearly on the wane. On 8 August the British made a major breakthrough at Amiens on what Ludendorff called the 'black day' of the German army. German fortunes in the west never recovered and the German army was steadily forced out of the occupied territories. Though the army maintained relative order, the retreat could not be checked and it continued into September.[259] On 29 September Germany's ally Bulgaria surrendered and this led Ludendorff to demand that the German government conclude an immediate armistice. The morale of Germany's military leaders had finally broken. All the gambles had failed and the war was lost.

The day before the Bulgarian surrender, 28 September, Scheer (now head of the entire navy) received word from Ludendorff that the army could no longer hold Flanders and that it should be immediately evacuated. On the 29th the Kaiser gave his assent and von Schröder was told to prepare to evacuate the Flanders coast.[260] The precise date at which it would become necessary to evacuate was still unknown. As a direct result of that message von Schröder took the prudent decision, on his own authority, to send the remaining naval forces in Flanders back to Germany. He ordered the five destroyers and two torpedo-boats that were seaworthy to leave Flanders that evening. All remaining vessels that could do so were ordered to assemble in Zeebrugge outside of the lock gates. The submarines currently in harbour were not able to go to sea but their repairs were accelerated in the hope that some of them could be saved.[261] At 11pm that evening von Schröder received word from Scheer that the Flanders position, with the exception of Antwerp, was to be evacuated as soon as possible.[262]

On the following day von Schröder issued his orders for the dismantling of the Flanders bases. The first priority was to save as many ships and as much war materiel as possible. Anything that could not be moved, including ships and submarines, was to be destroyed to prevent it falling into enemy hands. The dismantling of the coastal defences began that same day though the only guns that could safely be removed were those in the second line of defence. The larger coastal guns were still needed if the MarineKorps was to hold the coast as long as possible. The A-Is were ordered to tow barges full of ammunition and other war materiel through the canals to Antwerp. The remaining A-IIs were also ordered to proceed to Antwerp. Von Schröder hoped that they could be disassembled, put on trains and returned to Germany. He was convinced that these small craft would not have been able to survive the trip across the North Sea due to their slow speed. The aircraft of the naval air station were also ordered to return to Germany as soon as the weather permitted.[263]

On 1 October an additional six destroyers, two submarines and twelve torpedo-boats were successfully evacuated. That left only two destroyers which were being overhauled in Ghent and three others undergoing repairs in Bruges. The Germans hoped that the first two might still be able to escape but plans were put in place to destroy the other three. Two remaining submarines were expected to leave within two or three days. Three submarines that were too badly damaged to leave were destroyed in Ostend that same day. Plans were made to block both Ostend and Zeebrugge and to demolish all of the remaining dockyards and harbour facilities. The blocking of Ostend and the destruction of the lock gates there took place on 4 October.[264]

By 3 October the majority of the material that could be moved had been evacuated. One of the remaining destroyers was scuttled in the canal from Bruges to Ghent and the demolition work in Ostend and Bruges began. On 5 October the last of the escaping destroyers left for Germany and the remaining three were destroyed.[265] The evacuation had been a success. A total of eleven destroyers, fourteen torpedo-boats, seven submarines and thirty-three seaplanes escaped. Three submarines, four destroyers, and twelve torpedo-boats had to be scuttled.[266] The Flanders flotillas were officially dissolved on 14 October.[267]

The MarineKorps itself had been officially dissolved eight days earlier, on 6 October. The troops of the 1st MarineDivision were sent to the Black Sea to help man captured Russian warships[268] while the forces of the 2nd and 3rd MarineDivisions were turned over to the army. Von Schröder remained their commander but he was now subordinated to von Arnim and the IV army.[269] In the meantime the dismantling of the coastal defences continued. The remaining troops were able to evacuate ten 29cm guns but the remainder had to be destroyed in place.[270]

On 14 October von Schröder received orders to fall back as far as Ostend. He was also ordered to prepare for the blocking of Zeebrugge and Antwerp. That evening the remaining minelayers laid a new minefield before the entrances to Zeebrugge after which they were scuttled. On the 15th the lock gates at Zeebrugge were destroyed.[271] On the 16th the order came in to abandon Bruges and it was duly evacuated two days later.[272] The British had moved into Ostend on the 17th and they re-entered Zeebrugge on the 19th. By the 25th Bruges was in the hands of the Belgian army.[273] The long German occupation of the Belgian coastline had come to an end without the German navy and the MarineKorps Flandern ever taking full advantage of their opportunities.

CONCLUSION

In retrospect 1918 was in many ways an anti-climax for the MarineKorps. The war had essentially been decided by the failure of the German submarine campaign in 1917. Any chance for additional effective submarine activity in the Channel was prevented by the Channel Barrage devised by Admiral Keyes. The Barrage essentially closed the passage through the straits and it was allowed to function almost without interruption. The one German raid on 15 February, despite its great success, was never repeated and the British ships were allowed to continue their patrol work unhindered. Von Schröder and the MarineKorps were no longer able to act offensively without the assistance of forces from the High Seas Fleet because they were tied down guarding the minesweepers and escorting the Flanders submarines out to sea. By the latter part of 1918 they had suffered such heavy losses from mines and aircraft that the two flotillas stationed in Flanders were never close to full strength.

The most dramatic events of the entire war in Flanders, the raids on Ostend and Zeebrugge, had only a minor effect on the outcome of the war. While they boosted the morale of the British at a critical moment they failed in their main aim; blocking the canals. Ironically, the British were able to accomplish that later through air attacks and coastal bombardments though by that stage of the war even the complete closure of the Flanders harbours would not have made a critical difference. The offensive capability of the Flanders flotillas had already been crippled and it never recovered.

The air attacks on the Flanders harbours played a key role in disabling the Flanders flotillas. Those attacks, which increased in intensity from May on, dealt a heavy blow both by damaging ships directly and by damaging the facilities that were needed to repair and maintain them. The cumulative damage done to the harbour installations critically reduced the ability of the MarineKorps to repair their damaged ships. The incessant nature of the attacks proved to be the most important factor since they left the men of the dockyards no respite. Even though no single raid did tremendous damage, the cumulative impact of the repeated raids eventually disabled the support services of the MarineKorps and dealt a crushing blow to the Korps' ability to conduct operations.

By the end of September 1918 those operations had become purely defensive in nature and the MarineKorps Flandern had lost what little ability it had to affect the outcome of the war. The Germans had completely squandered the great opportunity that the Allies had given them when the latter failed to destroy the Belgian harbours in 1914.

Conclusion

When the First World War began the German navy found itself in a difficult position. The battle fleet that Admiral Tirpitz had been building was incomplete and as a result the Germans were at a numerical disadvantage against the Royal Navy. The Germans also suffered from a geographic disadvantage. Great Britain sat directly across the shipping lanes from Germany to the outside world. As a result it was relatively easy for the British to cut the Germans off from their international trade and isolate them. The Germans could do little in return. The major German naval bases were located within the Heligoland Bight, too far from Great Britain to pose a serious threat. The Germans needed a way to turn the tables on the British geographically, and at the same time, reduce the British superiority in surface forces.

To try and accomplish the latter goal the Germans implemented a strategy which they called *Kleinkrieg*. In theory this involved the aggressive use of destroyers, torpedo-boats and submarines against the British fleet and British commerce in an effort to whittle away at Great Britain's naval superiority. Then, once the scales had been balanced, the High Seas Fleet could seek out a decisive battle with the British Grand Fleet. The strategy had one fatal flaw; it could only be implemented from the Bight if the British instituted a close blockade of the German coast. The Germans confidently expected that this was exactly what the British would do, however, the British instead, realising the dangers of torpedoes and mines, implemented a distant blockade which gave the Germans control over the relatively unimportant southeastern North Sea. Britain's geographic position made this possible. Since they could block the exits from the North Sea with fleets based in Britain they did not need to opt for a close blockade. This made it even more imperative that the Germans find a way to turn the tables on the British geographically.

The conquest of Belgium by the German army in 1914 made this possible. When the British and Belgians abandoned the coast they left the harbours of Bruges, Ostend, and Zeebrugge in working condition because the British army believed that they would need the ports when they began their counter-attack and drove the Germans from Belgium. The counter-attack did not materialise and the Germans were left with a collection of bases from which they could properly implement the *Kleinkrieg*. The Royal Navy was aware of this and was very concerned over what the Germans would do with those bases.

One of the few members of the German navy who recognised the potential importance of the Flanders coast was Admiral Tirpitz. As a result he pushed for the creation of a naval station in Flanders. That in turn led to the creation of the MarineKorps Flandern. Tirpitz and the man he selected to lead the MarineKorps, Admiral Ludwig von Schröder, both realised that the Kleinkrieg could only be properly implemented from the Flanders bases. Unfortunately they were nearly alone in their opinions. Von Schröder had to fight for resources from the very beginning and all too often his command was third in priority behind the High Seas Fleet and the Baltic Sea command. Nonetheless, in 1915, von Schröder was able to eventually, after lengthy debates within the navy, acquire enough forces to create the Flanders Submarine, Torpedo-Boat and Destroyer Flotillas.

The Flanders submarines played a key role in the German submarine campaigns throughout the war, accounting for roughly 25 percent of the total number of sinkings. The destroyers and torpedo-boats though never had the impact that they could have done. The Germans launched two very successful destroyer raids against the British patrols in the Channel, one in October 1916 and the other in February 1918. Each of these raids caught the British by surprise and did significant damage to the smaller British patrol craft, the drifters and motor launches. However, the raids were a very rare occurrence. Why?

The classic criticism of the German navy in the First World War was that the High Seas Fleet rarely ventured to sea, fought the battles of Dogger Bank and Jutland and then never set sail again. This is an exaggeration, we know the fleet did have several other sorties, even after Jutland, but the implication that the German naval leaders were overly cautious has more than a grain of truth to it. The Germans were unwilling to suffer losses at sea. This attitude was passed down from the Kaiser in August 1914 and lingered throughout the entire war. It applied not only to the dreadnoughts of the High Seas Fleet but also to the light forces. Simply put, the Germans were not willing to run the risks that were necessary if their fleet was to have a positive impact on the war. Von Holtzendorff's memoranda to von Schröder in the spring of 1918 are a perfect example of this kind of thinking. In those memoranda von Holtzendorff urged von Schröder to support the navy's role in the great western offensive by sending his submarines into the Channel to attack the British troop convoys to France. The submarines had never had success attacking these transports and von Schröder pointed this out to von Holtzendorff, suggesting instead that he be reinforced with destroyers from the High Seas Fleet, so he could launch a major attack against those convoys with surface forces. He was told that this was 'too risky.' Even at that potentially decisive moment the naval leadership shrank from committing their surface forces to battle. This was one of the reasons why the Germans squandered the advantage presented to them by the Flanders bases. The leaders of the German navy either simply did not grasp the possibilities presented by their new position or were too afraid of losses to make proper use of it. The British for their part were seriously concerned over the German possession of these bases and feared what might happen if the Germans ever made proper use of the Flanders bases.

From 1915 on von Schröder argued that an aggressive destroyer campaign should be carried out from Flanders. He reasoned that such a campaign would force the British to send additional craft to the Harwich and Dover commands. By forcing the British to transfer forces to the south von Schröder would be providing the High Seas Fleet with targets of opportunity. His ideas though carried little weight with Ingenohl, von Pohl and Scheer, the heads of the High Seas Fleet. If von Schröder was to receive significant forces they would most likely have to come from the main battle fleet and none of the fleet's commanders were willing to significantly reduce their command. Even when the leaders of the navy did decide to send forces to Flanders they did not send enough to make a serious impact. Von Schröder never had enough destroyers permanently under his command to act freely. Most of the major raids that were launched by the Flanders flotillas were launched in conjunction with flotillas on loan from the High Seas Fleet. Successful as those raids were, they were too few and far between to be anything more than pinpricks.

The British feared that the Germans might implement such a destroyer campaign. They correctly understood what the Germans did not; that the Grand Fleet had to maintain its destroyer strength at all times if it was to be ready to sail against the High Seas Fleet. The High Seas Fleet, on the other hand, held the initiative. The Germans knew when their fleet was going to head to sea; when they did not have operations planned they could send their destroyers to Flanders to launch raids against the British. They squandered that advantage. Initially they feared that the passage across the North Sea would be too dangerous but, even after 1916 when the frequent transit of destroyers back and forth to Flanders had shown that this was not the case, they still kept the majority of their forces in the Bight to defend it against a British attack. Only in January 1918 did the Germans send a massed destroyer attack out from the Bight to the Channel. Despite that attack's brilliant success it was not repeated. Why not?

The documents provide little explanation. Clearly the Germans feared a British attack on the Bight. In his correspondence with von Schröder, Scheer repeatedly refers to the need to keep the destroyers in the Bight to defend it against a British attack. Apparently the Germans were traumatised by the British attack on the Bight in August 1914 and were determined to be ready if it ever occurred again. In their defence there was just enough British activity near the Bight, between seaplane raids and mine-laying, to keep the Germans concerned. Nonetheless, Ingenohl and his two successors were overly concerned with the defence of this area. Throughout the war they were unwilling to take the risks that were necessary to achieve victory. They preferred to preserve the fleet for either the peace table or for a naval armageddon with the Grand Fleet. The only logical conclusion aside from fear is that most of the German navy's leadership simply did not grasp their strategic situation. One is forced to wonder what might have happened had the unrestricted submarine campaign of 1917 been accompanied by an aggressive destroyer campaign from Flanders. Could the Germans have won the war had they made better use of the Flanders bases?

Perhaps. Certainly the presence of large numbers of destroyers raiding the Channel and the British coast on a regular basis, especially in the heart of the submarine crisis in April and May of 1917, would have posed a serious threat to both the British anti-submarine forces and to British commercial shipping. The Germans, however, preferred to leave their fate in the hands of the submarines, restricting their destroyers and torpedo-boats to mine-laying and minesweeping. Fortunately for the Entente, the German naval leadership took a defensive and essentially passive stance throughout the war. As a result the MarineKorps was never able to fully utilise its geographical advantages. Tirpitz's and von Schröder's hopes for the unit were never fulfilled. With the conquest of the Belgian coastline in October 1914 the Germans were given the opportunity to place significant pressure on the British. They did not. Germany began the war with Britain at a serious geographical disadvantage; they had the opportunity to turn the tables but did not. If, as has been frequently said, Belgium was the dagger pointed at the throat of Britain, one is forced to conclude that the Germans were incapable of wielding that dagger properly.

Appendices

Table 6: Aircraft in the MarineKorps[1]

Name	Type	Weaponry	Crew	Top Speed	Max Time Aloft
Brandenburg W.12	Seaplane	1 or 2 forward machine guns	2	160 kph	3½ hrs
Brandenburg W.29	Seaplane	1 or 2 forward guns and 1 rear machine gun	2	178 kph	4 hrs
Albatross D.III	Aeroplane	2 forward machine guns	1	165 kph	2 hrs
Albatross D.VA	Aeroplane	2 forward machine guns	1	186 kph	2 hrs
Fokker D.VII	Aeroplane	2 machine guns	1	187 kph	1½ hrs
Fokker D.VIII	Aeroplane	2 machine guns	1	205 kph	1½ hrs-
Rumpler CI	Seaplane	1 light machine gun; 1 machine gun and 1 rotating gun	2	150 kph	4 hrs
Albatross W4	Seaplane	1 or 2 forward machine guns	1	160 kph	3 hrs
Brandenburg KDW	Seaplane	2 forward machine guns	1	170 kph	2½ hrs

1 Technical data drawn from Ryheul, *MarineKorps*, pp261–68.

Table 7: MarineKorps' Order of Battle[2]

MarineKorps Flandern
   – Admiral Ludwig von Schröder
1st MarineDivision
   1. Strength at the end of 1914:
     – 1st Marine-Brigade
     – 1st Matrosen-Regiment
     – 1st Matrosen-Artillerie-Regiment
     – 2nd Marine-Brigade

     – 1st Landwehr-Eskadron
     – 1st Landwehr-Feld-Artillerie-Abteilung
     – 2nd Marine-Pionier-Kompagnie
     – 2nd Matrosen-Artillerie-Regiment

2nd MarineDivision
   2. Strength at the end of 1914:
     – 3rd Marine-Brigade
     – 3rd Marine-Infanterie-Regiment
     – 3rd Matrosen-Regiment
     – 4th Marine-Brigade
     – 4th Matrosen-Regiment

     – 5th Matrosen-Regiment
     – 3rd Landwehr-Eskadron
     – 1st Marine-Feldartilleriebatterie
     – 2nd Marine-Feldartilleriebatterie
     – 3rd Marine-Pionier-Kompanie

3rd MarineDivision
   3. Strength at creation on July 1, 1917
     – Marine-Infanterie-Brigade
     – 1st Marine-Infanterie-Regiment
     – 2nd Marine-Infanterie-Regiment
     – 3rd Marine-Infanterie-Regiment
     – 3rd Eskadron
     – 7th Husaren-Regiment

     – 9th Feldartillerie-Regiment
     – 115th Pioniere-Batallion
     – 1st Reserve-Kompagnie,
       24th Marinebattalion
     – 160th Minenwerfer-Kompagnie

2 Taken from Kriegsstarknachweisung des MarineKorps, December 1914, RM3:4614; Ryheul, *MarineKorps*, pp246–47; Gladisch, *Krieg der Nordsee*, vol VI: pp293–94.

Table 7a: Flotillas Order of Battle

III Destroyer Flotilla[3]
— Leader: *S-53*

— 5th Half-Flotilla	— 6th Half-Flotilla
– *V-71*	– *G-91*
– *V-81*	– *V-70*
– *V-73*	– *S-54*
– *G-88*	– *S-55*
– *G-85*	– *G-42*

Torpedoboat Flotilla Flanders
— Leader: *A-43*

— 1st Half-Flotilla	— 2nd Half-Flotilla
– *A-46*	– *A-42*
– *A-9*	– *A-39*
– *A-8*	– *A-40*
– *A-47*	– *A-44*
– *A-48*	– *A-45*

Destroyer Flotilla Flanders
— Leader: *V-47*

— 1st Half-Flotilla	- 2nd Half-Flotilla
– *V-67*	– *S-15*
– *G-95*	– *S-20*
– *V-68*	– *S-24*
– *G-96*	– *S-18*

3 Strengths given are from the beginning of the unrestricted submarine campaign.

Table 8: The Eastern Coastal Batteries - 1918[4]

Name	Number of guns	calibre
Kaiser Wilhelm II	Four	30.5cm
Hessen	Four	28cm
Braunschweig	Four	28cm
Freya	Four	21cm
Hertha	Four	21cm
Schleswig-Holstein	Two	17cm
Augusta	Three	15cm
Hamburg	Four	10.5cm
Bremen	Four	10.5cm
Lekkerbek	Two	8.8cm
Schützennest	Six	5cm
Friedrichsort	Four	17cm
Lübeck	Two	15cm
Mole	Four; Two; Four; Two	5cm; 8.8cm; 10.5cm; 15cm
Kanal	Four	8.8cm
Sachsen	Four	17cm
LeopoldKanal	Two	5.2cm
Kaiserin	Four	15cm
Groden	Four	28cm
Mittel	Three	10.5cm
Hafen	Four	8.8cm

Table 9: The Western Coastal Batteries-1918

Name	# of guns	Calibre
Deutschland	Four	38cm
Pommern	One	38cm
Tirpitz	Four	28cm
Preussen	Four	28cm
Hannover	Three	28cm
Oldenburg	Four	17cm
Gneisenau II	Four	17cm
Cecilie	Four	15cm
Aachen	Four	15cm
Beseler	Four	15cm
Antwerpen	Four	10.5cm
Hindenburg	Four	28cm
Schlesien	Four	17cm
Ludendorff	Four	15cm
Irene	Three	15cm
Blücher	Three; One; One	15cm; 8.8cm; 10.5cm
Eylau	Five; Three; Two; One	8.8cm; 3.7cm; 5cm; 10.5cm
Gneisenau I	Four	17cm
Seekamp	Two	17cm
Würtemberg	Four	10.5cm

4 Both of the following tables are taken from Ryheul, *MarineKorps*, pp157–69, 177–93. In general the eastern batteries extende from Knocke to the Dutch border and the western batteries extend from the land front to Knocke.

Bibliography

ARCHIVES
Bundesarchiv-Militärarchiv, Freiburg-im-Breisgau.
Reichsmarine 120 - Files of the MarineKorps Flandern
RM 120: 145-153, 241. Air Operations and Reinforcements
RM 120: 570, 601-2. Denkschrifts
RM 120: 1, 34-6, 54, 142, 283, 519. Naval Operations and Reinforcements
RM 120: 96, 98, 576-579, 587. Flanders Submarine Flotillas
RM 120: 282, 516, 518. War Diaries
RM 120: 60, 111-2. Coast Defence
RM 120: 275. The Ostend-Zeebrugge Attack
RM 120: 38. Fall K
RM 120: 45-7, 52-3, 55. Flanders Torpedo-Boat Flotilla
RM 120: 77. Correspondence with the High Seas Fleet
RM 120: 50-1. Flanders Destroyer Flotilla
Reichsmarine 3 - Files of the Reichs Marine Amt
RM 3: 5622-5637. Miscellaneous files concerning Belgium
RM 3: 5643-5651. Orders to the MarineKorps
RM 3: 5711-12. Daily communications on the naval war
RM 3: 4706-7. Bases in Belgium
RM 3: 5709-10, 3488. Daily activity reports from the Flanders Submarines
RM 3: 5703. Order of battle for the MarineKorps Flandern
RM 3: 5639. Creation of the MarineKorps
RM 3: 5708. Daily activity reports for the Flanders Torpedo-Boats
RM 3: 3487. Creation of the Flanders Flotillas
RM 3: 5704. Daily activity reports of the MarineKorps
RM 3: 5706. Coastal Defences
RM 3: 5707. Shipyard Activity Reports
RM 3: 11959. Tirpitz's denkschrift on the value of the Flanders harbours

REFERENCE WORKS
Bird, Keith W. *German Naval History: A Guide to the Literature* (NY: Garland Publishing, 1985).
Breyer, Siegfried. *Battleships and Battlecruisers, 1905–70* (Garden City, N.Y.: Doubleday, 1973).
Conway's All the World's Fighting Ships, 1860–1905 (London: Conway Maritime Press, 1979).
Conway's All the World's Fighting Ships, 1906–21 (London: Conway Maritime Press, 1985).
Dittmar, F.J. and J.J. Colledge. *British Warships 1914–19* (London: Ian Allen, 1972).
Gröner, Erich. *Die Deutschen Kriegschiffe, 1815–1945*, II vols (Munich: J.F. Lehmanns, 1966–68, rev. Eng. ed. (Annapolis, Md.: Naval Institute Press, 1990).
Jane, Fred T. (ed.) *Jane's Fighting Ships, 1914* (London: Sampson Low, Marston, 1914, reprint,

Newton Abbot, Devon: David & Charles, 1968).

Röhr, Albert. *Handbuch der deutschen Marinegeschichte* (Oldenburg: Gerhard Stalling Druck und Verlag, 1963).

Strachan, Hew. (ed.) *World War I: A History* (Oxford: Oxford University Press, 1998).

Taylor, John C. *German Warships of World War I* (London: Ian Allen, 1969).

Thetford, Owen. *British Naval Aircraft Since 1912*, 4th rev. ed. (London: Putnam, 1977).

OFFICIAL HISTORIES

Corbett, Julian S. and Henry Newbolt. *History of the Great War: Naval Operations*, V vols (London: Longmans, Green, 1920–31).

Falls, Cyril. *Military Operations: France and Belgium 1917*, III vols (London: HMSO, 1948).

Groos, Otto, and Walther Gladisch. *Der Krieg in der Nordsee*, VII vols Berlin (vol VII Frankfurt-on-Main), (Berlin: E.S. Mittler, 1920–65).

Raleigh, Sir Walter and H.A. Jones. *The War in the Air*, VI vols (Oxford: Clarendon Press, 1922–37).

Reichskrieg Ministerium. *Der Weltkrieg 1914–1918*, XV vols (Berlin: E.S. Mittler, 1925–42).

Spindler, Rear-Admiral Arno. *Der Handelskrieg mit U-Booten*, V vols Berlin (Vol V Frankfurt-on-Main): (Berlin: E.S. Mittler, 1932–66).

GERMANY

Bartz, Karl. *Zeebrügge: Der Englische Angriff auf die Deutsche U-Bootwaffe* (Berlin: Im Deutschen Verlag, 1938).

Bauer, Hermann. *Als Führer der U-Boote im Weltkrieg* (Leipzig: Kohler & Amelang, 1943).

_____ *Reichsleitung und U-Bootseinsatz 1914 bis 1918* (Lippoldsberg: Klosterhaus Verlag, 1956).

Bergen, Claus. (ed.) *U-Boat Stories: Narrative of German U-Boat Sailors* (London: Constable, 1931).

Berghahn, Volker. *Germany and the Approach of War in 1914*, 2nd ed. (NY: St. Martin's, 1993).

Bernhardi, Friedrich von. *Germany and the Next War*, Eng trans. (NY: Longmans, 1914).

Bethmann-Hollweg, Theobald. *Reflections on the World War*, II vols (London: Butterworth, 1920).

Blackbourn, David. *The Long Nineteenth Century: A History of Germany, 1780–1918* (NY: Oxford University Press, 1998).

Buchholz, Arden. *Moltke, Schlieffen and German War Planning* (NY: Berg Publishers, 1991).

Deist, Wilhelm. 'Die Politik der Seekriegsleitung und die Rebellion der Flotte Ende Oktober 1918' *Vierteljahrshefte für Zeitgeschichte*, vol XIV (October 1966): pp341–68.

Deseyne, Aleks A.M. 'The German Coastal Defenses in Flanders, 1914–18' in Steven Weingartner (ed.) *A Weekend with the Great War* (Shippensburg, PA: White Mane Publishing Company, 1995).

Drascher, Wahrhold. 'Zur Soziologie des deutschen Seeoffizierkorps', *Wehrwissenschaftliche Rundschau*, vol XII: pp555–69.

Endres, Franz Carl. 'Soziologische Struktur und ihr entsprechende Ideologien des deutschen Offizierkorps vor dem Weltkriege' *Archiv für Sozialwissenschaft und Sozialpolitik*, vol LXVIII: pp282–319.

Falkenhayn, Erich von. *General Headquarters and Its Critical Decisions*, (London: Hutchinson, 1919).

ste Verlag, 1961. English trans. NY: Norton, 1967.

Feldmann, Gerald. *Army, Industry and Labor in Germany 1914–18*, (Princeton: Princeton University Press, 1966).

Forstner, Georg-Günther Freiherr von. 'Torpedoboots-unternehmungen Flandern' *Krieg auf 7 Ozeanen*, vol II (Berlin: n.p, 1935).

Gayer, A. 'Summary of German Submarine Operations in the Various Theaters of War from 1914–1918' *United States Naval Institute Proceedings*. vol 52, no 4 (April 1926): pp621–59.

_____, *Die Deutschen U-Boote in ihrer Kriegführung 1914–18* (Berlin: E.S. Mittler, 1930).

Gatzke, Hans W. *Germany's Drive to the West (Drang nach Westen): A Study of Germany's Western*

War Aims During the First World War (Baltimore: Johns Hopkins Press, 1950).

Gemzell, Carl-Axel. *Organization, Conflict and Innovation: A Study of German Naval Strategic Planning, 1888–1940* (Lund: Esselte Studium, 1973).

Geyer, Michael. *Deutsche Rüstungspolitik 1860–1980* (Frankfurt: Suhrkamp, 1984).

Gibson, R.H. and Maurice Prendergast. *The German Submarine War, 1914 to 1918* (London: Constable, 1931).

Goetze, W. v. 'Das Marinekorps in Flandern 1914–18' *Marine-Rundschau*, vol XXXI (1–3, 1926): pp6–18, 48–58, 95–104.

Görlitz, Walter. (ed.) *The Kaiser and His Court: The Diaries, Notebooks and Letters of Admiral Georg Alexander von Müller, Chief of the Naval Cabinet, 1914–18* (London: MacDonald, 1961).

Hedde, P. 'Der Ausbau der flandrischen Küste zum Stützpunkt des Marinekorps' *Marine-Rundschau*, vol XXXIII. (4, 1928): pp145–58.

Herwig, Holger H. *The German Naval Officer Corps: A Social and Political History, 1890–1918* (Oxford: Clarendon Press, 1973).

_____ *The First World War: Germany and Austria-Hungary 1914–18* (London: Arnold, 1997).

_____ *'Luxury Fleet': The Imperial German Navy, 1888–1918* (London: Allen & Unwin, 1980).

_____ 'Admirals *versus* Generals: The War Aims of the Imperial German Navy 1914–1918' *Central European History*, vol V (September 1972): pp208–33.

_____ 'Zur Soziologie des kaiserlichen Seeoffizierkorps vor 1914', *Marine und Marinepolitik*: pp73–88.

_____ 'Soziale Herkunft und wissenschaftliche Vorbildung des Seeoffiziers der Kaiserlichen Marine vor 1914' *Militärgeschichtliche Mitteilungen*. no 2 (1971): pp81–111.

_____ and David F. Trask. 'The Failure of Imperial Germany's Undersea Offensive Against World Shipping, February 1917–October 1918' *The Historian*, vol XXXIII (August, 1971): pp619–32.

Herzog, Bodo. *60 Jahre Deutsche U-Boote, 1906–66* (Munich: J.F. Lehmanns Verlag, 1968).

_____ & Günter Schomaekers. *Ritter der Tiefe-Graue Wölfe: Die erfolgreichsten U-Boot Kommandanten der Welt des Ersten und Zweiten Weltkrieges* (Munich: Verlag Welsermühl, 1965).

Hildebrand, Hans H. and Ernest Henriot. *Deutschland's Admirale 1849–1945* (Osnabrück, Biblio Verlag, 1990)

Horn, Daniel. *The German Naval Mutinies of World War I* (New Brunswick, NJ: Rutgers University Press, 1969).

Hubatsch, Walther. *Die Ära Tirpitz: Studien zur Deutschen Marinepolitik 1890–1918* (Göttingen: Musterschmidt Verlag, 1955).

_____, *Die Admiralstab und die Obersten Marinebehörden in Deutschland, 1848–1945* (Frankfurt-on-Main: Bernard & Graefe Verlag, 1958).

Hülsen, B.V. 'Ruhmestage der Marinedivision in belgischer Darstellung (9–12 September 1914)', *Marine-Rundschau*, vol XXXII (1927): pp67–75.

_____ 'Das Marinekorps in Flandern 1914–1918 (Landkrieg)' *Marine-Rundschau*, vol XXXI (4–6, 1926): pp6–18, 45–58, 95–104.

Imrie, Alex. *German Naval Air Service* (London: Arms and Armour Press, 1989).

Jeschke, Hubert. *U-Boottaktik: Zur Deutschen U-Boottaktik, 1900–45* (Freiburg: Verlag Romach, 1972).

Kaulisch, Baldur. 'Zur überseeischen Stützpunktpolitik der kaiserlichen deutschen Marineführung am Ende des 19. Jahrhunderts und im ersten Weltkrieg', *Militärgeschichte*, no 5 (1980): pp585–98.

Kelly, Patrick J. 'The Naval Policy of Imperial Germany' (Ph.D. diss. Georgetown University, 1970).

Kennedy, Paul M. 'The Development of German Naval Operations Plans Against England, 1896–1914' in Paul M. Kennedy (ed.) *The War Plans of the Great Powers 1880–1914* (London: Allen & Unwin, 1979).

Kühlwetter, Kapitän z.S. a.D. von. 'The Personnel of the German Navy', *Brassey's Naval Annual* (1913): pp132–50.

Lambi, Ivo. *The Navy and German Power Politics, 1862–1914* (Boston: Allen and Unwin, 1984).
Ludendorff, Erich. *My War Memories, 1914–18*(London: Hutchinson, 1919).
_____*Kriegführung und Politik* (Berlin: E.S. Mittler, 1922).
_____*Urkunden der Obersten Heeresleitun über Ihre Tätigkeit 1916–18* (Berlin: E.S. Mittler, 1922).
Lundeberg, Philip K. 'The German Naval Critique of the U-Boat Campaign, 1915–18' *Military Affairs*, vol XXVII, no 3 (Fall 1983): pp105–18.
Morrow, John H. *Building German Airpower, 1909–14* (Knoxville: University of Tennessee Press, 1976).
_____ *German Air Power in World War I* (Lincoln: University of Nebraska Press, 1982).
Peters, Michael. *Der All-Deutsche Verband am Vorabend des Ersten Weltkrieges (1904–14)* (Frankfurt-am-Main: Peter Lang, 1992).
Philbin, Tobias R. *Admiral von Hipper: The Inconvenient Hero* (Amsterdam: B.R. Grüner, 1982).
Pohl, Admiral Hugo von. *Aus Aufzeichnungen und Briefen während der Kriegszeit* (Berlin: Karl Siegismund, 1920).
Ritter, Gerhard. *The Sword and the Scepter: The Problem of Militarism in Germany*, IV vols (Coral Gables: University of Miami Press 1969–73).
_____*Der Schlieffenplan. Kritik eines Mythos* (Munich: R. Oldenbourg 1956).
Robinson, Douglas H. *The Zeppelin in Combat: A History of the German Naval Airship Division 1912–18*, 3rd ed. (Seattle: University of Washington Press, 1980).
Röhl, J.C.G. and Nicolaus Sombart. (eds.) *Kaiser Wilhelm II: New Interpretations, the Corfu Papers* (Cambridge: Cambridge University Press, 1982).
Röhr, Albert. 'Die Luftabwehr des Marinekorps und der Luftkrieg in Flandern', *Marine-Rundschau*, vol XXVIII (8, 1923): pp341–48.
Rössler, Eberhard. *The U-Boat: The Evolution and Technical History of German Submarines*, Eng. trans (London and Melbourne: Arms and Armour Press, 1981).
Ruge, Friedrich. 'Die Verwendung der Mine im Seekrieg 1914 bis 1918. Ihre Erfolge und Misserfolge', *Marine-Rundschau* no 32 (June 1927): pp258–300.
Rhyheul, Johan. *MarineKorps Flandern 1914–18* (Hamburg: E.S. Mittler, 1997).
Scheer, Admiral Reinhard. *Germany's High Seas Fleet in the World War* (London: Cassell, 1919).
Schulze, E. 'Das Marinekorps in Flandern 1914–18', *Marine-Rundschau*, vol XXVII (8–10, 1922).
Spindler, Rear Admiral Arno. 'The Value of the Submarine in Naval Warfare', *U.S. Naval Institute Proceedings*. vol LII, no 5, (May 1926): pp835–54.
Stegemann, Bernd. *Die Deutsche MarinePolitik 1916–18* (Berlin: Duncker & Humblet, 1970).
Steinberg, Jonathan. 'A German Plan for the Invasion of Holland and Belgium' in Paul M. Kennedy (ed.) *The War Plans of the Great Powers* (London: Allen & Unwin, 1979).
Sutton, James E. 'The Imperial German Navy 1910-1914' (Ph.D. diss. Indiana University, 1953).
Thomas, Lowell. *Raiders of the Deep* (Garden City, NY: Doubleday, Doran, 1928).
Tirpitz, Admiral Alfred von. *My Memoirs*, II vols (NY: Dodd Mead, 1919).
_____*Deutsche Ohnemachtspolitik im Weltkriege* (Hamburg and Berlin: Hanseatische Verlagsanstalt, 1926).
Usher, Roland. *Pan-Germanism: From its Inception to the Outbreak of the War, a Critical Study* (NY: Grosset and Dunlap, 1914).
Waldeyer-Hartz, Hugo von. *Admiral von Hipper* (London: Rich & Cowan, 1933).
_____ 'Der Kampf um Ostend und Zeebrugge' *Was wir vom Weltkrieg nicht wissen* (Leipzig: n.p, 1936).
_____ *'Ein Mann'; das Leben des Admirals Ludwig v. Schröder* (Braunschweig: F. Viewig & Sohn, 1934).
Wegener, Vice Admiral Wolfgang. *The Naval Strategy of the World War*, trans. by Holger H. Herwig (Annapolis, MD: Naval Institute Press, 1989).
Weir, Gary E. *Building the Kaiser's Navy: The Imperial Naval Office and German Industry in the von Tirpitz Era, 1890–1919*, (Annapolis, MD: Naval Institute Press, 1992).

Weniger, Karl. 'Die Kämpfe an der belgischen Küste und um die belgischen Hafen im Herbst 1914' *Marine-Rundschau*, vol XLI (3, 1936): 105–17.

GREAT BRITAIN

Aspinall-Oglander, Cecil F. *Roger Keyes* (London: The Hogarth Press, 1951).

Bacon, Admiral Sir Reginald. *The Dover Patrol, 1915–17*, II vols (London: Hutchinson, 1919).

_____ *The Concise Story of the Dover Patrol* (London: Hutchinson, 1932).

Bell, A.C. *A History of the Blockade of Germany and of the Countries Associated with Her in the Great War, Austria-Hungary, Bulgaria, and Turkey* (London: HMSO, 1937).

Beesly, Patrick. *Room 40: British Naval Intelligence 1914–18* (London: Hamish Hamilton, 1982).

Buxton, Ian. *Gun Monitors* (Tynemouth, Northumberland: World Ship Society and Trident Books, 1978).

Carpenter, Captain A.F.B. *The Blocking of Zeebrugge* (London: Herbert Jenkins, 1922).

Chalmers, Rear Admiral W.S. *The Life and Letters of David, Earl Beatty* (London: Hodder and Stoughton, 1951).

Chatterton, E. Keble. *The Auxiliary Patrol* (London: Sidgwick & Jackson, 1923).

_____ *Fighting the U-Boats* (London: Hurst & Blackett, 1942).

_____*Beating the U-Boats* (London: Hurst & Blackett, 1943).

Churchill, Winston. *The World Crisis*, V vols (NY: Scribner's, 1923–31).

Doughty, Martin. *Merchant Shipping and War: A Study in Defence Planning in Twentieth Century Britain* (London: Royal Historical Society, 1982).

Fayle, Ernest C. *Seaborne Trade*. III vols (London: John Murray, 1920–24).

French, David. *British Strategy and War Aims 1914–1916* (London: Allen & Unwin, 1986).

_____ *The Strategy of the Lloyd-George Coalition* (Oxford: Oxford University Press, 1950).

Gilbert, Martin. *Churchill: A Life* (NY: Henry Holt, 1991).

Giles, John. *Flanders Then and Now: The Ypres Salient and Passchendaele* (London: Leo Cooper, 1970).

Goldrick, James. *The King's Ships were at Sea: The War in the North Sea August 1914–February 1915* (Annapolis, MD: Naval Institute Press, 1984).

Graham, Dominick and Shelford Bidwell. *Coalitions, Politicians and Generals: Some Aspects of Command in Two World Wars* (London: Brassey's, 1993).

Guinn, Paul. *British Strategy and Politics 1914–18* (London: Oxford University Press, 1965).

Halpern, Paul G. (ed.) *The Keyes Papers, Publications of the Navy Records Society*, vol CXVII and vol CXXI (London: Navy Records Society, 1972. Reprint. London: Allen & Unwin, 1979, 1980).

Hankey, Lord. *The Supreme Command 1914–18*, II vols (London: Allen & Unwin, 1961).

Hurd, Archibald. *The Merchant Navy*, III vols (London: John Murray, 1921–29).

Jellicoe, Admiral of the Fleet, Earl. *The Crisis of the Naval War* (London: Cassell, 1920).

_____ *The Submarine Peril* (London: Cassell, 1931).

Keegan, John. *The First World War* (NY: Alfred A. Knopf, 1999).

Kennedy, Paul M. *The Rise and Fall of British Naval Mastery* (NY: Scribner's, 1976).

Keble, Howard. *The Zeebrugge Affair*. (NY: George H. Doran, 1918).

Keyes, Roger. *The Naval Memoirs*, II vols (London: Thornton Butterworth, 1934–35).

Lloyd George, David. *War Memoirs of David Lloyd George*, 2nd ed. II vols (London: Oldhams, 1936).

Marder, Arthur J. *From the Dreadnought to Scapa Flow: The Royal Navy in the Fisher Era, 1904–19*, V vols (London: Oxford University Press, 1961–70).

Patterson, A. *Tyrwhitt of the Harwich Force* (London: MacDonald, 1973).

Pitt, Barrie. *Zeebrugge: St. George's Day 1918* (London: Cassell, 1958).

_____ (ed.) *The Jellicoe Papers, Publications of the Navy Records Society*, II vols vol CVIII and vol CXI (London: Navy Records Society, 1966–68).

Prior, Robin and Trevor Wilson. *Passchendaele: The Untold Story* (New Haven, CT: Yale University Press, 1996).

Ranft, B.M. (ed.) *The Beatty Papers Volume I: 1902–18, Publications of the Navy Records Society*, vol CXXVIII (Aldershot: Scolar Press for Navy Records Society, 1989).

Roskill, Stephen W. *The Strategy of Sea Power* (London: Collins, 1962).

_____'The U-Boat Campaign of 1917 and Third Ypres' *Journal of the Royal United Services Institute* 104, no 616, (November 1959): pp440–42.

_____*Earl Beatty: The Last Naval Hero* (London: Collins, 1962).

Taffrail [Captain Taprell Dorling]. *Endless Story: Being an Account of the Work of the Destroyers, Flotilla Leaders, Torpedo Boats and Patrol Boats in the Great War* (London: Hodder & Stoughton, 1931).

_____*Swept Channels: Being an Account of the Minesweepers in the Great War* (London: Hodder & Stoughton, 1935).

Terraine, John. *The Road to Passchendaele: The Flanders Offensive of 1917: A Study in Inevitability*, (London: Leo Cooper, 1970).

Warner, Phillip. *The Zeebrugge Raid* (London: William Kimber, 1978).

Wiest, Andrew. *Passchendaele and the Royal Navy, Contributions in Military Studies Series*, (Westport, CT: Greenwood Press, 1995).

Winton, John. *Convoy: The Defence of Sea Trade, 1890–1990* (London: Michael Joseph, 1983).

GENERAL

Abbott, G.F. *Greece and the Allies, 1914–22* (London: Methuen and Company, 1922).

Bennett, Geoffrey. *Naval Battles of the First World War*, rev. ed. (London: Batsford, 1968. Reprint. London: Pan, 1983).

Cowie, Captain J.S. *Mines, Minelayers and Minelaying* (London: Oxford University Press, 1949).

Friedman, Norman. *Submarine Design and Development* (Annapolis, MD: Naval Institute Press, 1984).

Grant, Robert M. *U-Boats Destroyed: The Effects of Anti-Submarine Warfare, 1914–18* (London: Putnam, 1964).

_____ *U-Boat Intelligence, 1914–18.* (London: Putnam, 1964).

Halpern, Paul G. *A Naval History of World War I* (Annapolis: Naval Institute Press, 1994).

Hermann, David G. *The Arming of Europe and the Making of the First World War* (Princeton: Princeton University Press, 1996).

Hough, Richard. *The Great War at Sea 1914–18* (Oxford: Oxford University Press, 1983).

Hezlet, Vice Admiral Sir Arthur. *Aircraft and Sea Power* (London: Peter Davies, 1970).

_____ *Electronics and Sea Power* (NY: Stein and Day, 1975).

_____, *The Submarine and Sea Power* (London: Peter Davies, 1967).

Kahn, David. *The Code Breakers: The Story of Secret Writing* (NY: MacMillan, 1967).

Killen, John. *A History of Marine Aviation 1911–68* (London:Muller, 1969).

Leontaritis, George B. *Greece and the First World War: From Neutrality to Intervention, 1917–18* (NY: Columbia University Press, 1990).

Lundeberg, Philip K. 'Undersea Warfare and Allied Strategy in World War I' *Smithsonian Journal of History*, vol I, nos I and II, (1966–67): pp1–30, 49–72.

Tanenbaum, Jan K. *General Maurice Sarrail, 1856–1929: The French Army and Left-Wing Politics* (Chapel Hill, NC: University of North Carolina Press, 1974).

Terraine, John. *Business in Great Waters: The U-Boat Wars 1916–45* (London: Leo Cooper, 1989).

Vandenbosch, Amry. *The Neutrality of the Netherlands During the World War* (Grand Rapids, MI: Wm. B. Eerdmans Publishing, 1927).

_____ *Dutch Foreign Policy Since 1815* (Hague: Martinus Nijhoff, 1959).

Van der Flier, M.J. *War Finances in the Netherlands up to 1918, Economic and Social History of the World War*, Dutch Series (Oxford: Clarendon Press, 1923).

Van Tuyll van Serooskerken, Hubert P. 'The Netherlands and World War I' in Kelly DeVries (ed.) *History of Warfare*, no 7 (Leiden: Brill, 2001).

Notes

Introduction

1 For the most detailed treatment of the growing rift between Germany and Britain see Paul Kennedy, *The Rise of the Anglo-German Antagonism, 1860–1914*, (London: Allen & Unwin, 1980).

2 The classic study of the Schlieffen Plan remains Gerhard Ritter's *Der Schlieffenplan. Kritik eines Mythos*, (Munich: R. Oldenbourg, 1956). More recent works touching on the topic include: David G. Herrmann, *The Arming of Europe and the Making of the First World War*, (Princeton: Princeton University Press, 1996); Arden Buchholz, *Moltke, Schlieffen and German War Planning*, (NY: Berg Publishers, 1991); and Paul Kennedy, ed. *The War Plans of the Great Powers, 18801914*, (London: Allen and Unwin, 1979).

3 For the best study of the German navy's preparations for war see Ivo Lambi, *The Navy and German Power Politics, 1862–1914*, (Boston: Allen and Unwin, 1984) and Carl-Axel Gemzell, *Organization, Conflict and Innovation: A Study of German Naval Strategic Planning, 1888–1940*, (Lund: Esselte Studium, 1973).

4 Jonathan Steinberg, 'A German Plan for the Invasion of Holland and Belgium,' in Kennedy, *War Plans*, p156.

5 Steinberg, 'German Plan', pp156–160. For further detail on this lack of cooperation see Lambi, *German Power Politics*.

6 For information on the strategic thought of the German naval High Command in August 1914 see the first volume of the German official history: Otto Groos and Walther Gladisch, *Der Krieg in der Nordsee*, VII vols (Berlin, E.S. Mittler, 1920–1965) I: pp1–63.

7 All of the following information in this section is drawn from: Alfred von Tirpitz, 'Die Bedeutung Belgiens und seiner Häfen für unsere Seegeltung', contained in ReichsMarine 3:11959, German Military Archives, Freiburg-im-Breisgau, Germany. ReichsMarine hereafter cited as RM.

8 For an examination of the varying types of German submarines see Eberhard Rössler, *The U-boat: the Evolution and Technical History of German Submarines*, Eng. trans. (Annapolis, MD: Naval Institute Press, 1981).

9 At the start of the occupation Ostend, Zeebrugge and Bruges were too small to be used by anything larger than light cruisers. Antwerp was of course a major harbour but German use of the port was limited by Dutch neutrality. Since the Dutch controlled the banks of the Scheldt it was not possible for the Germans to use the river for military purposes without violating Dutch neutrality. Therefore the naval forces of the MarineKorps Flandern were limited to the 'Triangle'.

10 'Little War'. The goal of this strategy was to slowly reduce British naval superiority by attacking the British battleships with torpedo craft. It was begun in the belief that the British would implement a close blockade of the German harbours in the event of war. For discussions of the policy see: Paul G. Halpern, *A Naval History of World War I*, (Annapolis, MD: Naval Institute Press, 1994), p23; Otto Groos, *Der Krieg in der Nordsee*, (Berlin: E.S Mittler, 1920), I: pp41–63; and Holger H. Herwig, *'Luxury Fleet': The Imperial German Navy 1888–1918*, (London: Allen & Unwin, 1980; reprint, London: Ashfield Press, 1987), pp. 160–61.

Chapter 1

1 Grosses Hauptquartier to Naval Staff, 23 August 1914, printed in Otto Groos, *Der*

Krieg in der Nordsee, (Berlin: E.S. Mittler, 1923), vol II: p119.

2 Edgar Erich Schulze, 'Das MarineKorps Flandern 1914–18' *Marine-Rundschau*, vol XXVII (8–10, 1922), p380.

3 Schulze, 'MarineKorps', p380. See also Groos, vol II: p117; and Admiral Alfred von Tirpitz, *My Memoirs* II vols (NY: Dodd Mead, 1919), vol I: p239.

4 Tirpitz, *Memoirs*, vol I: p239.

5 Tirpitz alludes to this briefly in his memoirs, as does Schulze in his article but the official history has very little to say on this subject.

6 Tirpitz, *Memoirs*, vol I: p239; Schulze, 'Das MarineKorps', p380.

7 The Reichs Marine Amt (or the Imperial Navy Office) was created in March 1889 by Kaiser Wilhelm II to be the administrative arm of the navy. It's primary responsibility was for the creation and maintenance of the ships of the fleet. The Admiralstab (or Naval Staff) was responsible for preparing strategic plans for the navy, conducting naval intelligence and the conduct of military operations in wartime. It was intended as the naval version of the Prussian General Staff though it never had the same power or prestige. For more information see Holger Herwig, *'Luxury Fleet': The Imperial German Navy 1888–1918*, (London: Allen & Unwin, 1980; reprint, London: Ashfield Press, 1987), p22.

8 Vice Admiral Eduard von Capelle to Kapitän zur See Albert Hopman, 24 August 1914, RM3:5638.

9 Capelle to Hopman, 24 August 1914, RM3:5638.

10 For a very detailed discussion of these events see Groos, *Krieg in der Nordsee*, vol II: pp120–22.

11 Tirpitz and Falkenhayn to Chancellor Theobald von Bethmann-Hollweg, 29 August 1914, RM3:5638.

12 This data can be found in several sources: Admiral Ludwig von Schröder, Order creating the MarineDivision, RM3:5642; Groos, *Krieg der Nordsee*, vol II:p121; Schulze, pp380–81. The request for individuals skilled in small craft is in a note from von Schröder to the Naval Staff contained in RM3:4706.

13 This debate is covered in detail in Groos, *Krieg der Nordsee*, vol II:pp120–124.

14 Tobias Philbin, *Admiral von Hipper: The Inconvenient Hero*, (Amsterdam: B.R. Grüner, 1982), p59.

15 Von Schröder to the MarineDivision, Order No. 2, 30 August 1914, RM3:4614.

16 Groos, *Krieg der Nordsee*, vol II: p124; Tirpitz, *Memoirs*, vol I: p80.

17 Admiral Ludwig von Schröder, MarineDivision Order #1, 29 August 1914 RM3:5642.

18 von Schröder to Tirpitz, 12 September 1914, RM3:5638.

19 Groos, *Krieg der Nordsee*, vol II: pp121–22.

20 Admiral Ludwig von Schröder, 'Study of Ostend and Zeebrugge as Possible Naval Bases', December 1914, RM120:259.

21 The bulk of the following information is taken from the only extant biography of von Schröder, written by a former officer of the MarineDivision as a memorial after von Schröder's death in 1933. Hugo von Waldeyer-Hartz, *'Ein Mann'; das Leben des Admirals Ludwig von Schröder*. (Braunschweig: F. Viewig & Sohn, 1934), pp29–53. What personal papers of von Schröder's there are in the archives deal with the war and the period from 1919 to his death in 1933.

22 Ibid., pp64–76.

23 Ibid., p77.

24 Ibid., pp107–9.

25 Ibid., pp110–11, 83–84.

26 Ivo Lambi, *The Navy and German Power Politics*, (Boston: Allen & Unwin, 1984), pp107, 122. See also von Waldeyer-Hartz, *Ein Mann*, p116.

27 Groos, *Krieg der Nordsee*, vol II: p125.

28 Holger Herwig, *The German Naval Officer Corps: A Social and Political History, 1890–1918*, (Oxford: Clarendon Press, 1973), p87. Also see Groos, *Krieg der Nordsee*, vol II: p119.

29 Von Schröder, MarineDivision Order No. 2, 30 August 1914, RM3:5642.

30 Groos, *Krieg der Nordsee*, vol II: p127; Reichskriegsministeriums, *Der Weltkrieg, 1914–18*, (Berlin: E.S. Mittler und Sohn, 1925–42); vol III: pp330–32,466. Most of the following narrative is taken from the official German history of the naval war, *Der Krieg in der Nordsee*.

31 Groos, *Krieg der Nordsee*, vol II: p128; Reichskriegsministeriums, *Weltkrieg*, vol III: pp330–32.

32 Groos, *Krieg der Nordsee*, vol II: p129.

33 Groos, *Krieg der Nordsee*, vol II: pp134–36; Reichskriegsministeriums, *Weltkrieg*, vol V: pp221–45.

34 Groos, *Krieg der Nordsee*, vol II: pp135–37; Reichskriegsministeriums, *Weltkrieg*, vol V: pp221–45.

35 Sir Julian Corbett and Henry Newbolt, *History of the Great War: Naval Operations*, V vols (London: Longmans, 1920–31), vol I: p181.

36 Corbett, *Naval Operations*, vol I: pp184–189. For Churchill's role see Winston S.

Churchill, *The World Crisis: an Abridgement of the Classic Four Volume History of World War I*, (NY: Charles Scribner's Sons, 1923-31; reprint, NY: Charles Scribner's Sons, 1992), pp196–211; and Martin Gilbert, *Churchill: A Life*, (NY: Henry Holt and Company, 1991), pp282,286.

37 Groos, *Krieg der Nordsee*, vol II: pp147, 155; Corbett, *Naval Operations*, vol I: pp184–89.

38 Kriegstagebüch of Admiral Ludwig von Schröder, 10 October 1914, RM120:515. The *Kriegstagebüch* was the Admiral's war diary recording the actions of first the MarineDivision and later the MarineKorps. It contains notes on the activities of the division and the corps as well as official communications from the RMA and Naval Staff. It also holds personal observations by Admiral von Schröder on the events with which he was involved. As such it provides much useful detail, especially on tactical matters.

39 Corbett, *Naval Operations*, pp194–95.

40 Groos, *Krieg der Nordsee*, vol II:p158.

41 Kriegstagebüch von Schröder, 13 October 1914, RM120:515; Groos, *Krieg der Nordsee*, vol II:pp157–58.

42 Karl Weniger, 'Die Kämpfe an der belgischen Küste und um die belgischen Hafen im Herbst 1914', *Marine-Rundschau*, vol XLI (1936): pp105–6.

43 Corbett, *Naval Operations*, vol I: pp214–15; Groos, *Krieg der Nordsee*, vol II: pp202–3. For further information see also the second volume of Arthur J. Marder, *From the Dreadnought to Scapa Flow: The Royal Navy in the Fisher Era, 1904–19*. V vols. (London: Oxford University Press, 1961–70).

44 For the most recent general treatments of these battles and their place in the war see John Keegan, *The First World War*, (NY: Alfred A. Knopf, 1999) and Holger Herwig, *The First World War: Germany and Austria-Hungary 1914–18*, (London: Arnold, 1997). See also Reichskriegsministeriums, *Weltkrieg*, vol V: pp295–345; vol VI: pp10–25, 35–49, 371–95.

45 Kriegstagebüch von Schröder, 23 October 1914, RM120:515.

46 Von Schröder to von Capelle, Tirpitz, and von Müller, 14 October 1914, RM3:5638.

47 Groos, *Krieg der Nordsee*, vol II: p221.

48 Von Schröder to the Tirpitz, 12 September 1914, RM3:5638.

49 Boedicker to von Schröder, 18 September 1914, RM3:5638.

50 Telephone conversation between Schröder and Kapitän zur See Hopman, 15 October 1914, RM3:5638.

51 Von Müller to the High Seas Fleet, North Sea station and Baltic station, 20 October 1914, RM3:5638.

52 Ibid.

53 Groos, *Krieg der Nordsee*, vol IV: pp291–92.

54 Von Schröder to von Falkenhayn, 25 October 1914, RM3:5639.

55 Groos, *Krieg der Nordsee*, vol II: p293; Schulze, 'MarineKorps', p382.

56 Kurt Boedicker, 'Proposal on the creation of a second MarineDivision', 5 November 1914, RM3:5638.

57 Kriegsliederung 2nd MarineDivision, RM3:5638. Also included in RM3:4614.

58 Allerhöchste Befehl to Chancellor von Bethmann-Hollweg and General von Falkenhayn, 8 November 1914, RM3:5639.

59 Allerhöchste Befehl, 9 December 1914, RM3:5639; Groos, *Krieg der Nordsee*, vol II: p292.

60 Ibid; Groos, *Krieg der Nordsee*, vol II: p293; Schulze, 'MarineKorps', p382.

61 Exchange of notes between Falkenhayn and Tirpitz, 28 February–6 March 1915, RM3:5639.

62 Memoranda by Hopman, 18–23 February 1915, RM3:5639.

63 Tirpitz to von Schröder, n.d. [early 1915], RM3:5638.

64 Von Capelle to Tirpitz, 22 March 1915, RM3:4614.

65 Minutes of a meeting between MarineKorps Chief of Staff von Hülsen and four members of the Government-General of occupied Belgium, 20 February 1915. Contained in both RM3:4614 and RM3:5639.

Chapter 2

1 Rear-Admiral Arno Spindler, *Der Handelskrieg mit U-booten*, V vols (Berlin: E.S. Mittler und Sohn, 1932–66), vol II: p2.

2 Memorandum by Rear-Admiral Paul Behncke, 14 October 1914, RM120:1.

3 Naval Staff to von Schröder, n.d., RM3:5638.

4 The following is based on a three-part study completed by Rear Admiral Paul Behncke on 24 October 1914 entitled 'Kriegführung gegen England von den belgisch-französischen Häfen und der Schelde aus.' The study is in RM120:1.

5 For a full discussion of the British and Belgian efforts in Antwerp see Sir Julian Corbett and Henry Newbolt, *History of the Great War: Naval Operations*, V vols (London: Longmans, 1920–31), vol I: pp178–201; and Winston S. Churchill, *The World Crisis: an Abridgement of the Classic Four Volume History of World War I*, (NY: Charles Scribner's Sons, 1923–31; reprint, NY: Charles Scribner's Sons, 1992), pp196–211.

6 Otto Groos, *Der Krieg in der Nordsee*, (Berlin: E.S. Mittler, 1923), vol IV: p122.

7 Bartenbach Commission, 'Report on the feasibility of ports for construction of small submarines and torpedo-boats', 25 October 1914, RM3:5638.

8 Notes on a visit to Flanders by Vice-Admiral Albert Hopman, 18 February to 23 February 1915, RM3:5639.

9 Von Schröder, "Report on the feasibility of using Ostend and Zeebrugge as naval bases", 14 October 1914, RM120:1.

10 Bartenbach Commission, 'Report on naval bases', 25 October 1914, RM3:5638.

11 Bartenbach Commission, 'Report on naval bases', 25 October 1914, RM3:5638; Edgar Erich Schulze, 'Das MarineKorps Flandern 1914–18', *Marine-Rundschau*, vol XXVII (8–10, 1922), p383; P Hedde, 'Der Ausbau der flandrischen Küste zum Stützpunkt des MarineKorps', *Marine-Rundschau*, vol XXXIII (4, 1928), p147.

12 Report on Zeebrugge, n.d., RM3:5638.

13 Groos, *Krieg der Nordsee*, vol IV: p122.

14 Bartenbach Commission, 'Report on naval bases', 25 October 1914, RM3:5638.

15 Von Schröder, Order creating the Abteilung Hafenbau, 17 November 1914, RM3:4614. See also Hedde, 'Ausbau', p148.

16 Schulze, 'MarineKorps', p465.

17 Pohl to von Schröder, n.d., RM3:5638.

18 Groos, *Krieg der Nordsee*, vol II: pp287–88.

19 Kapitän zur See Hans Zenker to Tirpitz, 20 October 1914, RM3:5638; Behncke to Tirpitz, 28 October 1914, RM3:5638; Kriegsliederung MarineKorps, n.d., RM120:33.

20 Kaiserliche Werft to RMA, 18 March 1915, RM120:96; Johann Ryheul, *MarineKorps Flandern 1914-1918*, (Hamburg: E.S Mittler und Sohn, 1997), pp31–48. The latter has a complete listing of all of the facilities constructed in the harbours and the precise numbers of Belgian and German workers used to build them.

21 Hedde, 'Ausbau', 148, 153; Ryheul, *MarineKorps*, pp31–48.

22 Aleks A.M. Deseyne, 'The German Coastal Defenses in Flanders, 1914–18' in *A Weekend With the Great War*, ed. Steven Weingartner, (Shippensburg, PA: White Mane Publishing Company, 1995), p43.

23 For a full treatment see Corbett and Newbolt, *Naval Operations*, vol I: pp1–20, and Groos, *Krieg der Nordsee*, vol II: pp202–29.

24 Corbett, *Naval Operations*, vol II: pp12, 19. For a full discussion of the various plans being discussed see Arthur J. Marder, *From the Dreadnought to Scapa Flow: The Royal Navy in the Fisher Era, 1904–19*, V vols (London: Oxford University Press, 1961–70), vol II: pp349–67.

25 Admiral Friedrich von Ingenohl to von Schröder, 6 December 1914, RM120:1.

26 Vice-Admiral Hermann Jacobsen, 'Evaluation of a possible English blocking attack on Zeebrugge', 9 December 1914, RM120:1.

27 Unsigned document from the office of the military attaché to the Netherlands to War Ministry, 4 April 1915, RM120:47.

28 See chapter five for a full discussion of German plans regarding the Netherlands.

29 Behncke to the RMA, 17 October 1914, RM3:5638.

30 Zenker to the Naval Staff forwarded to Tirpitz, 20 October 1914, RM3:5638.

31 Telephone conversation between Tirpitz and Schröder, n.d., RM3:5638.

32 Herwig, *Luxury Fleet*, p169.

33 MarineDivision to Tirpitz, 20 October 1914, RM3:5638.

34 Von Schröder, 'Erwägungen über die Kriegführung gegen englisch Seestreitkräfte von Zeebrügge and Ostend aus,' 13 December 1914, RM120:259.

35 Notes by Hopman on a trip to Flanders, 18 February to 23 February 1915, RM3:5639.

36 Von Schröder to von Tirpitz and Kaiser Wilhelm II, 31 March 1915, RM3:5639. Also contained in RM120:1.

37 Ibid. For an exceptionally well-detailed treatment of the precise workings of the coastal batteries see Deseyne, 'German Coastal Fortifications.'

38 Von Schröder to Tirpitz, 3 April 1915, RM3:5639.

39 Ibid.

40 Schulze, 'MarineKorps', p385.

41 A brief history of each battery is included in Ryheul, *MarineKorps*, pp157–95.

42 Kriegstagebüch von Schröder, RM120:515.

43 Unsigned report on a British air attack on Zeebrugge, n.d., RM120:145.

44 See Chapter 3 for a full discussion of this matter.

45 Unsigned report on a British air attack on Zeebrugge, n.d., RM120:145.

46 Boedicker to MarineKorps, 8 February 1915, RM3:5639. See also Hopman's notes on his trip to Flanders, 18 February to 23 February 1915, RM3:5639.

47 Albert Rohr, 'Die Luftabwehr des Marinekorps und der Luftkrieg in Flandern', *Marine-Rundschau*, vol XXVIII (8, 1923): p342.

48 Ibid., p392.

49 Ibid., p342.

50 From an unsigned and undated document

entitled 'Defense Against Air Attacks'
contained in RM120:145. See also Schulze,
'MarineKorps', p463.

51 See chapter 1.

52 Unsigned Naval Staff proposal for the
creation of a western air station, 26 August
1914, RM120:145; Kaiser Wilhelm II to
Tirpitz, 29 August 1914, RM120:145.

53 Zenker to Naval Staff, forwarded to Tirpitz,
20 October 1914, RM3:5638.

54 Tirpitz to Admiral Hugo von Pohl, Admiral
Georg Alexander von Müller, Admiral
Friedrich von Ingenohl, and Prince Heinrich
von Preussen, 22 October 1914, RM120:145.

55 Schulze, 'MarineKorps', p461; Groos, *Krieg
der Nordsee*, vol IV: p116.

56 Schulze, "MarineKorps", 461; Groos, *Krieg
der Nordsee*, vol IV: p116; Ryheul,
MarineKorps, p109. Herr was not actually
the first commander. He took over when the
original commander was shot down in early
1915.

57 MarineKorps memorandum on the
organization of the naval air station, 17
December 1914, RM120:145.

58 Befehlshaber der Marine Luftfahr
Abteilungen Flandern to Commander North
Sea Station, 28 May 1915, RM120:145.

59 Herwig, *Luxury Fleet*, p213. Useful
diagrams of both types are in Ryheul,
MarineKorps, pp261–62. As we will see that
conclusion is debatable.

60 Groos, *Krieg der Nordsee*, vol IV: p120;
Schulze, 'MarineKorps', p462.

61 The pilots generally used two methods to
communicate with their gunners. The first
method involved having the observer in the
aircraft use signal flags to communicate with
the batteries. However, they also made use of
pigeons to relay messages. Von Schröder,
Orders for artillery commanders, 28 January
1915, RM120:145.

62 Ibid.

63 MarineKorps to Tirpitz, memorandum on
the possible uses for aircraft in Flanders,
undated but the contents of the
memorandum put its probable origin in late
October or early November of 1914,
RM120:146.

64 Führer der U-Boote Fregatten-Kapitän
Hermann Bauer to von Ingenohl, 7
November 1914, RM120:145; Von Ingenohl
to von Schröder, 29 December 1914,
RM120:145.

65 Schulze, 'MarineKorps', p462.

66 Ibid., p461.

67 See Schulze, 'MarineKorps', for a
discussion of the successes of the Flanders
aircraft. See also Groos, *Krieg der Nordsee*,
vol IV: pp116–22, 326–28.

68 Kapitänleutnant von Moltke to von Pohl, 7
October 1914, RM120:145. I was unable to
determine any relation to either the great
Moltke or his less illustrious namesake.

69 Von Moltke to von Pohl, 10 October 1914,
RM120:145.

70 Admiral Gustav Bachmann to von Pohl, 12
February 1915, RM120:145.

71 Ibid.

72 XIII Reserve Korps to von Schröder, 7
March 1915, RM120:145.

73 Behncke to Tirpitz, 3 September 1914,
RM120:145.

74 Bachmann to Falkenhayn, 23 March 1915,
RM120:146.

75 Tirpitz to War Ministry, 10 April 1915,
RM120:145.

76 Ibid.

77 Ibid.

78 Von Schröder to Tirpitz, 22 April 1915,
RM120:145.

79 Tirpitz to von Schröder, 23 April 1915,
RM120:145.

Chapter 3

1 Rear-Admiral Paul Behncke, memorandum
14 October 1914, RM120:1.

2 Ibid.

3 Otto Groos and Walther Gladisch, *Der Krieg
in der Nordsee*, VII vols (Berlin: E.S. Mittler,
1920–1965), vol II: pp202–29; Sir Julian
Corbett and Henry Newbolt, *History of the
Great War: Naval Operations*, V volumes.
(London: Longmans, 1920–31), vol I:
pp213–35, 249–56; vol II:1–21.

4 Groos, *Krieg der Nordsee*, vol III: pp46–47;
Edgar Erich Schulze, 'Das MarineKorps
Flandern 1914–18', *Marine-Rundschau*, vol
XXVII (8–10, 1922), p417.

5 Schulze, 'MarineKorps', p417.

6 Von Ingenohl to von Pohl, 18 November
1914, RM120:1.

7 Kriegstagebüch von Schröder, 22 November
1914, RM120:515.

8 Groos, *Krieg der Nordsee*, vol IV:pp1–2.

9 Von Schröder, Study of Ostend and
Zeebrugge as possible submarine bases,
December 1914, RM120:259.

10 Von Schröder to Ingenohl, 4 December
1914, RM120:1.

11 Von Pohl to von Schröder, 5 December
1914, RM120:1.

12 Von Ingenohl to von Pohl, 8 December
1914, RM120:1.

13 Von Ingenohl to von Schröder, 11 December
1914, RM120:1. See also Groos, *Krieg der
Nordsee*, vol IV:pp1–2. For the details on the
construction of the *UB* and *UC*-class
submarines see Eberhard Rössler, *The U-
boat: The Evolution and Technical History of*

German Submarines, trans. Harold Erenberg, (Annapolis: Naval Institute Press, 1981), pp39–44.

14 Von Ingenohl to von Schröder, 11 December 1914, RM120:1.

15 Von Pohl to von Ingenohl, 12 December 1914, RM120:1.

16 Von Pohl to von Ingenohl, 13 December 1914, RM120:1.

17 Von Ingenohl to von Pohl, 14 December 1914, RM120:1.

18 Ibid.

19 Von Pohl to von Schröder, 13 December 1914, RM120:1.

20 Von Schröder to von Pohl, 18 December 1914, RM120:1.

21 Von Ingenohl to von Schröder, 23 December 1914, RM120:1.

22 Ibid.

23 Groos, *Krieg der Nordsee*, vol IV: pp22–23; Schulze, 'MarineKorps', p384. On the night of October 17th the Germans had sent the 7th Half-Flotilla (*S-115, S-117, S-118,* and *S-119*) to lay mines at the mouth of the Thames. They were intercepted by the light cruiser *Undaunted* and four British destroyers (*Lance, Loyal, Legion,* and *Lennox*). The entire German force was destroyed. See also Paul G. Halpern, *A Naval History of World War I*, (Annapolis, MD: Naval Institute Press, 1994), p35.

24 Von Pohl to von Schröder, 2 January 1915, RM120:1.

25 Schulze, 'MarineKorps', p385; and Groos, *Krieg der Nordsee*, vol IV: pp23–24.

26 Kriegstagebüch von Schröder, 7 January 1915, RM120:515.

27 Von Schröder to von Pohl, 30 January 1915, RM120:1. The *Siegfried*'s were old coastal defence battleships built between 1890 and 1896. They displaced just over 3,700 tons and were capable of a top speed of roughly fifteen knots. The main armament of the vessels consisted of three 24cm guns with a range of roughly 13,000 metres. They also had six to eight 8.8cm and six machine guns as an additional armament.

28 Kapitän zur See Friedrich Boedicker, 'Bemerkungen von der Dienstreise von A nach Flandern', January 1915, RM3:5639. At the time he was serving in the Allgemeine Marine-Department of the RMA.

29 Behncke to von Schröder, 6 February 1915, RM120:587.

30 For an excellent examination of the military and political discussions surrounding the decision for unrestricted submarine warfare see Gerhard Ritter, *The Sword and the Scepter: The Problem of Militarism in Germany*. IV vols (Coral Gables: University

of Miami Press, 1969–73), vol III: pp119–50. For the naval background and the feelings in the fleet that led toward the campaign see Halpern, *Naval History*, 287–292.

31 Von Ingenohl to von Pohl, 22 January 1915, RM120:587.

32 Von Pohl to von Ingenohl, 4 February 1915, RM120:1.

33 Von Schröder to Tirpitz, 6 February 1915, RM120:95. The original is not in the files of the MarineKorps and therefore it cannot be determined if this was to include UB and UC boats or not.

34 Kriegstagebüch von Schröder, 11 February 1915, RM120:515.

35 Führer der Untersee-boote Hermann Bauer, 'Allgemeine Anordnungen für die Blockade der englisch-irischen Gewässern', 8 February 1915, RM120:587.

36 Von Pohl to von Schröder, 7 February 1915, RM120:587.

37 See Chapter Two.

38 von Pohl to Kaiser Wilhelm II, 14th February 1915, RM120:1.

39 Ibid.

40 Bachmann to von Pohl, 18th February 1915, RM120:1.

41 Von Schröder to Tirpitz, 22nd February 1915, RM120:1.

42 See Chapter Two.

43 Von Schröder to Tirpitz, 22nd February 1915, RM120:1.

44 Notes of Kapitän zur See Albert Hopman on his trip to Flanders, 18 February to 23 February 1915, RM3:5639. At the time Hopman was serving as the chief of the Zentralabteilung of the RMA.

45 Bachmann to von Pohl, 24 February 1915, RM120:1.

46 Groos, *Krieg der Nordsee*, vol IV: pp22–23. I was unable to find a reply from von Pohl or any official documentation stating the reason for the Kaiser's apparent change of mind.

47 Von Schröder to Kaiser Wilhelm II, 12 April 1915, RM120:1.

48 Bachmann to von Schröder, 18 April 1915, RM120:1.

49 Also, it should be pointed out that von Schröder's main supporter, Tirpitz, had by this time fallen out of favour with the court.

50 See Tables two and three for details on the ships.

51 Tirpitz to von Pohl, von Schröder, Bachmann, von Müller, and Bauer, 25 February 1915, RM120:98.

52 Rössler, *U-Boat*, 39–44.

53 Boedicker to Tirpitz, forwarded to von Schröder, 'Report on the construction of the Flanders naval station', 4 November 1914, RM3:5638.

54 Ibid. For the characteristics of the boats see also John Terraine, *Business in Great Waters: The U-Boat Wars 1916–1945*, (London: Leo Cooper, 1989), p20; Admiral Reinhard Scheer, *Germany's High Seas Fleet in the World War*, (London: Cassell, 1919), pp259–60; Holger H. Herwig, *'Luxury Fleet': The Imperial German Navy 1888–1918*, (London: Allen & Unwin, 1980; reprint, London: Ashfield Press, 1987), pp218–19; Rear Admiral Arno Spindler, *Der Handelskrieg mit U-Booten*, V vols (Berlin: E.S. Mittler, 1932–66), vol II: p64; Rössler, *U-boat*, 39–44; and Erich Gröner, *German Warships 1815–1945*, II vols. (Annapolis: Naval Institute Press, 1992), vol II: pp22–34.

55 Herwig, *Luxury Fleet*, pp218–19; Scheer, *High Seas Fleet*, p288; Rössler, *U-boat*, pp39–44; Gröner, *Warships*, vol II:22–34.

56 Herwig, *Luxury Fleet*, pp218–19; Gröner, *Warships*, vol II:p35; Rössler, *U-boat*, pp,76–80.

57 Scheer, *High Seas Fleet*, p260; Rössler, *U-boat*, pp76–80; Gröner, *Warships*, vol II:34–35.

58 Herwig, *Luxury Fleet*, pp218–19; Terraine, *Business*, p20; Gröner, *Warships*, vol II:25–6; Rössler, *U-boat*, 54–9.

59 Herwig, *Luxury Fleet*, p 169; Spindler, *Handelskrieg*, vol II:p64; Rössler, *U-boat*, pp39–44.

60 Inspektion des Untersee-bootswesens to Tirpitz, 8 December 1914, RM120:1. For a very detailed discussion of the planning that went into the creation of the various *UB* and *UC*-classes see Rössler, *U-boat*, pp39–59.

61 Inspektion des Untersee-bootswesens, Transport protocol for UB and UC boats, n.d., RM120:95.

62 Kaiserliche Werft Antwerp to von Schröder, 13 February 1915, RM120:588; Rössler, *U-boat*, pp39–44.

63 RMA to Marinekorps, 4 March 1915, RM120:588.

64 Groos, *Krieg der Nordsee*, vol IV: p121.

65 Inspektion des Untersee-bootswesens to von Schröder, 16th March 1915, RM120:96.

66 Kriegstagebüch von Schröder, RM120:515; Schulze, 'MarineKorps', p417; Groos, *Krieg der Nordsee*, vol IV: p121. See also Halpern, *Naval History*, p297.

67 Spindler, *Handelskrieg*, vol II: p64.

68 Schulze, 'MarineKorps', p419.

69 Scheer, *High Seas Fleet*, 260–61; Spindler, *Handelskrieg*, vol IV: pp2–3. Scheer actually credits the Flanders flotillas with thirty-eight submarines in May 1917.

70 Scheer, *High Seas Fleet*, pp233, 340. According to Spindler the numbers are somewhat higher with the Flanders flotillas accounting for just over one-third of all the shipping lost in the war. See chapters six and seven below for an elaboration of the role played by the Flanders flotillas during the unrestricted campaign of 1917 and 1918.

71 Groos, *Krieg der Nordsee*, vol IV: p123.

72 Boedicker to Tirpitz and von Schröder, 'Report on construction of the Flanders naval station', 5 November 1914, RM3:5638. For specs on the ships see Gröner, *Warships*, p161.

73 Boedicker to von Schröder, 22 May 1915, RM120:47.

74 Spindler, *Handelskrieg*, vol II: p64.

75 Corbett, *Naval Operations*, vol II: p401.

76 Groos, *Krieg der Nordsee*, vol IV: pp123, 127–28.

77 Spindler, *Handelskrieg*, vol II:136–137.

78 This is not the place for a discussion of the details of this debate. For a full in-depth discussion of these issues see Gerhard Ritter, *The Sword and the Scepter: The Problem of Militarism in Germany*, IV vols (Coral Gables: University of Miami Press, 1969–73), vol III: pp119-50. For an excellent discussion of the German navy and its views on submarine warfare see Halpern, *Naval History*, pp295–303, as well as Spindler, *Handelskrieg*, vol II:pp86–103, 159–75, 176–94.

79 Kriegstagebüch von Schröder, 1 June 1915, RM120:515.

80 Spindler, *Handelskrieg*, vol II:136–37.

81 Ibid, pp143–46.

82 Ibid.

83 Ibid.

84 Ibid.

85 Ibid, 154–156.

86 Kriegstagebüch von Schröder, 28 June 1915, RM120:515.

87 Spindler, *Handelskrieg*, vol II: p143.

88 Von Schröder to RMA, 8 May 1915, RM120:588.

89 Kriegstagebüch von Schröder, 26 May 1915, RM120:515.

90 Bachmann to von Pohl, 22 May 1915, RM120:588.

91 Herwig, *Luxury Fleet*, p219.

92 Von Schröder to Bachmann, 4 August 1915, RM120:588. Also in Kriegstagebüch von Schröder, RM120:515.

93 Spindler, *Handelskrieg*, vol II: pp217–18.

94 Ibid, p236.

95 Ibid., p219.

96 Von Schröder to von Holtzendorff, 5 October 1915, RM120:588.

97 Kriegstagebüch von Schröder, 6 November 1915, RM120:515.

98 Spindler, *Handelskrieg*, vol IV: p81.

99 Spindler, *Handelskrieg*, vol III: pp48–49.

100 Kriegstagebüch von Schröder, 2 May 1915, RM120:515; Corbett, *Naval Operations*, vol II: p401.

101 Groos, *Krieg der Nordsee*, vol IV: p125; Corbett, *Naval Operations*, vol II: p401; Kriegstagebüch von Schröder, 2 May 1915, RM120:515.

102 Kriegstagebüch von Schröder, 7 May 1915, RM120:515.

103 Kriegstagebüch von Schröder, 10 May 1915, RM120:515.

104 Corbett, *Naval Operations*, vol III: p148.

105 Groos, *Krieg der Nordsee*, vol IV: p306.

106 Groos, *Krieg der Nordsee*, vol IV: p306; Corbett, *Naval Operations*, vol III:pp149–51.

107 Kapitänleutnant Kurt Assmann 'Report on the battle between *A15* and two enemy destroyers', 25 August 1915, RM120:47; Kriegstagebüch von Schröder, 27 August 1915, RM120:515; Corbett, *Naval Operations*, vol III: p149; Johan Ryheul, *MarineKorps Flandern 1914–18*, (Hamburg: E.S. Mittler, 1997), p84. Ryheul attributes the damage to the French destroyer to fire from the coastal batteries. Given the poor armament of the German torpedo-boats his explanation seems much more likely than that contained in Assmann's report.

108 Groos. *Krieg der Nordsee*, vol IV: p306; Corbett, *Naval Operations*, vol III: pp149–51; Kriegstagebüch von Schröder, 24 August 1915, RM120:515.

109 Corbett, *Naval Operations*, vol III:149–51.

110 Kriegstagebüch von Schröder, 19 September 1915, RM120:515; Corbett, *Naval Operations*, vol III: pp151–52.

111 Kriegstagebüch von Schröder, 25 September 1915, RM120:515; Corbett, *Naval Operations*, vol III: p151; Groos, *Krieg der Nordsee*, vol IV: pp312–15, 319.

112 Groos, *Krieg der Nordsee*, vol IV: pp312–15; Ryheul, *MarineKorps*, pp127–28.

113 Kriegstagebüch von Schröder, 30 December 1915, RM120:515.

114 Boedicker to North Sea station and MarineKorps, 14 June 1915, RM120:146.

115 Groos, *Krieg der Nordsee*, vol IV: p119.

116 Chief of Staff of IV Army to von Schröder, 13 September 1915, RM120:147.

117 Von Schröder to Luftfahrwesens, 19 September 1915, RM120:147.

118 Von Holtzendorff to Tirpitz and von Schröder, 28 October 1915, RM120:147; von Holtzendorff to Tirpitz and von Schröder, 29 October 1915, RM120:147.

119 Boedicker to von Schröder, 7 October 1915, RM120:147.

120 Tirpitz to von Schröder, 6 May 1915, RM120:47.

121 Boedicker to North Sea Station and MarineKorps, 22 May 1915, RM120:47.

122 Groos, *Krieg der Nordsee*, vol IV: pp125–26.

123 Von Schröder to Tirpitz, 10 June 1915, RM120:142.

124 Ibid.

125 Von Schröder to Torpedo-Boat Flotilla, 28 July 1915, RM120:47.

126 Bachmann to von Schröder, 9 August 1915, RM120:47. For details on the new ships see Appendix four.

127 Ibid.

128 Von Schröder to Bachmann, 27 August 1915, RM120:47. See Appendix four for the details on the German destroyers.

129 Rear-Admiral Ernst Ritter von Mann to Tirpitz, von Pohl, von Schröder, and Prince Heinrich von Preussen, 1 November 1915, RM120:47.

130 Torpedowesens to RMA, 4 November 1915, RM120:47.

131 Tirpitz to von Pohl and Prince Heinrich von Preussen, 9 November 1915, RM120:47.

132 Von Mann to von Schröder, 12 November 1915, RM120:47.

133 Though they formed the Destroyer Half-Flotilla these craft were not technically destroyers. That category only applied to the ships of the *B-97*, *S-113*, and *V-170*-class. The *S-113*-class displaced over 2,400 tons and carried four 15cm deck guns but the *V-170*-class only displaced 1,500 tons and had a main armament of four 10.5cm guns. The *B-97*-class were 1,800 ton ships with four 8.8cm deck guns, later changed to 10.5cm. All had a top speed in the range of thirty-four to thirty-six knots. The distinction therefore is somewhat artificial. The primary difference was that the destroyers were generally built from 1916 on though here the *B-97*-class is an exception since they were built in 1914–15. For full details see Gröner, *Warships*, 169–87.

134 Von Mann to von Schröder, 11 November 1915, RM120:47.

135 Von Schröder to Tirpitz, 25 November 1915, RM120:47.

136 Von Schröder to the RMA, 21 December 1915, RM120:47.

137 Groos, *Krieg der Nordsee*, vol V: pp56–57; Kriegstagebüch von Schröder, 3 March 1916, RM120:515.

138 Groos, *Krieg der Nordsee*, vol IV: p329.

Chapter 4

1 Holger H. Herwig, *'Luxury Fleet': The Imperial German Navy, 1888-1918*, (London: Allen & Unwin, 1980), p290; Rear Admiral Arno Spindler, *Der Handelskrieg mit U-Booten*, V vols, (Berlin: E.S. Mittler, 1932–66), III: 284-5; Erich Gröner, *Die*

Deutschen Kriegschiffe, 1815–1945, II vols, (Munich: J.F. Lehmanns, 1966–68), vol II: pp22–24; Eberhard Rössler, *The U-boat: The Evolution and Technical History of German Submarines,* Eng. trans. (London and Melbourne: Arms and Armour Press, 1981), pp50–53. The deck gun was later replaced with a larger 8.8cm model.

2 Spindler, *Handelskrieg,* vol III: pp284–85; Rössler, *U-boat,* 50–53.

3 Spindler, *Handelskrieg,* p122.

4 Paul G. Halpern, *A Naval History of World War I,* (Annapolis, MD: Naval Institute Press, 1994), p306.

5 Spindler, *Handelskrieg,* vol III:p123.

6 Ibid., 121–22.

7 Halpern, *Naval History,* p311. Tyrwhitt was not onboard at the time.

8 Halpern, *Naval History,* p307; Spindler, *Handelskrieg,* vol III: p125; Sir Julian Corbett and Henry Newbolt, *History of the Great War: Naval Operations,* V volumes, (London: Longmans, 1920–31), vol III: p285.

9 Halpern, *Naval History,* p307.

10 Admiral Reinhard Scheer, *Germany's High Seas Fleet in the World War,* (London: Cassell, 1919), p117.

11 Scheer, *High Seas Fleet,* p127; Scheer to von Schröder, 10 April 1916, RM120:34.

12 Otto Groos and Walther Gladisch, *Der Krieg in der Nordsee,* VII volumes, (Berlin: E.S. Mittler, 1920–65), vol VI: pp130–32.

13 Kriegstagebüch von Schröder, 25 April 1916, RM120:515.

14 Scheer to von Schröder, 12 May 1916, RM120:34.

15 Kriegstagebüch von Schröder, 30 May 1916, RM120:516.

16 Kriegstagebüch von Schröder, 16 March 1916, RM120:515.

17 The type of the aircraft was not specified.

18 One of these was certainly the *Lance.* The other was unnamed but was one of the *Lance*'s sisters; Lookout, Lucifer, and Linnet. All were in the area to escort the seaplane carriers *Riviera* and *Vindex* which were launching a raid against Zeebrugge that same day. Corbett, *Naval Operations,* vol III: p290.

19 'Report of seaplane 547 on the battle between the Destroyer Half-Flotilla and four enemy destroyers', 21 March 1916, RM120:47. The author's signature was too badly faded to be legible. Presumably it was written by the pilot of seaplane 547. See also von Schröder to von Holtzendorff, 'Report on the battle of March 20 1916', 21 March 1916, RM120:47; Kriegstagebüch von Schröder, 20 March 1916, RM120:515;

Corbett, *Naval Operations,* vol III: p290.

20 Kriegstagebüch von Schröder, 20 March 1916, RM120:515.

21 Kriegstagebüch von Schröder, 28 March 1916, RM120:515.

22 Assmann to von Schröder, 22 April 1916, RM120:45; Kriegstagebüch von Schröder, RM120:515.

23 Assmann to von Schröder, 22 April 1916, RM120:45.

24 Ibid.

25 Von Schröder, 'Assessment of the Position at Sea,' sent to the IV army Command, 24 April 1916, RM120:34.

26 Admiral Sir Reginald Bacon, *The Concise Story of the Dover Patrol,* (London: Hutchinson, 1932), pp41,53.

27 Gladisch, *Krieg der Nordsee,* vol VI: p199. According to Corbett Tyrwhitt had available five light cruisers, and between fifty-two and fifty-four destroyers. Corbett, *Naval Operations,* vol II: pp419–20.

28 Ibid., p198.

29 Corbett and Newbolt, *Naval Operations,* vol III: p299.

30 Bacon, *Dover Patrol,* pp141–42.

31 Bacon, *Dover Patrol,* pp141–42; Corbett and Newbolt, *Naval Operations* vol III: p299; Edgar Erich Schulze, 'Das MarineKorps in Flandern 1914–18', *Marine-Rundschau,* vol XXVII, (8–10, 1922): p415; Halpern, *Naval History,* p291; Gladisch, *Krieg der Nordsee,* vol VI: pp202–3.

32 Gladisch, *Krieg der Nordsee,* vol VI: p133; Corbett, *Naval Operations,* pp299–300.

33 Gladisch, *Krieg der Nordsee,* vol VI: pp133, 202–3.

34 Kriegstagebüch von Schröder, 7 May 1916, RM120:516.

35 The request was mentioned by von Holtzendorff in a letter to Scheer. Von Holtzendorff to Scheer, 8 May 1916, RM120:34. The original request from von Schröder is not in the files of the MarineKorps.

36 Ibid.

37 Gladisch, *Krieg der Nordsee,* vol VI: pp202–3.

38 Von Schröder, 'Report on the position at sea', sent to the IV army, 14 May 1916, RM120:34; Kriegstagebüch von Schröder, 12 May 1916, RM120:515.

39 Assmann to von Schröder, 'Activity Report for April 1916', 30 April 1916, RM120:45; Archibald Hurd, *The Merchant Navy,* III vols, (London: John Murray, 1921–29), vol II: p257.

40 Kriegstagebüch von Schröder, 5 May 1916, RM120:516; Newbolt, *Naval Operations,* vol IV: pp1–23.

41 Assmann to von Schröder, 'Activity Report for May 1916', 31 May 1916, RM120:45; Newbolt, *Naval Operations*, vol IV: pp1–23.

42 Assmann to von Schröder, 26 May 1916, RM120:34.

43 Kriegstagebüch von Schröder, 29 May 1916, RM120:516.

44 Kriegstagebüch von Schröder, 7 June 1916, RM120:516.

45 Schulze, 'MarineKorps', p461. Schulze does not specify the make of the planes simply calling them Landkampfeinsitzers. However, according to Ryheul, the only land-based planes the MarineKorps had until 1917 were Albatross D-IIIs. Therefore, it would seem that these planes were of the latter type. Johan Ryheul, *MarineKorps Flandern 1914-1918*, (Hamburg: E.S. Mittler, 1997), pp263–66.

46 Gladisch, *Krieg der Nordsee*, vol VI: pp213–14; Kriegstagebüch von Schröder, multiple entries commending the importance of the air arm, RM120:515 and RM120:516.

47 Kriegstagebüch von Schröder, several entries commending the air station for its assistance in minesweeping, RM120:515.

48 Rear-Admiral Otto Philipp, Befehlshaber der Marine-Luftfahr Abteilungen to the North Sea and Baltic naval stations, 14 March 1916, RM120:148.

49 Kriegstagebüch von Schröder, 19 March 1916, RM120:515. No mention of these raids were made in the British Official History. Jones, H.A. and Sir Walter Raleigh, *The War in the Air*, VI vols (Oxford: Clarendon Press, 1928–37).

50 Philipp to von Schröder, 16 May 1916, RM120:148; Von Schröder to Philipp, 24 May 1916, RM120:148.

51 Von Schröder to Philipp, 25 May 1916, RM120:148.

52 Gladisch, *Krieg der Nordsee*, vol VI: pp213–14.

53 Von Schröder to all subordinate commands, orders for air operations for late May, 19 May 1916, RM120:148.

54 Gladisch, *Krieg der Nordsee*, vol VI: p194.

55 Von Falkenhayn to von Holtzendorff, 15 April 1916, RM120:34.

56 Ibid.

57 Von Holtzendorff to von Falkenhayn, forwarded to von Schröder, Scheer, von Capelle and Prince Heinrich von Preussen, 20 April 1916, RM120:34.

58 Ibid.

59 Von Falkenhayn to von Holtzendorff, 24 April 1916, RM120:34.

60 Von Holtzendorff to the Baltic station, forwarded to the MarineKorps and the North Sea station, 9 May 1916, RM120:34.

61 Scheer to von Holtzendorff, forwarded to von Schröder, 21 June 1916, RM120:34.

62 Gladisch, *Krieg der Nordsee*, vol VI: p195-96.

63 Kriegstagebüch von Schröder, 16 July 1916, RM120:516.

64 Spindler, *Handelskrieg*, vol IV:p183.

65 Ibid.; Rössler, *U-boat*, 50–53; Gröner, *Warships*, vol II: pp31–34.

66 For the sake of simplicity, the phrase UB from this point forward refers to *both* UB-Is and UB-IIs unless otherwise specified.

67 Halpern, *Naval History*, p332; Spindler, *Handelskrieg*, vol IV: p22.

68 Spindler, *Handelskrieg*, vol IV: p222.

69 Ibid., p22.

70 Ibid., p222.

71 Spindler, *Handelskrieg*, vol IV: pp222–23; Kriegstagebüch von Schröder, 12 August 1916, RM120:516.

72 Ibid., 218–21. The escorts were assigned as part of a commercial treaty signed by the Netherlands and Great Britain.

73 Spindler, *Handelskrieg*, vol IV: pp218–21; Gladisch, *Krieg der Nordsee*, vol VI: p209.

74 Gladisch, *Krieg der Nordsee*, vol VI: p195–96; Kriegstagebüch von Schröder, 13 August 1916, RM120:516.

75 Kriegstagebüch von Schröder, 14 September 1916, RM120:516.

76 Ibid., p225–29.

77 Ibid.

78 Ibid., p229–30.

79 Ibid., p244.

80 Bartenbach to von Schröder, 17 October 1916, RM120:52.

81 Von Schröder to all subordinate commands, 'Regulations for the transfer of the II Torpedo-Boat Flotilla', 31 May 1916, RM120:34.

82 Ibid.; Gladisch, *Krieg der Nordsee*, vol VI: p203.

83 Gladisch, *Krieg der Nordsee*, vol VI: pp205–6. The British forces consisted of the monitor *Lord Clive* and several 'Tribal'-class destroyers. Newbolt, *Naval Operations*, vol IV: pp22–23.

84 Gladisch, *Krieg der Nordsee*, vol VI: pp205–6; von Schröder to von Holtzendorff and Scheer, 8 June 1916, RM120:50; Kriegstagebüch von Schröder, 8 June 1916, RM120:516.

85 Gladisch, *Krieg der Nordsee*, vol VI: pp205–6; Kriegstagebüch von Schröder, 8 June 1916, RM120:516; Newbolt, *Naval Operations*, vol IV:pp22–23.

86 Ibid.

87 Gladisch, *Krieg der Nordsee*, vol VI: pp205–6; Kriegstagebüch von Schröder, 8 June 1916, RM120:516.

88 Corbett and Newbolt, *Naval Operations*, vol

IV: p22. Doubtless had things worked out otherwise and the Destroyer Half-Flotilla been destroyed, this probably would have ended any hope of getting naval reinforcements in the future.

89 Gladisch, *Krieg der Nordsee*, vol VI: pp210–11.

90 Ibid., pp194–95.

91 Ibid., pp196–97; Assmann to von Schröder, 'Torpedo-Boat Flotilla Activity Report for 1 June 1916 to 8 July 1916', 9 July 1916, RM120:145; Kriegstagebüch von Schröder, 28 June 1916, RM120:516.

92 Gladisch, *Krieg der Nordsee*, vol VI: pp207–8; Kriegstagebüch von Schröder, 28 June 1916, RM120:516; Assmann to von Schröder, 'Torpedo-Boat Flotilla Activity Report for 1 June 1916 to 8 July 1916', 9 July 1916, RM120:45.

93 Kriegstagebüch von Schröder, 23 June 1916, RM120:516.

94 III Torpedo-Boat Half-Flotilla, signature illegible, 'Report Concerning the Journey of the III Torpedo-Boat Half-Flotilla and the Mine Explosion of Torpedo-Boat *G-102*', 13 July 1916, RM120:52.

95 Kriegstagebüch von Schröder, 12 July 1916, RM120:516l; III Torpedo-Boat Half-Flotilla, 'Report Concerning the Journey of the III Torpedo-Boat Half-Flotilla and the Mine Explosion of Torpedo-Boat *G-102*', 13 July 1916, RM120:52.

96 Corbett and Newbolt, *Naval Operations*, vol IV: pp27–29; Gladisch, *Krieg der Nordsee*, vol VI: pp208–9; A. Temple Patterson, *Tyrwhitt of the Harwich Force: The Life of Admiral of the Fleet Sir Reginald Tyrwhitt*, (London: MacDonald, 1973), pp266–7.

97 Corbett and Newbolt, *Naval Operations*, vol IV: pp27–29; Gladisch, *Krieg der Nordsee*, vol VI: pp208–9; Kriegstagebüch von Schröder, 23 July 1916, RM120:516; Patterson, *Tyrwhitt*, pp266–67.

98 Schulze, 'MarineKorps', p414.

99 Kapitän zur See Titus Türk, Kommando des Minen und Sperrwesens des MarineKorps Flandern, 'Report on the Activity and Experiences of the Minesweepers of the MarineKorps from 1 April 1916 to 1 August 1916', 21 August 1916, RM120:45.

100 Assmann to von Schröder, 'Torpedo-Boat Flotilla Activity Report for 9 July to 8 August 1916', 9 August 1916, RM120:45; Assmann to von Schröder, 'Torpedo-Boat Flotilla Activity Report for 9 August to 8 September 1916', 10 September 1916, RM120:45.

101 Kriegstagebüch von Schröder, numerous entries, RM120:516.

102 Von Schröder to von Capelle, 14 September

103 Kriegstagebüch von Schröder, several entries, RM120:516.

104 Gladisch, *Krieg der Nordsee*, vol VI: p212.

105 Kriegstagebüch von Schröder, 9 July 1916, RM120:516.

106 Kriegstagebüch von Schröder, 22 July 1916, RM120:516.

107 Bacon, *Dover Patrol*, p105.

108 Kriegstagebüch von Schröder, 8 September 1916, RM120:516.

109 Naval Attaché Netherlands to von Schröder, von Holtzendorff and von Capelle, 5 October 1916, RM3:5639.

110 See Chapter Five.

111 Gladisch, *Krieg der Nordsee*, vol VI: p192.

112 Von Schröder to von Holtzendorff, 'Report on the Needs of the MarineKorps for Torpedo-Boats in the Fall of 1916', 12 June 1916, RM120:34.

113 Ibid.

114 Von Schröder to von Holtzendorff, 'Report on the Needs of the MarineKorps for Torpedo-Boats in Fall 1916', 12 June 1916, RM120:34; Gröner, *Warships* vol I:pp169–71. See Chapter Two for exact details on the A-boats.

115 Minutes of a meeting of the Harbour Department of the Naval Staff on June 16th 1916 concerning the building of torpedo-boats, 16 June 1916, RM120:34.

116 Gröner, *Warships*, vol I:pp163–65.

117 Minutes of a meeting in the Harbor Department of the Naval Staff on June 16th 1916 concerning the construction of torpedo-boats, 16 June 1916, RM120:34.

118 Ibid.

119 Von Mann to von Schröder, 20 June 1916, RM120:45.

120 Von Holtzendorff to von Schröder and Prince Heinrich von Preussen, 20 June 1916, RM120:45.

121 Von Holtzendorff to von Schröder and Prince Heinrich, 20 June 1916, RM120:45; von Capelle to von Schröder, 8 August 1916, RM120:45.

122 Von Mann to von Schröder, 12 July 1916, RM120:45.

123 Von Schröder to von Capelle, 10 August 1916, RM120:45.

124 Von Mann to von Schröder, 26 August 1916, RM120:45.

125 Von Schröder to von Capelle and von Holtzendorff, 12 June 1916, RM120:34.

126 Von Holtzendorff to von Schröder, 21 June 1916, RM120:34.

127 Von Schröder to von Holtzendorff, 7 July

1916, RM120:34.
128 Scheer to von Schröder, 15 July 1916, RM120:52.
129 Kriegstagebüch von Schröder, 31 July 1916, RM120:516.
130 Von Schröder to Scheer, 31 July 1916, RM120:34.
131 Kapitän zur See William Michaelis (head of Abteilung MobilMachung of the RMA) to von Schröder, 3 August 1916, RM120:52.
132 Naval Staff, unsigned, to von Schröder, 5 August 1916, RM120:45.
133 Von Holtzendorff to von Schröder, 6 September 1916, RM120:50. In the letter von Holtzendorff informed von Schröder of his request to von Capelle. The original was not in the files of the MarineKorps.
134 Spindler, *Handelskrieg*, vol IV:pp184–87.
135 Ibid., pp300–23.
136 Ibid.
137 Ibid., pp184–7, 300–23.
138 Spindler, *Handelskrieg*, vol III: pp288–99.
139 Spindler, *Handelskrieg*, vol III: pp283–84; Arthur J. Marder, *From the Dreadnought to Scapa Flow: The Royal Navy in the Fisher Era, 1904–1919*, V vols, (London: Oxford University Press, 1961–70), vol IV: pp137–52; Patterson, *Tyrwhitt*, pp166–67.
140 A.C. Bell, *A History of the Blockade of Germany and of the Countries Associated with Her in the Great War, Austria-Hungary, Bulgaria, and Turkey*, (London: HMSO, 1937), pp475–78.
141 Spindler, *Handelskrieg*, vol III: pp283–4.
142 Scheer, *High Seas Fleet*, p187.
143 Scheer, *High Seas Fleet*, p187; Corbett and Newbolt, *Naval Operations*, vol IV: p52; Halpern, *Naval History*, pp333, 346, 349; Gladisch, *Krieg der Nordsee*, vol VI:pp147–48.
144 Corbett and Newbolt, *Naval Operations*, vol IV: p53; Kriegstagebüch von Schröder, 23 October 1916, RM120:516; Gladisch, *Krieg der Nordsee*, vol VI: pp147–48.
145 Gladisch, Krieg der Nordsee, VI:218-9.
146 Kriegstagebüch von Schröder, 26 October 1916, RM120:516.
147 The Downs is the area along the southeastern British coast between Ramsgate and Dover. It forms a natural cove, with narrow entrances to north and south and the British used it as a mooring place for merchant shipping.
148 Kriegstagebüch von Schröder, 26 October 1916, RM120:516.
149 Gladisch, *Krieg der Nordsee*, vol VI: pp219; Corbett and Newbolt, *Naval Operations*, vol IV: pp52-65. Unless otherwise noted the following narrative of the battle of 26 October comes from these two sources.

150 Corbett and Newbolt, *Naval Operations*, vol IV:pp52–53.
151 Ibid.
152 Gladisch, *Krieg der Nordsee*, vol VI: p223. Unless noted all times are GMT.
153 Corbett and Newbolt, *Naval Operations*, vol IV: pp60–61.
154 Michelsen to von Schröder, 'Zusammenstellung der Angaben aus den Kriegstagebüchern über Verluste des Feindes bei dem Vorstoss unserer Torpedoboote in den Kanal am 26/27 Oktober 1916', n.d., RM120:52.
155 Ibid.
156 Scheer, *High Seas Fleet*, p188; Kriegstagebüch von Schröder, 27 October 1916, RM120:516; Von Schröder to Scheer and von Holtzendorff, 27 October 1916, RM120:52.
157 Bacon, *Dover Patrol*, pp122–3.
158 Halpern, *Naval History*, p346; Schulze, 'MarineKorps', p415.
159 Von Schröder to Scheer and von Holtzendorff, 27 October 1916, RM120:52; Kriegstagebüch von Schröder, 27 October 1916, RM120:516.
160 Corbett and Newbolt, *Naval Operations*, vol IV: p67; Gladisch, *Krieg der Nordsee*, vol VI: pp147–48.
161 For the best discussion of this decision see Marder, *Dreadnought*, vol III:pp308–20.
162 See Chapter Two.
163 Halpern, *Naval History*, p347; Scheer, *High Seas Fleet*, p188.
164 Scheer, *High Seas Fleet*, p188.
165 Kriegstagebüch von Schröder, 29 October 1916, RM120:516.
166 Gladisch, *Krieg der Nordsee*, vol VI: p233.
167 Gladisch, *Krieg der Nordsee*, vol VI: p233; Kriegstagebüch von Schröder, 2 November 1916, RM120:516.
168 The British did have the ability to read the German codes but there is no evidence that they had done so on this particular occasion. For an in-depth look at British code-breaking during the war see Patrick Beesly, *Room 40: British Naval Intelligence, 1914–1918*, (London: Hamish Hamilton, 1982).
169 Kriegstagebüch von Schröder, 2 November 1916, RM120:516; Gladisch, *Krieg der Nordsee*, vol VI: p233.
170 Gladisch, *Krieg der Nordsee*, vol VI: p233; Von Schröder to Scheer and von Holtzendorff, 2 November 1916, RM120:52.
171 Kriegstagebüch von Schröder, 3 November 1916, RM120:516; Assmann von Schröder, 'Activity Report of the Flanders Torpedo-Boat Flotilla from 9 October to 8 November 1916', 10 November 1916, RM120:45.

172 Gladisch, *Krieg der Nordsee*, vol VI: pp154, 233.
173 Kriegstagebüch von Schröder, 7 November 1916, RM120:516; 'Torpedo-Boat Flotilla to MarineKorps, Bruges wireless station, *G-91*, Destroyer Half-Flotilla, XVII Half-Flotilla and XVIII Half-Flotilla', unsigned, 9 November 1916, RM120:52.
174 Halpern, *Naval History*, p347; Gladisch, *Krieg der Nordsee*, vol VI: pp235–37; Corbett and Newbolt, *Naval Operations*, vol IV: pp64–70.
175 Gladisch, *Krieg der Nordsee*, vol VI: pp235–37; Kriegstagebüch von Schröder, 22 November 1916, RM120:516.
176 Bacon, *Dover Patrol*, pp180–90.
177 The best source of information on this topic is Beesly, *Room 40* and he does not mention any intercepts dealing with this German raid.
178 Gladisch, *Krieg der Nordsee*, vol VI: pp235–37.
179 Ibid., p237; Kriegstagebüch von Schröder, 27 November 1916, RM120:516.
180 Kriegstagebüch von Schröder, 27 November 1916, RM120:516.
181 Gladisch, *Krieg der Nordsee*, vol VI: p237.
182 Kriegstagebüch von Schröder, several entries, RM120:516.
183 Gladisch, *Krieg der Nordsee*, vol VI: p238. See Chapter Six for a discussion of the decision to send new forces to Flanders in 1917.
184 Assmann to von Schröder, 'Activity Report of the Torpedo-Boat Flotilla from 9 November to 8 December 1916', 10 December 1916, RM120:45.
185 Assmann to von Schröder, 'Activity Report of the Torpedo-Boat Flotilla from 9 December 1916 to 8 January 1917', 10 January 1917, RM120:45.
186 Corbett and Newbolt, *Naval Operations*, vol IV: pp66–67; Marder, *Dreadnought*, vol III: pp309–11.
187 Von Schröder to Jacobsen, 31 October 1916, RM120:45.
188 Von Schröder to von Holtzendorff, 15 November 1916, RM120:45.
189 Ibid.
190 Ibid.
191 Von Holtzendorff to Scheer, von Capelle, von Schröder, von Mann and Prince Heinrich, 27 November 1916, RM120:45.
192 Von Mann to Marinewerft Antwerpen, Bauwerft Ostende, Kaierlichewerft Danzig, Kaiserlichewerft Wilhelmshaven, and Kaiserlichewerft Kiel, forwarded to von Schröder, 7 December 1916, RM120:45.
193 Kommando der Luftstreitkräfte MarineKorps to MarineKorps, unsigned, 1 November 1916, RM120:149.
194 Ibid.
195 Ibid.
196 Minutes of a meeting between representatives of the MarineKorps, the RMA and the Naval Staff held in Berlin on November 11, 1916, RM120:149. Presumably their reference to the Netherlands is meant to refer to 'Fall K', the German plan to intervene in the Netherlands. For full information on the latter see Chapter Five. The type of plane was not specified in the document. Most likely they were Albatross D-VAs. According to Ryheul the only Albatross' assigned to Flanders were the older D-IIIs and the D-VAs. Ryheul, *MarineKorps*, p263.
197 'Report over the Necessary Increase in the Aircraft of the MarineKorps', unsigned report stamped by the MarineKorps, 25 November 1916, RM120:149.
198 IV army to Kommandierenden General der Luftstreitkräfte, forwarded to von Schröder, unsigned, 15 December 1916, RM120:149. The change was caused by the extreme losses the army had incurred at the Somme and Verdun.
199 Von Holtzendorff to Kommandierenden General der Luftstreitkräfte, forwarded to von Schröder, 6 December 1916, RM120:149. These were strictly land-based planes.
200 Vice-Admiral Reinhard Koch, Deputy Chief of the Naval Staff to Befehlshaber der Marine Flieger Abteilungen, forwarded to von Schröder, 24 December 1916, RM120:149.
201 See Chapter Six.
202 'Experiences of fighting aircraft with defensive guns, spotlights, and cooperation between fighters and batteries', unsigned document stamped by the MarineKorps air command, 25 October 1916, RM120:149.
203 Ibid.
204 Kriegstagebüch von Schröder, several entries from November 1916, RM120:516; Kommandierenden General der Luftstreitkräfte to von Schröder, 9 December 1916, RM120:149; Jacobsen to von Schröder, 6 December 1916, RM120:149; Jacobsen to von Schröder, 12 December 1916, RM120:149.
205 Jacobsen to von Schröder, 12 December 1916, RM120:149.
206 Kriegstagebüch von Schröder, 17 November 1916, RM120:149.
207 Schulze, 'MarineKorps', p386.
208 Jacobsen to von Schröder, 14 November 1916, RM120:35.
209 Ibid.

210 Jacobsen, 'Overview of the measures taken to defend against a landing', 16 November 1916, RM120:35.
211 Von Schröder to all subordinate commands, 21 December 1916, RM120:35. All of the information in the following paragraphs, unless otherwise noted, comes from these orders.
212 Von Schröder to all subordinate commands, 21 December 1916, RM120:35.
213 Scheer to von Schröder, 26 December 1916, RM120:35.
214 Von Schröder to von Holtzendorff and von Capelle, 28 December 1916, RM120:35.
215 See Chapter Five for a full discussion of 'Fall K.'
216 Von Schröder to von Holtzendorff and von Capelle, 28 December 1916, RM120:35.
217 Von Holtzendorff to von Capelle, 21 June 1916, RM3:5639.
218 Von Schröder to von Capelle, 23 August 1916, RM3:5639.
219 Von Schröder to IV army, 9 September 1916, RM3:5639; Von Schröder to von Capelle, 21 September 1916, RM3:5639.
220 For the best discussion of the effects of the Hindenburg Plan and of German industry as a whole see Gerald F. Feldman, *Army, Industry, and Labor in Germany 1914-1918*, (Princeton: Princeton University Press, 1966).
221 Von Schröder to von Capelle, 27 September 1916, RM3:5639.
222 Von Capelle to von Schröder, 10 October 1916, RM3:5639.
223 War Ministry to von Capelle, unsigned document stamped by the War Ministry, 5 October 1916, RM3:5639.
224 Von Schröder to von Capelle, 17 October 1916, RM3:5639.
225 Von Schröder to von Capelle, 17 October 1916, RM3:5639.
226 Rear-Admiral Gisberth Jasper, Commander of the 2nd MarineDivision to von Schröder, 21 October 1916, RM3:5639.
227 Von Capelle to von Holtzendorff, 28 October 1916, RM3:5639; von Holtzendorff to von Capelle, 30 October 1916, RM3:5639.
228 Torpedo-Boat Inspectorate to Baltic and North Sea naval stations, forwarded to von Schröder, 13 October 1916, RM120:145.
229 Kapitän zur See Otto Kranzbühler, Naval Staff liaison officer to the Oberste Heeres Leitung to von Holtzendorff, 16 December 1916, RM120:35.
230 Ibid.
231 Von Holtzendorff to von Capelle, forwarded to von Schröder, 30 December 1916, RM120:35. Von Hindenburg's argument was repeated in this letter. I did not find the original from von Hindenburg.
232 Ibid.
233 Von Schröder to von Holtzendorff, 8 January 1917, RM120:35.
234 Allerhöchste Befehl, 18 January 1917, RM120:35.
235 The classic study of German war aims remains Fritz Fischer, *Germany's Aims in the First World War*, (Düsseldorf: Droste Verlag, 1961. English trans. NY: Norton, 1967).
236 Fischer, *Germany's Aims*, p104.
237 Ibid., 106.
238 Hans W. Gatzke, *Germany's Drive to the West (Drang nach Westen): A Study of Germany's Western War Aims During the First World War*, (Baltimore: Johns Hopkins Press, 1950), p114.
239 Fischer, *Germany's Aims*, pp106, 172.
240 Ibid., p181.
241 Ibid., p112.
242 Ibid., p260.
243 Ibid., p112. For a full discussion of that denkschrift see the introduction.
244 Holger Herwig, 'Admirals *versus* Generals: The War Aims of the Imperial German Navy 1914–1918', *Central European History*, (September 1972): pp212–13.
245 Von Schröder to Tirpitz and Kaiser Wilhelm II, 31 March 1915, RM3:5639.
246 Ibid.
247 Ibid. Here we see the idea of the 'risk fleet' writ even larger.
248 Herwig, 'Admirals vs. Generals', pp214–15.
249 Oberbaurat von Eich, 'Bereisung die Hafen Belgiens in den Tagen 1 October bis zum 8 October', 18 November 1915, RM3:5639.
250 Fischer, *Germany's Aims*, p105.

Chapter 5

1 For the most recent discussion of the position of the Netherlands and the way in which they dealt with their situation see Hubert P. van Tuyll van Serooskerken, 'The Netherlands and World War I', *History of Warfare*, ed. Kelly DeVries, no 7 (Leiden: Brill, 2001). For more specific discussions of issues pertaining to Dutch see Amry Vandenbosch, *The Neutrality of the Netherlands During the World War*, (Grand Rapids, MI: Wm. B. Eerdmans Publishing, 1927); Amry Vandenbosch, *Dutch Foreign Policy Since 1815*, (Hague: Martinus Nijhoff, 1959); and M.J. van der Flier, *War Finances in the Netherlands up to 1918. Economic and Social History of the World War*, Dutch Series, (Oxford: Clarendon Press, 1923).
2 This is not to say that the British intended to force the Dutch into the war. In fact they were quite happy for them to maintain neutrality. Their greatest concern over the

Netherlands was that the Dutch might be forced to join the Central Powers. If that were to happen the Germans would then have access to Antwerp as a naval base and this would present the British with a very dangerous situation. Arthur J. Marder, *From the Dreadnought to Scapa Flow: The Royal Navy in the Fisher Era, 1904–19*, V vols (London: Oxford University Press, 1961–70), vol IV: p247–49; vol V: p163. For information on the British negotiations with the Dutch see A.C. Bell, *A History of the Blockade of Germany and of the countries Associated with Her in the Great War, Austria-Hungary, Bulgaria, and Turkey*, (London: HMSO, 1937), pp277–87, 473–78.

3   Vandenbosch, *Dutch Foreign Policy*, p274.
4   For a full discussion of all these matters see Vandenbosch, *Neutrality*, and van Serooskerken, *Netherlands and WWI*.
5   Nachrichten Offizier IV army to von Holtzendorff and von Schröder, unsigned, 20 August 1917, RM120:38.
6   Ibid.
7   Von Holtzendorff to Scheer, von Schröder, and Bauer, 13 October 1917, RM120:38.
8   Vandenbosch, *Dutch Foreign Policy*, p132.
9   Kriegstagebüch von Schröder, 28 March 1916, RM120:515.
10 Kriegstagebüch von Schröder, 15 September 1916, RM120:515.
11 Kriegstagebüch von Schröder, 15 December 1916, RM120:515.
12 Von Holtzendorff to von Schröder and Arthur Zimmermann, State Secretary for Foreign Affairs, 28 June 1917, RM120:38. This is not mentioned in the British official history of the air war.
13 Ibid.
14 Vandenbosch, *Dutch Foreign Policy*, pp125–26. Vandenbosch does not specify who made the demands and I was unable to find any correlation in the German sources for this demand.
15 Agent's report from Holland forwarded from von Holtzendorff to Scheer, von Capelle, von Schröder, and von Hindenburg, 10 May 1918, RM120:38.
16 Emphasis added.
17 Schweinitz, military attaché to the Netherlands, Militär-Bericht no. 27 'Das Anflieger unserer militärischen Anlagen in Belgien über Holland', 28 May 1918, RM120:38.
18 E. von Müller, naval attaché to the Netherlands to von Holtzendorff and von Capelle, 8 June 1918, RM120:38.
19 Gerhard Ritter, *The Sword and the Scepter: The Problem of Militarism in Germany*, 4 vols (Coral Gables: University of Miami Press,

1969–73), vol III: pp264–318.
20 At the start of the war the Dutch army was quite small compared to the major armies; they had 200,000 men under arms. Over the course of the war the Dutch did mobilise their army and go onto a war footing. By 1918 their army had increased to 450,000 men. Van der Flier, *War Finances*, pp36–37.
21 That was rectified by late 1916. By the end of that year the Germans had expanded their coastal batteries and had built new batteries that were specifically placed to reach all three of these channels.
22 Von Schröder, 'Considerations over the possibilities of an English landing in the Scheldt', 22 September 1915, RM3:5639.
23 Ibid.
24 Ibid.
25 Ibid.
26 Ibid.
27 Ibid.
28 Ibid; Otto Groos and Walther Gladisch, *Der Krieg in der Nordsee*, VII volumes. (Berlin: E.S. Mittler, 1920–65), vol IV: pp317–18.
29 Von Schröder, 'Considerations over the possibilities of a British landing in the Scheldt', 22 September 1915, RM3:5639.
30 Kriegstagebüch von Schröder, 3 February 1916, RM120:515.
31 Kriegstagebüch von Schröder, 4 February 1916, RM120:515.
32 Kriegstagebüch von Schröder, 30 March 1916, RM120:515.
33 Vandenbosch, *Dutch Foreign Policy*, p124. Vandenbosch clearly states that the Dutch understood this as a veiled German threat.
34 Ibid..
35 Nachrichten Abteilung des Generalstabes des Feldheeres to Kapitän zur See Friedrich von Bülow, Naval Staff representative at General Head Quarters, forwarded to von Holtzendorff, 7 January 1917, RM120:38.
36 See chapter Four.
37 Rear-Admiral Hermann Nordmann to the Chef des Generalstabes des Feldheeres–Nachrichten Abteilung, 21 January 1917, RM120:38.
38 Ibid.
39 This was true. See Admiral Sir Reginald Bacon, *The Concise Story of the Dover Patrol*, (London: Hutchinson, 1932), pp184–206. Bacon and Sir Douglas Haig planned a landing near Westende as part of the battle of Third Ypres. See Chapter Six for a complete discussion of the intended landing and German measures to meet it.
40 Von Müller to von Holtzendorff, 24 January 1917, RM120:38.
41 Walter Townley, British Legation Secretary in the Hague to the Foreign Office, 9 May

1917, RM120:38. Intercepted by the Germans and forwarded to the Naval Staff. The date is that of the original transmission. It appears that the Germans also had some limited ability to read British communications. I found several intercepts in the MarineKorps archives but did not find any discussion of a code-breaking service.

42 unsigned, 'Denkschrift betr. Möglichkeit einer englischen Landung auf den seeländischen Inseln und deren Abwehr', 29 June 1917, RM120:38.

43 Ibid.

44 Von Holtzendorff to von Schröder, 15 October 1916, RM120:38.

45 The Entente in that year had exploited differences between the pro-Entente Prime Minister of Greece and the pro-German King and had sent an army to Salonika to provide assistance to the Serbians. Greece itself remained neutral until late in the war while the Entente armies created a base at Salonika from which they carried on the war in the Balkans once Serbia had been defeated. See George B. Leontaritis, *Greece and the First World War: From Neutrality to Intervention, 1917–18*. (NY: Columbia University Press, 1990) for a recent look at these events and G.F. Abbott, *Greece and the Allies, 1914–22*. (London: Methuen and Company, 1922) for a more distant examination of the issues. For a look at the French aspects of the mission see Jan K. Tanenbaum, *General Maurice Sarrail, 1856–1929: The French Army and Left-Wing Politics*. (Chapel Hill, NC: University of North Carolina Press, 1974).

46 Von Holtzendorff to von Schröder, 15 October 1916, RM120:38.

47 Von Holtzendorff to von Schröder, Scheer and the commander of the North Sea Naval Station, 14 October 1916, RM120:38.

48 Ibid.

49 Nordmann to Scheer, 15 January 1917, RM120:38.

50 Scheer to von Holtzendorff, forwarded to von Schröder, 19 January 1917, RM120:38.

51 Von Holtzendorff to von Hindenburg forwarded to von Schröder, 2 February 1917, RM120:38.

52 Fourth Army Orders for the creation of "Gruppe Ghent", 29 April 1917, RM120:38; Reichskriegsministeriums, *Weltkrieg*, vol XII: pp436–37.

53 Von Holtzendorff to von Schröder and Scheer, 19 February 1917, RM120:38.

54 Generalstabes des Feldheeres, unsigned, 'Opinions on operations against Holland', n.d., RM120:38. The document is undated

but most likely was written after April 1917 since it refers to Gruppe Ghent which was only created in late April.

55 Scheer to MarineKorps, I–IV Squadrons, F.d.T., F.d.U., North Sea station, Cmdr. Reconnaissance Forces, Admiral Staff, CinC Coastal Defence, 31 March 1917, RM120:38.

56 Ibid.

57 General von Kirchbach, commanding general of Gruppe Ghent, 'Kriegsspiel Fall K', the document was undated but from internal evidence it appears to have taken place in the summer of 1917, certainly after the creation of Gruppe Ghent but also before the onset of the Passchendaele offensive. RM120:38.

58 Naval attaché to the Netherlands, unsigned, to von Holtzendorff, 23 May 1917, RM120:38.

59 Agent's report from Holland to the Naval Staff, 28 May 1917, RM120:38.

60 Gruppe Antwerp consisted of six divisions but unlike Gruppe Ghent these troops were not permanently stationed along the border. Gruppe Antwerp was only to come into existence if the expected attack actually took place. Once that occurred these troops would be sent from the IV army to the Netherlands. Reichskriegs Ministerium, *Der Weltkrieg 1914–18*, XV vols (Berlin: E.S. Mittler, 1925–42), vol XII: pp436–37.

61 Von Schröder to all subordinate commands, 21 July 1917, RM120:38.

62 Ibid.

63 Ibid.

64 Ibid.

65 German intercept of a message from Vice-Admiral Smit, Kommandant der Stellungen der Maas und Scheldemündungen, to Oberbefehlshaber der Land und Seestreitkräfte, August 1917, RM120:38. The intercept was acquired by the Naval Staff and sent from von Holtzendorff to both von Schröder and Scheer.

66 Von Holtzendorff to Scheer, von Schröder, and CinC coastal defence, 25 August 1917, RM120:38.

67 Von Holtzendorff to von Schröder and Scheer, 1 September 1917, RM120:38. The number seems to be a clear overestimation since the Dutch army did not exceed 500,000 men during the war. Van der Flier, *War Finances*, pp36–37.

68 General Staff intelligence section to the Naval Staff, n.d., RM120:38. The Dutch defences consisted of two 12cm, four 7.5cm, and two 5.7cm guns with six 15cm howitzers in reserve.

69 German intercept from CinC Scheldt to the

Dutch Naval Staff, Report on defences in the Scheldt and intentions for the fleet in the event of invasion, n.d., RM120:38. Once again the report was intercepted by the Germans and distributed to von Schröder and Scheer by the Naval Staff.

70 The type was not specified in the report.

71 Generalstabes des Feldheeres, 'Report on Holland's military position', August 1917, RM120:38.

72 Von Holtzendorff to Scheer, von Schröder, von Hindenburg, CinC coastal defence, and commander North Sea station, 25 February 1918, RM120:38.

73 Von Lossberg to all subordinate commands, 29 April 1918, RM120:38.

74 Marder, *Dreadnought*, vol IV: pp247–49; vol V: p163.

Chapter 6

1 Holger H. Herwig, *The First World War: Germany and Austria-Hungary 1914-1918*, (London: Arnold, 1997), pp289–91.

2 For an introduction to conditions in Germany during the war see Herwig, *First World War*. For a very detailed and in-depth discussion of Germany's internal problems see Gerald Feldmann, *Army, Industry, and Labor in Germany 1914-1918*; (Princeton: Princeton University Press, 1966) and Michael Geyer, *Deutsche Rüstungspolitik 1860-1980*; (Frankfurt: Suhrkamp, 1984).

3 Herwig, *First World War*, p292.

4 For full discussions of both sides of the issues involved in the resumption of the campaign see Fritz Fischer, *Germany's Aims in the First World War*, (NY: W.W. Norton, 1967), 280–310; Gerhard Ritter, *The Sword the and Scepter: The Problem of Militarism in Germany*, IV vols (Coral Gables: University of Miami Press, 1969–73), vol III: pp264–318; and for the purely naval end of the discussion see Paul G. Halpern, *A Naval History of World War I*, (Annapolis, MD: Naval Institute Press, 1994), pp335–340.

5 Cited in Herwig, *First World War*, p314. The emphasis is mine.

6 Von Holtzendorff to GeneralStabes des Feldheeres, 12 January 1917, RM120:35.

7 Von Holtzendorff to von Schröder, 20 January 1917, RM120:35.

8 Kriegstagebüch von Schröder, 16 January 1917, RM120:518.

9 Jacobsen to von Schröder, 18 January 1917, RM120:35.

10 Marine Luftfahrwesens des MarineKorps to the MarineKorps, 27 January 1917, RM120:149; von Schröder to Luftfahrwesens, 11 January 1917, RM120:149. Once again the type of plane

was not specified.

11 Marine Luftfahrwesens to MarineKorps, 3 January 1917, RM120:149.

12 Von Schröder to Marine Luftfahrwesens, 11 January 1917, RM120:149.

13 Von Schröder does not specify what these are, calling them only Fokker einsitzers. Since Ryheul mentions only Fokker D VII and Fokker D VIII as being part of the Flanders air contingent and the latter were not in Flanders until 1918, it seems logical that von Schröder was talking about D VIIs. Johan Ryheul, *MarineKorps Flandern 1914-1918*, (Hamburg: E.S. Mittler, 1997), pp264–65.

14 Von Schröder's notes for a meeting with von Holtzendorff, 16 January 1917, RM120:35.

15 Ibid.

16 Michelsen to von Schröder, 29 December 1916, RM120:52.

17 Kriegstagebüch von Schröder, 19 February 1917, RM120:518.

18 Otto Groos and Walther Gladisch, *Der Krieg in der Nordsee*, VII vols (Berlin: E.S. Mittler, 1920–65), vol VI: p156.

19 Gladisch, *Krieg der Nordsee*, vol VI: p157; Halpern, *Naval History*, p347; Kriegstagebüch von Schröder, 22 January 1917, RM120:518.

20 The following details of the engagement are drawn from Gladisch, *Krieg der Nordsee*, vol VI: pp157–70; Julian S. Corbett and Henry Newbolt, *History of the Great War: Naval Operations*, V vols, (London: Longmans, 1920–31), vol III: pp73–79; Patrick Beesly, *Room 40: British Naval Intelligence 1914–18*, (London: Hamish Hamilton, 1982), p275; and A. Patterson, *Tyrwhitt of the Harwich Force*, (London: MacDonald, 1973), pp176–80.

21 The other leading German destroyers were unable to get within range due to British gunfire. The only exception was *S-50* which suffered a mechanical breakdown and was unable to fire.

22 Gladisch, *Krieg der Nordsee*, vol VI: p170; Newbolt, *Naval Operations* vol III: p79; Halpern, *Naval History*, p347; Patterson, *Tyrwhitt*, pp176–80.

23 Von Schröder to von Holtzendorff, 23 January 1917, RM120:519; von Schröder to Scheer, 23 January 1917, RM120:52.

24 Kriegstagebüch von Schröder, 23 January 1917, RM120:518; von Schröder to IV army, 23 January 1917, RM120:52.

25 Kriegstagebüch von Schröder, 23 January 1917, RM120:518.

26 Von Schröder to von Holtzendorff, U-boat flotilla activity report for January 1917, 17 February 1917, RM120:577.

27 Halpern, *Naval History*, p335.
28 Rear-Admiral Arno Spindler, *Der Handelskrieg mit U-Booten*, V vols, (Berlin: E.S. Mittler, 1932–66), vol IV: pp2–3.
29 Kriegstagebüch von Schröder, 3 February 1917, RM120:518; von Schröder to von Holtzendorff, 'U-Boat Flotilla Activity Report for February 1917', 10 March 1917, RM120:577.
30 Spindler, *Handelskrieg*, vol IV:pp2–3. Spindler's numbers do not agree with those in the submarine activity reports for the first phase. The reports list the Flanders strength as: March thirty-three; April thirty-five; May thirty-five.
31 Spindler, *Handelskrieg*, vol IV: pp2–3. These figures include all the submarine types under the command of the MarineKorps.
32 Ibid., pp2–3.
33 Ibid., pp2–3.
34 All of the above information is drawn from the activity reports of the submarine flotillas for February - May 1917. Von Schröder to von Holtzendorff, 'U-Boat Flotilla Activity Report for February 1917', 10 March 1917, RM120:577; von Schröder to von Holtzendorff, 'U-Boat Flotilla Activity Report for March 1917', 17 April 1917, RM120:577; von Schröder to von Holtzendorff, U-Boat Flotilla Activity Report for April 1917, 18 May 1917, RM120:577; von Schröder to von Holtzendorff, U-Boat Flotilla Activity Report for May 1917, 16 June 1917, RM120:577.
35 Von Schröder to von Holtzendorff, 'U-Boat Flotilla Activity Report for February 1917', 10 March 1917, RM120:577.
36 Spindler, *Handelskrieg*, vol IV: pp194–95. The official British history lists a higher figure of 540,000 tons; Newbolt, *Naval Operations*, vol IV: p359. The latest estimate is that of Herwig, *First World War*, p314, which lists the total as 499,430 tons. Throughout this work I use the numbers from Spindler and Halpern unless otherwise noted.
37 Spindler, *Handelskrieg*, vol IV: p197.
38 Von Schröder to von Holtzendorff, 10 March 1917, RM120:577.
39 Von Schröder to von Holtzendorff, 'U-Boat Flotilla Activity Report for March 1917', 17 April 1917, RM120:577.
40 Spindler, *Handelskrieg*, vol IV: pp194–95.
41 Spindler, *Handelskrieg*, vol IV: p197.
42 Von Schröder to von Holtzendorff, 'U-Boat Flotilla Activity Report for March 1917', 17 April 1917, RM120:577.
43 Spindler, *Handelskrieg*, vol IV: pp194–95.
44 Spindler, *Handelskrieg*, vol IV: p197.

45 Von Schröder to von Holtzendorff, 'U-Boat Flotilla Activity Report for April 1917', 18 May 1917, RM120:577.
46 Robert M. Grant, *U-Boats Destroyed: The Effect of Anti-Submarine Warfare 1914–18*, (London: Putnam, 1964), p152.
47 Von Schröder to von Holtzendorff, 28 April 1917, RM120:576.
48 Spindler, *Handelskrieg*, vol IV:pp194–95.
49 Ibid., p.197.
50 Von Schröder to von Holtzendorff, 'U-Boat Flotilla Activity Report for May 1917', 16 June 1917, RM120:577.
51 Ibid.
52 Ibid.
53 Spindler, *Handelskrieg*, vol IV: pp107–14; Halpern, *Naval History*, p349. Halpern gives figures for the year of 253 passages by submarines with only one being sunk by a mine.
54 Kriegstagebüch von Schröder, 25 January 1917, 29 January 1917, 30 January 1917, 11 February 1917, RM120:518.
55 Von Holtzendorff to von Schröder, 6 February 1917, RM120:50.
56 Rear-Admiral Adolf von Trotha, Chief of Staff to Admiral Scheer, to all subordinate commands and to the MarineKorps, 9 February 1917, RM120:50.
57 Kriegstagebüch von Schröder, 18 February 1917, RM120:518.
58 Gröner, *Warships*,vol I: pp176–83.
59 Kriegstagebüch von Schröder, 14 February 1917, 20 February 1917, RM120:518; Gladisch, *Krieg der Nordsee*, vol VI: p297.
60 Gladisch, *Krieg der Nordsee*, vol VI: pp297, 299–302; Halpern, *Naval History*, p348; Kriegstagebüch von Schröder, 25 February 1917, RM120:518.
61 Kriegstagebüch von Schröder, 25 February 1917, RM120:518.
62 Newbolt, *Naval Operations*, vol IV: p352.
63 Gladisch, *Krieg der Nordsee*, vol VI: pp299–302.
64 The entire narrative here is taken from the Kriegstagebüch von Schröder, 25 February 1917, RM120:518; Gladisch, *Krieg der Nordsee*, vol VI: pp299–302; and Newbolt, *Naval Operations*, vol IV: pp352–53. All information specific to one particular source is duly noted.
65 Kriegstagebüch von Schröder, 25 February 1917, RM120:518; Gladisch, *Krieg der Nordsee*, vol VI: pp299–302.
66 Gladisch, *Krieg der Nordsee*, vol VI: p303; Kriegstagebüch von Schröder, 17 March 1917, RM120:518; Halpern, *Naval History*, p348.
67 Newbolt, *Naval Operations*, vol IV: p361.
68 Gladisch, *Krieg der Nordsee*, vol VI: pp303–

5; Newbolt, *Naval Operations*, vol IV: pp361–62; Kriegstagebüch von Schröder, 17 March 1917, RM120:518.

69 Newbolt, *Naval Operations*, vol IV: pp361–62; Gladisch, *Krieg der Nordsee*, vol VI: pp303–5.

70 Newbolt, *Naval Operations*, vol IV: pp361–63; Gladisch, *Krieg der Nordsee*, vol VI: pp303–5.

71 Gladisch, *Krieg der Nordsee*, vol VI: p307.

72 Kriegstagebüch von Schröder, 29 March 1917, RM120:518; Gladisch, *Krieg der Nordsee*, vol VI: p309.

73 Gladisch, *Krieg der Nordsee*, vol VI: p291. This was true with one exception. The flotilla was returned to the High Seas Fleet for the operation against the Baltic islands in the fall of 1917.

74 Scheer to von Schröder, date not included on the copy preserved in the Kriegstagebüch, Kriegstagebüch von Schröder, 17 April 1917, RM120:518.

75 Kriegstagebüch von Schröder, 24 March 1917, RM120:518.

76 Halpern, *Naval History*, p348.

77 Gladisch, *Krieg der Nordsee*, vol VI: pp292–93.

78 Assmann to von Schröder, 22 March 1917, RM120:53.

79 Von Capelle to von Holtzendorff, 4 February 1917, RM120:45. Essentially what happened was that the needs of the Torpedo-Boat Flotilla could not be met because they came after those of the army and the submarines.

80 Von Holtzendorff to von Capelle, forwarded to von Schröder, Scheer, Prince Heinrich and von Müller, 26 February 1917, RM120:45.

81 Von Schröder to von Holtzendorff, 22 February 1917, RM120:45. The original plan had been to take the A-Is out of service unless it became necessary to implement 'Fall K.'

82 Von Holtzendorff to von Schröder, 4 March 1917, RM120:45.

83 Von Capelle to all naval commands, 'Changes to the Kriegsstarknachweisung des MarineKorps', 11 April 1917, RM3:4615.

84 Assmann to von Schröder, 'Activity Report of the Flanders Torpedo-Boat Flotilla for the period from 9 January 1917 to 8 February 1917', 11 February 1917, RM120:45.

85 Gladisch, *Krieg der Nordsee*, vol VI: p308; Assmann to von Schröder, 'Activity Report of the Flanders Torpedo-Boat Flotilla for the period from 9 March 1917 to 8 April 1917', 12 April 1917, RM120:45. The latter document dates the attack as having taken place on 26 March, but since there is no other evidence to support a raid on that date

it most likely refers to the events of the 24th.

86 Gladisch, *Krieg der Nordsee*, vol VI: pp322–23; Kriegstagebüch von Schröder, 25 April 1917, RM120:518; Assmann to von Schröder, 'Activity Report of the Flanders Torpedo-Boat Flotilla for the period from 9 April 1917 to 8 May 1917', 9 May 1917, RM120:45.

87 Kriegstagebüch von Schröder, 2 May 1917, RM120:518; Assmann to von Schröder, 'Activity Report of the Flanders Torpedo-Boat Flotilla for the period from 9 April 1917 to 8 May 1917', 9 May 1917, RM120:4.

88 Gladisch, *Krieg der Nordsee*, vol VI: p329. Once again the British Official History does not mention this event, perhaps because the Germans escaped the notice of the British forces.

89 Kriegstagebüch von Schröder, 19 May 1917, RM120:518; Gladisch, *Krieg der Nordsee*, vol VI: pp334–35.

90 Gladisch, *Krieg der Nordsee*, vol VI: pp334–35.

91 Gladisch, *Krieg der Nordsee* vol VI: pp318–22; Newbolt, *Naval Operations*, vol IV: p372; Halpern, *Naval History*, p348; Marder, *Dreadnought to Scapa Flow*, vol IV: p107; Kriegstagebüch von Schröder, 21 April 1917, RM120:518. All of the following information is drawn from these sources. They all agree on the events of the evening.

92 Gladisch, *Krieg der Nordsee* vol VI: pp318–22; Newbolt, *Naval Operations*, vol IV: p372; Halpern, *Naval History*, p348; Marder, *Dreadnought to Scapa Flow*, vol IV:p107; Kriegstagebüch von Schröder, 21 April 1917, RM120:518. All the reports of the event agree except that in von Schröder's war diary the Germans report having engaged a force of eight British destroyers and leaders.

93 Gladisch, *Krieg der Nordsee*, vol VI: pp323–24; Kriegstagebüch von Schröder, 26 April 1917, RM120:518.

94 Kriegstagebüch von Schröder, 30 April 1917, RM120:518.

95 Gladisch, *Krieg der Nordsee*, vol VI: p329; Kriegstagebüch von Schröder, 10 May 1917, RM120:518. The skirmish was not mentioned in Newbolt.

96 Gladisch, *Krieg der Nordsee*, vol VI: pp333; Kriegstagebüch von Schröder, 17 May 1917, RM120:518.

97 Kriegstagebüch von Schröder, 23 May 1917, RM120:518.

98 Kriegstagebüch von Schröder, 26 May 1917, RM120:518.

99 Kriegstagebüch von Schröder, 1 February 1917, RM120:518.

100 Gladisch, *Krieg der Nordsee*, vol VI: p294;

Kriegstagebüch von Schröder, 2 February 1917, RM120:518.

101 Ibid., p26; Kriegstagebüch von Schröder, 16 February 1917, 1 March 1917, RM120:518.

102 Kriegstagebüch von Schröder, 8 February 1917, RM120:518; Gladisch, *Krieg der Nordsee*, vol VI: p294.

103 Kriegstagebüch von Schröder, 4 April 1917, RM120:518.

104 Ibid.; Gladisch, *Krieg der Nordsee*, vol VI: pp313–14; Newbolt, *Naval Operations*, vol IV: p371. Oddly, Newbolt dates this attack as occurring on March 7th.

105 Gladisch, *Krieg der Nordsee*, vol VI: p311.

106 Kriegstagebüch von Schröder, 1 May 1917, RM120:518.

107 Gladisch, *Krieg der Nordsee*, vol VI:pp324–27.

108 Halpern, *Naval History*, p425; John Terraine, *Business in Great Waters: The U-Boat Wars 1916–1945*, (London: Leo Cooper, 1989), p74.

109 Gladisch, *Krieg der Nordsee*, vol VI: p331; Newbolt, *Naval Operations*, vol IV:pp40–43; Kriegstagebüch von Schröder, 11 May 1917, RM120:518.

110 Admiral Sir Reginald Bacon, *The Concise Story of the Dover Patrol*, (London: Hutchinson, 1932), p216.

111 Ibid., pp 210–13..

112 The belief that the Royal navy lacked sufficient destroyers to protect all of Britain's shipping stems from the fact that the British had been manipulating their shipping figures to mislead the Germans. Once that mistake had been discovered resistance to convoy lessened. Up until that point it was believed that an insufficiently guarded convoy would be worse than no convoy at all. For the details see especially Halpern, *Naval History*, pp351–70; and Arthur J. Marder, *From the Dreadnought to Scapa Flow: The Royal Navy in the Fisher Era, 1904–19*, V vols (London: Oxford University Press, 1961–70), vol IV: pp115–52.

113 For fully detailed discussions of the convoy system and how it was implemented along with the problems that attended its early creation see Halpern, *Naval History*, pp351–70; Terraine, *Business*, pp57–105; and Marder, *Dreadnought*, vol IV: pp115–67, 181–92, 256–93.

114 Allerhöchste Befehl, 11 April 1917, RM3:4615.

115 Kapitän zur See Carl Tägert, Commander of the II Marine Brigade, 'Report on current defences in Ostend', to Flanders Flotillas, 1st MarineDivision, 2nd Naval Artillery Regiment and Harbour Captain Ostend, 23

April 1917, RM120:35. Tägert did not include the larger coastal guns such as the *Tirpitz* battery as part of the immediate defences of the port.

116 Jacobsen to von Schröder, 23 April 1917, RM120:35.

117 Von Schröder to Jacobsen, 30 April 1917, RM120:35.

118 All of the above is drawn from a memo sent from Admiral von Schröder to the IV army, 12 May 1917, RM120:111.

119 Crown Prince Rupprecht to IV army, 20 May 1917, RM120:111.

120 Kriegstagebüch von Schröder, 21 May 1917, RM120:518.

121 All of the above comes from an unsigned study by the MarineKorps entitled 'Möglichkeiten feindlicher Unternehmungen von see aus gegen die Küste', 22 May 1917, RM120:519.

122 Jacobsen to von Schröder, 'Overview of the defences of the coast', 26 May 1917, RM120:111.

123 Ibid.

124 Jacobsen to von Schröder, 22 May 1917, RM120:111; Jacobsen to von Schröder, 26 May 1917, RM120:111.

125 Kriegstagebüch von Schröder, 24 May 1917, RM120:518.

126 Scheer to all subordinate commands, forwarded to von Schröder and von Holtzendorff, 25 May 1917, RM120:77.

127 Jacobsen to von Schröder, 26 May 1917, RM120:111.

128 Spindler, *Handelskrieg*, vol IV:pp377–78; Marder, *Dreadnought*, vol IV:pp181–82; Newbolt, *Naval Operations*, vol V: p42; Herwig, *WWI*, p314. Once again the totals given differ. Newbolt reports losses nearing 700,000 tons while Marder reports 683,325 and Herwig 669,218 tons respectively. The numbers cited in the text are from Spindler.

129 Von Schröder to von Holtzendorff, 'U-Boat Flotilla Activity Report for June 1917', 16 July 1917, RM120:577.

130 Von Holtzendorff to von Schröder, 17 June 1917, RM120:576.

131 Von Schröder to von Holtzendorff, 7 June 1917, RM120:576.

132 Naval Staff, unsigned, 'Massnahmen zur wirksameren Durchführung des U-bootskrieg,' 26 June 1917, RM120:576.

133 Von Holtzendorff to von Schröder, 17 June 1917, RM120:576; Naval Staff, unsigned, 'Massnahmen zur wirksameren Durchführung des U-bootskrieg', 26 June 1917, RM120:576.

134 Von Holtzendorff to von Schröder, 15 June 1917, RM120:576.

135 Naval Staff, unsigned, 'Massnahmen', 26

June 1917, RM120:576. In a modern and updated version, this ofcourse became known as the 'wolfpack' and it was standard operating procedure for German submarines in World War II.

136 Spindler, *Handelskrieg*, vol IV:pp294–95. Once again varying numbers are given by the other authorities.

137 Von Schröder to von Holtzendorff, 'U-Boat Flotilla Activity Report for July 1917', 18 August 1917, RM120:577.

138 Marder, *Dreadnought*, vol IV: p277; Newbolt, *Naval Operations*, vol V: p139; von Schröder to von Holtzendorff, 'U-Boat Flotilla Activity Report for July 1917', 18 August 1917, RM120:577.

139 Von Holtzendorff to von Schröder, 7 July 1917, RM120:577.

140 Kriegstagebüch von Schröder, several entries in June and July 1917, RM120:518; Gladisch, *Krieg der Nordsee*, vol VII:pp116–17.

141 Kriegstagebüch von Schröder, 5 June 1917, RM120:518; Newbolt, *Naval Operations*, vol V: p45; Gladisch, *Krieg der Nordsee*, vol VII: p105.

142 It was the force from Harwich which encountered the two German destroyers. The Germans mistook the four light cruisers for additional destroyers.

143 Kriegstagebüch von Schröder, 5 June 1917, RM120:518; Newbolt, *Naval Operations*, vol V: p45; Gladisch, *Krieg der Nordsee*, vol VII: p105.

144 Kriegstagebüch von Schröder, 8 July 1917, RM120:518; Gladisch, *Krieg der Nordsee*, vol VII: p121.

145 Jacobsen to the 1st and 2nd Naval Brigades, 9 June 1917, RM120:35.

146 See *Planning Passchendaele*.

147 Assmann, 'Activity Report for the Flanders Torpedo-Boat Flotilla for the period from 9 May 1917 to 8 June 1917', 12 June 1917, RM120:45; Kriegstagebüch von Schröder, 26 June 1917, RM120:518; Gladisch, *Krieg der Nordsee*, vol VII: p127.

148 Bacon, *Dover Patrol*, p143.

149 Kriegstagebüch von Schröder, 25 July 1917, RM120:518; Gladisch, *Krieg der Nordsee*, vol VII: p141.

150 Kriegstagebüch von Schröder, 19 June 1917, RM120:518. The incident was not mentioned by Newbolt.

151 Von Schröder, orders for a bombardment of the coastal sector at Nieuport Bad, 5 July 1917, RM120:519.

152 Führer der Torpedobootstreitkräfte Flandern Korvettenkapitän Kahle to von Schröder, 21 June 1917, RM120:55.

153 Von Schröder did not specify the class of the

vessels but it appears that he is discussing the *S-113*-class of destroyers. These were 2,400 ton vessels armed with four 15cm guns and capable of nearly thirty-seven knots. Most were only completed in 1918 and hence saw only limited action.

154 Von Schröder to Kahle, 7 July 1917, RM120:55.

155 Scheer to Kahle, 20 July 1917, RM120:55.

156 Von Schröder to Scheer, 28 July 1917, RM120:55.

157 Von Holtzendorff to von Capelle, 27 July 1917, RM120:51

158 Von Holtzendorff to von Schröder, 14 February 1917, RM120:45.

159 Von Schröder to von Holtzendorff, 22 February 1917, RM120:45.

160 Von Holtzendorff to von Capelle, Scheer, von Müller, von Schröder, commander Baltic station, and commander North Sea station, 26 February 1917, RM120:45.

161 Von Schröder to von Holtzendorff, 1 June 1917, RM120:45.

162 Von Holtzendorff to von Schröder, 5 June 1917, RM120:145.

163 Von Schröder to Kahle, 7 July 1917, RM120:55.

164 Graf von Moltke, operational orders for 'Strandfest', 4 July 1917, RM120:54.

165 Graf von Moltke, revised orders for 'Strandfest', 7 July 1917, RM120:54.

166 Graf von Moltke, operational orders for 'Strandfest', 4 July 1917, RM120:54.

167 John Giles, *Flanders Then and Now: The Ypres Salient and Passchendaele*, (London: Leo Cooper, 1970), p161; Gladisch, *Krieg der Nordsee*, vol VII: p147.

168 Andrew Wiest, *Passchendaele and the Royal Navy*, Contributions in Military Studies Series (Westport, CT: Greenwood Press, 1995), p133.

169 Von Schröder to Crown Prince Rupprecht, 6 June 1917, RM120:111.

170 Army Group Crown Prince Rupprecht to von Schröder, 7 June 1917, RM120:35.

171 Jacobsen to all battery commanders, 14 June 1917, RM120:35.

172 Von Arnim to Jacobsen, 26 June 1917, RM120:112.

173 Kriegstagebüch von Schröder, 27 June 1917, RM120:518.

174 Von Schröder to von Arnim, 'Study of the of the possibility of an enemy landing on the coast', 15 July 1917, RM120:112.

175 Von Arnim to von Schröder, 18 July 1917, RM120:112.

176 Rear-Admiral Georg von Ammon, Commander of the 1st Naval Brigade to Jacobsen, 20 July 1917, RM120:112.

177 Von Schröder, 'Regulations for a

MarineKorps war-game to test the coastal defences against a British landing', 25 July 1917, RM120:111.

178 'Results of the war-game', 3rd MarineDivision to MarineKorps, 25 July 1917, RM120:111.

179 Kommando des Luftfahrwesens des MarineKorps to the MarineKorps, 29 July 1917, RM120:35.

180 The number of works dealing with Passchendaele is immense. Those which the author found to be most useful were: Robin Prior and Trevor Wilson, *Passchendaele: The Untold Story*, (New Haven, CT: Yale University Press, 1996); Andrew A. Wiest, *Passchendaele and the Royal Navy*, Contributions in Military Studies Series (Westport, CT: Greenwood Press, 1995); John Terraine, *The Road to Passchendaele: The Flanders Offensive of 1917: a Study in Inevitability*, (London: Leo Cooper, 1977); John Giles, *Flanders Then and Now: The Ypres Salient and Passchendaele*, (London: Leo Cooper, 1970); and Cyril Falls, *Military Operations: France and Belgium 1917*, III vols, vol II (London: HMSO, 1948).

181 Wiest, *Passchendaele*, 24-25.

182 Ibid., 35-6. This is essentially the plan adopted by Haig in 1917.

183 Ibid., 41-3.

184 Wiest, *Passchendaele*, 55; Marder, *Dreadnought*, IV:200.

185 Wiest, *Passchendaele*, 59-60; Marder, *Dreadnought*, IV:200.

186 There is still a controversy in the historiography of the Third Battle of Ypres concerning the roles of Haig and Lloyd-George. Following the war Lloyd-George, in his memoirs, tried to absolve himself of any blame for the offensive and relentlessly attacked Haig and his generals for glory-seeking and idiocy. It is not my intention to enter that debate. An excellent overview of the historiographical argument is included in Prior and Wilson, *Passchendaele*, and an excellent portrayal of the problems faced by both Lloyd-George and Haig in 1917 is presented in Dominick Graham and Shelford Bidwell, *Coalitions, Politicians and Generals: Some Aspects of Command in Two World Wars*, (London: Brassey's, 1993).

187 Quoted in Marder, *Dreadnought*, vol IV: p202.

188 Wiest, *Passchendaele*, pp109-10.

189 Ibid., p104; Marder, *Dreadnought*, vol IV: p194.

190 There were other reasons given for the attack as well, the most common being the need to attack the Germans to keep them from attacking the French. In the event, however, the Germans were unaware of the mutinies and had no plans whatsoever for anything other than small localised attacks. The bulk of historiographical weight now accepts the key role played in the genesis of the Third Ypres campaign by the concerns of the Royal Navy. The traditional claim though had always been, prior to Wiest, that it was the submarine campaign that made the seizure of Ostend and Zeebrugge so vital. Though the submarine campaign would have been hurt by the loss of the bases, it would hardly have been crippled. Clearly, as Wiest points out, the greatest danger to the British from the Flanders bases was the destroyer flotillas. Had the Germans used the bases in the ways envisioned by Jellicoe and Bacon, the results might have been disastrous for the British. It seems clear that Bacon and Jellicoe would have agreed with von Schröder's assessment of the potential for the Flanders bases.

191 Marder, *Dreadnought*, vol IV: p205. Two of the most outspoken critics were Admiral David Beatty and Rear Admiral John Michael de Robeck, the commander of the British naval force in the eastern Mediterranean that had supported the Gallipoli landing. De Robeck in fact called the landing 'impossible'.

192 Prior and Wilson, *Passchendaele*, p45; Wiest, *Passchendaele*, p93; Herwig, *WWI*, p330.

193 Prior and Wilson, *Passchendaele*, p69.

194 Bacon, *Dover Patrol*, 192; Wiest, *Passchendaele*, p137.

195 Out of necessity this has been a very brief survey of what went into the planning of the Third Ypres operation and what was hoped for from it. The best recent work for the operation in general is Prior and Wilson, *Passchendaele* and Wiest's work is excellent on the role played by the navy. He also gives a very clear description of the planned amphibious assault and is fairly confident it would have succeeded. Clearly, had it gone forward and succeeded it might have ended the war. What this author thinks its chances of success were is elaborated below.

196 The best discussion of these events remains Ritter, *Sword and Scepter*, vol III: pp457–89.

197 Daniel Horn, *The German Naval Mutinies of World War I*, (New Brunswick, NJ: Rutgers University Press, 1969), pp94–138; Herwig, *WWI*, pp376–78; Herwig, *Officer Corps*, p208; Interestingly, according to Herwig in *Officer Corps*, several of the ratings tainted by the revolt were sent to join the MarineKorps, though no explanation is given as to why. Unfortunately no record of this exists in the files of the MarineKorps for

clarification, though it is interesting to note that, when the MarineKorps was disbanded in early November 1918, von Schröder was sent to Kiel to deal with the revolts there. It is unknown if this was because of the way he handled the ratings in 1917 or if they were originally sent to him because he had a reputation for discipline. No mention of the event is made at all in von Schröder's biography.

198 The above breakdown is taken directly from Falls, *Military Operations 1917*, vol II: piii.

199 Von Arnim to von Schröder and GeneralKommando des GardeKorps, 28 July 1917, RM120:35; Reichskriegsministeriums, *Weltkrieg*, vol XII: pp425–26, 436–37.

200 Von Schröder to von Arnim, 30 July 1917, RM120:35.

201 Jacobsen to von Arnim and von Schröder, 'Erläuterungsbericht zu dem weiterem Ausbau der Küste', 4 August 1917, RM120:112.

202 2nd Infanterie-Radfahrer Brigade to MarineKorps, 13 August 1917, RM120:112.

203 Jacobsen to von Schröder, 17 August 1917, RM120:112.

204 Ludendorff, 'Auffassung der Lage,' 22 August 1917, RM120:35.

205 Von Arnim to von Schröder, 26 September 1917, RM120:150.

206 Kommando des Marine Luftfahrwesens to MarineKorps, 30 September 1917, RM120:150.

207 Kriegstagebüch von Schröder, 19 October 1917, RM120:518; General von Krosigk, Gruppe Nord, 'Measures intended to meet an English Fleet Attack', 19 October 1917, RM120:111. Von Krosigk was directly under von Schröder who was the commander of Gruppe Nord.

208 Kriegstagebüch von Schröder, 21 October 1917, RM120:518.

209 Ludendorff, 'Auffassung der Lage', 1 November 1917, RM120:35.

210 Von Arnim to von Krosigk, 1 November 1917, RM120:112.

211 Von Schröder to Jacobsen, 5 November 1917, RM120:112.

212 Von Schröder to von Holtzendorff, 12 November 1917, RM120:35.

213 Jacobsen to von Arnim and von Schröder, 19 November 1917, RM120:35.

214 Ludendorff to von Holtzendorff, 16 November 1917, RM120:111.

215 Von Schröder to von Holtzendorff, 17 November 1917, RM120:111.

216 Von Holtzendorff to Ludendorff, forwarded to von Schröder, 22 November 1917, RM120:111.

217 Von Schröder to von Arnim, 19 December 1917, RM120:35.

218 Von Schröder to von Holtzendorff, 'U-Boat Flotilla Activity Report for August 1917', 17 September 1917, RM120:577; von Schröder to von Holtzendorff, 'U-Boat Flotilla Activity Report for September 1917', 18 October 1917, RM12:577; von Schröder to von Holtzendorff, 'U-Boat Flotilla Activity Report for October 1917', 20 November 1917, RM120:577; von Schröder to von Holtzendorff, 'U-Boat Flotilla Activity Report for November 1917', 22 December 1917, RM120:578; von Schröder to von Holtzendorff, 'U-Boat Flotilla Activity Report for December 1917', 16 January 1918, RM120:578.

219 Spindler, *Handelskrieg*, vol IV: pp21–30; Rössler, *U-boat*, pp54–59.

220 Von Schröder to von Holtzendorff, 'U-Boat Flotilla Activity Report for August 1917', 17 September 1917, RM120:577; von Schröder to von Holtzendorff, 'U-Boat Flotilla Activity Report for September 1917', 18 October 1917, RM120:577; von Schröder to von Holtzendorff, 'U-Boat Flotilla Activity Report for October 1917', 20 November 1917, RM120:577; von Schröder to von Holtzendorff, U-boat flotilla activity report for November 1917, 22 December 1917, RM120:578; von Schröder to von Holtzendorff, U-boat flotilla activity report for December 1917, 16 January 1918, RM120:578.

221 Spindler, *Handelskrieg*, vol IV: pp294–95.

222 Ibid.

223 Von Schröder to von Holtzendorff, 'U-Boat Flotilla Activity Report for August 1917', 17 September 1917, RM120:577; von Schröder to von Holtzendorff, 'U-Boat Flotilla Activity Report for September 1917', 18 October 1917, RM120:577.

224 Von Schröder to von Holtzendorff, 'U-Boat Flotilla Activity Report for August 1917', 17 September 1917, RM120:577.

225 Von Schröder to von Holtzendorff, 'U-Boat Flotilla Activity Report for September 1917', 18 October 1917, RM120:577.

226 Von Holtzendorff to Scheer and von Schröder, 21 September 1917, RM120:576.

227 Ibid.

228 Halpern, *Naval History*, p365; *Spindler, Handelskrieg*, vol IV: p497.

229 Von Schröder to von Holtzendorff, 'U-Boat Flotilla Activity Report for October 1917', 20 November 1917, RM120:577.

230 Von Holtzendorff to von Schröder, 26 October 1917, RM120:576.

231 Halpern, *Naval History*, p365; Spindler, *Handelskrieg*, vol IV: p497.

232　Von Schröder to von Holtzendorff, 'U-Boat Flotilla Activity Report for November 1917', 22 December 1917, RM120:578.

233　Marder, *Dreadnought*, vol IV: p285.

234　Halpern, *Naval History*, p365; Spindler, *Handelskrieg*, vol IV: p497.

235　Von Schröder to von Holtzendorff, 'U-Boat Flotilla Activity Report for December 1917', 16 January 1918, RM120:578.

236　Kriegstagebüch von Schröder, 29 November 1917, RM120:518. The torpedoes had a faulty seal that apparently caused them to take on water and sink before reaching their targets. Several submarines reported torpedoes losing depth and running underneath their intended targets.

237　Von Schröder to von Holtzendorff, 'U-Boat Flotilla Activity Report for December 1917', 16 January 1918, RM120:578.

238　Halpern, *Naval History*, p407; Terraine, *Business*, pp109–10; Newbolt, *Naval Operations*, vol V:178–82; Herwig, *Luxury Fleet*, p206; Marder, *Dreadnought*, vol IV: p317–18; Bacon, *Dover Patrol*, pp158–60.

239　Terraine, *Business*, pp109–10.

240　Marder, *Dreadnought*, vol IV: p347. The exact dates were December 28th for Bacon's removal and January 1st for Keyes' appointment.

241　See Chapter Seven.

242　Spindler, *Handelskrieg*, vol IV: p318.

243　Herwig, *WWI*, p318.

244　Kriegstagebüch von Schröder, multiple entries for August 1917, RM120:518.

245　Kriegstagebüch von Schröder, 17 November 1917, RM120:518.

246　Kahle to von Schröder, 2 November 1917, RM120:46.

247　Kriegstagebüch von Schröder, 22 September 1917, RM120:518.

248　Kriegstagebüch von Schröder, 22 October 1917, 25 October 1917, RM120:518.

249　Kriegstagebüch von Schröder, 16 August 1917, 22 August 1917, RM120:518.

250　Kriegstagebüch von Schröder, 3 September 1917, 4 September 1917, RM120:518.

251　Von Arnim to von Schröder, 24 August 1917, RM120:150.

252　Kommando Marine Luftfahrwesens to von Schröder, 9 September 1917, RM120:150.

253　Gruppenführer der Flieger 4 to von Schröder, 16 September 1917, RM120:150.

254　Kommando Marine Luftfahrwesens to von Schröder, 14 September 1917, RM120:150.

255　Von Holtzendorff to von Schröder, 5 October 1917, RM120:150.

256　Von Schröder to von Holtzendorff, 15 October 1917, RM120:150.

257　Kriegstagebüch von Schröder, 6 September 1917, RM120:518; Gladisch, *Krieg der Nordsee*, vol VI: p126.

258　Kriegstagebüch von Schröder, 28 October 1917, RM120:518; Gladisch, *Krieg der Nordsee*, vol VI: p126.

259　Kriegstagebüch von Schröder, 27 September 1917, RM120:518; Gladisch, *Krieg der Nordsee*, vol VI: pp129–30. *U-70* was later found by *UC-71* and towed into harbour.

260　Kriegstagebüch von Schröder, 27 October 1917, RM120:518; Gladisch, *Krieg der Nordsee*, VI:130.

261　Kriegstagebüch von Schröder, 18 October 1917, RM120:518. No mention of the incident is made in either of the official histories.

262　Kriegstagebüch von Schröder, 11 September 1917, RM120:518.

263　Scheer to von Schröder, n.d., RM120:55. Internal evidence suggests that this dates to either September or October 1917.

264　Von Holtzendorff to von Schröder and Scheer, 1 October 1917, RM120:55.

265　Kriegstagebüch von Schröder, 11 November 1917, RM120:518.

266　Kriegstagebüch von Schröder, 28 November 1917, RM120:518.

267　Kriegstagebüch von Schröder, 22 November 1917, RM120:518.

268　Kriegstagebüch von Schröder, 23 November 1917, RM120:518. These were vessels that had been damaged in the attack on the Gulf of Riga.

269　Kriegstagebüch von Schröder, 18 December 1917, RM120:518.

270　Assmann to von Schröder, 9 August 1917, RM120:46.

271　Transcript of a phone conversation between Assmann and the Kriegsleitung in Berlin, 21 September 1917, RM120:46.

272　Von Holtzendorff to von Schröder, 25 September 1917, RM120:46.

273　Kriegstagebüch von Schröder, 17 November 1917, RM120:518. Why it was considered necessary to escort destroyers with torpedo-boats remains unknown.

274　Kriegstagebüch von Schröder, 18 December 1917, RM120:518.

275　See especially Newbolt, *Naval Operations*, vol IV: pp360–378; Marder, *Dreadnought*, vol IV:pp99–108.

Chapter 7

1　For the fullest discussion of the effects of Brest-Litovsk and the role of war aims in Germany's continuation of the war, see Fritz Fischer, *Germany's Aims in the First World War*, (Düsseldorf, Droste Verlag, 1961. Eng trans. NY: Norton, 1967), pp475–510.

2　For a discussion of the conflict between the two forces see Holger H. Herwig, 'Admirals *versus* Generals: The War Aims of the Imperial German Navy 1914-1918', *Central European History*, (September 1972): 212–13.

3 Ibid., p220.

4 Fischer, *Germany's War Aims*, pp594–95.

5 Ibid..

6 All of the following information is drawn from a denkschrift written by von Schröder entitled, 'The Military Value of the Flanders Coast', dated 14 February 1918. The document is contained in file RM120:36. The emphasis is mine.

7 Ibid.

8 Von Schröder denkschrift supplement, 'Flanders and the North Sea', 14 February 1918, RM120:36.

9 Von Holtzendorff to Ludendorff, response to a conversation held on 8 April 1918, 13 April 1918, RM120:36. The document is also cited in Herwig, 'Admirals vs. Generals', p223.

10 Von Holtzendorff to Ludendorff, 13 April 1918, RM120:36.

11 Herwig, 'Admirals vs. Generals', p223.

12 Rear Admiral Arno Spindler, *Der Handelskrieg mit U–Booten*, V vols (Berlin: E.S. Mittler, 1932–66), vol V: p64.

13 Ibid., p104.

14 Ibid., pp426–27.

15 Von Schröder to von Holtzendorff, 6 February 1918, RM120:579.

16 Von Schröder to von Holtzendorff, 'U-boat Flotilla Activity Report for January 1918', 17 February 1918, RM120:578.

17 Spindler, *Handelskrieg*, vol V: p364.

18 Ibid., pp426–27.

19 Paul G. Halpern, *A Naval History of World War I*, (Annapolis: Naval Institute Press, 1994), p423.

20 Arthur J. Marder, *From the Dreadnought to Scapa Flow: The Royal Navy in the Fisher Era, 1904–19*, V vols (London: Oxford University Press, 1961–70), vol V: p78.

21 Von Schröder to von Holtzendorff, 'U-Boat Flotilla Activity Report for February 1918', 26 March 1918, RM120:578. According to Spindler the flotillas only accounted for 65,461 tons. Spindler, *Handelskrieg*, vol V: p364.

22 Marder gives a total of 318,174 tons and Spindler 243,152 tons. Marder, *Dreadnought*, vol V: p78; Spindler, *Handelskrieg*, vol V: pp426–27.

23 Halpern, *Naval History*, p423.

24 Von Schröder to von Holtzendorff, 'U-Boat Flotilla Activity Report for March 1918', 22 April 1918, RM120:578. Spindler credits them with 99,395 tons. Spindler, *Handelskrieg*, vol V: p364.

25 Halpern, *Naval History*, p423.

26 Spindler, *Handelskrieg*, vol V: p364. No flotilla activity report for April remains in the naval records.

27 Halpern, *Naval History*, p416.

28 Spindler, *Handelskrieg*, vol V: pp104–49.

29 Von Schröder to von Holtzendorff, 'U-Boat Flotilla Activity Report for February 1918', 26 March 1918, RM120:283.

30 Halpern, *Naval History*, pp406–7.

31 For a detailed look at this argument between the two men see Marder, *Dreadnought*, vol IV: pp315–23; Admiral Sir Roger Keyes, *The Naval Memoirs of Admiral of the Fleet Sir Roger Keyes*, (London: Thornton Butterworth, 1935) vol II; and Bacon, *Dover Patrol*.

32 Halpern, *Naval History*, p406. Keyes, *Memoirs*, vol II: p143.

33 Halpern, *Naval History*, p406; Marder, *Dreadnought*, vol V: pp39–40.

34 Keyes, *Memoirs*, vol II: p160; Otto Groos and Walther Gladisch, *Der Krieg in der Nordsee*, VII vols, (Berlin: E.S. Mittler, 1920–65), vol VII: p148.

35 Kriegstagebüch von Schröder, several entries throughout 1918, RM120:282; Gladisch, *Krieg der Nordsee*, vol VII: pp229–30.

36 John Terraine, *Business in Great Waters: The U-Boat Wars 1916–45*, (London: Leo Cooper, 1989), p111; Julian S. Corbett and Henry Newbolt, *History of the Great War: Naval Operations*, V vols (London: Longmans, 1920–31), vol V: 209–10.

37 Gladisch, *Krieg der Nordsee*, vol VII: p148.

38 Minutes of a phone conversation between von Holtzendorff and von Schröder, 7 January 1918, RM120:35.

39 Inspektion des Torpedowesens to MarineKorps, 4 January 1918, RM120:46.

40 Von Holtzendorff to von Schröder, 12 March 1918, RM120:46.

41 Kriegstagebüch von Schröder, 16 February 1918, RM120:282.

42 Admiral Reinhard Koch, deputy chief of the Naval Staff, to von Capelle and von Schröder, 27 February 1918, RM120:55.

43 Kommando III Flotilla to *V-71*, *V-73*, *G-91*, and *S-55*, 11 April 1918, RM120:53.

44 Kommando III Flotilla to High Seas Fleet, Führer der Torpedoboote, and Führer der Torpedoboote Flandern, 20 April 1918, RM120:53.

45 Kommando der III Flotilla to Führer der Torpedoboote Flandern, Führer der Torpedoboote, and IV Reconnaissance group, 21 April 1918, RM120:53; Führer der IV Aufklärungsgruppe to Scheer, 20 April 1918, RM120:53; Scheer to von

Holtzendorff, April 24 1918, RM120:53. No mention of the skirmish was made in either official history.

46 Gladisch, *Krieg der Nordsee*, vol VII: p132; Kriegstagebüch von Schröder, 14 January 1918, RM120:282.

47 Keyes, *Memoirs*, vol II: p169.

48 Kriegstagebüch von Schröder, 14 January 1918, RM120:282.

49 Keyes, *Memoirs*, vol II:p169.

50 Gladisch, *Krieg der Nordsee*, vol VII:p132; Kriegstagebüch von Schröder, 14 January 1918, RM120:282; Newbolt, *Naval Operations*, vol V: p208; Keyes to Beatty, 18 January 1918, in Paul Halpern, ed. *The Keyes Papers*, Publications of the Naval Records Society, (London: Navy Records Society, 1972), vol I: p445.

51 Newbolt, *Naval Operations*, vol V: p208; Kriegstagebüch von Schröder, 23 January 1918, RM120:282.

52 Keyes to Beatty, 7 February 1918, cited in Halpern, *Keyes Papers*, vol 451.

53 Admiral Reinhard Scheer, *Germany's High Seas Fleet in the World War*, (London: Cassell, 1919), pp314–17; Halpern, *Naval History*, p408; Gladisch, *Krieg der Nordsee*, vol VII: pp189–95.

54 Gladisch, *Krieg der Nordsee*, vol VII: pp189–95; Halpern, *Naval History*, p408; Kriegstagebüch von Schröder, 13 February 1918, 14 February 1918, RM120:282.

55 Newbolt, *Naval Operations*, vol V: pp210–23; Keyes, *Memoirs*, vol II: pp160–61.

56 Gladisch, *Krieg der Nordsee*, vol VII: pp189–95.

57 Gladisch, *Krieg der Nordsee*, vol VII: pp189–95; Newbolt, *Naval Operations*, vol V: pp210–23.

58 Gladisch, *Krieg der Nordsee*, vol VII: pp189–95; Newbolt, *Naval Operations*, vol V: pp210–23.

59 Gladisch, *Krieg der Nordsee*, vol VII: pp189–95; Newbolt, *Naval Operations*, vol V: pp210–23.

60 Keyes, *Memoirs*, vol II: p174.

61 Newbolt, *Naval Operations*, vol V: pp210–23; Gladisch, *Krieg der Nordsee*, vol VII: pp189–95.

62 Kriegstagebüch von Schröder, 14 February 1918, RM120:282.

63 Scheer, *High Seas Fleet*, pp314–17.

64 Halpern, *Naval History*, pp408; Newbolt, *Naval Operations*, vol V: pp210–23; Keyes, *Memoirs*, vol II: p174; Terraine, *Business*, p111; Barrie Pitt, *Zeebrugge: St.George's Day, 1918*, (London: Cassell and Company, 1958), p42.

65 Gladisch, *Krieg der Nordsee*, vol VII: pp189–95; Kriegstagebüch von Schröder, 14

February 1918, RM120:282.

66 Keyes to Beatty, 22 February 1918, in Halpern, *Keyes Papers*, p459.

67 Kriegstagebüch von Schröder, 15 February 1918, RM120:282.

68 Gladisch, *Krieg der Nordsee*, vol VII:189–95; 225–26.

69 Keyes, *Memoirs*, vol II: p174; Keyes to Beatty, 19 February 1918, in Halpern, *Keyes Papers*, p458.

70 Von Schröder to von Holtzendorff, 'U-Boat Flotilla Activity Report for February 1918', 26 March 1918, RM120:283.

71 Von Schröder to von Holtzendorff, 'U-Boat Flotilla Activity Report for March 1918', 22 April 1918, RM120:578.

72 Admiral Ludwig von Schröder, 'Erwägungen und Massnahmen für den Fall einer Besetzung der französischen Nordostküste', 7 January 1918, RM120:602.

73 Ibid.

74 Von Schröder, MarineKorps Gruppenbefehl, n.d., RM120:36. Since the introduction alludes to German forces crossing the Somme a few days earlier, a best guess would put the date of the document as late March or very early April.

75 Kriegstagebüch von Schröder, 19 March 1918, RM120:282; Gladisch, *Krieg der Nordsee*, vol VII: p234.

76 The following narrative comes from: Newbolt, *Naval Operations*, vol V: pp223–30; Halpern, *Naval History*, p410; Gladisch, *Krieg der Nordsee*, vol VII: pp234–37; Keyes, *Memoirs*, vol II: pp193–98; Pitt, *Zeebrugge*, pp53–56; and Kriegstagebüch von Schröder, 21 March 1918, RM120:282.

77 Newbolt, *Naval Operations*, vol V: pp223–30; Keyes, *Memoirs*, vol II: pp193–98.

78 Kriegstagebüch von Schröder, 21 March 1918, RM120:282.

79 Kriegstagebüch von Schröder, 9 April 1918, 18 April 1918, RM120:282.

80 Naval staff, [Scheibe], 'Further Observations on the Position of the War', 29 March 1918, RM120:36.

81 Scheibe, 'Further Observations', 29 March 1918, RM120:36.

82 Kriegstagebüch von Schröder, 30 March 1918, RM120:282.

83 The author would like to thank the *Journal of Military History* for allowing parts of this section, which originally appeared in their journal, to be reprinted.

84 Pitt, *Zeebrugge*, pxiii.

85 For a detailed discussion of these various schemes see Marder, *Dreadnought*, vo II:pp349–67.

86 Marder, *Dreadnought*, vol V: pp46–47.

87 Halpern, *Keyes Papers*, p412.

88 Captain A.F.B. Carpenter, *The Blocking of Zeebrugge*, (London: Herbert Jenkins, 1922), p18.

89 Pitt, *Zeebrugge*, p13.

90 Keyes to Beatty, 5 December 1917; Halpern, *Keyes Papers*, pp422–23.

91 Carpenter, *Blocking*, p43.

92 'Plan for Operation Z.O', 25 February 1918, contained in Halpern, *Keyes Papers*, pp460–78.

93 Newbolt, *Naval Operations*, vol V: p246.

94 Pitt, *Zeebrugge*, p25; Newbolt, *Naval Operations*, vol V: p246.

95 Carpenter, *Blocking*, pp24–28.

96 The current account is taken primarily from the following: Keyes, *Memoirs*, vol II: pp204–26; 'Plan for Operation Z.O.', 25 February 1918, contained in Halpern, *Keyes Papers*, 460–78; Gladisch, *Krieg der Nordsee*, vol VII: pp238–71; Halpern, *Naval History*, pp411–12; and Carpenter, *Blocking*, p74.

97 Gladisch, *Krieg der Nordsee*, vol VII:238–71.

98 The following narrative relies on: Keyes, *Memoirs*, vol II: pp262–291; Carpenter, *Blocking*, pp176–210, 233–52; Newbolt, *Naval Operations*, vol V: pp241–65; Gladisch, *Krieg der Nordsee*, vol VII: pp238–71; and Pitt, *Zeebrugge*.

99 Kriegstagebüch von Schröder, 11 April 1918, RM120:282; Carpenter, *Blocking*, p151.

100 Kriegstagebüch von Schröder, 11 April 1918, RM120:282; Edgar Erich Schulze, 'Das MarineKorps in Flandern 1914–1918', *Marine-Rundschau*, vol XXVII (8–10, 1922): p387; Halpern, *Naval History*, pp411–12; Gladisch, *Krieg der Nordsee*, vol VII: pp238–71.

101 Kriegstagebüch von Schröder, 11 April 1918, RM120:282; Gladisch, *Krieg der Nordsee*, VII:pp238–71.

102 Keyes, *Memoirs*, vol II: p262; Pitt, *Zeebrugge*, p90.

103 MarineKorps Luftabwehr report to the MarineKorps on the events of 22/23 April 1918, 23 April 1918, RM120:275; Gladisch, *Krieg der Nordsee*, vol VII: pp238–71; Kapitänleutnant Gunther Lütjens, Führer der II Torpedoboote HalbFlotille Flandern, to von Schröder, 'Report on the attack of 22 April 1918', 25 April 1918, RM120:275; Kapitänleutnant Konrad Zander, Führer der II Zerstörer Halbflotille, to the Kaiser, 'Report on the British Attack on Zeebrugge on the Night of 22/23 April 1918', n.d., RM120:275.

104 Gladisch, *Krieg der Nordsee*, vol VII: p251; Newbolt, *Naval Operations*, vol V: p254; Carpenter, *Blocking*, pp233–40.

105 MarineKorps Luftabwehr, 'Report', 23 April 1918, RM120:275.

106 'Battle Report of the Zeebrugge Mole Battery', 23 April 1918, RM120:275.

107 Ibid.

108 Gladisch, *Krieg der Nordsee*, vol VII: p253; Lütjens, 'Report', 25 April 1918, RM120:275.

109 Lütjens, 'Report', 25 April 1918, RM120:275.

110 Gladisch, *Krieg der Nordsee*, vol VII: pp255–57.

111 Battle report of the mole battery, 23 April 1918, RM120:275.

112 Pitt asserts that at the time of the explosion a column of German bicycle troops was trying to cross the viaduct and they were supposedly destroyed by the explosion. There is no mention of this in the German documents. Pitt, *Zeebrugge*, pp114–15.

113 Newbolt, *Naval Operations*, vol V: p26.

114 Gladisch, *Krieg der Nordsee*, vol VII: p265.

115 Carpenter, *Blocking*, p270; Halpern, *Naval History*, p411–12.

116 Kriegstagebüch von Schröder, 3 May 1918, RM120:282.

117 Zander, 'Report', n.d., RM120:275.

118 Kriegstagebüch von Schröder, 22 April 1918, RM120:282.

119 Gladisch, *Krieg der Nordsee*, vol VII: p266; Pitt, *Zeebrugge*, p166.

120 Halpern, *Naval History*, p414; Newbolt, *Naval Operations*, vol V: pp265–77; Pitt, *Zeebrugge*, p177; Keyes, Memoirs, II:321–336.

121 Kommando des Minen und Sperrwesens der MarineKorps to von Schröder, 12 May 1918, RM120:275.

122 Gladisch, *Krieg der Nordsee*, vol VII: pp275–81.

123 Gladisch, *Krieg der Nordsee*, vol VII: pp275–81; Newbolt, *Naval Operations*, vol V: pp265–77; Pitt, *Zeebrugge*, p177; Keyes, *Memoirs*, vol II: pp321–336; von Schröder to von Holtzendorff and Scheer, 10 May 1918, RM120:275; von Schröder to Presseabteilung des Admiralstabes, 10 May 1918, RM120:275; Kriegstagebüch von Schröder, 10 May 1918, RM120:282; 1st MarineDivision Battle Report, 11 May 1918, RM120:275.

124 Kriegstagebüch von Schröder, 10 May 1918, RM120:282.

125 Gladisch, *Krieg der Nordsee*, vol VII: pp275–81.

126 Gladisch, *Krieg der Nordsee*, vol VII: pp267–68.

127 Von Schröder to von Holtzendorff and Scheer, 23 April 1918, RM120:275; von Schröder to von Arnim and Crown Prince Rupprecht, 23 April 1918, RM120:275.

128 Von Schröder to von Holtzendorff, 23 April 1918, RM120:275.

129 Kaiser Wilhelm II to Ludendorff, 23 April 1918, RM120:275.

130 Von Schröder to von Holtzendorff, 25 April 1918, RM120:275. Von Holtzendorff's original message to von Schröder was not in the files but the questions he asked are indicated on the reply by von Schröder. Ludendorff's attitude is cited in Gladisch, *Krieg der Nordsee*, vol VII: p267.

131 Von Schröder to von Holtzendorff, 25 April 1918, RM120:275.

132 Von Schröder to von Holtzendorff, 25 April 1918, RM120:275; Admiral Ludwig von Schröder, 'Judgment of the position on 25 April', 25 April 1918, RM120:275.

133 Von Holtzendorff to von Schröder, 29 April 1918, RM120:275.

134 Gladisch, *Krieg der Nordsee*, vol VII: p267.

135 Von Arnim to von Schröder, 27 April 1918, RM120:111.

136 Edgar Erich Schulze, Chief of Staff of the MarineKorps, to von Schröder, 24 April 1918, RM120:275.

137 Kriegstagebüch von Schröder, 24 April 1918, RM120:282.

138 Kriegstagebüch von Schröder, 25 April 1918, RM120:282; Gladisch, *Krieg der Nordsee*, vol VII: pp270–71.

139 Kriegstagebüch von Schröder, 1 May 1918, RM120:282; Gladisch, *Krieg der Nordsee*, vol VII:270–71.

140 Kriegstagebüch von Schröder, 4 May 1918, RM120:282.

141 Kriegstagebüch von Schröder, 14 May 1918, RM120:282; Gladisch, *Krieg der Nordsee*, vol VII: 270–71.

142 Gladisch, *Krieg der Nordsee*, vol VII: p274; Kriegstagebüch von Schröder, 8 June 1918, RM120:282.

143 Von Schröder, MarineKorps Gruppenbefehl, 3 May 1918, RM120:60; Kriegstagebüch von Schröder, 5 May 1918, RM120:282; von Schröder, MarineKorps Gruppenbefehl, 8 May 1918, RM120:60.

144 Schultz, 'Regulations for the mole commander', 31 May 1918, RM120:111.

145 Gladisch, *Krieg der Nordsee*, vol VII: p271; Kriegstagebüch von Schröder, 5 May 1918, RM120:282.

146 Kriegstagebüch von Schröder, 5 May 1918, RM120:282.

147 Gladisch, *Krieg der Nordsee*, vol VII: p271; Kriegstagebüch von Schröder, 9 May 1918, RM120:282; Schultz to von Schröder, 26 April 1918, RM120:60.

148 Kriegstagebüch von Schröder, 8 June 1918, RM120:282; Schultz to von Schröder, 26 April 1918, RM120:60.

149 Kriegstagebüch von Schröder, 5 May 1918, RM120:282.

150 Schultz to von Schröder, 26 April 1918, RM120:60; Kriegstagebüch von Schröder, 1 May 1918, RM120:282.

151 Kriegstagebüch von Schröder, 5 May 1918, RM120:282.

152 Kriegstagebüch von Schröder, 14 May 1918, RM120:282; Kriegstagebüch von Schröder, 25 May 1918, RM120:282; Gladisch, *Krieg der Nordsee*, vol VII: p274.

153 Kriegstagebüch von Schröder, 25 May 1918, RM120:282.

154 Gladisch, *Krieg der Nordsee*, vol VII: p271.

155 Schultz to von Schröder, 26 April 1918, RM120:60.

156 Schultz, 'Defensive plan of Zeebrugge mole', May 1918, RM120:111. The specific date was so badly smudged as to be illegible. From internal evidence it appears that the plan came into effect in late May.

157 'Regulations for the mole garrison', n.d., RM120:111.

158 Halpern, *Naval History*, p412.

159 Hans H. Hildebrand and Ernest Henriot, *Deutschland's Admirale 1849–1945*, (Osnabrück, Biblio Verlag; 1990), III vols, vol III: p270.

160 Von Schröder to Naval Staff Press Section, 25 April 1918, RM120:275; MarineKorps press release, 27 April 1918, RM120:275.

161 Von Schröder to Naval Staff Press Section, 25 April 1918, RM120:275; MarineKorps press release, 27 April 1918, RM120:275.

162 OHL Official Statement 'The English Attack on Ostende and Zeebrugge', n.d., RM120:275.

163 Keyes, *Memoirs*, vol II: pp313–20.

164 Scheer, *High Seas Fleet*, p339.

165 Bacon, *Dover Patrol*, p223.

166 Kriegstagebüch von Schröder, 1918, RM120:282. In his war diary von Schröder lists the numbers of submarines entering and leaving the harbours each day. This information was used to try and assess the impact of the raid. On the two days immediately following the raid, no submarines entered or left Bruges. These were not the only days of the year in which no submarine activity was recorded, so it is not incontrovertible evidence but nevertheless the numbers would seem to indicate that the raid certainly had some effect.

167 Newbolt, *Naval Operations*, vol V: pp265–77. In actuality this was due the declining numbers of torpedo craft available to the Flanders flotillas and Scheer's unwillingness to send additional flotillas out from the Bight.

168   See particularly Halpern, *Naval History*,
      p415; and Marder, *Dreadnought*, vol V: p65.
169   Cited in Marder, *Dreadnought*, vol V: pp48–
      49.
170   Gladisch, *Krieg der Nordsee*, vol VII: p272.
171   Kriegstagebüch von Schröder, 9 June 1918,
      RM120:282; Gladisch, *Krieg der Nordsee*, vol
      VII: p320.
172   Kommando des Fliegers to von Schröder, 5
      April 1918, RM120:151.
173   Von Arnim to von Schröder, later sent on to
      the commander of the air forces in Flanders,
      16 April 1918, RM120:151.
174   Kriegstagebüch von Schröder, 17 February
      1918, RM120:282; Gladisch, *Krieg der
      Nordsee*, vol VII: p230.
175   Gladisch, *Krieg der Nordsee*, vol VII: p230.
176   Kriegstagebüch von Schröder, 23 March
      1918, RM120:282; Gladisch, *Krieg der
      Nordsee*, vol VII: p230.
177   Kriegstagebüch von Schröder, 1 April 1918,
      RM120:282; Gladisch, *Krieg der Nordsee*, vol
      VII: p230.
178   Kriegstagebüch von Schröder, 9 April 1918,
      RM120:282.
179   Kriegstagebüch von Schröder, 17 May 1918,
      RM120:282; Gladisch, *Krieg der Nordsee*, vol
      VII: p272.
180   Kriegstagebüch von Schröder, 30 May 1918,
      RM120:282.
181   Gladisch, *Krieg der Nordsee*, vol VII: pp319,
      326; Kriegstagebüch von Schröder, 6 June
      1918, RM120:282; Kriegstagebüch von
      Schröder, 12 June 1918, RM120:282;
      Kriegstagebüch von Schröder, 15 June 1918,
      RM120:282; Kriegstagebüch von Schröder,
      31 July 1918, RM120:282.
182   Gladisch, *Krieg der Nordsee*, vol VII: pp326–
      28; Kriegstagebüch von Schröder, 29 August
      1918, RM120:282; Kriegstagebüch von
      Schröder, 30 August 1918, RM120:282.
183   Kriegstagebüch von Schröder, 21 March
      1918, RM120:282.
184   Gladisch, *Krieg der Nordsee*, vol VII: pp326–
      28.
185   Kriegstagebüch von Schröder, 1 June 1918,
      RM120:282; Kriegstagebüch von Schröder,
      August 1918, RM120:282; Gladisch, *Krieg
      der Nordsee*, vol VII: p319.
186   For assertions that the German defences
      kept damage to a minimum see Albert Rohr,
      'Die Luft Abwehr des MarineKorps und der
      LuftKrieg,' *Marine-Rundschau*, vol XXVIII
      (8, 1923), p347.
187   Rohr, 'Luftabwehr', p342.
188   Rohr, 'Luftabwehr', p346.
189   Crown Prince Rupprecht to von Schröder, 6
      June 1918, RM120:241; Gladisch, *Krieg der
      Nordsee*, vol VII: p320; Kriegstagebüch von
      Schröder, 2 June 1918, RM120:282.

190   Kriegstagebüch von Schröder, 5 June 1918,
      RM120:282.
191   Keyes, *Memoirs*, vol II: p341.
192   Kriegstagebüch von Schröder, 7 July 1918,
      RM120:282.
193   Kriegstagebüch von Schröder, 9 June 1918,
      RM120:282; Kriegstagebüch von Schröder,
      23 June 1918, RM120:282.
194   Kommando des Fliegers to von Schröder, 29
      June 1918, RM120:282.
195   Von Schröder to von Holtzendorff, 16 July
      1918, RM120:152; Scheer to von Schröder,
      25 August 1918, RM120:152. On August
      11th von Holtzendorff was removed as head
      of the naval staff and the former tripartite
      structure of the German navy was replaced
      by the Seekriegsleitung, under the united
      command of Admiral Scheer. Scheer
      effectively took over the duties of both the
      head of the Naval Staff and the head of the
      RMA. His place as commander of the High
      Seas Fleet was taken by Admiral Hipper. For
      details see Halpern, *Naval History*, p422.
196   Von Schröder to Scheer, n.d., RM120:152.
197   Schulze, 'MarineKorps', p463.
198   Record of a phone conversation between
      Edgar Erich Schulze and Kommando des
      Fliegers, 16 June 1918, RM120:152; von
      Schröder, regulations for Gruppe 12, 18
      June 1918, RM120:152.
199   Record of a phone conversation between
      Edgar Erich Schulze and the Kommando
      des Fliegers, 16 June 1918, RM120:152.
200   Von Holtzendorff to von Schröder, 6 May
      1918, RM120:60.
201   Kriegstagebüch von Schröder, 12 May 1918,
      RM120:282; Gladisch, *Krieg der Nordsee*, vol
      VII: p275.
202   Commander of III Torpedo-Boat Flotilla
      (unsigned) to von Schröder, 14 May 1918,
      RM120:53.
203   Kriegstagebüch von Schröder, 22 August
      1918, RM120:282; Gladisch, *Krieg der
      Nordsee*, vol VII: p324. Newbolt did not
      mention the skirmish.
204   Hall to Keyes, 7 January 1918; Halpern,
      Keyes Papers, p440.
205   Kriegstagebüch von Schröder, August 1918,
      RM120:282.
206   Kriegstagebüch von Schröder, 27 August
      1918, RM120:282.
207   Kriegstagebüch von Schröder, 30 May 1918,
      RM120:282; Kriegstagebüch von Schröder,
      27 June 1918, RM120:282.
208   Kriegstagebüch von Schröder, 21 April
      1918, RM120:282.
209   Tyrwhitt to Keyes, 13 August 1918, in
      Halpern, *Keyes Papers*, p505; Keyes,
      Memoirs, vol II: p350.
210   Kriegstagebüch von Schröder, 8 August

1918, RM120:282; Gladisch, *Krieg der Nordsee*, vol VII:p322.

211 Kriegstagebüch von Schröder, 11 August 1918, RM120:282; Gladisch, *Krieg der Nordsee*, vol VII: p322.

212 Kriegstagebüch von Schröder, 15 August 1918, RM120:282; Gladisch, *Krieg der Nordsee*, vol VII: p322.

213 Newbolt, *Naval Operations*, vol V: pp426–27. The numbers for October only include the first two weeks of the month. The harbours had been evacuated by the third week of October.

214 Halpern, *Naval History*, p416.

215 Von Holtzendorff to von Schröder, 1 August 1918, RM120:578.

216 Kriegstagebüch von Schröder, 21 September 1918, RM120:282.

217 Gladisch, *Krieg der Nordsee*, vol VII: p325.

218 Halpern, *Keyes Papers*, p415.

219 Kriegstagebüch von Schröder, 30 May 1918, RM120:282.

220 Gladisch, *Krieg der Nordsee*, vol VII: p325.

221 Kriegstagebüch von Schröder, 26 September 1918, RM120:282.

222 Von Schröder to von Holtzendorff, 'U-Boat Flotilla Activity Report for May 1918', 23 June 1918, RM120:578.

223 Spindler, *Handelskrieg*, vol V: p364.

224 Von Schröder to von Holtzendorff, 'U-Boat Flotilla Activity Report for May 1918', 23 June 1918, RM120:578.

225 Spindler, *Handelskrieg*, vol V: p364.

226 Von Schröder to von Holtzendorff, 'U-Boat Flotilla Activity Report for June 1918', 20 July 1918, RM120:578.

227 Spindler, *Handelskrieg*, vol V: p364.

228 Ibid. The flotilla reports cease in July 1918.

229 Spindler, *Handelskrieg*, vol V: pp364–65.

230 Halpern, *Naval History*, p423; Marder, *Dreadnought*, vol V: p113.

231 Von Schröder to von Arnim, 28 April 1918, RM120:578. The amount of tonnage sunk is almost certainly too high.

232 Von Holtzendorff to von Schröder and Scheer, 3 May 1918, RM120:578.

233 Ibid.

234 Von Holtzendorff to von Schröder and Scheer, 3 May 1918, RM120:578.

235 Von Holtzendorff to von Schröder, 26 May 1918, RM120:578.

236 Von Holtzendorff to the Kaiser, 'Naval Support for Operation Michael', June 1918, RM120:578.

237 Ibid..

238 Minutes of a phone conversation between von Schröder and von Holtzendorff, 2 June 1918, RM120:578.

239 Von Holtzendorff to von Schröder, 18 July 1918, RM120:578.

240 Von Schröder to von Holtzendorff, 29 July 1918, RM120:578.

241 Von Holtzendorff to the Kaiser, 1 August 1918, RM120:578. Again, this is probably an overestimation.

242 Von Holtzendorff to von Hindenburg, 7 May 1918, RM120:60.

243 Schultz to von Schröder, 25 April 1918, RM120:111.

244 Von Schröder to Schultz, 3 May 1918, RM120:60.

245 Von Schröder, MarineKorps Gruppenbefehl, 1 July 1918, RM120:111.

246 Kriegstagebüch von Schröder, 9 July 1918, RM120:282; Kriegstagebüch von Schröder, 16 July 1918, RM120:282.

247 OHL Intelligence Officer Dresden to the General Staff, forwarded to the Naval Staff and the MarineKorps, 20 July 1918, RM120:111. There was no corroborating evidence in the British accounts.

248 Kriegstagebüch von Schröder, 15 August 1918, RM120:282.

249 Kriegstagebüch von Schröder, 23 September 1918, RM120:282.

250 Kriegstagebüch von Schröder, 23 September 1918, RM120:282.

251 11th Bavarian Division (unsigned) to MarineKorps, 11 August 1918, RM120:111.

252 Von Schröder, MarineKorps Gruppenbefehl, 17 August 1918, RM120:60.

253 Albrecht, 'Measures for the Naval Forces in the Event of an Attack on the Coast', 28 August 1918, RM120:36.

254 See Chapter Six.

255 Admiral Ludwig von Schröder, 'Defence of the Flanders coast', 4 September 1918, RM120:570.

256 Von Schröder to Scheer, 10 September 1918, RM120:36.

257 Schultz to von Schröder, 12 October 1918, RM120:111.

258 Von Schröder to Schultz, 14 October 1918, RM120:111.

259 For the most recent overview of these events from the German perspective see Herwig, *First World War*, pp433–50.

260 Gladisch, *Krieg der Nordsee*, vol VII: p329.

261 Schulze, 'MarineKorps', 466; Kriegstagebüch von Schröder, 29 September 1918, RM120:282l; Gladisch, *Krieg der Nordsee*, vol VII: p329.

262 Kriegstagebüch von Schröder, 29 September 1918, RM120:282; Scheer, *High Seas Fleet*, p343.

263 Kriegstagebüch von Schröder, 30 September 1918, RM120:282.

264 Kriegstagebüch von Schröder, 1 October 1918, RM120:282; Gladisch, *Krieg der Nordsee*, vol VII: p330.

265 Kriegstagebüch von Schröder,
     3 October 1918, RM120:282;
     Kriegstagebüch von Schröder,
     5 October 1918, RM120:282.
266 Halpern, *Naval History*, p444. Scheer gives
     slightly different figures in his memoirs
     claiming that four submarines and two
     destroyers had to be scuttled. Scheer, *High
     Seas Fleet*, p346.
267 Spindler, *Handelskrieg*, vol V: p149.
268 Herwig, 'War Aims', p227.

269 Scheer, *High Seas Fleet*, p345; Gladisch,
     Krieg der Nordsee, vol VII: p330.
270 Scheer, *High Seas Fleet*, p346.
271 Kriegstagebüch von Schröder, 14 October
     1918, RM120:282; Kriegstagebüch von
     Schröder, 15 October 1918, RM120:282.
272 Schulze, 'MarineKorps', p467;
     Kriegstagebüch von Schröder, 16 October
     1918, RM120:282; Kriegstagebüch von
     Schröder, 18 October 1918, RM120:282.
273 Keyes, *Memoirs*, vol II: p377.

Index